SANDINO

SANDINO
THE TESTIMONY OF
A NICARAGUAN PATRIOT
1921–1934

Compiled and Edited by Sergio Ramírez

Edited and Translated with an Introduction

and Additional Selections by

Robert Edgar Conrad

•

PRINCETON UNIVERSITY PRESS

Published by Princeton University Press, 41 William Street,
Princeton, New Jersey 08540
In the United Kingdom: Princeton University Press, Oxford

Library of Congress Cataloging-in-Publication Data

Sandino, the testimony of a Nicaraguan patriot: 1921–1934 / compiled
and edited by Sergio Ramírez; translated and edited, with an
introduction and additional selections by Robert Edgar Conrad.
p.   cm.
"Based on the expanded 1984 edition of Sandino's writings
assembled and edited by Sergio Ramírez and published in Managua in
two volumes under the title El pensamiento vivo."
Includes bibliographical references.
ISBN 0-691-07848-3 (alk. paper)—ISBN 0-691-02319-0
(pbk.: alk. paper)
1. Sandino, Augusto César, 1895–1934.   2. Nicaragua—Politics and
government—1909–1937.   3. Nicaragua—History—Revolution,
1926–1929.   4. Revolutionists—Nicaragua—Biography.   5. Sandino,
Augusto César, 1895–1934.   Pensamiento vivo.   I. Ramírez, Sergio,
1942–   . II. Conrad, Robert Edgar, 1928–   .
F1526.3.S24S28   1990
972.8505'1—dc20   89-48567

This book has been composed in Linotron Sabon and Gill Sans

Princeton University Press books are printed on acid-free paper,
and meet the guidelines for permanence and durability of the
Committee on Production Guidelines for Book Longevity of the
Council on Library Resources

Printed in the United States of America by Princeton University Press,
Princeton, New Jersey

10 9 8 7 6 5 4 3 2 1
(Pbk.) 10 9 8 7 6 5 4 3 2 1

Designed by Laury A. Egan

CONTENTS

Documents

• CHILDHOOD AND YOUTH •

• 1926–1927 •

CONTENTS

CONTENTS

CONTENTS

CONTENTS

CONTENTS

CONTENTS

CONTENTS

CONTENTS

ILLUSTRATIONS

Illustrations follow p. 516.

1. Family portrait. Source: Jorge Eduardo Arellano and Eduardo Pérez-Valle, eds., *Sandino: Iconografía básica* (Managua, 1979).

2. Sandino's mother, Margarita Calderón. Courtesy Instituto de Estudio del Sandinismo.

3. Photo taken following the inauguration of Adolfo Díaz as president. Source: Rafael del Nogales, *The Looting of Nicaragua* (New York, 1928).

4. Henry L. Stimson, President Coolidge's special envoy to Nicaragua. Source: *The Literary Digest* 93, no. 8 (21 May 1927), 5.

5. General José María Moncada. Source: Harold Norman Denny, *Dollars for Bullets: The Story of American Rule in Nicaragua* (New York, 1929).

6. Sailors and marines collecting rifles from Nicaraguan soldiers for ten dollars each, in accordance with the Tipitapa agreement. Source: *The Outlook* 146, 10 (6 July 1927), 316.

7. Captain G. D. Hatfield, commander of the marine garrison at Ocotal. Source: *The Literary Digest* 49, no. 5 (30 July 1927), 5.

8. Augusto C. Sandino in 1926 or 1927, during the Constitutionalist War. Courtesy Library of Congress.

9. Blanca Aráuz de Sandino. Source: *Time* 13, no. 8 (25 February 1929), 26.

10. "A Bandit Hut," photo taken by U.S. Marine Robert E. Moody, "Just before It was Burned." Source: Moody's album of Nicaraguan photos, courtesy Library of Congress.

11. Sandinista soldiers. Source: Arellano and Pérez-Valle, *Sandino: Iconografía básica*.

12. Augusto C. Sandino in Mérida, Yucatan, in July 1929, with his general staff. Source: Arellano and Pérez-Valle, *Sandino: Iconografía básica*.

13. Sandino with the family of Pedro José Zepeda, holding his godchild, Zepeda's son César Augusto. Source: Arellano and Pérez-Valle, *Sandino: Iconografía básica*.

14. Blanca Aráuz de Sandino traveling on a *pipante* (longboat) on the Coco River. Source: Arellano and Pérez-Valle, *Sandino: Iconografía básica*.

15. Members of a crew of army engineers surveying the Nicaraguan canal route in 1930, with Nicaraguan workers. Courtesy National Archives, 111–SC–96910.

16. Sandino and President Juan B. Sacasa in the Presidential Palace in Managua on February 4, 1933, after the signing of the peace agreement. Source: Arellano and Pérez-Valle, *Sandino: Iconografía básica*.

17. Sandinista and National Guard soldiers assembled in the plaza of San Rafael del Norte for the purpose of disarming part of Sandino's army in compliance with the peace agreement of February 1933. Source: Arellano and Pérez-Valle, *Sandino: Iconografía básica*.

18. In San Rafael del Norte in February 1933. Courtesy Instituto de Estudio del Sandinismo.

19. Sandino and Ramón de Belausteguigoitia. Source: Ramón de Belausteguigoitia, *Con Sandino en Nicaragua* (Managua, 1981).

20. Sandino and his general staff near the end of his life. Source: Arellano and Pérez-Valle, *Sandino: Iconografía básica*.

ACKNOWLEDGMENTS

I wish to call attention, as Sergio Ramírez did in the 1984 edition, to the participation of Flor de María Monterrey, director of the Instituto de Estudio del Sandinismo (IES), and other researchers at that institution, in the expansion and improvement of that edition, and consequently of this one. I also wish to thank the following people who made important contributions: Mr. Sanford G. Thatcher, formerly of Princeton University Press, for his help in getting me started on this project; my wife Ursula for her work on the illustrations; Diane Didier of Baton Rouge, Louisiana, for drawing the maps; and Julie Marvin of Princeton University Press for her fine editing. My thanks go as well to *The Nation* magazine/The Nation Company, Inc., for allowing me to publish parts of Carleton Beals's articles on Sandino: "With Sandino in Nicaragua: Sandino Himself," "Send the Bill to Mr. Coolidge," and "Sandino—Bandit or Patriot," all copyright 1928. And finally, I wish to express my sincere gratitude to Sergio Ramírez, distinguished novelist, historian, literary critic, and vice-president of Nicaragua, for granting me permission to translate these writings by his country's national hero.

NOTE ON THE ORGANIZATION
AND EDITING OF
THE ENGLISH-LANGUAGE EDITION

The collection of documents presented in this volume is based on the expanded 1984 edition of Sandino's writings assembled and edited by Sergio Ramírez and published in two volumes in Managua under the title *El pensamiento vivo*. This work has not only gone through many Spanish editions (the first published in San José, Costa Rica, in 1974), but has also appeared in several foreign languages, including German, Italian, and Swedish. A number of Sandino's writings have been published in English, but this is the first attempt to offer a comprehensive English-language edition.

In order to provide a more accessible single-volume edition, it was necessary to delete many items from the 1984 edition. However, this has been done, I believe, wihout eliminating anything vital for understanding Sandino and his times. In the 1984 edition two long accounts of the Constitutionalist War (1926–1927) and events leading to Sandino's rebellion were published in an appendix. Their inclusion in the body of the work (Documents 8 and 9) has enabled me to remove several items (Documents 7, 9, 10, and 15 of the 1984 edition), which were, in fact, excerpts from those two narratives.

Elsewhere I have been able to shorten some documents, especially when they contained material not written by Sandino. This was true, for example, of the old Document 241 (my Document 184). Document 242 of the 1984 edition (my Document 185) also contains some material that appears elsewhere in the 1984 edition, and therefore these sections have been removed from that longer selection. For the record, others deleted from the 1984 edition are old Documents 8, 12, 13, 23, 32, 40, 46, 51, 55, 56, 58, 62, 65, 70, 71, 72, 81, 85, 87, 91, 101, 103, 108, 113, 114, 115, 119, 120, 121, 122, 123, 128, 129, 130, 133, 141, 145, 146, 147, 148, 150, 151, 153, 156, 157, 158, 162, 165, 167, 177, 179, 182, 183, 187, 188, 193, 201, 202, 214, 217, 218, 223, 225, 253, 254, 256, 257, and 261. Also omitted from this volume are Sergio Ramírez's introductory essay, "El Muchacho de Niquinohomo," his analytical article, "Sandino: Clase e ideología," his chronology of events, his biographical index, and three brief introductory notes to earlier editions. When making abridgments I have been guided by a desire to avoid repetition and to include as much of Sandino's thought as possible within the limits of a single volume.

Where necessary, I have added explanatory footnotes, attaching the initials RC to distinguish my notes from those written by Sergio Ramírez. His practice of placing source notes after the documents has been retained. The numbers in these notes refer to the numbered sources in the List of Sources. These include some basic studies of Sandino and Nicaragua and are supplemented by a selected bibliography. Ellipsis points have been placed in brackets to indicate editorial abridgment; if they are not in brackets they appear in the 1984 edition.

In order to round out certain aspects of Sandino's life, I have added a few documents not in the 1984 edition. These include a letter addressed to the All-America Anti-Imperialist League published in English in *The New York Times* (Document 70); an eyewitness account of the events leading to Sandino's assassination, carried out by members of the National Guard under orders of the Guard commander and later dictator, General Anastasio Somoza (Document 200); and several excerpts from José Román's *Maldito país*, a book written in 1933 and published at last in 1979. The latter selections (Documents 2, 29, 58, 120, 179, and 201) deal with Sandino's childhood, his second journey to Mexico, and aspects of his military struggle and its aftermath. Document 201, the final item in this collection, is introspective and reveals Sandino's hopes and fears in the last year of his life.

Finally, the title of this edition reflects what I regard as Sandino's basic motivation during his long struggle: the great love he felt for his country and his constant wish to see it sovereign and free.

MAPS

NICARAGUA

SANDINO'S AREA OF OPERATIONS

SANDINO

TRANSLATOR'S INTRODUCTION

Since 1979, the year the Sandinista Front for National Liberation (FSLN) won its military victory over the Nicaraguan National Guard and the Somoza family dictatorship, Nicaragua has achieved a prominence in world affairs not normally attained by a small country of some two and a half million people. Few of the world's nations have been the object of more conflict and debate during those ten years than this poor, underdeveloped land, which for most of its history as an independent country has experienced more than its share of oppression, war, and foreign domination. Few governments have been more criticized by sectors of American society than the Sandinista regime, and few have aroused more sympathy among large segments of the world's population than this same government of scholars, writers, priests, poets, and dedicated revolutionaries.

Despite this worldwide interest—which had its counterpart in the 1920s and 1930s—many people in Western countries are still little acquainted with the background of the current Nicaraguan revolution. Many remain unaware, for example, of the deep and direct economic, political, and military involvement of the United States in Nicaragua's affairs in this century, and perhaps even fewer are conscious of the damage inflicted upon the Nicaraguan people by decades of U.S. domination. Few people outside Nicaragua know, for example, that, beginning in 1909, the year the Taft administration helped foment a pro-business revolution on the east coast of Nicaragua, the United States installed a whole series of unpopular Nicaraguan regimes, meanwhile imposing unwanted treaties and other burdensome relationships upon that country, aided by those same governments of its own creation. Indeed, few citizens of the United States know that from 1927 until 1933 U.S. armed forces were engaged in a bitter jungle war in Nicaragua, much like that fought in Vietnam, against an army of Nicaraguan and Latin American patriots led by one Augusto C. Sandino, a man whose name and acts have since inspired generations of his fellow-citizens.

Clearly Nicaragua's tragic story is not sufficiently known, and for the general public many questions remain unanswered. What are the causes of the current Nicaraguan revolutionary phenomenon? What events in their history impelled the Nicaraguan people toward revolution, and what has given their small country the strength and determination to resist the economic, diplomatic, and military pressure imposed upon them during the eight years of the Reagan administration? Going back in time, who were the Sandinistas of the 1920s and 1930s, and who was Augusto C. Sandino, the man who gave the Nicaraguan Revolution its name? What induced him and a small band of followers to initiate a guerrilla struggle against powerful U.S. armed forces and their Nicaraguan allies and to continue this unequal conflict for nearly six years?

The answers to these questions lie in the history of Nicaragua's relations with the United States in this century.[1] By its very presence, the United States has helped to determine the course of events in every Latin American country, but toward such countries as Cuba, Haiti, Panama, the Dominican Republic, Mexico, and Nicaragua (all to be found, as some would say, "in America's own backyard"), the United States has often pursued policies of direct and prolonged intervention. In the case of Nicaragua this has taken many forms, including conspiracies to topple governments, military and diplomatic threats, direct involvement in civil wars, establishment of so-called neutral zones by U.S. armed forces in order to frustrate the plans of political groups not favored by the United States, the establishment of American-trained and -equipped military forces, imposition of onerous treaties and economic and administrative controls that in effect all but nullified the nation's sovereignty, and, perhaps most intolerable to Augusto Sandino and other Nicaraguan patriots, outright occupation by U.S. armed forces.

A brief review of the turbulent history of Nicaragua from 1909 until 1927—the year Sandino began his personal crusade against one more large-scale military intrusion—will uncover the roots of the conflicts that have racked that country and, more relevantly, will prepare the reader to understand the documents contained in this book—documents which reveal one man's uncompromising responses to foreign domination of his native land.

•

After the revolution for independence against Spain and the failure of efforts to unite Central America early in the nineteenth century, political affairs in Nicaragua were of the Liberal-versus-Conservative kind that consumed the energies of Latin American countries well into the twentieth century.[2] In 1909, however, a new and dynamic force entered the Nic-

---

[1] "One has to study history and to find in history . . . the elements of this revolution," wrote Humberto Ortega, brother of President Daniel Ortega of Nicaragua and a leading member of the Sandinista government. Cited by Donald C. Hodges, *Intellectual Foundations of the Nicaraguan Revolution* (Austin, Texas, 1986), 195.

[2] For accounts of the political and economic history of Nicaragua and Central America see Thomas L. Karnes, *The Failure of Union: Central America, 1824-1960* (Chapel Hill, N.C., 1961); Miles L. Wortman, *Government and Society in Central America, 1680–1840*

araguan political arena, upsetting traditional alignments and permanently changing the nature of the political contest. In that year the Liberal president of Nicaragua, José Santos Zelaya, was overthrown by a Conservative rebellion with the undisguised support of the U.S. government, in the first of a series of American interventions that would end only in the 1930s with the establishment of the American-trained and -financed National Guard under the leadership of General Anastasio Somoza.

From its beginning, the Conservative revolt of 1909 enjoyed the moral and financial support of U.S. business interests in Nicaragua, as well as that of the State Department under the direction of President Taft's secretary of state, Philander C. Knox. On October 7 the U.S. consul at Bluefields on Nicaragua's Caribbean coast, Thomas F. Moffat, revealing his own close association with the conspirators, predicted in a cable to the State Department "that a revolution will start in Bluefields on the 8th." The following day, Emiliano Chamorro, a Conservative Party general, Juan Estrada, the co-opted Liberal governor of the province who was promised the presidency of his country in exchange for his cooperation, and Adolfo Díaz, an employee of the nearby U.S.-owned La Luz and Los Angeles Mining Company, began the predicted revolt with the help of the local garrison under Estrada's command. On October 12, Moffat, who enjoyed the confidence of the rebel leaders, sent one more optimistic cable to the State Department to announce that "foreign business interests are enthusiastic," that "immediate reduction of the tariff was assured," and that all concessions not owned by foreigners had been annulled.[3] According to undisputed assertions from Liberal Party sources, three weeks after this revolt began, Adolfo Díaz, who would soon become president of Nicaragua, personally made loans to the rebels totaling $600,000, although his mining-company salary at that time was not more than $1,000 per year.[4] On December 1, 1909, Secretary of State Knox, who was also a legal consultant to the La Luz and Los Angeles Mining Company and a major stockholder in that same firm, withdrew U.S. recognition of the

(New York, 1982); and Jaime Wheelock Román, *Imperialismo y dictadura*, 5th ed. (Mexico, D.F., 1980).

[3] U. S. Department of State, *Papers Relating to the Foreign Relations of the United States, 1909* (hereafter *Foreign Relations* with dates), 452; Harold Norman Denny, *Dollars for Bullets: The Story of American Rule in Nicaragua* (New York, 1929), 74–76; Richard Millett, *Guardians of the Dynasty* (Maryknoll, New York, 1977), 23–24. The tariff Moffat referred to was a tax on exports, and the annulled concessions were large grants of territory held by Nicaraguans, including President Zelaya himself, which until then had blocked the expansion of foreign agricultural, lumbering, and mining interests in the vast eastern zone of Nicaragua. See T. Lane Carter, "The Gold Mining Industry in Nicaragua," *The Engineering and Mining Journal*, 17 December 1910, 1204.

[4] Denny, *Dollars for Bullets*, 78; Amy Woods, "Nicaragua and the United States," *Congressional Record, 1928*, 7615. Sandino, who was interested in all aspects of the U.S. intervention, put this figure at $800,000. See Doc. 79.

Zelaya government in a diplomatic note that has been described as "a virtual declaration of war."[5]

Expressing the hope that his fall from power might bring peace to Nicaragua and "above all, the suspension of the hostility manifested by the American government," President Zelaya resigned his office on December 17, 1909, naming as president another Liberal, José Madriz, a prestigious lawyer and member of the Central American Court of Justice, who did not, however, receive diplomatic recognition from the Taft administration. The war continued, and by May 1910, President Madriz's Liberal forces were demanding the surrender of the rebels at the port of Bluefields, a development that led to direct U.S. military intervention. On May 16, 1910, the American commander of the warship *Paducah* declared the town and port of Bluefields a "neutral zone," thwarting a Liberal victory. American marines were quickly landed at Bluefields "to protect American lives and property," and during the following weeks, the United States supplied arms to the Conservative forces while insisting that customs duties at Bluefields be paid to the Conservative faction. The result was President Madriz's resignation after nearly a year of civil war and the entry of Estrada's army into Managua on August 27, 1910.[6]

Many causes for these intrusions into Nicaragua's internal affairs have been proposed. Zelaya had canceled or threatened to cancel certain U.S. concessions in Nicaragua, including that held by the La Luz and Los Angeles Mining Company. U.S. businessmen had complained that the Nicaraguan president had kept Central America in a state of turmoil, a situation allegedly prejudicial to U.S. interests in Panama. Zelaya, moreover, had negotiated a large loan in London, a bold display of independence in the face of the policy of "dollar diplomacy," which sought to discourage European investments in strategic areas of Latin America. And finally, the Nicaraguan president, who had refused to grant the United States the right to build an interoceanic canal across Nicaragua, was said to be ready to offer that privilege to Germany or Japan. As was soon apparent, the United States was in fact clearly interested in acquiring the exclusive right to build a Nicaraguan canal, both to forestall potential competitors and, if warranted, to construct such a canal for the economic and strategic advantages it might offer.[7]

[5] Mario Ribas, "A Central American Indictment of the United States," in *Current History*, September 1927, 919; Woods, "Nicaragua," 7615; Gregorio Selser, *Sandino* (New York, 1981), 27; Hodges, *Intellectual Foundations*, 120; Millett, *Guardians*, 25–26. For Knox's note, see *Foreign Relations, 1909*, 455–57.

[6] *Foreign Relations, 1909*, 458–59; Rafael de Nogales, *The Looting of Nicaragua* (New York, 1928), 8; Denny, *Dollars for Bullets*, 84–90.

[7] Sergio Ramírez, "Sandino: Clase e ideología," in Augusto C. Sandino, *El pensamiento vivo* (Managua, 1984), 2:424–25; Wheelock Román, *Imperialismo y dictadura*, 107–8; Woods, "Nicaragua," 7615; Neill Macaulay, *The Sandino Affair* (Chicago, 1967), 23; Selser, *Sandino*, 26; Millett, *Guardians*, 20–23.

But events following the Conservative military victory of 1910 offer more concrete evidence of the aims of the United States in Nicaragua. Thomas G. Dawson, U.S. minister to Panama and a member of Knox's law firm, went to Managua soon after the Conservative regime took power, there inducing Estrada and his associates to agree to certain conditions prior to U.S. diplomatic recognition. These conditions were contained in the so-called Dawson Agreements, which provided for the election of a new Constituent Assembly that would adopt a constitution intended to guarantee the rights of foreigners. A claims commission was to be set up to rehabilitate the public finances, and the good offices of the United States were to be solicited by the Nicaraguan government for negotiation of a loan to be guaranteed by a certain percentage of the customs receipts of the Republic. It was also stipulated that the newly established Constituent Assembly would elect Juan Estrada and Adolfo Díaz as president and vice president respectively.[8]

To carry out the loan provision of the Dawson Agreements, the Knox-Castrillo Treaty was signed in June 1911. This pact provided for aid in securing a loan of $15,000,000 from U.S. bankers, and for the appointment of a collector general of customs (the nation's most important source of funds) to be named by the bankers and appointed by the Nicaraguan president subject to State Department approval. The refusal of the U.S. Senate to ratify the Knox-Castrillo Treaty did not prevent the interested parties from implementing some of its provisions. On the strength of the proposed treaty alone, the Estrada government signed contracts with the New York banking firms of Brown Brothers and Company and J. and W. Seligman. An advance of $1,500,000 (a tenth of the proposed loan) was arranged, to be secured by the customs revenues of Nicaragua, assuring the lenders "timely repayment of principal and interest." Moreover, as stipulated in the unratified Knox-Castrillo Treaty, a collector general of customs was appointed—not a Nicaraguan, but a U.S. citizen named Clifford D. Ham who held the position until 1928. The amenable Nicaraguan government never received the bulk of the loan, but the stock of a new Nicaraguan bank and of the National Railway was also turned over to the bankers "in lieu of other security."[9] Furthermore, with the change of government there was new optimism among U.S. citizens in the

---

[8] U.S. Department of State, *A Brief History of the Relations between the United States and Nicaragua, 1909–1928* (Washington, D.C., 1928), 6; John A. Booth, *The End and the Beginning: The Nicaraguan Revolution* (Boulder, Colorado, 1982), 32; Denny, *Dollars for Bullets*, 92–93; Woods, "Nicaragua," 7615.

[9] For these and later complex dealings of this kind, see U.S. Department of State, *A Brief History*, 11–17; for an analysis of the financial and other economic advantages attained by the American bankers in Nicaragua through these proceedings, and their effects on Nicaragua's economy, see Nogales, *The Looting of Nicaragua*, 21–25; and especially Booth, *The End and the Beginning*, 32–34.

gold-mining districts of eastern Nicaragua. "The first act of the Estrada revolutionists," wrote the mining expert, T. Lane Carter, "was to reduce the outrageous tariff imposed by Ex-President Zelaya," which was "of great assistance to the miners." Large tracts of land formerly held by Nicaraguan concessionaires would soon be opened to gold prospectors, Carter predicted, and U.S. firms would have more incentive to establish themselves in Nicaragua.[10]

By 1911, then, the purposes of the intervention—or at least its results—were reasonably clear. U.S. companies had acquired new opportunities and new advantages in mining, agriculture, and lumber. U.S. citizens had taken control of the National Railway, customs revenues, the National Bank, and the Claims Commission. A former member of Teddy Roosevelt's Rough Riders was reorganizing the Nicaraguan armed forces, and the American minister in Managua was advising the Conservative government. Thus, considering the ever-present threat of a new military intervention, Nicaragua had become a ward of U.S. business, if not of the U.S. government itself. Sergio Ramírez sums up the situation: "There did not remain a single strategic sector of that wholly backward economy that was not under American power, so that the oligarchic Conservative faction that returned to government in [1910] was nothing more than a bureaucratic intermediary of the American occupation."[11]

•

Under these circumstances, resistance to the Conservative government was inevitable. In 1912, the newly elected and surprisingly independent Constituent Assembly adopted a new constitution, parts of which seemed intended to defend the nation's independence. Article 2, for example, declared that sovereignty "is one, inalienable and imprescriptible, and resides essentially in the people," and therefore no treaties were to be agreed to that would be "contrary to the independence and the integrity of the nation, or which in any way affect its sovereignty, except such as may look toward union with one or more republics of Central America." And article 55 gave the Congress alone the power to "authorize loans and levy direct or indirect taxes."[12]

Adolfo Díaz, who had succeeded Estrada to the presidency, dissolved the Assembly soon after it promulgated the new constitution, and in response, General Luis Mena, who had himself taken part in the 1909 re-

---

[10] T. Lane Carter, "Mining in Nicaragua in 1910," *The Engineering and Mining Journal*, 7 January 1911, 74. Noteworthy was his remark: "Great interest was taken [in 1910] in La Leonesa Mine which is being developed under the direction of H. C. Hoover." This, of course, was Herbert Clark Hoover, the mining engineer who later as president continued President Coolidge's military intervention in Nicaragua for almost his entire four years in office.

[11] Millet, *Guardians*, 30–31; Ramírez, "Sandino," 425–26.

[12] Cited in Nogales, *The Looting of Nicaragua*, 17.

volt against Zelaya, established an anti-Díaz government in the town of Masaya twenty miles southeast of Managua. Civil war broke out anew, with Liberal forces led by General Benjamín Zeledón besieging the capital. Díaz repeated an earlier appeal for a treaty allowing U.S. intervention in Nicaraguan affairs, and during the first weeks of August 1912, American sailors landed at the ports of Corinto and Bluefields and 354 marines moved eastward along the rail line to Managua, relieving the beleaguered Conservatives in the capital. By the end of the summer more than 2,700 sailors and marines had taken up positions on Nicaraguan soil in support of the unpopular government of Adolfo Díaz.[13]

U.S. forces quickly went into action, capturing rebel ships, threatening the city of Granada, and forcing the surrender of General Mena. Marine artillery next shelled the rebel stronghold of Masaya and the nearby volcanic fortress of Coyotepe. After a brief but bloody battle, U.S. forces captured Coyotepe, eliminating Zeledón and setting the stage for the capture of Masaya by Conservative forces. American marines then occupied León, the last major position under Liberal control, bringing the war to an end and assuring the supremacy of Adolfo Díaz.[14] With American sailors and marines keeping the peace, with the U.S. government supporting Díaz for the presidency and discouraging the candidacy of General Emiliano Chamorro, and with the Conservatives in charge of the electoral machinery and even denying Liberals the right to vote, Adolfo Díaz was "unanimously" elected president late in 1912, receiving three or four thousand votes from a population of some 700,000. To compensate for his political sacrifice, General Chamorro was given the coveted post of Nicaraguan minister to the United States.[15]

Thus the stage was set for the next major event in U.S.-Nicaraguan relations: the Bryan-Chamorro Treaty. Signed in Washington on August 5, 1914, by Secretary of State William Jennings Bryan and General Chamorro, this remarkable treaty granted "in perpetuity to the Government of the United States, forever free from all taxation or other public charge, the exclusive proprietary rights necessary and convenient for the construction, operation and maintenance of an interoceanic canal by way of the San Juan River and the great Lake of Nicaragua or by way of any route over Nicaraguan territory." For protection of this acquisition, the Nicaraguan government agreed to lease to the United States, for a term of ninety-nine years, the Caribbean Corn Islands, while it granted the United States the right to establish a naval base on the Gulf of Fonseca to

[13] Ibid., 18–20; Bernard C. Nalty, *The United States Marines in Nicaragua* (Washington, D.C., 1968), 7; Selser, *Sandino*, 35; Rafael Ramírez Delgado, *Jornada Libertaria de 1912 en Nicaragua* (Tegucigalpa, 1951), 31–36.

[14] *Report of the Secretary of the Navy, 1913*, 38; Nalty, *United States Marines*, 9; Millett, *Guardians*, 31–33; Wheelock Román, *Imperialismo e dictadura*, 110–11.

[15] Nalty, *United States Marines*, 9–10; Denny, *Dollars for Bullets*, 122–23.

be "subject exclusively to the laws and sovereign authority of the United States," these provisions to be renewable by the United States for an additional ninety-nine years.

In exchange, the United States agreed to pay $3,000,000 to the Nicaraguan government, to be deposited in the bank or banks "as the Government of the United States may determine" and to be applied to the Nicaraguan debt "or other public purposes . . . , all such disbursements to be made by orders drawn by the Minister of Finance and approved by the Secretary of State of the United States or by such person as he may designate." This token sum, for which Nicaragua, contrary to its constitution, had not only ceded specific national territories, but any part of the national territory that the United States might find useful for its purposes, was not even to be entrusted outright to the Nicaraguan government, but was to be held instead in U.S. banks and disbursed only with State Department approval.[16]

•

In the years following this agreement, the Conservative Party ruled in Nicaragua, its power resting, in the words of a Marine Corps historian, "on the presence of a strong Marine detachment at the Managua legation," which remained in Nicaragua after the 1912 intervention.[17] General Chamorro succeeded Adolfo Díaz to the presidency as a result of the "election" of 1916, allegedly because Díaz prevented the would-be Liberal candidate, Julián Irías, from returning from exile to campaign, and because the United States itself imposed unacceptable conditions upon Irías.[18] General Chamorro in turn was succeeded by his uncle, Diego Manuel Chamorro, whose election was assured by his nephew's control of the electoral machinery.

In the elections of 1924, however, in part as a result of an U.S.-inspired electoral reform, a Liberal-Conservative coalition opposed to the ruling Díaz-Chamorro faction was victorious. Carlos Solórzano, a moderate Conservative, and Dr. Juan Bautista Sacasa, a Liberal, were elected president and vice president respectively by a nearly two-to-one majority in what was then regarded as the fairest election ever held in Nicaragua.[19] On January 1, 1925, Solórzano and Sacasa took office, and in August the U.S. Marines were at last withdrawn.

Nevertheless, the interference of Díaz and Chamorro and the involvement of the United States in Nicaragua's internal affairs were far from finished. Just weeks after the marine withdrawal, followers of Chamorro

[16] For this treaty see U.S. Department of State, *A Brief History*, 75–77.

[17] Nalty, *United States Marines*, 9–10. Despite the marine guard, however, no fewer than ten incidents of rebellion occurred between 1912 and 1924 in opposition to the Conservative governments. See Wheelock Román, *Imperialismo y dictadura*, 112.

[18] Nalty, *United States Marines*, 10; Selser, *Sandino*, 46.

[19] U.S. Department of State, *A Brief History*, 21–26; Woods, "Nicaragua," 7617.

and Díaz seized La Loma Fortress, which dominated Managua, forcing Solórzano to replace Liberal members of his cabinet and to make other concessions leading to Chamorro's assumption of full power. Vice President Sacasa, the Liberal vice president, was compelled to leave the country, and soon after, Chamorro forced President Solórzano himself to resign, then had himself named president by a Congress packed with his own supporters. Reversing its former policy toward Chamorro, the State Department refused to recognize his illegal government, though U.S. officials in Managua continued to deal with him.[20] Furthermore, on flimsy constitutional grounds, Washington withheld recognition of Sacasa, who, as vice president, was claiming the presidency from outside the country.

At this point, the events of 1909 seemed to repeat themselves. In May 1926, a revolt broke out on the Caribbean coast, with the Liberals this time seizing the port of Bluefields. The inevitable warship arrived "to protect American lives and property," and predictably its commander declared Bluefields a "neutral zone." Not long afterward the Nicaraguan Congress, packed with Chamorro supporters, elected Adolfo Díaz president of Nicaragua. Thus the old State Department favorite, an accomplice in Chamorro's 1924 coup d'état, had again risen to power with State Department support, and three days later his government was recognized by the Coolidge administration.[21]

In the weeks that followed, civil war spread throughout the country, culminating in December 1926 with Juan Sacasa's establishment of a "Constitutionalist Government" at the Caribbean town of Puerto Cabezas. U.S. forces soon landed there and at other strategic points along the coast, establishing "neutral zones," isolating Sacasa's government, and even denying him the right to possess weapons, some of which the Americans tossed into the sea.[22] Then early in January and February 1927, in response to a request for military support from Adolfo Díaz, U.S. armed forces returned to Nicaragua, occupying the nation's railroads, ports, and major cities, establishing neutral zones, and, wherever possible, blocking the progress of Sacasa's Liberal forces. A prominent Nicaraguan historian and labor leader, Sofonías Salvatierra, described the arrival of the U.S.

[20] U.S. Department of State, *A Brief History*, 28–30; Booth, *The End and the Beginning*, 38; Marvin Goldwert, *The Constabulary in the Dominican Republic and Nicaragua: Progeny and Legacy of United States Intervention* (Gainesville, Florida, 1962), 27; Woods, "Nicaragua," 7617. Major Calvin B. Carter, the American head of a newly established Nicaraguan constabulary (forerunner of the National Guard), was supplied with weapons by Chamorro during this period of nonrecognition and took part in fighting against the Liberals. See C. B. Carter, "The Kentucky Feud in Nicaragua: Why Civil War Has Become Her National Sport," *The World's Work* 54 (1927), 320; Millet, *Guardians*, 47–48.

[21] Woods, "Nicaragua," 7617–18; Millett, *Guardians*, 49–50.

[22] For Sacasa's own description of the establishment of "neutral zones" at his provisional capital and elsewhere along the Caribbean coast, see *The New York Times*, 31 December 1926.

forces in Managua on January 6, 1927: "The war elements that they transported were so numerous that they spent the entire night of the 6th to the 7th moving them from the railroad station to the Campo de Marte, which was where the North American forces always quartered themselves when they were in Nicaragua. A little later they took possession of the Tiscapa fortress, and on February 23 the stars and stripes were seen waving over that stronghold."[23]

Against a barrage of criticism President Coolidge defended this latest U.S. intervention, reminding the world of "the proprietary rights of the United States in the Nicaraguan canal route" and "the obligation flowing from the investment of all classes of our citizens in Nicaragua." A week earlier, in fact, Undersecretary of State Robert Olds had justified U.S. support of Díaz on the grounds that Central America and Panama together constituted "a legitimate sphere of influence for the United States." The United States controlled the destiny of Central America, Olds asserted, because this was essential to American interests. "Until now," he claimed, "Central America has always understood that governments which we recognize and support stay in power, while those which we do not recognize and support fall. Nicaragua has become a test case. It is difficult to see how we can afford to be defeated."[24] Despite such arguments, however, and despite U.S. military aid to the Díaz government, Liberal forces led by General José María Moncada marched westward from the Caribbean coast and by April 1927, had crossed the central mountains and were threatening the cities of the western highlands, including Managua itself.[25]

In that month, President Coolidge asked Major Henry L. Stimson, a former secretary of war, to undertake a mission to Nicaragua to investigate the situation, to report his views to the U.S. government, and, if possible, "to straighten the matter out." Stimson surveyed the conditions of the war-torn country and, after conferring with U.S. military and diplomatic officials, with Díaz and his cabinet, and with Conservative and Liberal party leaders, quickly agreed with Díaz on terms to be offered the nearly victorious Liberals. These included an immediate end to the war, simultaneous delivery of weapons by both armies into U.S. custody, a general amnesty and return of exiles, Liberal participation in the Díaz cabinet, organization of a constabulary or National Guard to be commanded by U.S. citizens, supervision of the 1928 election and subsequent

[23] *Report of the Secretary of the Navy, 1927,* 7–8; Macaulay, *The Sandino Affair,* 28–29; Carroll Binder, "On the Nicaraguan Front: How the American Intervention Looks to an Eye-Witness," *The New Republic,* 16 March 1927, 87–90; Sofonías Salvatierra, *Sandino o la tragedia de un pueblo* (Madrid, 1934), 40.

[24] U.S. Congress, "Conditions in Nicaragua and Mexico, Hearings before the Committee on Foreign Affairs" (House of Representatives, 69th Cong., 2d session. [1927]), 9.

[25] Macaulay, *The Sandino Affair,* 28–29; *Foreign Relations 1927,* 3:328.

elections by Americans, and the stationing of marines in the country to enforce the agreement. Stimson then traveled to the town of Tipitapa just east of Managua where, "under a large blackthorn tree near the dry river bed," as he described the site, he met with General Moncada and a delegation of Liberals representing the Constitutionalist president, Dr. Juan Sacasa.[26]

Sofonías Salvatierra describes this fateful meeting:

> Colonel Stimson announced to the Constitutionalist delegates that Coolidge's policy naturally could not be allowed to fail because of the prestige of the United States government, and that the disarming of the two armies, that is, the total disarming of the Republic, was a condition sine qua non of peace; that Mr. Díaz would have to complete the constitutional term of Mr. Solórzano; that future elections would be supervised by the American government; and that if this was not accepted the armed forces of the United States would in fact impose it. The three delegates of the Constitutionalist government declared that they did not have instructions to accept those conditions for peace. Then Colonel Stimson and General Moncada, separating themselves from the other three, spoke together alone, and the result of this was that, without agreeing to anything with the delegates, they all went to Managua, including General Moncada. By force of logic everything indicated that he [Moncada] had arranged the peace with Stimson with the understanding that he would be the future president.[27]

Moncada had, in fact, accepted Stimson's demands at Tipitapa, though as Sacasa's subordinate he had no authority to make an agreement with a foreign representative, particularly an agreement to disband the Liberal army and to allow Adolfo Díaz to retain the presidency.[28] None of this, however, prevented Stimson, Moncada, and Díaz from implementing the "Peace of Espino Negro."[29] To speed up disarmament, Stimson and Díaz had previously agreed that each soldier of either army who surrendered a weapon to the U.S. forces would receive a bounty of ten U.S. dollars, a large sum of money for the peasant soldiers of Nicaragua who, in the

[26] Henry L. Stimson, *American Policy in Nicaragua* (New York, 1927), 42–77.

[27] Salvatierra, *Sandino*, 50–51. Sandino and other Nicaraguans believed that Moncada had been offered the presidency at Tipitapa in exchange for his army's capitulation. See Booth, *The End and the Beginning*, 41. For an expression of this opinion in Sandino's writings, see Doc. 8.

[28] Already on April 7 it had been decided in Washington that U.S. recognition of Diaz would not be a subject for negotiation with Nicaraguan Liberals. See Lejeune Cummins, *Quijote on a Burro: Sandino and the Marines, a Study in the Formulation of Foreign Policy* (Mexico, D.F., 1958), 16.

[29] In Nicaragua the agreement made between Stimson and Moncada at Tipitapa is known as the "la Paz del Espino Negro" (the Peace of the Blackthorn Tree).

words of one Marine Corps officer, "have worked a lifetime and never seen ten dollars."[30] With this inducement, and with a promise from Díaz to appoint Liberal governors in six departments (positions later held by several of Moncada's former generals), Moncada informed his ragged soldiers that their efforts to win freedom and honor "had been annulled in the final hour by order of the Government of the United States and by its army, one of the largest in the world," that it was not humanly possible to oppose the marines, and that therefore "we should be able to bow to force and give up our weapons, but not our dignity and self-respect. . . . It may be," he added prophetically, "that someday justice will prevail."[31]

All of Moncada's generals but one, Augusto Sandino, accepted the Tipitapa agreement and surrendered their weapons. Within a week more than nine thousand rifles, 296 machine guns, and nearly six million rounds of ammunition had been surrendered to the Marine Corps from both sides, and many more weapons were collected later in remote parts of the country.[32] In public statements Sacasa strongly protested against the Stimson-Moncada agreement and the disarming of his soldiers, but on May 20, 1927, he and twenty-six of his followers abandoned their provisional capital at Puerto Cabezas and departed for Costa Rica.[33] Probably as a reward for his easy compliance with Stimson's demands, General Moncada became president of Nicaragua in January 1929, through an election supervised by U.S. Marines, and in accordance with the Tipitapa agreement, the Marine Corps began to organize and train Stimson's new and "impartial" National Guard. This force soon joined U.S. soldiers in a long and costly campaign against Augusto Sandino and his small army of peasants, workers, and foreign volunteers, which the marines and the National Guard never defeated in almost six years of jungle warfare.

•

The people of the United States and their representatives in Congress did not allow these events to occur without opposition and protest. In fact,

[30] "More Letters from Nicaragua," *Outlook*, 6 July 1927, 317.

[31] Stimson, *American Policy*, 80, 82; José María Moncada, *Estados Unidos en Nicaragua* (Managua, 1942), 12–14.

[32] Stimson, *American Policy*, 84; Cummins, *Quijote on a Burro*, 19.

[33] *The New York Herald Tribune*, 10, 15, 17 May 1927. In rejecting the Stimson plan, Sacasa stated publicly:

Mr. Stimson, instead of investigating the real situation and doing justice to the Nicaraguan people, seems to have been sent for the express purpose of ramming down their throats the presidency of Díaz, the same Díaz who, with Chamorro, plotted the coup d'état which violated the constitution. . . . I do not believe, as Mr. Stimson has said, that the retention of Díaz in the Presidency is still to the honor and prestige of the United States; on the contrary, my belief is that a great nation acquires honor and prestige by respect for the sovereignty of small and weak countries instead of the oppression of those which struggle for the security of their institutions.

both before and after Sandino's rise to prominence, members of Congress and elements of the press often criticized or condemned the Nicaraguan policies of Presidents Coolidge and Hoover, and those of Taft before them. To better understand the gravity of these events, and to make Sandino's writings and his rebellion more comprehensible, it will be useful to quote members of Congress whose condemnations of U.S. policies were sometimes as vituperative as those of Sandino himself.

In January 1927, for example, as U.S. armed forces again moved into Nicaragua, Senator Burton K. Wheeler of Montana used these words to describe that country's plight:

> The State Department has literally gutted Nicaragua. . . . Its sovereignty is a ghastly mockery. . . . The country in its every aspect is absolutely under the merciless heel of the State Department and the New York bankers. Every strategic post, fiscal and military, is in the hands of appointees of the State Department. Nicaragua is this moment in the bitterest bondage in which any free people ever found themselves.[34]

On March 3, 1927, some two months before the onset of Sandino's rebellion, Senator Lynn J. Frazier of North Dakota declared:

> Every well-informed Senator on this floor knows that from first to last our dealings with Nicaragua have been of such a character that they have earned the world-wide designation of "dollar diplomacy." . . . In regard to Nicaragua, the Department of State not only has acted as a debt collector but as a bond broker. . . . Two great firms of international bankers—Brown Bros. and W. & J. Seligman, of New York City—have wound their financial tentacles about the unfortunate Nicaraguan Nation and are sucking it dry. . . . it is a curious coincidence, to say the least, that for a long period of time the Department of State always has seen fit to invoke the might of the American marines to put down the Liberals, whose policy is to develop Nicaragua for the Nicaraguans, and never yet has deposed one of these dictators who have betrayed their country to the American banking interests.[35]

Concerning the Knox-Castrillo and Bryan-Chamorro treaties, Senator William E. Borah, Republican Chairman of the Senate Foreign Relations Committe, stated in 1927:

> Mr. President, we made the loan treaty and we made the canal treaty with ourselves. Díaz . . . owed his political life, if not his physical life, to the presence of the force supplied by the United States; and while

---

[34] *Congressional Record*, 69th Cong., 2d sess., 1927, 68, pt. 2:2290.
[35] Ibid., 68, pt. 5:5523–24.

that force was there we made a loan which he approved, and we made a canal treaty. Mr. President, that transaction is as pronounced and unconscionable an act of imperialism as ever disgraced the records of any nation. It was a violation of the most primary precepts of international decency.[36]

In an article published in the *Congressional Record*, Senator Wheeler alluded to some unsavory Dickens characters to illustrate "the useful function" performed by Díaz for the American bankers and the State Department. "Those of you who have read Oliver Twist," he wrote,

> will recall old Fagin and his training school for juvenile burglars. Bill Sykes and other kindred spirits used the graduates of this school by putting them through windows too small for a man to enter. It was then the business of the little burglar to unlock the door so the big burglar could get in and get the stuff. . . . [Díaz] is an agile little Nicaraguan who has been thrust through the little window of the presidency several times to unlock the house of Nicaragua to certain American bankers and their faithful servant, our State Department.[37]

As Sandino's rebellion attracted growing world attention, some members of Congress expressed sympathy for the Nicaraguan people and even praise for Sandino himself. In March 1928, Senator J. Thomas Heflin of Alabama, a frequent critic of the administration's Nicaraguan policies, likened Sandino to the American founding fathers. "Sandino crying for liberty," he said,

> begging for the deliverance of his country from the invader, sounds like the cries our fathers made in the days of the Revolution when they were asking that the British forces be withdrawn. They asked him [Sandino] upon what conditions he would surrender. Here is his reply: "I demand the immediate withdrawal of the [American] invading troops. I shall never recognize a government imposed by a foreign power." That is good American doctrine. . . . We are seeking this man out to kill him for fighting for principles that we fought for in 1776.[38]

•

Sandino's rebellion began in May 1927, in direct response to the Stimson-Moncada agreement. That rebellion, however—and the many letters, manifestoes, proclamations, battle reports, interviews, and other documents that he wrote or dictated during the next seven years, many of which are included in this book—can only be understood in light of the

[36] Ibid., 68, pt. 2:1557.
[37] Ibid., 68, pt. 5:5794.
[38] Ibid., 70th Cong., 1st sess., 1928, 69, pt. 5:5037–38.

events that had plagued his country since his childhood. Motivated by intense patriotism and obsessed with Nicaragua's plight, Sandino had witnessed memorable events: the sight of Benjamín Zeledón, hero of the Mena War of 1912, tossed over the back of a horse and paraded to his grave; the arrest of his father for protesting the Bryan-Chamorro treaty; the landing of American naval forces at Puerto Cabezas in December 1926 and their seizure of Sacasa's arsenal; the costly battles of the Constitutionalist War of 1926–1927 in which he had himself played a commanding role; and, finally, the humiliating decision at Tipitapa, which had halted the Liberal army's advance on Managua, denying a Liberal victory and the hoped-for restoration of Nicaraguan sovereignty and self-respect.

During the first weeks after Tipitapa, as Sandino's army dwindled to a handful of followers, he perhaps envisioned only a brief display of defiant patriotism almost certain to end in death and intended to prove that some Nicaraguans at least would fight and die for their country. A broader mission soon crystallized, however, and seeking support he made it known to the world. His grievances, we learn from his writings, encompassed the entire spectrum of abuses committed since 1909 by "the traitors and invaders" of Nicaragua, but his attention also reached out to such areas of human concern as worker organization and legislation, the rights of women and children, the protection and development of Nicaragua's Indians, Central American unification, construction of a Nicaraguan canal for the benefit of Nicaraguans and the world in general, Indo-Hispanic cooperation for defense and the common welfare, and land reform and the establishment of peasant cooperatives—little of which is surprising considering the hard experiences of his childhood and youth as a member of the American peasant class and a migrant worker in Mexico and other Central American countries.

Despite such widespread interests, the essential purpose of Sandino's rebellion was to defend Nicaragua's basic right to exist as a free and independent country, a goal he expressed with the slogan, *Patria y Libertad* (fatherland and freedom), and with the name he chose for his columns of ragged soldiers: "the Army in Defense of the National Sovereignty of Nicaragua."[39] Throughout his revolt, in fact, Sandino insisted upon only two

---

[39] In *Intellectual Foundations of the Nicaraguan Revolution*, Donald C. Hodges alleges that Sandino was a conspiratorial "anarcho-communist" who disguised the real aims of his movement "behind a bizarre and mysterious symbolism that even the Sandinistas have failed to decipher" (xi). However, it is in his writings that we must search for the true Sandino. Nowhere in those writings does he mention such revolutionary leaders as the Mexican Ricardo Flores Magón, who, according to Hodges, made a lasting impression on him (5), and nowhere does he refer to such anarchist or communist thinkers as Mikhail Bakunin, Pierre Proudhon, Leon Trotsky, or even the martyrs of the era, Sacco and Vanzetti. In fact, the men he looked up to and even imitated were not anarchists or contemporary radical or revolutionary leaders. They were the heroes of the independence movement, of Latin Amer-

basic conditions for disbanding his army and retiring to private life: total withdrawal of U.S. armed forces from Nicaragua and the establishment of a constitutional government free of foreign domination, essentially the same demands mentioned by Senator Heflin in 1928. In spite of ever-changing circumstances, Sandino reiterated these positions again and again, until in February 1933, a month after the marines withdrew and Dr. Juan B. Sacasa was inaugurated constitutional president of Nicaragua, he made peace with the newly elected Liberal government and brought his war to an end.

The documents that follow tell Sandino's story in great detail, but additional comments are needed. Sandino's writings constitute much more, I believe, than one man's protest against tyrannical government and foreign intervention. Often eloquent and inspirational, poetic or picaresque, sometimes cruel or impertinent, at times mystical, but always defiant and motivated by a deep love of country, his writings have inspired a generation of Nicaraguan leaders and, with their victory in 1979, a nation in search of progress and independence. Sandino's thought, to quote Sergio Ramírez,

> is not a theoretical proposition, but the consequence of experience. Those who would hope to find in Sandino clear ordered statements about the means of production or class struggle will fail, because Sandino was not a theoretician, but rather a man of action who as a result of that action translated his war experience, his revolutionary experience, his political experience, into words. And even in those writings we do not find the thought of a man who is scientifically prepared, but rather that of a "well-read artisan," as we would say in good Nicaraguan, that of a peasant who transformed himself into a politician during the struggle and in the midst of the struggle discovered the forms of his political expression, which were based upon his fundamental class interest; because it is necessary to see whose side he was on and whom he was against to define his true position.[40]

Taken as a whole, I would add, Sandino's writings make a memorable self-portrait, the spontaneous autobiography of one of the most unusual personalities in the history of Latin America, whose physical life ended

---

ican liberalism, and of Central American unity, such as Simón Bolívar, Father Hidalgo, Francisco Morazán, and Benito Juárez. Merely to list possible radical influences in Mexico or elsewhere on the assumption that Sandino "could not have escaped" them is highly speculative unless proven by facts. Therefore we must continue to accept the opinions of most scholars who have studied Sandino: that his philosophy combined patriotic and anti-imperialist tenets directed mainly against U.S. intervention in Nicaragua with a deep concern for the lot of the Latin American peasant and working classes, both tendencies affected by strong spiritist overtones. See Booth, *The End and the Beginning*, 236–37, n. 26.

[40] Ramírez, "Sandino," 433–34.

with his assassination at the hands of those he fought, but whose message is still relevant today. Equally important, this is a detailed first-hand account of a long and destructive war told from the point of view of one of its principal combatants—a war that, though little known to the people of the United States, is almost as relevant to them today as it is to Nicaraguans, not only because citizens of the United States fought and died in that war, but because when a nation knows what it did in the past it may have the power to change the future. One of the best lessons to be taken from this book was expressed in a letter that Sandino wrote to President Hoover at the start of his term in 1929: "As long as you continue the policies of Coolidge and Kellogg," he warned the new American president, "you will continue to encounter Sandinos."

DOCUMENTS

· CHILDHOOD AND YOUTH ·

I. LETTER TO THE HONDURAN POET FROYLÁN TURCIOS, APRIL 1, 1928

In view of the interest that our independent brothers of the Americas have shown in learning something accurate about the life of the soldier, Augusto C. Sandino, and obligated by the slanderous campaign that cowardly sellouts have unleashed against me in my own country, which I am seeking to liberate while accepting every sacrifice, I take this opportunity to send you in brief form some facts about my early life, which you may use as you see fit.

I was born at four o'clock in the morning on the 18th of May, 1895, in the town of Victoria, department of Masaya, Nicaragua. Two youngsters less than eighteen years of age were my parents. I studied my first letters in the public schools opened by General J. S. Zelaya, the constitutional president of that period.

At the age of twelve I left my parents and set off in search of adventure. I traveled through the principal cities of Central and North America, as well as in the most important industrial centers, remaining the longest time in Mexico.

I have in my possession many letters of recommendation offering proof of my honorable conduct from the companies for which I worked. The profession of mechanic was the one in which I distinguished myself.

During my long absence from my country there was never any tranquility in my soul, because when I got to know a place, I longed to find myself in a better one, everywhere suffering disappointment by imagining myself superior to the reality that I was beginning to know. Likewise I confess that in our profane world I never found happiness, and for this reason, and because I was in search of spiritual consolation, I read mythological books and searched for teachers of religion, the last one of which was the honorable gentleman, Justino Barbiaux, who lives in Álamo, Veracruz, Mexico.

I have always been inclined to read everything that in my opinion is moral and instructive. One of the things I have concluded, according to my latest observations and way of thinking, is that the men to whom God has granted great minds often become conceited, and I can't figure out why they forget that they are mortal human beings, falling into the unpardonable crime of trafficking with justice and human flesh as if people were a herd of pigs. In this way the degradation of ninety-five percent of my fellow citizens has come about.

I have also realized that good doctrines are both condemned and invoked by unscrupulous men, merely to achieve advantages, without a true regard for Humanity or for God.

In short, from the knowledge I have acquired I have concluded that humanity can never live in dignity as long as it deviates from sound reason and the laws that honor requires.

Thus, seeing that the United States of North America, with the sole right granted by brute force, would deprive us of our Fatherland and our Freedom, I have accepted the unjustified challenge that tends to throw our sovereignty to the ground, imposing upon my acts my responsibility before History. To remain inactive or indifferent, like most of my fellow citizens, would be to add myself to the rude crowd of mercenary assassins of their own country.

Thus my acts will justify me, since my ideal feeds upon a broad horizon of international opinion.

I love Justice and for it I will sacrifice myself. Material treasures do not exercise any power over my person; the treasures I long to possess are spiritual.

[12, vol. 4, no. 65 (May 1928), 1213]

2. THE BOY FROM NIQUINOHOMO: SANDINO'S CHILDHOOD AS TOLD TO JOSÉ ROMÁN IN 1933[1]

Socially the Sandino family occupies one of the most prominent places, perhaps the most prominent, in Niquinohomo and in the history of the town going far back into the past.

A certain Señor Sandino arrived in Nicaragua from Spain, and he belonged to the same family as two other Sandinos who had also emigrated from Spain, one to Colombia and the other to Campeche, in Mexico. The one who came to Nicaragua managed to make some money, got married, and had several children, among them: José María, Ofreciano, and Santiago. This last in turn married a pure Indian girl named Agustina Múñoz, with whom he had the following children: the girls Asunción, Cayetana, and Isabel, and the boys Pedro, Cleto, and Gregorio, who was my father. My father was born on March 12, 1869, in Niquinohomo, in the hereditary family home, where the family has resided until this day. He inherited some money, coffee farms, and houses, and he is still the richest man in the place.

My father is short and strong. In him predominates the blood of his mother, because he is markedly of the Indo-Hispanic type and a man of good manners and sober behavior. From early youth he dedicated himself to the cultivation of his inherited property, and he married Doña América Tiffer, with whom he had the following children: Asunción, América, and Sócrates, who is the oldest and was born in October 1898. As can be seen, I am not the son of that marriage, but rather I was born four years earlier, in 1894.[2]

My mother's name is Margarita Calderón, and she was a worker on one of of my father's farms. I am, then, Román, the son of love, in other words a bastard, according to social conventions. After I came into the world my father forgot the woman who was the mother of his first child, because she was a farm worker, and he married Doña América Tiffer, a member of the provincial bourgeoisie.

And so I opened my eyes in misery and was brought up in misery, without even a child's necessities, and while my mother picked coffee I was left to myself. From the time I could walk I did so on the coffee plantations, helping my mother to fill her basket in order to earn a few centavos.

I was badly dressed and fed even worse in those cold cordilleras. That was how I grew up, and maybe that was why I didn't grow. When it wasn't coffee they sent us out to harvest, it was wheat, corn, or other cereals, with wages so minimal and the work so hard that living was sorrow for us, true sorrow! And, yet, to be permitted to work we had to get registrations—which my mother and I never stopped paying for. And, aside from that, keep in mind that my mother often gave birth, which further aggravated our situation. Believe me, it's terrible to remember all that, but it's the simple truth.

There were times when just to eat we had to hock some trinket for a few centavos. And there were days, many days, very many days, in fact, when, with my mother completely disabled, I had to go out at night to steal on the plantations so that I wouldn't have to let her die of hunger. And this is how I grew toward manhood, standing up to a cruel and merciless life and the will of destiny by means of a fierce and tenacious effort. Fortunately, nature endowed me with thought and willpower. Very early I began to understand the great tragedy of my life, which gnawed at my innermost self with my recognition of my awful misery. Misery and powerlessness at my tender age. I didn't depend at all on my father, and it was I myself who had to take care of my mother.

When once, by chance, my half brother Sócrates met me on the street, he gave me an old piece of clothing that I exchanged for my rags. When I compared my brother's situation with my own, I was infuriated by the injustices of life. Even though I was such a hard worker, what could a creature less than ten years old earn in a place where even adults' wages were only a few centavos a day? I was at a period in life when I needed—not, let's say, the most basic things for the comfort of the body—but rather what was even more essential, the warmth of a home for spiritual peace and the formation of character and personality. I lacked both of these, and the worst of it was that I was entirely conscious of my situation.

Now, Román, I'm going to relate a specific detail I'll never forget. Something terrible happened that made my life even worse. My mother and I worked on a farm that belonged to the village mayor, my father being the judge. She had received an advance payment of a few pesos, but since she got an offer of better pay on another coffee plantation, she decided to accept that offer, to be able to pay her debt back even sooner, but the mayor, fearing he would lose his advance, ordered her arrested. And so one fine afternoon some soldiers appeared and put us in the local jail. My mother's grief and the cruel mistreatment she had received caused her to abort, which brought on a copious hemorrhage that nearly killed her. And it was left to me, all by myself, to care for her. All by myself! In that cold dirty village prison. As biological secrets, which were unknown to me until then, since I was hardly nine years old, were revealed to me, my mother's groans and the fact that she was near death restrained my anger. And though I was only a child, with my mother already asleep and I unable to sleep, I lay down beside her on that bloody floor and thought of a thousand atrocious and fierce acts of revenge. I clearly remember how, as I understood my own lack of power, I began to ponder over things with my childish philosophy.

Why would God act like this? Why do people claim that authority is the right arm of the law? And what kind of law is that? If, as the priest says, law is the voice of God intended to protect the people, why is it that authority, instead of helping us poor people, favors society's drones? Why does God love Sócrates more than he loves me, if I have to work and he doesn't? Then God damn it, I thought to myself, God and life are pure shit. It's only us poor people who are getting screwed!

Soon after that my mother went off with a man to Granada and I refused to follow her. Since I've always been a person with a decisive character, I went to live with my maternal grandmother, who was extremely poor and did any kind of work she could get.

Alone I continued my hand-to-mouth struggle with life. Knowing that my mother was far away with a string of children and that my father, on the other hand, was married to a woman who couldn't even see me, with my childish reasoning and my sentimental heart, I began to think that life didn't make any sense, that I had no reason to exist, because the same people who had brought me into the world treated me like this, and I wasn't in any way to blame. [. . .]

What's certain is that when I might have become a vagabond or a criminal, I decided to make myself into somebody. The fact is that one day, hungry, dressed in rags and carrying some packages in order to earn a few centavos, I met my father on the street entirely by chance. I put the packages down on the ground, walked up to him and, crying but with spirit, asked him, "Listen, sir, am I your son or am I not?"

And my father answered, "Yes, son, I am your father."

Then I replied: "Sir, if I'm your son, why don't you treat me the way you treat Sócrates?"

Tears appeared in the old man's eyes. He took me into his arms. He kissed me and hugged me hard and long. And he took me to his house. I was almost eleven at the time.

Despite my young age, by hard work and good behavior I made myself indispensable in my paternal home. They sent me to school, but instead of attending regularly, Sócrates and I and some other boys went off to play war. With stones, lemons, and green oranges. And if it happened that we were surprised by the police, because in the period when General Zelaya was president education was compulsory, we had even more fun annoying them and making fun of them and then running for safety inside the school. I was a very bad student, because I spent almost all my time making wax soldiers with which we fought real battles in miniature, which were witnessed by neighborhood friends. Since my ignorance was well known in the entire school and since there was a little girl whom I had settled my eyes on, one day when leaving class she came up to me with a book in her hand and, as a way to torment me, asked me to read it to her. My first impulse was to admit my ignorance, but I made up some excuse and saved myself from shame.

When I got home I decided I would never again find myself in such a situation, and I devoted myself to study with a stubborn tenacity, though I didn't boast about it. Soon I was one of the most diligent students in the school. I remained studious, and as I grew older I assisted my father more with the management of his business. I was even able to establish a little business of my own, dealing in grains. With my help my father eventually controlled the bean business in that whole region, and he doubled his capital. [. . .]

The first trip I ever made was on foot to Costa Rica. I worked as a mechanic's assistant in the Ceilán hacienda near the border, which was the property of a relative of yours, Don Pablo Jiménez Román, a great gentleman who treated me with affection and decency. When I arrived there I deposited a large sum of money with Don Pablo, and during the four months I worked for him, I didn't touch a penny of my wages, so that I was able to increase what I'd brought with me. I left Ceilán for Rivas and Rivas for San Juan del Sur. There, in that port, I signed onto a ship, also as a mechanic's assistant. I wandered for a long time, changing ships, and I learned the machinist's trade. I traveled to many countries, indeed half the world. I saved my money, and then I returned to Niqui-nohomo near the end of 1919. My cousin Mercedes attracted me like a magnet. Not for a single day had I stopped thinking about her, although she of course didn't know that.

In Niquinohomo I went into the grain business, independently of my family. I traded with the villages and with Managua and Granada. Because I didn't have any vices and practiced orderly habits, my small capital grew constantly. And, aside from that, the people I did business with soon put their trust in me.

At last, after a long romantic history, in 1921, a month before I was to marry my cousin Mercedes, I experienced an incident of great importance to my life, since it sent my destiny in another direction. Dagoberto Rivas was an individual of my same village with whom I had always had a good friendship and even some business dealings. One day Dagoberto heard that a sister of his, a widow, appeared to be involved with me in an amorous relationship, or at least it was popularly rumored that she was. A neighbor of Dagoberto, a man who liked to make trouble, was the person who spread this bit of gossip. One Sunday in June, without any knowledge of any of this, when I arrived for mass unfortunately I sat down on a bench behind Dagoberto and several of his friends. When they noticed my arrival, Rivas and his friends began to whisper various personal insults at me, while all the time I remained impassive. Interpreting my calm manner as cowardliness, Rivas got more and more upset, and at the very moment that the priest began to elevate the host, Rivas turned halfway around and struck at my face, which, though I was able to deflect it, resulted in a blow to my forehead. In a spontaneous and thoughtless act, I took out my revolver and shot him, fortunately only wounding him in the leg.

Naturally, Román, as you can imagine, this was a scandal of the kind that epic tales are made of in a village like Niquinohomo. Bullets in the church during mass and at the moment of the elevation of the host! To avoid a trial and other undesirable results, despite being about to get married, I left at once for the Atlantic coast, taking only the money I had in cash. I spent a month on the coast, using another name, and from there I left for La Ceiba, Honduras, where I worked at the Montecristo sugar plantation. In La Ceiba, in the hotel where I was staying, another Nicaraguan also lived, a young man named Montenegro, with whom I developed a very good friendship. Years later, wandering about in life, Montenegro joined the United States Marine Corps and it was his fate to come to fight against me in Nicaragua, and he was wounded. I was always a good friend of Montenegro.

[7, 35–40, 46–48]

1. Sandino gave this account of his early life to the young poet and reporter Jose Román in 1933, soon after the signing of the peace treaty with President Sacasa that ended the military struggle. RC

2. In the previous document and elsewhere Sandino claims to have been born in 1895. RC

3. LETTER TO MARÍA SANDINO, JULY 1921[1]

Señorita Maríta S. Sandino
Niquinohomo

My never-forgotten Maríta,

I think that by this time you should know that I am leaving the place where I am now, because I don't want to lose time.

My love, I was very upset about your note, to the point that I wanted to go to speak with all of you personally and explain my motives and ask you to forgive me and to tell you that you were right about me, but today I feel differently about things because, according to what Fernando tells me, I didn't understand your note correctly, and if that is true, then my heart has been made a bit more tranquil.

I want to tell you about the difficulties I had on the day I went to see you and couldn't. I left from the place where I was at six o'clock, by a road called El Negro, and I reached Masaya at eight. I passed through the edge of town and left by way of San Sebastián, and after walking for a while I found myself on a corner with three policemen, but I went by them so fast that when they tried to look at me I had already passed out of the light and into the darkness. At last I reached the Catarina road and when I managed to get pretty far away from Masaya, I felt happy, because in just a few minutes I would see you again.

But all my happiness was in vain. I reached Catarina and was surprised by a group of people who were out walking on the occasion of the feast of Saint Peter. I changed streets and there was no lack of people there, but they said nothing to me. I arrived at my beloved Niquinohomo and left my mule at the place that seemed best to me, and I went into Braulia's coffee estate on foot to where my mother was, and Fernando was waiting for me. I asked if you expected me, and he said yes, that he had been told that you did. But on the street a music band was marching and I couldn't go through there, but instead through Luisa Blanco's place. I entered the woods by way of the Alvarado spring, and I went through with a thousand difficulties, because, though I knew the woods so well, I lost my way because it was so dark. I walked for about half an hour without knowing where I was, but at last I was able to get out of the woods, and I took the road I wanted, which is the one leading to the house of Victoriano Campos, to his orchard. Later I hoped to pass that house, but some dogs came out that wanted to bite me or at least seemed to know that I was there. I turned back and went into the woods through a little pasture, and when I reached my aunt's well I was happy, because the hour was near when I could greet you and your family.

Finally I approached the fence of your house, lifting myself up over the wire, not feeling how damp I was, but thinking only that the moment was near when all my sacrifices would be repaid. I made out your gloomy house, the animals whinnied as if to greet me, and at last I approached quickly and tapped on the door, softly, then harder, but nothing happened; again and again I knocked, but nothing happened. I felt sad. I wasn't happy anymore, and I considered myself a wretch. I'm not much for feeling sorry for myself, but I felt a knot in my throat when I realized that the doors of the house where the mistress of my heart lives had been closed to me. I went out onto the street, and while passing in front of your window, I remembered the place where you sleep and gave you a kiss.

I reached the plaza and found myself among a small cluster of people and greeted them, and they didn't say anything to me, and so I left. I reached the place where my father was and left him after a long conversation. It was 1:30, all was calm, and I felt no fear of any kind. The moon was already casting its light, but opaque, and as I looked at the town at that dark hour it seemed like a church, and its houses mausoleums.

I left at 2:30 and reached the place where I was staying at 6:05 in the morning, sad and grieved.

But when Fernando arrived, my life was already different.

Accept the sincerity of my heart.

A.C.S.

Greetings to my forever-remembered Don Mateo and Doña Beatriz, to Doña María and the other members of the family.

[20, 3 pp.]

1. María or Mariíta Sandino and Mercedes Sandino are clearly the same person, that is, Sandino's cousin and fiancée, who remained in Niquinohomo and never married. This letter is an account of Sandino's movements immediately after the incident with Dagoberto Rivas described in the previous document. RC

4. LETTER TO
DON GREGORIO SANDINO, 1922

Señor Don Gregorio Sandino
La Victoria

My dearest father:

I have received your esteemed letter. In it you say I should pay Don
Florencio. Yes, papa. Don't think that my unhappiness about that isn't
very great, but I haven't done it yet because of the bad effect this terrible
climate has had upon me, and only in the last few months have I been
able to get a few pesos together, but at the cost of some privations and of
keeping up the illusion that I might travel to a more civilized country
where, even if I couldn't make some money, I could at least gaze upon the
full and clear light of civilization, from which I might have something to
gain.

This place is picturesque and one can earn a great deal of money, but
what isn't spent with sighs is spent with tears. Listen. Life in these places
is entirely bohemian, and the climate is truly a focal point of disease. As
a result, many of us don't make any money because of the many illnesses,
and others because they don't know how to control their disorderly pas-
sions.

If I decided to settle my debts, it would mean not leaving here, because
you should understand that it isn't so easy to go from one country to
another with very little money. When a man reaches his destination, upon
landing, he has thousands of different impressions, and everything seems
so strange. Nobody speaks to him, and if he doesn't have any money he
doesn't have anything. After asking for a room at some hotel, he arranges
things as best he can and then goes out looking for work. The people size
him up from head to toe and ask a thousand questions, including what
does he know how to do and why did he leave the place where he was
before, and, in the end, he even gets insulted most of the time. Now you
will see the importance of arriving in a place with a little money and a
good appearance, instead of being penniless, and looking like some kind
of eccentric.

Here there are thousands of men who want to go back where they came
from but can't. They don't have the means because, even if they earn

hundreds of dollars, they squander it. In these places, wherever one goes, one hears music of every kind. There are great dance halls, many distractions, today one thing, tomorrow another, and so those who have gotten themselves patched up are the owners of the countless canteens and gambling houses. This life is not for a man who wants to distinguish himself at something, and so I am doing what I can to get out of here as soon as I possibly can.

Greetings to my sisters and to my stepmother, and for you a strong embrace from your indefatigable but unfortunate

AUGUSTO

Greetings to Don J. M. Sandino and to Don César. Tell them I remember them with affection.

[20, 2 pp.]

5. LETTER TO MARÍA SANDINO,
JUNE 3, 1922

Honduras Sugar & Distilling Co.
Paid-up capital: 250,000 in Gold Property of
the Great Central Mill "Abeja" and Distill-
ery Located in Dutuville, Estates of Palmyra,
Montecristo, Corinto, and Victoria
La Ceiba and Dutuville, June 3, 1922

Señorita Mariíta S. Sandino
LaVictoria

My love:

I am finishing one year of absence from you, my life, but neither that difficult year nor twenty more would be enough to diminish the unchanging love I profess for you. This year of sad separation has been nothing less than a year of remorse for me, and one of countless adventures. Neither you nor anyone else who hasn't gone out into the world can understand how difficult an adventurer's life can be.

Do not take the word *adventurer* in its unfavorable sense as far as I'm concerned, because an adventurer can be any man forced into such a life by his circumstances. You should also understand that anyone who has traveled such roads is four times as much a man as one who, having left his country, has been supported by his wealth. And so it can be said that anyone who has traveled such hard roads thinks when he finds himself among such small birds that they still don't know what the world is all about. It's like the value of a hundred-dollar bill compared with a few small copper pennies.

Mariíta, I feel very sad when I remember the letters I have sent to you that you have not answered, and your silence has forced me to reach several conclusions. I am very wicked, and during my hours of meditation I have imagined what all of you must think about me. I'm going to tell you what I imagine you are all saying.

For example, you must think the following: This man has been my headache. He is my trickster. Maybe it's also true that he loves me because some years have gone by and he hasn't forgotten me. But my biggest problem is that I don't love him very much, since I don't believe he will come back, and it's better for me not to dignify him by answering his letters because otherwise he will go on with his foolishness and then maybe I will suffer. Yes, yes, no, no, yes . . . it would be better to forget him. Oh, God, grant me what I ask! No, not this anymore. How I regret! How I repent . . . And something more: What did I fall in love with? He isn't a model person, he isn't rich, and most important, he went away . . . But it's better so, better! And if he comes back? If he does, I'll just ignore him. Yes, I'm determined, and what difference would it make to me if that fool cracked his head thinking about me?

What your esteemed father says among you: "This guy will not do for my daughter; she is not a burden to me, and so why should I sacrifice her to this vagabond who no longer wants to stay in his own place? And it's clear that the crazy act he committed was intentional, so that he could leave. There's no way I will let her respond to this vagabond, this pervert, this deceiver."

What your grandmother says: "I don't say anything. All I say is that he's not bad and that if they'd gotten married he would have made a splendid husband, but misfortune followed him around."

What your mother says: "He won't return. He likes the wanderer's life, and I always knew he was a liar."

What your Aunt Mariíta says: "I didn't believe they would get married because I always looked upon him as being very unreliable."

Mateíto and Zoilita, I'm sure, lean neither one way nor the other. At most they might say sometimes that they like the way things turned out, and at times what a poor man I am.

This is what I imagine from all of you. I beg you to pardon me if my wicked conjectures offend you, and I want you to know that as long as I live I will never forget you.

Greetings to those about whom I have lied in my malicious letter.

And you, my life, my angel, accept the endless kisses and embraces of your

AUGUSTO

My Mayan, If you love me, send greetings to my father in my name, and to my mother, and for this I give you another kiss. Good-bye. Yours.

[17, 2 pp.]

· 1926–1927 ·

6. THE RETURN TO NICARAGUA, 1926

This is an opportune time, I believe, to make it known that I was born in a little town in the Department of Masaya on May 18, 1895; that as I grew up I lacked even the most essential things; and that I never imagined that I would come to assume, in the name of the Nicaraguan people, the position in which I now find myself as head of the Army in Defense of the Sovereignty of Nicaragua. When I reached the Segovias, I was still unaware of the task awaiting me. Events have revealed to me the stand that I should take. In Mexico I was working for a Yankee company, the Huasteca Petroleum Company, when I realized that I should come to Nicaragua to take part in the struggle against North American power[. . . .]

Back in the year 1925 I wanted to believe that everything in Nicaragua had become ignominious and that honor had disappeared entirely from the people of that land. At that time, because of my sincere character, I succeeded in surrounding myself with a group of spiritualist friends, with whom day after day I discussed the submission of our Latin American peoples before the hypocritical or forceful advance of the murderous Yankee empire. On one of those days I told my friends that if in Nicaragua there were a hundred men who loved their country as much as I do, our nation would restore its absolute sovereignty, threatened by that same Yankee empire. My friends replied that perhaps there were in Nicaragua that many men or more, but that the difficulty was finding out who they were. From that moment I wanted to search for those hundred men, and chance wished me to assume the posture you now witness, and with that posture I continue to search with the hope of learning where those hundred legitimate sons of Nicaragua may be[. . . .]

Nevertheless, here in the theater of events, I realized that the political leaders, both Conservatives and Liberals, are a pack of dogs, cowards and traitors, incapable of guiding a patriotic and courageous people. We have abandoned those leaders and among ourselves, workers and peasants, we have improvised our leadership. And yet, in these days of such splendor and good examples, the ruinous politicians continue to vie for the caresses of the foreign whip, and, like dogs and cats in a sack, they are fighting to reach the presidency on the basis of a foreign supervision that we would not accept. Spiteful people say that Sandino and his army are bandits, which means that within a year all of Nicaragua will be converted into a nation of bandits, because, before then, our army will have taken the reins of national power, for the greater welfare of our country. Nicaragua will be freed only by bullets, and at the cost of our own blood. [. . .]

[1, 35–38]

7. THE DECISION TO RETURN: FRAGMENT OF AN INTERVIEW

[. . .] This same intervention has been the reason why the other peoples of Central America and Mexico detest us Nicaraguans. And that hatred was confirmed for me during my travels in those countries.

I felt most deeply wounded when they said to me, "Sell-out of your own country, shameless, a traitor."

At first I responded to these phrases. I said that since I was not a statesman, I didn't think I deserved such dishonorable terms. But later I began to think and I understood that they were right, because, as a Nicaraguan, I had a right to protest, and I knew then that in Nicaragua a revolutionary movement had broken out. I worked then for the Huasteca Petroleum Company in Tampico. It was May 15, 1926. I possessed my savings, which amounted to five thousand dollars.

I took from those savings three thousand dollars and I came to Managua. I learned what had been going on and I went to the mines of San Albino, beginning my active political life, the details of which everybody knows.[. . .]

[3, 89–90]

8. SANDINO AND THE CONSTITUTIONALIST
WAR OF 1926–1927[1]

For the Honored Press of the World in General:

On February 2, 1927, I returned to the Segovias from Puerto Cabezas, where I had gone to request weapons from Dr. Juan Bautista Sacasa, so that soldiers under my command might provide better service in the Constitutionalist War that had broken out that year in Nicaragua. I stayed in Puerto Cabezas for forty days, asking for weapons without receiving any during that time.

On December 24, 1926, the Yankees declared Puerto Cabezas a neutral zone, ordering Dr. Sacasa to evacuate the entire Constitutionalist Army from that port within forty-eight hours, along with any Nicaraguan war matériel located there. Having received this rude order, the Constitutionalists began to abandon the town within the brief specified period. Since they were unable to remove all the weapons stored there, many of them were thrown into the sea by the Yankees. As a result of this terrible humiliation, Sacasa's forces abandoned forty rifles and seven thousand rounds of ammunition along the stretch of coast from Puerto Cabezas to Prinzapolka.

My six aides and I didn't want to go another step without taking those abandoned weapons with us. With the help of some natives of Mosquitia we transported the weapons and ammunition by land to Prinzapolka. Moncada was in Prinzapolka, and the arms I gathered together came again under his control.

I had written several letters to General Moncada asking him for weapons to give impetus to the Great Constitutionalist War in the Segovias, but he had deceptively put me off. In my eagerness to do something for my country, I petitioned General Moncada to allow me at least to take those forty rifles and the ammunition, which would have been lost if I had not recovered them. Moncada replied that I was to do nothing in the Segovias and that the best thing I could do would be to join one of the units he was ordering into the interior.

My reply was that I didn't anticipate any success for the army that he was sending into the interior if at the same time the enemy weren't confronted in the Segovias. Otherwise, the Constitutionalist Army would be destroyed in the neighborhood of Chontales.

My reasoning didn't please Moncada. He denied me the weapons, and so I began my return trip to the Segovias along with my six aides. At the port of Wonta on the return trip I met Doctors Arturo Baca and Onofre Sandoval, who were on their way to Prinzapolka to speak to General Moncada. The first of these two gentlemen was Undersecretary of War and the second Minister of Development in Sacasa's government. The said ministers invited me to return to Prinzapolka, promising that they would urge Moncada to allow me to take those few rifles and the ammunition, which they themselves had considered lost.

I returned to Prinzapolka, received the rifles, and, after a month of navigation on the Coco River, arrived on February 2 at the town of Wiwilí. At exactly the moment I was returning to the Segovias, the battle of Chinandega took place, under the leadership of General Francisco Parajón. As a result of this battle, enemy forces had greatly reduced their defenses in the towns of Ocotal, Estelí, Jinotega, and Matagalpa, the capitals of the four departments of the Segovias. Rapidly I extended myself over the Segovias with the help of those few rifles, and suddenly the enemy evacuated those four departments.

The battle of Chinandega ended in the enemy's favor, and they recovered the towns of Matagalpa and Jinotega. They couldn't do the same, however, with Ocotal and Estelí, where they came under pressure from forces commanded by General Camilo López Irías, with whom we were cooperating independently. In Ocotal I had an interview with General López Irías, and we agreed that he would control the department of Estelí and I the department of Jinotega. Estelí was soon brought under control, without any trouble whatsoever, because there were no enemy forces there. I controlled the entire department of Jinotega with the exception of its capital.

I camped on the plains of Yucapuca, two leagues from the departmental capital. On the plains of Yucapuca we endured three hard-fought battles, in which we won the most glorious victories for our army. My column grew in men and weapons.

I had already met Blanca Aráuz, telegraph operator of San Rafael del Norte. (She was a very pleasant young girl of nineteen years of age.)

The cold on the plains of Yucapuca was almost polar, and so after the three battles, I was forced by the cold to abandon my positions there, concentrating my forces in San Rafael del Norte. From there I planned new activities. We had reestablished the telegraphic communications of the two departments, with the exception of the city of Jinotega itself.

I resided with my general staff in Blanca's house, and the telegraph office was also installed there. During many long daylight hours and even at night I sat before the table where Blanca worked. Many of my conferences with the different parts of the departments were carried on by telegraph. In this way I fell in love with Blanca, and she became my fiancée.

During my stay in San Rafael del Norte I was in contact with General Camilo López Irías, and we were in agreement on all our columns' movements. The forces under my command had another clash between Saraguazca and San Gabriel with good success. General López Irías captured from the enemy two trucks loaded with rifle ammunition in a place called Chagüitillo, on the road between Managua and Matagalpa. His forces were made up of seven hundred fully equipped men, and his weapons were those left over from the Cosigüina expedition and the battle of Chinandega.[2] My forces were made up of two hundred fully equipped men.

General López Irías informed me by telegraph that, reacting to the capture of the trucks, a powerful enemy column was approaching Estelí. I offered him my cooperation. That same day, my men had captured food supplies in the valley of Apanás from the enemy force that had occupied Jinotega. I concentrated all my forces in the great plaza of the church of San Rafael del Norte, and from among the soldiers I considered the best, I chose eighty cavalrymen, sending them to the command of General López Irías, who, as stated earlier, was occupying Estelí.

During a night and half a day General José León Díaz marched to the place where his column was needed. The enemy was taking up positions in front of General López Irías's forces in the place called Los Espejos. At dawn the following morning a formidable battle took place between the Constitutionalist forces and the Conservatives. General López Irías's column was torn to pieces by the enemy.

My men, whose aim was to protect General López Irías, defeated the enemy on his flank and sent him cargoes of food, ammunition and other objects.

General López Irías traveled by automobile from Los Espejos to Estelí, informing me by telegraph that his column had been destroyed, that he had no information about my men, and that, considering their courage, he feared another disaster. I answered him angrily, and he didn't contradict me. I ordered a regrouping in San Rafael del Norte of the cavalry under the command of General José León Díaz, which at that time was in Estelí.

While all this was going on, I had sent out several dispatches to put myself in contact with General Moncada's forces. This I had now accomplished, and General Moncada's letters to me were desperate. (Several such letters are preserved in our army's archive.)

In the last of these letters there is a paragraph that I am not copying from the original since I don't have it at hand, but which more or less says the following: "If you do not soon come to the aid of my army, we will hold you responsible for any disaster that may occur." Signed by Luis Beltrán Sandoval and José María Moncada.

The enemy had now gained control of Estelí and still held the city of Jinotega, Matagalpa, and the principal places through which the forces of the Segovias might be moved in the direction of Chontales, which was where Moncada was located. I was more or less surrounded by the enemy's columns, and there was no news at all of General López Irías.

In the area of the Segovias that I controlled, I ordered the employees whom I had left in the towns of Quilalí and El Jícaro to organize units of unarmed volunteers who might be sent to General Moncada's encampments in Chontales. My order was quickly obeyed by the employees of the said towns. During those same days, while Moncada was in a state of desperation, two columns of unarmed volunteers arrived where I was, one under the command of Colonel Antonio López and the other under the command of Colonel Pompilio Reyes. These columns had been about to turn back before they reached San Rafael del Norte, where I was camped. The news about General López Irías's disaster had been alarming.

Blanca and I discussed in private the combined plan that would allow us to send forces to General Moncada and to capture the city of Jinotega. With the aid of a sketch of the city of Jinotega, given to me by Dr. González of Matagalpa, I completed this two-pronged plan.

On an afternoon in the month of March of that same year, I brought together my entire force in the plaza of San Rafael del Norte. There I announced that the first leader of the unarmed volunteers would be Colonel Simón Cantarero, and the second leader Colonel Pompilio Reyes. I organized the force into four companies, a general staff, and a field command, and I circulated the news that we were on our way to join General Moncada.

We left the town of San Rafael del Norte at seven o'clock, and that same night we reached the plains of Yucapuca for the second time. There I gave the necessary orders to the leaders of the column of unarmed volunteers, to the effect that they were to march to Tierra Azul, the place where Moncada was, with a letter from me. I also ordered them to make their group useful there until my arrival. At the same time I told them of my plan to capture Jinotega, and that the enemy would not try to prevent their march, but would prefer instead to protect the town of Jinotega, which we would attack that same night.

I gave the plan and the orders in written form to each of the unit leaders who were to take part in the battle of Jinotega. The column commanded by Colonel Salvador Bosque and Colonel Clemente Torres would enter the town by way of La Montañita; General José León Díaz, Colonel Joaquín Lobo, and Colonel Coronado Maradiaga would enter with their columns by way of Peña de la Cruz; Colonel Ignacio Talavera would enter with his force by way of La Cabaña; the column of Major José Morales and Captain Juan López would enter by way of La América; the general staff would enter by way of La Puerta. An order was also given to Colonel Rufo Antonio Marín to enter with his column of reinforcements by way of El Chirinagua. The people who went to Chontales and the others who went to fight at Jinotega broke out in enthusiastic cheers, and then they all set out by different routes.

At five in the morning of the second day, our men began to fire against the enemy's positions.

The city was gloomy. With the first rays of dawn, the electric lights that illuminated it seemed very pale. The town church was distinguished by its white mausoleums. The moment was perfect for lifting Rubén Darío into a state of ecstasy.[3] It was the first time I had seen that city. I fell in love with it as I would fall in love with a bride, and I'll never forget it.

At nine in the morning the column commanded by Colonels Salvador Bosque and Clemente Torres gained control of the fortress of El Cubulcán, which was defended by General Gabriel Artola. The fighting continued in the city during the entire day. Because of the distance that separated one column from another, orders had not been given to the conquerors of El Cubulcán to advance over the city. But when I discovered with my telescope that our red and black flag fluttered on the summit of El Cubulcán, I gave the appropriate order. At two o'clock in the afternoon the previously mentioned leaders fell upon the city. The fighting was bitter until our forces entered the enemy's command posts and other positions.

At four in the afternoon the town, where we found a large quantity of military stores, was entirely in our hands. During that whole night I removed all the supplies and sent them to San Rafael del Norte so that I could reorganize my forces, because many people had volunteered to join us, and a complete understanding of everything we had accomplished was needed.

At half past five in the afternoon of that same day of combat, forty Yankees arrived to protect the enemy. In El Mal Paso, in the neighborhood of Jinotega, they were convinced that we held the city, and so they went back the way they had come.

I left to reorganize my forces, and on the third day I returned to occupy militarily the city of Jinotega.

From San Rafael del Norte, Blanca informed me by telegraph in Jinotega that she had learned that General Francisco Parajón had returned from El Salvador and was reorganizing his forces in the west. The news was soon confirmed. I sent a man by the name of Quintero in search of General Parajón with a letter telling him how important it was that he was approaching the Segovias and that I would not abandon Jinotega until his arrival. (I feared the Yankees would declare Jinotega a neutral zone and for that reason I could not travel to where General Parajón was.) If my memory doesn't fail me, I used Engineer Félix Fajardo, a resident of Estelí, as my secretary for the writing of that letter.

The capture of the city of Jinotega and the approach of General Parajón's forces demoralized the enemy forces in Estelí. Enemy forces evacuated Estelí, and General Parajón traveled without incident, reaching Jinotega on Holy Tuesday. Once I had gained control of Jinotega I began to organize the departmental government, naming Dr. Doroteo Castillo as the department's governor. Also a town band was established, and on the occasion of the arrival of the new units commanded by General Parajón there was a concert on the Jinotega plaza.

After I had come to an agreement with General Parajón and other leaders, I left for Chontales, where Moncada was. On Holy Wednesday, April 13 of that year, at two in the afternoon, I set out on the march. My entire column was made up of eight hundred cavalrymen. We were the advance guard because we were the best-equipped force, and we left two days ahead of the columns that had just arrived. This was the agreement we had made with the leaders who remained in the rearguard.

When I arrived in the vicinity of Palo Alto, I was told that General Moncada had evacuated all his positions in Palo Alto and that the enemy had encircled him at Las Mercedes. In General Moncada's evacuation from Palo Alto to go to Las Mercedes, the cooperation given by the column of unarmed volunteers that I had sent was of great importance to our cause.

I changed directions, and on Easter Sunday at two o'clock in the afternoon I approached the village of San Ramón, spreading my forces out in sixteen squads so that they might make camp in a proper manner. The enemy in San Ramón fired upon our column, but the distance was so great that we didn't even know at the time that the firing was directed at us. Not a bullet reached us. From a delegation that I had sent out to a man named Vita under the command of Colonel Humberto Torres, chief of the general staff, I knew that the enemy had evacuated San Ramón and was marching toward Matagalpa. On April 18 at nine in the morning that town came under our control.

I received a note bearing the same date from the leader of the Yankees camped in Matagalpa, in which I was told that from that time on the city of Matagalpa was to be declared a neutral zone. The distance between that city and San Ramón is two and a half leagues. My reply to the Yankee leader was to tell him that if the neutrality was for the Liberals as well as for the Conservatives, it would be accepted, but that if I should hear that they were acting with partiality toward the Conservatives, I would attack that city even if they were there. For this letter I used as my secretary Don Adán Medina, a resident of Jinotega.

The Yankee officer, having received my note, replied that he would comply with the promise of neutrality. These notes are preserved in our army's archive.

After this exchange, General Parajón's column arrived along with those of the other leaders who had stayed in Jinotega.

On April 19 I left San Ramón, with the forces who served as the rear-guard staying behind. On the road it occurred to me to send a note to the same Yankee officer informing him that citizens of Liberal affiliation should take control of the civil authority in the department of Matagalpa, since the entire department was dominated by our forces, and so it wasn't possible for Conservatives to continue to hold that authority. This note was carried by Colonel Humberto Torres. The Yankees replied, informing me that they would consult with their superior and that they would let me know how the question was decided.

But these notes didn't alter my march toward Chontales. Colonel Humberto Torres reached me in the town of Terrabona, informing me that the Matagalpa Conservatives had imprisoned him and that four Yankee officers had accompanied him from Ciudad Darío to the outskirts of Terrabona, suspecting that the Conservatives intended to assassinate Colonel Torres on the road. The Yankees who accompanied Colonel Torres had told him of their desire to meet me, but they weren't able to do so, because I had left at the head of my column. They spoke with Parajón and the other rearguard leaders.

In the village of San José de los Remates, we were again reunited, and an officer of the rearguard columns told me that one Castro Wassmer had said that the Yankees ought not to have negotiated with me, but with him instead, because he was the executive's representative. I smiled, feeling pity for this Wassmer fellow.

Making use of the information acquired in that village, we continued our march, with my column always in the advance. General Porfirio Sánchez H., then a colonel, was head of my column's vanguard, and so he was in charge of the guide who was to lead us to Las Mercedes, the place occupied by General Moncada. Las Mercedes was the place where Moncada was held in the famous *ring of steel*, to use the enemy's term.

When the guide arrived at a certain place, he halted, telling General Sánchez the following: "El Bejuco is the place where those hills can be seen up ahead there, and people say they are occupied by the enemy. Las Mercedes is in those other hills farther out. That's all I know. Inform your leader of this, because I can't go on." General Sánchez waited for me, telling me what had happened. I suspected that the enemy was very near and that for this reason the campesino had refused to go on.

I ordered the occupation of all the appropriate places. At that very moment we noticed at a distance of about four hundred yards a force of cavalry wending its way down over some pastures. We didn't know whether they were Moncada's forces or those of the enemy. I ordered General Porfirio Sánchez H. to go with the seventy cavalrymen he commanded to find out what we had seen. Twenty minutes later a clash began between General Sánchez's forces and those of the enemy. One could hear the firing from more than forty machine guns.

When the shooting stopped, since it happened so fast, I asked for a squad from General Parajón's column to protect our flank. The squad arrived and as soon as it was understood that General Sánchez's exchange of fire with the enemy had stopped, many members of the squad went toward the spot where the battle had taken place to search for better weapons. All this happened between five and six o'clock.

After taking the necessary precautions, I went in search of General Sánchez. Quite sensibly, General Parajón wanted to prevent me from going personally to that area without first investigating it carefully. He said that retiring from the field might have been a military trick, that the enemy might have set up some machine guns that could greatly damage our columns if they entered the area without taking precautions.

To be brief, I turned down his advice, remaining just behind my men, with the others well prepared in their positions.

At eight o'clock that night I arrived at the place where the enemy had their field hospital and staff headquarters. There we found many wounded, a great deal of medicine, and a large quantity of rifles. Concerning the latter, the enemy had piled them up and set fire to them, but our men extinguished the fire and pulled the weapons out. The wounded men told me that the enemy army that had fled that place totaled more than a thousand men commanded by ten generals and several dozen minor officers.

Many of our people who were under the command of the other rear-guard leaders didn't have weapons, and so we equipped all of them with those we had captured.

There wasn't a single death or wounded man on our side. At a faraway place on the other side of some hills one of General Parajón's men, who had been serving as a cook, was wounded.

On the second day, at dawn, we noticed a little red flag on a mountain peak, and I went with a squad of men to find out what kind of force it was. From the peak a delegation also came down. We met and recognized Moncada's force. They told us that they had been waiting for us for several days, and there was great enthusiasm on both sides.

They explained how to get to the camp where Moncada was. When I arrived at the camp, Castro Wassmer was already there with General Moncada, lying in a hammock. Since that time I have been conscious of Castro Wassmer's tremendous vanity.

I told General Moncada how much I had wanted to reach him sooner, and he said that if we had been held up for just one more day, we would have had to search for him farther away, because on that same day he had been about to break his line of defense, since it was known that this was the day the enemy had planned to start their general offensive. We embraced each other, and then I went in search of my people whom I had left in El Bejuco.

That same day, in the evening, I left with my eight hundred cavalrymen for Boaco, under General Moncada's orders.

The column of unarmed volunteers, which earlier I had put under the command of Colonels Cantarero and Reyes, told me of their wish to rejoin my column. Moncada had sent out an Order of the Day prohibiting the heads of columns who had arrived there from having more than three hundred men under their command, because there were many leaders who didn't command any forces at all. But none of the men of my cavalry wanted to join another leader, and so because of this attitude I was allowed to continue commanding my entire cavalry unit and part of the column I had sent out earlier, including Colonel Cantarero and Dr. González. The latter was the special courier whom I had used to communicate with Moncada between San Rafael del Norte and Tierra Azul.

I marched to Boaco. Moncada had told me that the enemy had evacuated that town, and that we should not be surprised if we saw some soldiers there because they were our people. We left with this understanding, but when we reached the Boaco area, we saw a very powerful electric spotlight which lit up the landscape nearly a league beyond the town. General Porfirio Sánchez knew that this force could not be one of ours, and so he ordered a halt in the march and told me what he had seen. I ordered the retreat of all our forces and the occupation of some heights which we had passed earlier.

The next morning we discovered fourteen enemy reserve units in the hills on our flank. It seemed obvious to me that Moncada had not been well informed about the town when he had assured me that there were no enemy forces there. It was a real fortress and we could not capture it without preparing an entirely new strategy. I sent a messenger to Moncada at Las Mercedes, where he normally spent the night, informing him that Boaco was in enemy hands, and that if he so ordered, I would prepare an appropriate plan of attack.

The messenger returned to inform me that Moncada was no longer in Las Mercedes, that he had left in the direction of Boaquito, that in the camps where Moncada had been he found only a great multitude of flies, and that he had been frightened and so had returned.

Under these circumstances, I decided to take the road that Moncada had taken, and we slept on a hill called El Chillón. On the morning of the second day I made contact with Moncada, who approved of my decisions. I remained on El Chillón for two days until I received orders to occupy the hill called El Común, a league south of the town of Teustepe.

The enemy was in Teustepe and its vicinity. They made several attacks for the purpose of opening a breach between Teustepe and Boaco, but they couldn't break through our lines.

The last shots of the Constitutionalist War were fired by part of my cavalry.

The enemy's last attack was made against one of General Parajón's columns. I sent a hundred mounted men commanded by Colonel Ignacio Talavera to support him, but when my reinforcements arrived, General Parajón had already repulsed the enemy. My men didn't want to be denied the opportunity to take part, and so they furiously attacked an enemy column that was spending the night at the hacienda of Los Cocales.

Not another shot was fired.

On the second day of that battle, I received a note from General Moncada informing me that a forty-eight hour truce had been established, because he had agreed to attend a conference in Managua or Tipitapa. I replied informing him that we did not agree that he should go alone, that he should be accompanied by the rest of us, with all of us fully armed. I feared treachery on the part of the Yankees.

The messenger came back, telling me, "General Moncada has left and right now he must be licking the Yankees' boots." There was a lot of disapproval and suspicion in the whole army about that trip. After the first forty-eight hours of the armistice a new order came for another forty-eight hours.

On May 5 of that year, I received a verbal order from Moncada sent through Colonel Pompilio Reyes, telling me to concentrate the forces under my command in the town of Santa Lucía, that henceforth there would be no further need to organize reserves, and that the men could now begin to sleep under a roof because everything had been settled. I considered that order very irregular, and so I went at once with my general staff to La Cruz, jurisdiction of Teustepe, which was the place where Moncada was.

I found him lying in a hammock that he had hung under a leafy tree. When we saw each other, he got up and saluted me, and I repeated the order that Colonel Reyes had brought me. I asked him for an explanation of the way the peace agreement had been made.

Before replying, he arranged himself in his hammock, at the same time adjusting a gold American Marine Corps cross that hung about his neck on a little white ribbon. His explanation was that a representative of the United States had told him that his government was ready to end the war in Nicaragua, that that government had accepted Adolfo Díaz's request to supervise the presidential elections, and that, therefore, that government had constituted itself as custodian of Adolfo Díaz's weapons and of those of the Constitutionalist Army. In exchange for surrendering the weapons, each person turning one in was to get ten dollars, and anyone who didn't peacefully dispose of his weapon in this way would be disarmed by force.

I smiled maliciously.

My smile seemed to surprise General Moncada, and so he added, "Also, they will give us control of seven departments of the Republic. You

are the candidate chosen to be governor of Jinotega. Díaz's government will pay for all the animals in the army's service, and you may round up all you can, and legally they will belong to you."

I asked Moncada whether or not the whole army had agreed to this, and he replied, "It has to be, because everybody will be paid the salary he has earned. You are to receive ten dollars for each day you were under arms."

Again I smiled sarcastically.

Moncada invited me to go to some conferences that were to be held on the 18th of that month in Boaco, promising that at that time everyone's opinion would be heard, because he had asked Stimson for a period of eight days in which to respond.

It should be kept in mind that Moncada told the unit leaders that he had asked Stimson for a period of eight days, beginning on May 5, to seek the army's opinion and then to reply. Despite this, President Moncada later declared May 4 a national holiday because that was the day the peace pact was signed, which proves that the army's opinion was of little importance to him, and that when he returned from Tipitapa to our camps he already had the treaty and the presidency in his pocket.

Indeed, May 4 ought to be a national holiday, but not because that was the day that Moncada sold out the Liberal Army that he commanded as though it were a herd of animals. It should be a holiday because it was the day that Nicaragua proved to the world that our national honor cannot be humiliated, that she still has sons who would offer their blood to wash out the stains the traitors would cast upon her.

I told Moncada that I opposed the arrangement.

In his easy manner, he tried to convince me to accept the surrender, telling me that it would be madness to fight against the United States because it is a very powerful country with a hundred million inhabitants, that I couldn't do anything with the three hundred men under my command, that the same thing that would happen to a lamb in the clutches of a tiger would happen to us: "The more it moved, the deeper the claws would enter its flesh."

From then on I felt profound disgust for Moncada. I told him that I thought it was my duty to die for Liberty, and that this was the meaning of the red and black flag that I had raised—*Freedom or Death*—and that the Nicaraguan people had expected to gain their freedom from the Constitutionalist War.

He smiled sarcastically and said the following words, "No, man, why would you want to sacrifice yourself for the people? The people aren't grateful. I know this from my own experience. Life ends and the country remains. The duty of every human being is to enjoy his life, to live well and not to get too worked up about things."

I said good-bye to him and went to the place where my forces were.

Since my general staff was there during that whole meeting with Moncada, each member could testify to the truth of this account.

When we went out onto the road, my general staff and I cried death to the Yankees, and on the way we debated the reasons for Moncada's surrender, and we all understood that he carried the presidency of Nicaragua in his pocket.

I arrived at the hill of El Común where my soldiers were, and I told them what I had heard from Moncada's own mouth and our opinion of him. Colonel Simón Cantarero, the oldest and wittiest man in the army, told me that Moncada was a dog, that his life was a long chain of treasonous acts, that he himself had never believed in Moncada, but that he had helped in the Constitutionalist War without any real belief in victory, imitating certain women who, disgraced before the world, give away their love hoping for reciprocation, then begin to experiment with one man after another without getting anything but disappointment in return.

I ordered my cavalry to break camp in order to reorganize it. We didn't go where Moncada had ordered us to go, that is, to Santa Lucía, because we were expected to surrender our rifles there. I ordered my men to return to Jinotega, and with fifty men I myself went toward Boaco, the place where the conferences Moncada had mentioned were to take place.

In Boaco I left my animals on the edge of town, going on foot with my staff to where Moncada was, one of Boaco's principal houses. Moncada was sitting in a rocking chair placed on a carpet, speaking to a priest. The room was small, but there were many pictures on the walls and fine furniture and curtains. The floor was mosaic, and in the hall there were pots of flowers and a garden in the patio. Moncada was no longer dressed in a field uniform, but wore instead a light Palm Beach suit and polished shoes. He apologized to the priest, then told me that the conference of army leaders had already taken place, that all had agreed to disarm, and that my duty was to conform to the opinion of the majority.

In my mind I was well prepared for this. I had convinced myself through conversations with my column's leaders of the inadvisability of seriously contradicting Moncada, since he was in a position to disarm me by force and to arrest me. This way Nicaragua couldn't regain her freedom.

I told Moncada that I had thought about the matter and had decided to support the position of the other leaders, but that I wanted him to let me surrender my weapons in the city of Jinotega, because I had established the departmental government in that place and had left more than two hundred rifles in custody there.

He told me that this would have to be discussed with the marines, and that I should wait three days for their decision.

Again I asked him to let me wait for those three days at the hacienda El Cacao de los Chavarría, which is located on the road between Teustepe and Jinotega. He agreed, but added that I would also have to sign the disarmament agreement, which had already been signed by the other officers. At that moment it seemed to me that my dreams of freedom had been lost because if Moncada insisted that I sign that document I was prepared to shoot him. I made a great effort to control myself as the situation required, and I spoke these exact words: "You are in command. I fully authorize you to sign for me."

No doubt he felt victorious, because he spoke of how he had converted me to his way of thinking, and yet I was the only opponent of the Moncada-Stimson pact among all the army's leaders. He agreed to my suggestion and said he would sign for me. I said good-bye to him, and we mounted our animals to follow the rest of my forces, who were already on their way to Jinotega.

From the hacienda of El Cacao de los Chavarría, I sent a note to Moncada, which said the following: "I wish to inform you that upon my arrival here my entire force, because of a lack of food, has left for Jinotega. As a result, it's not important for me to stay here. I'm also leaving for that city, where I will await your orders and subject myself to the wishes of the others."

When I reached that city, there was a great threat to the place from a group of Conservatives who had kept their weapons. The enthusiasm in Jinotega was great when they saw us arriving with all our weapons, perhaps better equipped than when we had left. They gave us many flowers, and I received many portraits from young ladies with their dedications, and many objects that I still treasure. I told the people of Jinotega about my plan to fight the Yankee piracy, and by means of a telegraphic circular I made this known in the three departments of Jinotega, Estelí, and Nueva Segovia.

On the second night I shipped several machine guns, six hundred rifles, and a large amount of ammunition to the Segovian mountains to the care of trusted leaders. I invited many members of the army under my command to remain at home, because I knew that they were not ready to sacrifice themselves. Leaving intact Jinotega's departmental government, I set out with three hundred cavalrymen for San Rafael del Norte, while the weapons that I ordered hidden in the Segovian jungle were sent by another route.

We arrived in San Rafael del Norte at five in the afternoon. After giving orders to the leaders of the three hundred cavalrymen, I went again with my general staff to occupy Blanca's house, where the telegraph office was located. Blanca already knew of my arrival, and she didn't want to work at the telegraph table. Her brother, also a telegraph operator, had taken her place. I turned my horse over to an assistant and went without my aides to the parlor, expecting to find Blanca there. But she was not there, and instead Lucila, one of her sisters, received me. I asked her for Blanca, and she offered me dinner, which she herself prepared.

Blanca received me with a kiss, telling me that Lucila had offered a mass for the troops to the Virgin of May if I should return unharmed. I thanked her for her sister's kind feelings and said that in two days, at eight in the morning, my army would be prepared to attend the mass that they had offered. We left to suggest the idea to the town priest, and he happily agreed to celebrate the mass. He was a young priest, hardly twenty-two years of age.

I paid for the mass myself, and on the second day at the hour agreed to my army respectfully attended mass. During the ceremony we heard salvoes of rifle and machine gun fire. The mass was splendid, and I myself attended.

The day after the ceremony, I ordered certain forms of mobilization and remained in the town as if in time of peace.

The 18th of that month was my birthday, and on that day I married Blanca in the church of San Rafael del Norte.

At two in the morning on the 18th I went to the church with Blanca and our sponsors, accompanied by her entire family. The townspeople didn't know we were getting married, though I had ordered the officer of the day not to interfere if he noticed that somebody was opening the church doors in the small hours of the night. At the appointed time, as I walked to the church, the air was cold and foggy. We found the building lit up profusely. I breathed odors of incense and burning candles. The scent of flowers adorning the temple and the various perfumes filling the air reminded me of my childhood.

The priest invited me to confess, and I did so sincerely. Blanca and I and the sponsors knelt before the altar. She wore a white dress and a veil and a crown of orange blossoms, and I wore my pistols at my belt and a coffee-colored gabardine riding uniform and high dark boots. Six of my aides accompanied me to the church. We didn't invite the public to take part in the ceremony because we wanted it to be an act of absolute intimacy.

We left the church and outside in the street I felt like a new man, as if walking on air. Ten saddled horses belonging to the officer of the day and his aides stood in the church atrium. At the corner of a nearby street many of the young men of my army congratulated us as we passed. As we entered Blanca's house we could hear rifle, pistol, and machine-gun fire from every part of town, carried out without my permission, though I understood the shooting was motivated by my men's enthusiasm and so said nothing. From every side came the sound of enthusiastic cheering, and we received countless statements of congratulation.

Two days later I left my wife to enter the Segovian jungles, where I have continued to defend my country.

Almost all the people who accompanied me at that time have proved themselves to be weak and can be found serving the invader. With pride, and to the honor of those who have remained, let me cite their names. They are Generals José León Díaz and Porfirio Sánchez H., and Colonel Coronado Maradiaga.

Two years after my wedding I read in a national newspaper that Blanca has been arrested and taken to Managua, and put at the pirates' disposition by order of Moncada.

Oh infamous Moncada, torturer of defenseless women, you have complied with your masters' orders. You have accomplished what you wanted most, destroying my home forever!

Wicked man, be damned!

General Headquarters, El Chipotón, March 18, 1929
Patria y Libertad.
A. C. SANDINO

[19, 17 pp.]

1. Sandino wrote this document on March 2, 1929, as a protest against the arrest and imprisonment of his wife, Blanca Aráuz, by the National Guard. It is an account of events between December 1926, when Sandino arrived on the Atlantic coast in an attempt to acquire weapons from Sacasa's government, and May 21, 1927, the date he began his separate military campaign against the U.S. intervention. Two elements stand out in this chronicle: first, the development of the Constitutionalist War and Sandino's important role in that struggle, and, secondly, the personality and activities in cooperation with Sandino of Blanca Aráuz, a telegraph operator in the town of San Rafael del Norte. RC

2. The Cosigüina expedition was a largely unsuccessful Liberal attempt in May 1926 to land men and supplies on the Pacific coast. The battle of Chinandega took place early in 1927 and resulted in the destruction of much of the city, in part as the result of bombing attacks by two American pilots. See "American Pilot in the Nicaraguan Air Service," in *The New York Times*, March 5, April 10, and May 29, 1927. RC

3. A reference to the Nicaraguan poet. RC

9. THE ORIGINS OF ARMED RESISTANCE BEGUN ON MAY 4, 1927: MESSAGE TO GABRIELA MISTRAL[1]

For Gabriela Mistral

In my previous narratives[2] I mentioned the note, dated May 3, 1927, that General José María Moncada sent me, which today I find it convenient to copy from the original, along with my reply:

Boaquito, May 3, 1927

General Augusto C. Sandino
His Encampment

I have the honor to inform you that through two North American officers I have agreed to a conference in Managua or in Tipitapa with Mr. Henry Stimson, personal representative of the government of the United States of America. I will agree to nothing without the consent of the commanding officers of the army. I am sending an identical copy of this message to all the other commanders.

Your most affectionate fellow party member,

J. M. MONCADA

Las Limas, May 3, 1927

General José María Moncada
Boaquito

Esteemed General:

I am in possession of your message and suppose that by now you have named the delegates who will represent you at the conference to which you refer, because we will not accept your attending the conference except with all of us together and with our weapons in hand.

Your most affectionate coreligionist and friend,

A. C. SANDINO
Adán Medina
Secretary

There was no reply to my note because General Moncada had already left for Tipitapa accompanied only by his aides.

In narratives previously published, I have revealed the remarks of members of our Constitutionalist Army after General Moncada's return from Tipitapa.

With the same easy manner with which in earlier days General Moncada had filled our hearts with enthusiasm and patriotism, he now told us just the opposite, urging us to be timid and to look with horror upon the havoc caused by the war.

After his return from Tipitapa he was no longer recognizable. Instead of a soldier, he was like a man clothed with a priestly gentleness, and with that change of conduct he was able to freeze even those hearts most disposed toward patriotism.

On the night of May 6, after having spoken on the 5th of that month with General Moncada, I, along with my general staff, considered the idea of attacking the city of Matagalpa, where only two hundred Yankees were guarding the neutral zone. My plan to attack the city of Matagalpa was not carried out. Instead, my reason for making such public calculations was to gauge the level of determination of the members of my force. I was bitterly disappointed. All were cool to the idea, and no one supported my point of view. That same night more than sixty men deserted my column, including many members of my general staff.

I recall among the deserters a young man from Matagalpa named Prasling, who had served us as a guide in the territory where we had been operating. When I arrived at Boaco on the 18th for the conferences announced by General Moncada, I was told that young Prasling had spread the news that at that very moment I was on my way to attack Matagalpa, and this he had told General Moncada.

I reached Boaco with fifty cavalrymen and left it with only nineteen; all the rest had deserted.

Among the deserters were Colonel Humberto Torres, a resident of Estelí, Sergeant Major Pedro López of Jinotega, first and second officers, respectively, of my general staff; Sergeant Major Celestino Cantarero and Don Adán Medina, the first of whom was provisional judge advocate and the second secretary of my unit, both residents of the city of Jinotega.

The desertion of such individuals caused further discouragement in my force's camps. With every passing minute it became more difficult to control the shirking and the wave of desertions. In that awful crisis of our nation's honor, emotional events took place that, but for the requirements of history, I would keep entirely secret.

I'll mention some of them.

Many subordinate officers and soldiers not yet known to me approached me for advice crying like children. Some spoke to me of their desire to commit suicide. Others said that they had no place to go, because in their native towns they risked being murdered by Conservatives. Others asked me "for God's sake" not to give up our weapons, pledging to accompany me until either I or they succumbed.

A few minutes before the desertion of Sergeant Major Pedro López, he spoke these words to me: "There's nothing I can do. I don't have enough money to emigrate from Nicaragua, but I'll sell what I can and find some place to go. But I won't stay in Jinotega."

Moments later he disappeared as if in a trance, exactly as he had said he would.

There's something else. During those moments when our national dignity was under such humiliating attack, tears gushed forth in torrents from my own eyes as well.

Everyone in the army who knew me at that time sensed my disapproval of Moncada's treason, and it was for this reason that they asked for my advice.

I shared the sorrow that had taken hold of the hearts of some of my fellow countrymen, and meanwhile Moncada and Beltrán Sandoval had ordered the firing of machine guns against personnel of our army who were already disarmed, because they had asked for clothing for their bodies, which were covered with filthy rags. The incident I'm referring to took place in Boaco, and the main witnesses were the people from the Atlantic coast, many of whom returned to their homes hungry and sick.

I've pointed out in previous writings that by promising Moncada to await his orders in El Cacao de los Chavarría, I was able to free myself from his grasp. From there I sent Moncada a note, which I take from my copy of it in the archive of our Liberating Army.

El Cacao, May 9, 1927

General José María Moncada
Boaco

I have the pleasure to inform you that upon arriving at this place I was told that, because of a shortage of food, my column had dispersed and marched toward Jinotega. Therefore I have decided that there is no further reason to stay here, and so I am also leaving for the place where I will await your orders, subject as always to the majority opinion.

Most affectionately,
A. C. SANDINO

This was the note that prevented Moncada from halting my march.

My column was surrounded by other units of the Liberal Army. Those nearest to my forces were those of Generals Augusto Caldera and Francisco Parajón, the first in Teustepe and the second in San José de los Remates. Those two generals were among those who had signed Moncada's surrender and remained under his command.

I have also mentioned the movements I carried out after sending that note to General Moncada, up to May 8, 1927. In the city of Jinotega I had left Colonel Joaquín Lobo as chief political officer of the department of that name, with instructions to inform me in San Rafael del Norte of the movements of the Yankees toward that same city of Jinotega.

On May 20, at eight in the evening, I returned again to Jinotega from San Rafael del Norte, where I was told that the invaders were spending the night a league from that city, intending to attack it at dawn.

Because Colonel Lobo didn't have any weapons available, since I had sent all of them away, I repeated my order that there was to be no resistance in the city of Jinotega and that, once the enemy had occupied it, he was to let them know that I was occupying San Rafael del Norte. As soon as I had repeated my orders to Colonel Lobo, I left Jinotega at one in the morning of the 21st for San Rafael del Norte, accompanied by my four aides.

That day Colonel Lobo informed me by telegram at ten in the morning that he had obeyed my orders and that the Yankee pirates had taken control of the city after some pretense of attacking it. The telegraph operator I had left behind in Jinotega accepted the responsibility of informing me of all the invaders' movements and plans and those of Moncada. Moncada entered Jinotega by automobile after the pirates' fake attack. By telegraph he insisted upon asking me to join the surrender. Those telegraphic messages were sent and received by Blanca.

In response to my rejection of the surrender, the Yankees and Moncada asked my father to travel to San Rafael del Norte to persuade me to accept it.

In the town of San Rafael del Norte I was able to convince only twenty-nine cavalrymen, with four machine guns, to accompany me. I have already revealed to the world the names of those twenty-nine brave men.[3]

In the final hours of the 21st news reached me through private channels that General Moncada had arranged to come to me for a conference. I waited for him for about two days, intending to capture him and to take him with me into the mountains.

At five in the morning on the 23d, one of the spies I had left in Jinotega arrived where I was on horseback, informing me that he had spoken personally with my father, whom he had also seen leaving Jinotega with the intention of meeting me, and that General Moncada would not leave Jinotega.

After receiving this positive news, I ordered the mobilization of my twenty-nine men. I kissed my wife good-bye, and we began our march toward the mountains, where in the not too distant future thousands of the adventurous pirates of Wall Street were to lie buried as payment for their deeds.

On that same May 23 we reached the village of Yalí, where, on entering the town, I received a telegram from Blanca. In it she informed me that my father was in San Rafael del Norte, and in her own name and that of my father she begged me to wait for him in Yalí, because he wanted to see and embrace me before I went into the mountains. I agreed to her request, and we halted for the day. That same afternoon at three o'clock my father's arrival was announced, and I went out to the street to receive him.

Before me was a group of about ten men mounted on good horses. Among those men, all of whom were wearing cavalry uniforms since they were ex-members of my column, was the conspicuous silhouette of an olive-skinned man of average height wearing a blue cashmere suit, a Panama hat with a black silk ribbon, and a bow tie of the same color.

This man was my father.

We exchanged enthusiastic greetings with the entire group, and then, after an affectionate exchange between my father and myself, I invited them into the house where I was staying. My father's first words were to ask me on his own behalf, and on behalf of my mother and other relatives, not to undertake armed resistance against the Yankee invaders. He told me that he was very sad about the Liberal Army's capitulation, and that if every officer of our Constitutionalist Army had adopted the attitude that I was attempting to assume, Nicaragua would have been spared humiliation; but that nobody else had done so, and that if I did not desist from my plans, I would die without success, as General Benjamín Zeledón had died in 1912 when the Yankees attacked the town of Masaya, defended by that indomitable general.[4]

I replied to my father that the posture I was trying to assume was none other than that of General Benjamín Zeledón, in that era. The one difference was that that fraternal patriot had been the first to lift the stone that, with its great weight, would someday drive the dynamo that would bring the light of freedom to our peoples, and I would carry that stone as far as I could and, even after I had fallen in battle, others would come to carry it wherever it had to be taken.

When my father understood my determination to sacrifice myself, I saw that he felt greater affection for me at that moment, and he spoke these exact words: "If you are determined to sacrifice yourself, you ought to do so with full honor. After you have fired the first shot against the enemy, you can expect nothing but death or victory. You must never surrender on the weak pretexts of hunger, deprivation, or exhaustion. In such a situation it would be better to kill yourself than to accept a shameful surrender."

With the best words I could find, based on reason, right, and justice, I told my father of the blind faith I had in my heart that I would drive the thieves from our territory. Night came, the talk of surrender ended, and my father and I limited ourselves to talking about our family and reminiscing about the people of the town where we both were born.

In the town of Yalí lives a gentleman of Spanish nationality whose name is José Moral, who for some time was the priest of that place and who had renounced the priesthood about ten years before, dedicating himself to agriculture and to trade. The gentleman I refer to has been one of my best friends, and for the same reason he looked after my father with great courtesy the day he arrived in Yalí.

In earlier paragraphs of this account, I revealed the sorrow weighing upon the hearts of some of my comrades in arms, because of Moncada's double-dealing in Tipitapa, and that many of my comrades had begged me not to lay down our weapons, swearing to accompany me until victory or death. Only sixteen days had passed since the day I saw those men inconsolable, and since they had made me the promises that I've mentioned. And yet, on that May 23 when my father arrived in Yalí, there was not a single one of those men who had appeared irreconcilable with José María Moncada's treason who still remained in my army's ranks.

On May 20, when I arrived in Jinotega from San Rafael del Norte, it was for the purpose of organizing the departmental government of Jinotega and Estelí. Those who were elected governor of Estelí and as chief of police of the same department were Dr. Doroteo Castillo and Colonel Federico Torres; as governor of Jinotega, Colonel Joaquín Lobo and as director of police, Sergeant Major Pedro López (the deserter). As I said, I left Jinotega for San Rafael del Norte at one o'clock in the morning of May 21, and I've never returned to that town again.

After the conversation I had with my father on the afternoon of May 23, which I have already related, I have not concerned myself with giving further explanations for the attitude taken by me against the invaders. That night I slept with the tranquility of a child, and I didn't think at all about preparing a written reply to the Yankees or to Moncada.

When I awoke on the 24th, I got yet another disappointment. The twenty-nine men who had come with me and who I had thought possessed hearts of tempered steel had clearly awakened in the morning full of doubts, and almost all were thinking about asking me for a leave of absence, explaining that at some later time they would come after me.

Eight of those twenty-nine men took the trouble to approach me personally, and they left for their homes, promising to catch up with me on the road. Our column was no longer made up of twenty-nine men, but only twenty-one, and there was a real possibility that I would find myself alone.

The twenty-one men who remained with me had various opinions. Some thought I should reply in writing, and others seemed to lack interest in any solution. The latter, because of their indifference, inspired less trust, and it seemed to me that I might better pay heed to those who took a real interest in the matter. Generally—and I didn't intend to put this in writing—I told my companions that I knew full well how hypocritical the Yankees are, and that their intervention in Nicaragua was based on nothing but brute force. Briefly I told them something about the abuses the Yankees have committed in various small countries of our America and against the people of our race and the need to give them a lesson marked in blood.

Very early that morning my father left the house where we had slept, and after I had spoken to my men I went to a nearby house to have breakfast with four of my aides. In the hall of the house where we went to eat my father was speaking with this gentleman, José Moral, and after greeting one another, I spoke to Señor Moral about the appropriateness of a written reply in terms that might seem reasonable to me, but said that, in any event, it would be a good idea to respond. My father had exchanged thoughts with Señor Moral, and they both agreed, as did my men, that I should reply in writing.

Convinced as I am of how hypocritical the Yankees are and of the underhanded and macabre policies which they have fostered in Nicaragua, I spoke these words: "To the thief one must offer the keys. Let's open the doors wide to them and see if they will come in. Then you will be convinced that those bandits aren't sincere."

I continued: "Señor Moral, I would like you to write a note in which it will be stated that the defensive weapons that protect our national rights do not have a price, also pointing out that the proposals put forward by the Yankees and accepted by General Moncada will not guarantee an effective peace as long as Adolfo Díaz remains in the presidency, since he can count on a majority chosen by himself in the Congress, the Senate, and the Supreme Court, and that, in that event, in the not too distant future, there will be another civil war. Tell them also that the two political parties should refrain from all interference in the Republic's affairs, and that an American governor should assume power until the elections that they've referred to are carried out, and that in this case neither I nor my soldiers will accept one cent in exchange for our weapons, as they have offered."

Pleased and happy, Señor Moral agreed to my request.

I sensed in my men, who stood all about me, a brighter spirit than I had seen just before I had decided to respond in writing.

Speaking to my men, I told them that this note would not be answered by the Yankees, but that I hoped that when it wasn't, that negative fact would convince them that the Yankees are bandits, that when the doors are opened to them they won't come in, because they are accustomed to murdering people under cover along the highways.

Señor Moral and my father stayed there to draw up the note, and I went with my four aides to the table where breakfast was being served. By the time we had finished eating, the letter had already been prepared in Señor Moral's own handwriting, and what it said was this:

Yalí, May 24, 1927

To the Leader of the American Detachment camped in Jinotega:

Considering that the treaty proposals accepted by General Moncada will not guarantee the peace and tranquility of the country under the presidency of Adolfo Díaz, possessing as he does a majority elected by him in the Congress and in the Senate and Supreme Court, and that eventually this would cause new troubles for the Liberal Party and a new civil war, keeping in mind the desire for peace that animates all of us, and so that this peace may last and be effective, we suggest as indispensable conditions the abstention of the two political parties from all involvement in the Republic's affairs for as long as there are no absolutely free elections; and that therefore, if the United States has intervened in good faith in our country, we propose as a condition sine qua non for the surrender of our weapons, that a United States military governor take power, while the presidential elections are being carried out, supervised by them. If these proposals are accepted, let me point out that neither I nor any of my soldiers will accept any money whatsoever for the surrender of our weapons.

Leader of the Mountaineers

This note was handed to me by Señor Moral, and after I had looked it over I shrugged my shoulders slightly, because it pleased me and yet it didn't, and nevertheless it was necessary to act in this way in order to continue winning the minds of my men. For this reason I signed it.

The slight shrugging of my shoulders was perhaps a reflection of my own misgivings about the subterfuge I had made use of in the note. It was necessary, however, to sacrifice something in order to save our national honor. With this note I sacrificed my own feelings, but at that moment I was prepared, as I am today, to sacrifice those feelings along with my energy and my life itself, without any regard for the drivel that foolish, cowardly and faint-hearted people would spill upon my name.

Two miserable and cowardly intellectuals of Managua, whose names I will not give here because of my scorn for them, have carefully followed each step I've taken in life. And not finding anything to accuse me of, they have pounced upon two letters of a political nature that I wrote during the Constitutionalist War. These are the note written to General Moncada from El Cacao de los Chavarría on May 9, 1927, the motives of which I have already explained, and the note written in Yalí to the leader of the Yankee pirates in Jinotega on May 24, 1927, the motives of which I have also now explained.

With eyes fired up like two wild animals, tongues extended and dripping, they have sat over those two notes, unable to understand or appreciate the sacred breath that quickens the minds of men willing to sacrifice their lives in fateful times, to save from disgrace those same creatures who themselves would destroy and diminish everything with their cruel and hateful minds, branded with the gold their masters gave them so that their services may provide additional profits for the safes of the Wall Street bankers.

But enough for now. I will stop here.

Las Segovias, General Headquarters, El Chipotón, Nicaragua, Central America, April 10, 1929, and Seventeenth Year of the Anti-Imperialist Struggle in Nicaragua
Patria y Libertad.
A. C. SANDINO

[19, 9 pp.]

1. Written on April 10, 1929, this document, like the previous one, is a chronicle of the events of 1927 leading to Sandino's rebellion. The recipient, Gabriela Mistral, was the Chilean poet and winner of the Nobel Prize for Literature who once referred to Sandino's guerrilla fighters as "el pequeño ejército loco" (the crazy little army). RC

2. See Doc. 8.

3. Their names, ages, and places of origin are as follows: Augusto C. Sandino, 33, Niquinohomo, Nicaragua; Rufo Marín, 26, and Santiago Ditri, 17, El Jícaro, Nicaragua; Francisco Estrada, 28, and Ramón Uriarte, 45, Managua, Nicaragua; Simón González, 32, Porfirio Sánchez, 33, Pastor Ramírez, 20, Rufino Ramírez, 24, José de la Rosa Tejada, 18, Carlos Fonseca, 24, and Sixto Maradiaga, 12, Honduras; José León Díaz, 40, El Salvador; Coronado Maradiaga, 54, Pedro A. Irías, 40, Juan Gregorio Colindres, 38, and Manuel Moncada, 20, Murra, Nicaragua; Abraham Centeno, 40, Yalí, Nicaragua; Lorenzo Blandón, 25, and Ferdinando Quintero, 28, Estelí, Nicaragua; Leopoldo Téllez, 25, Matagalpa, Nicaragua; Pedro Cabrera, 25, and Rodolfo Sevillano, 28, León, Nicaragua; Marcial Salas, 37, Costa Rica; Francisco Centeno, 24, La Concordia, Nicaragua; Cipriano Tercero, 22, Pueblo Nuevo, Nicaragua; Genaro Gómez, 22, Somoto, Nicaragua; Fernando Maradiaga, 46, and Alejandro Pérez, 12, El Chipote, Nicaragua.

4. On July 29, 1912, the Conservative general Luis Mena rebelled against the regime of Adolfo Díaz, also a Conservative, a situation of which the Liberal Party, led by General Benjamín F. Zeledón, took advantage as a way to recover the power lost some years before. This rebellion motivated the open military intervention of the United States in Nicaragua. What had been a civil war became a heroic anti-interventionist campaign, forerunner of the anti-imperialist struggle. On October 4, 1912, General Zeledón, the political and military leader of the Liberals, was overwhelmed by the numerical and technical superiority of the invading forces.

10. CIRCULAR TO THE AUTHORITIES OF THE SEGOVIAS, MAY 19, 1927

San Rafael del Norte
May 19, 1927

CIRCULAR TO THE AUTHORITIES OF THE SEGOVIAS

By means of the present statement I will make known my final decision in respect to the political situation in our country. It seems that the Constitutionalist movement, led by Moncada, has been displaced, and our people have become victims of the Yankee intrusion and of a lack of resolve on the part of our principal leaders. If good has been done and the peaceful manner by which this movement has been ended deserves applause, we owe that applause directly to Moncada. But if it deserves criticism and if someone should be accused of responsibility, it is this same Moncada because of the way he demoralized the army after he returned from Managua, which he did in the following way: he concentrated his forces and the supply convoy that was in Teustepe and the other groups still under his control into Las Banderas and Boaco, and he did this without the overall approval of the army. Then, inviting the leaders to a conference in Boaco where he was to discuss whether it would be convenient or not to accept the Yankee proposals, he did everything in his power to see to it that those proposals which the "machos"[1] had made would be accepted.

I was present to hear him speak to a group of my companions, and I listened without responding, because psychologically I understood how determined he was in the depths of his being to surrender the weapons. Ironically, in his presence, I asked my men whether they were ready or not to give up their weapons. And they replied with an outburst and turned their backs. When Moncada realized that I didn't accept his opinion, he stared at me almost threateningly, telling me that my duty was to conform to the majority opinion, because otherwise it would be madness for me to try to fight the "machos."

Realizing it wouldn't be wise to contradict him because he could still deny me my freedom, I answered that it was my wish to follow the majority opinion. I understood, however, that the majority had been won over by him, because by regrouping the forces he had demoralized the army. I went to the conference. When I arrived at the session it had ended. All this I did by rote, and not through faith or obedience. I asked him to allow me, if I was to turn over my weapons, to do so in Jinotega, but he told me I had to communicate this to the Yankees, and that for this purpose it would be necessary to wait for three days. I agreed to wait in the place called El Cacao, but when I arrived there I sent a letter to General Moncada telling him that my column had arrived late because of hunger, and that I myself would leave for Jinotega where I would stay to await his orders, as always subject to the opinion of the majority of the leaders. But I did all this to prevent him from putting obstacles in my way, and so that I could collect the weapons, which is what I did. Arriving in Jinotega I summoned the prinicipal persons of that town to inform them of my decision to fight the Yankees, telling them, however, that before taking action we would launch a protest against the United States in the name of the Liberal Party of Nicaragua, because already in those days we were divided.

. . . Since there were not enough men determined to throw down the gauntlet by an act of heroism, I decided to rid myself of the people whom I knew to be property owners, who would not want to leave their homes. In Jinotega I have about one hundred men, and in Estelí the same.

I have now given orders to the forces in Jinotega and elsewhere not to enter into action against the North American forces if they should invade those towns, and to regroup themselves in the place where I am, which is San Rafael, so that the civil authorities may hear of the Yankee pretensions, and that meanwhile I can keep informed of everything by telegraph and go to wait for them wherever I may choose, in this way ending the Constitutionalist movement with a display of Yankee blood.

It doesn't matter if the world collapses down upon me. We will comply with a sacred duty. Based on all I have said, I will protest on my own account if there is nobody to support me.

Your most affectionate companion and friend,
A. C. SANDINO

[9, 236–38]

1. In Spanish the word *macho* means *masculine* or *vigorous* but can also refer to a male animal such as a goat or a mule, or to a stupid person. In Central America it can refer to blonds, and in Sandino's time it was often applied pejoratively to U.S. soldiers or to North Americans in general. RC

11. LETTER TO GENERAL JOSÉ MARÍA MONCADA, CIRCA MAY 24, 1927

To José María Moncada:

I do not know why you now wish to order me about. I remember that you always frowned upon me when you were commander in chief. You always opposed my requests for troops to fight the enemy, and when Dr. Sacasa gave me forty-five men and some weapons, you were angry about it. It appears that you were jealous of me. No doubt you know my temperament, and you know that I am unbreakable. I want you to come now and disarm me. I am in my position and I await you. Otherwise, no one can make me give up. *I will not sell myself, nor will I surrender.* I must be conquered. I must comply with my duty and I hope that my protest will remain for the future written in blood.

[9, 240–41]

12. LETTER TO THE GOVERNOR OF OCOTAL, DON ARNOLDO RAMÍREZ ABAUNZA, JUNE 14, 1927

El Verruguillo
June 14, 1927

To the Governor of Ocotal
Dr. Arnoldo Ramírez Abaunza

My dear sir:

I am pleased to inform you by means of the present letter that we accept you as political head of Ocotal, but that we will not permit the intervention of any authority in the following places: San Fernando, Ciudad Antigua, Telpaneca, Quilalí, El Jícaro, Murra, and Jalapa, since we are adequately equipped to provide security in those places, the inhabitants of which are entirely Liberal and do not regard themselves as secure as long as Adolfo Díaz remains in power.

We *will not surrender a single rifle* if his government is not replaced by a Liberal government, as well as an honorable one. Inform your government of our attitude, and tell them that if the Yankees want to disarm us we will know how to kill those who wish to take away the rifles that we seized from the "cachurecos"[1] with so much honor, and that if this does not suit them, then so be it.

Most affectionately,
A. C. SANDINO

[11, 45]

---

1. A word normally meaning *twisted* or *deformed*, used in Central America to refer to Conservatives. RC

13. NOTE TO COLONEL FRANCISCO ESTRADA, JUNE 18, 1927

General Headquarters of the Defenders of
the National Law

To Lieutenant Colonel Don Francisco Estrada:
Presente.

By a decision reached today you have been named political head of the departmental capital of Nueva Segovia, recognized today in El Jícaro, which hereafter will be known as Ciudad Sandino. And for all legal purposes, please take possession of the post to which you have been assigned.

Patria y Libertad.
El Chipote, June 18, 1927
A. C. SANDINO
General and Leader of the
Defenders of the National Law

[11, 46]

14. LETTER TO BENITO LÓPEZ, JUNE 25, 1927

Ciudad Sandino
June 25, 1927

Señor Don Benito López
Ocotal

Esteemed friend:

None of the things the Yankees say are true; even if they say that six-teen planes will come to fight me, and even if they send thirty-six or a hundred and six, to me they will appear weak, because I am ready in my mountains to repel any number of drug-dependent Yankees or denatural-ized armed policemen who would attack me.

Tell the sell-out Frixiones that if he comes here where I am, he will get my rifles without paying me one cent for them, and that it won't be nec-essary for him to announce himself, because my men will come out on the road to receive him and to give him every attention he has made himself worthy of.

With nothing further for the moment, I am your most affectionate friend and companion.

A. C. SANDINO

P.S. I will give you the animals which you ask for with the greatest pleasure just as soon as the cavalry unit that stole them arrives here.

Farewell.

[19, 1 p.]

15. MANIFESTO, JULY 1, 1927

To the Nicaraguans, to the Central Americans, to the Indo-Hispanic Race:[1]

The man who doesn't ask his country for even a handful of earth for his grave deserves to be heard, and not only to be heard, but also to be believed.

I am a Nicaraguan and I am proud because in my veins flows above all the blood of the Indian race, which by some atavism encompasses the mystery of being patriotic, loyal, and sincere.

The bond of nationality gives me the right to assume responsibility for my acts, without being concerned that pessimists and cowards may brand me with a name that, in their own condition as *eunuchs*, would be more appropriatly applied to them.

I am a mechanic, but my idealism is based upon a broad horizon of *internationalism*, which represents the right to be *free* and to establish *justice*, even though to achieve this it may be necessary to establish it upon a foundation of blood. The oligarchs, or rather, the *swamp geese*, will say that I am a plebeian, but it doesn't matter. My greatest honor is that I come from the lap of the oppressed, the soul and spirit of our race, those who have lived ignored and forgotten, at the mercy of the shameless hired assassins who have committed the crime of high treason, forgetful of the pain and misery of the Liberal cause that they pitilessly persecuted, as if we did not belong to the same nation.

Sixteen years ago Adolfo Díaz and Emiliano Chamorro ceased to be Nicaraguans. Ambition killed their right to their nationality because they ripped from its staff our country's flag, the symbol that envelops all Nicaraguans. Today that flag flies limply and in shame because of the ingratitude and indifference of its sons, who do not make a superhuman effort to free it at once from the claws of the enormous eagle with its curved beak bloody with the blood of Nicaraguans. Meanwhile in the Campo de Marte military base that flag that murders weak nations now waves, the enemy of our race and of our language.

Who bound our Fatherland to this pillar of infamy? Díaz and Chamorro. And those mercenaries still demand the right to rule over us as oligarchs, supported by the invader's Springfields.

No. A thousand times *no*.

For myself and for my companions in arms who have not betrayed the

Liberal revolution, who have not faltered and who have not sold our weapons to satisfy our own ambition, the revolution continues, and today more than ever before it is powerful because only those who have displayed the valor and self-denial that every Liberal should possess remain involved in it.

If, sadly, Moncada failed in his duties as a soldier and patriot, it was not because most of the Liberal army leaders were illiterates and because of this he could impose his boundless ambition like some emperor.

In the Liberal ranks there are men of conscience who understand the duties that a soldier's rectitude imposes upon him, such as the nation's honor, it being understood that the Army is the foundation upon which the nation rests, for which reason it cannot personalize its acts without violating its basic responsibilities. I judge Moncada before history and before the Fatherland as a deserter from our ranks, with the added aggravation of having gone over to the enemy.

Nobody gave him the authority to abandon the ranks of the revolution to make secret agreements with the enemy, and this is especially true of the invaders of the Fatherland. His high position obliged him to die like a man before accepting his country's humiliation, the humiliation of his party, and of his coreligionists.

An unpardonable crime demanding revenge!

Pessimists will say that we are very small to undertake a task of this magnitude, but I am convinced that, however insignificant we may be, our pride and patriotism are very great. For that very reason, before the Fatherland and before history, I swear that my sword will defend the national honor and redeem the oppressed.

I accept the challenge of the dastardly invader and the nation's traitors. Our breasts will be ramparts against which their hordes will shatter themselves, because I am firmly convinced that when they have killed the last of my soldiers, more than a batallion of their own men will have died in my wild mountains. I will not be like Mary Magdalene, who implored her enemies' pardon on her knees, because I believe that no one in this land has the right to be a human demigod.

I hope to convince my compatriots, the Central Americans, and the Indo-Hispanic race that in the mountains of the Andean Cordillera there exists a group of patriots who will know how to die like men, in open battle, in defense of their national honor.

Come, morphine addicts, come and kill us in our own land. I await you before my patriotic soldiers, feet firmly set, not worried about how many of you there may be. But keep in mind that when this happens the Capitol Building in Washington will shake with the destruction of your greatness, and our blood will redden the white dome of your famous White House, the cavern where you concoct your crimes.

I wish to assure the governments of Central America, especially that of

Honduras, that my attitude should not cause them concern. They should not think that, because my forces possess more than enough strength to invade their territory, I would do so with the intention of overthrowing them. No. I am not a mercenary, but rather a patriot who does not allow outrageous assaults upon our sovereignty.

Since nature has granted our country enviable riches and has placed us at the crossroads of the world, and since it is that same natural advantage that has made our land coveted to the point that our enemies would even enslave us, I would like to sever the ties to which the sinister Chamorro movement has bound us.

Our young country, this dark beauty of the tropics, should wear on her head the Phrygian cap of liberty bearing the magnificent slogan symbolized by our *red and black* flag. She should not be a victim violated by the Yankee adventurers who were invited here by the four horrid individuals who still claim to have been born in this land.

The world would be an unbalanced place if it allowed the United States of America to rule alone over our canal, because this would mean placing us at the mercy of the Colossus of the North, forcing us into a dependent and tributary role to persons of bad faith who would be our masters without justifying such pretensions in any way.

Civilization requires that a Nicaraguan canal be built, but that it be done with capital from the whole world, and not exclusively from the United States. At least half of the cost of construction should be financed with capital from Latin America, and the other half from other countries of the world that may want to hold stock in this enterprise, but the share of the United States should be limited to the three million dollars that they paid to the traitors Chamorro, Díaz, and Cuadra Pasos. And Nicaragua, my Fatherland, will then receive the taxes that by right and by law belong to it, and we will then have income enough to crisscross our whole territory with railroads and to educate our people in a true environment of effective democracy. Thus we will be respected and not looked upon with the bloody scorn we suffer today.

Fellow citizens:

having expressed my ardent desire to defend my country, I welcome you to my ranks without regard to your political tendencies, with the one condition that you come with good intentions to defend our nation's honor. Because keep in mind that you can fool all of the people some of the time, but not all of the people all of the time.

San Albino Mine, Nueva Segovia, Nicaragua, Central America, July 1, 1927

Patria y Libertad.
AUGUSTO CÉSAR SANDINO

[19, 4]

1. In editions prior to 1981 this document was presented with the name "Manifiesto político" (political manifesto). Its present title is Sandino's original one, according to a copy in the archive of the IES. Moreover, there exist some editorial differences between this version and the one published earlier.

16. LETTER TO U.S. MARINE CAPTAIN G. D. HATFIELD, JULY 12, 1927

Camp of El Chipote
Via San Fernando

To Captain G. D. Hatfield[1]
El Ocotal

I received your message yesterday, and I fully understand it. I will not surrender, and I await you here. I want *a free country or death*. I am not afraid of you. I rely upon the patriotic ardor of those who accompany me.

Patria y Libertad.

A. C. SANDINO

HATFIELD'S CIRCULAR, CIRCA JULY 13, 1927

To whom it may concern:

Augusto C. Sandino, formerly a general of the Liberal Armies, is now an individual outside the law, in rebellion against the government of Nicaragua. Consequently, those who accompany him or remain in territory occupied by his forces do so at their own risk, and neither the government of Nicaragua nor that of the United States of America will be responsible for deaths or injuries that may result from the military operations of the Nicaraguan or American forces in territory occupied by Sandino.

G. D. HATFIELD
Captain, Marine Corps.,
Commanding Nueva Segovia

[11, 47–49]

1. Sandino's brief but energetic reply to Captain G. D. Hatfield (USMC) was the result of his message of July 11, 1927. The complete text is included in Doc. 18. Upon receiving Sandino's reply, Hatfield issued a circular declaring Sandino "outside the law." Its contents are included here in full.

17. MANIFESTO TO NICARAGUAN COMPATRIOTS, CIRCA JULY 14, 1927

To my Nicaraguan compatriots:

It is not necessary to justify my acts to those persons who could never understand my views, or who in any event have refused to do so, unable to submit to that which honor and patriotism demand. I make no attempt to excuse myself to those who are unqualified to judge my actions, the countless adulators, for example, who live from the scraps their master throws them, and who have assumed the task of censuring my acts, reviling them and making me appear irresponsible and lacking in judgement in regard to the positions I have taken in defense of the national honor and our country's sovereignty, or in regard to the rights of the people, so terribly cheated by those who have come here to our land to make excessive profits, dealing with other people not as honorable businessmen of one kind or another, but like slave traders or dealers in human flesh. Such critics cannot judge or censure because they do not look at the causes that justify the drastic measure that has been taken to make amends or to stop an abuse, no matter who may have committed that abuse or thought he had a right to do so, merely because he is a citizen of the United States.

According to information I have received, Moncada, taking advantage of the distance that separates us, wants to make me look like the enemy of the people, and not like the defender of the rights of my fellow citizens.

I am going to make a statement about the causes that led to the measure I took in the name of my country and my fellow citizens:[1]

The American Alexander, who lives in Murra, department of Nueva Segovia, has been a gold smuggler for several years, producing great profits for himself and the luxurious life-style of a nabob, cheating the mine workers who live at the mercy of the dangers peculiar to that kind of work. The American Alexander pays his miners not with cash, *but rather with vouchers, worth from one cent to five pesos, which are valid only in Charles Butters's commissary in exchange for merchandise at exorbitant prices that the workers must accept.*

Alexander is a habitual drunkard and, as such, is harmful to the society in which he lives, and his punishable acts should cease and be corrected, because it is to them that he owes his cynicism.

Charles Butters, American, who for a number of years has called himself the owner of the San Albino mine, who cheats my fellow countrymen out of their salaries, forcing them to work twelve hours a day, paying them with vouchers worth from one cent to five pesos, which are acceptable only in his commissary in exchange for merchandise at twice the normal price, *thinks himself authorized by his nationality* to commit such abuses, and thinks that they should not be stopped by those who have a duty to do so. But being an American does not mean being invulnerable; the real people of my country also have their law and their justice, intended to prevent such abuses carried out with the support of our traitors.

General Moncada does not know about and disregards the needs and suffering of the working class because he does not belong to that community of people who are forced to earn their living by their physical labor, with their bare hands, in order to eat and dress themselves badly. Moncada is not qualified to speak in defense of ideals unknown to his experience. Moncada disregards these things because his myopia does not allow him to see the hard social problems of his fellow citizens who, cheated and offended, have demanded the justice heretofore denied to them. You should understand, Señor Moncada, that any foreigner of whatever nationality who transgresses or commits reprehensible acts in the country where he lives falls under the sanction of the laws and must suffer the consequences, especially if that country is in a state of war. The gold produced in the bowels of the Nicaraguan earth belongs to Nicaragua, and it is extracted by the hands of Nicaraguan workers. Where, then, is the guarantee behind that enormous debt of 45,000 dollars that is owed to the holders of the vouchers with which they pay the worker's labor, the worker who lives from day to day and who at any time and without any cause can be fired, having in his pocket as his pay some bits of paper, which, though they have the number five stamped on them, are not worth a cent beyond the district of the mine? How will Charles Butters convert the sacred debt that he owes to his worker who, miserable, half-naked and sick with malaria, has nothing with which to return to the refuge of his home because everything he has saved is represented by bits of paper that are not worth a penny outside the place where he has worked?

Moncada, the people know what justice is, and when it is denied to them they seize it! And since I am of the people and know what law and justice are, I have seized it myself in Butters's name, taking those assets that belong to my country in order to convert that longstanding debt into real value, paying it with that same gold which the enterprise produces.

With this done, the property will be returned to the swindling company, if it is able to prove to the people that it is in fact the legitimate owner.

I want nothing for myself; I am a mechanic, *the sound of my hammer on its anvil echoes at a great distance, and it speaks every language in matters of labor.* I aspire to nothing. I desire only the redemption of the working class.

Aside from this, I defy Moncada himself to respond to other charges. I do not take orders from any foreign leader, and much less do persons of foreign nationality serve with me. You, Moncada, cannot say the same, and, in regard to your aspirations, I remember your words written in a letter that you sent me, which I have in my possession: "There is no reason to sacrifice yourself for your country. Life comes to an end, but the country remains." This made me lose confidence in you and made me understand the dimensions of your moral personality.

I take this opportunity to respond to the conduct of the adventuring invader whose name is G. D. Hatfield.

"Who are you, miserable servant of Wall Street, to threaten the genuine sons of my country and myself with such impudence? Do you perhaps think that you are in the heart of Africa to come here to impose your will merely because you are Coolidge's paid assassin? No, degenerate pirate, you do not even know your father or your real language. I do not fear you. If you would like to avoid your countrymen's loss of blood, they having no interest in our political affairs, make up your mind like a man. Come to me personally, choose the terrain you prefer outside your control, and I will do the same, so that we may measure the power of our weapons in the following way. Either you will fill yourself with glory killing a patriot, or I will make you eat the dust in the manner demonstrated by the official seal of my army."[2]

Patria y Libertad.
A. C. SANDINO

[19, 3 pp.]

1. The measure to which Sandino refers is the intervention that he carried out on June 30, 1927, at the San Albino mine, property of North Americans, where he had worked in 1926 upon his return from Mexico. At this mine he also began his first activities of a political nature, including organization of the first Sandinistas, the embryo of the Segovian Column and the Army in Defense of the National Sovereignty.

2. This paragraph is Sandino's complimentary response to the "insolent note from the little Yankee captain" who on July 11, 1927 had demanded Sandino's surrender. The original answer appears in this edition in Document 18.

18. A STATEMENT BY SANDINO TO
HIS RACIAL BROTHERS,
CIRCA JULY 15, 1927

The Yankee cowards and criminals protect themselves with the mask of hypocrisy, raising a white flag in order to murder my fellow countrymen without risk to themselves.

All Central Americans are now aware of our position of sacred protest against the punishable Yankee invasion and against the Nicaraguan traitors, who march like boy scouts in the invaders' vanguard. For this reason, I believe it will now be useful to inform my racial brothers of the most recent developments in the area outside the control of the cynical traitor Adolfo Díaz, which is made up of the following towns in the Department of Nueva Segovia: San Fernando, Ciudad Antigua, Telpaneca, San Juan de Segovia, Quilalí, Murra, Jalapa, and Ciudad Sandino, which formerly was called El Jícaro.

In each of these towns we have a small security force for the maintenance of public order as well as the functioning of our administration, which is based on the purest democracy, since we grant even our enemies every kind of guarantee to their persons and interests. In addition to these security forces, we have six cavalry units composed of fifty soldiers each, who patrol the zone we control, and our war arsenal is located in a place called El Rempujón, which has only one entrance, that from the hill called El Chipote. On July 11 I received from the man who calls himself the leader of the punishable Yankee expedition, now based in Ocotal, the note that I here reproduce, which was sent by telegraph from Ocotal to San Fernando at 11 A.M. on July 11, 1927 and received at noon on the same day:

General Augusto C. Sandino, El Jícaro

It seems impossible that you still remain deaf to a reasonable proposal, and in spite of your insolent replies in the past I am giving you another opportunity to surrender with honor.

As you no doubt know, we are prepared to hunt you to your stronghold and destroy your troops and yourself should you stand your ground. On the other hand, should you escape to Honduras or elsewhere you will have a price upon your head and will never be able to return in peace to the country you claim to love, but can at best make forays as a bandit upon your peaceful countrymen.

If you will come to Ocotal with all or part of your armed forces and surrender your arms peacefully, you have the guarantee of safety from me, a representative of a country that does not win battles by treachery. Furthermore, you will then be able to live an honorable and useful life in your native land and be able to help your people by setting an example of rectitude and the qualities of leadership.

Otherwise you will be an exile and outlaw, wanted nowhere, and in constant danger of death, not the death of a soldier in battle but the death of a criminal or of treacherous shooting in the back by one of your own followers.

No outlaw has ever prospered or died contentedly, but as an example of one who was in your position twenty-five years ago, but came to his senses in time, I invite your attention to Aguinaldo of the Philippines, who eventually became one of its greatest leaders and a firm friend of the United States.[1]

In conclusion I wish to inform you that Nicaragua has had its last revolution and that the soldier of fortune will find no opportunity to employ his talents here in the future.

You have but two days to give me an answer that will save the lives of many of your people, and if you are the patriot you claim to be I will expect you to be in Ocotal at eight o'clock in the morning of July 14, 1927.

Please advise me of your intentions in one word, either yes or no, and I sincerely hope it will be yes.

G. D. HATFIELD

The mere reading of that letter caused my blood to boil as a legitimate son of my beloved country, and yet I restrained the hatred aroused in me by the leader of the adventurous Yankees, who are trampling Nicaragua's sovereignty under foot, responding in the following terms:

El Rempujón, July 12, 1927

Mr. G. D. Hatfield:

I have in my possession your telegram dated the 11th of this month, which I am now answering.

When I joined the Constitutionalist movement I did so with the firm idea of either having a free country or death. And since we have not succeeded in gaining an effective freedom, and since I have not died, I will maintain my firm resolve to struggle against you. Our arms shall not be given up because they represent the energetic protest of my country, and for that reason your threats seem very pallid to me, and I care very little what you represent. The first to pass the boundary that we have marked out will have to leave several tons of bodies on the battlefields. If you are determined to do this you may come soon, and we will have the honor of sprinkling the soil of our country with the blood of traitors and invaders.

I must also inform you that if the United States wants peace in Nicaragua, they will have to turn the presidency over to a legitimate Nicaraguan. At that time I will give up my weapons peacefully without the need for anyone to force this upon me.[2]

A. C. SANDINO

The adventurous leader had laid down his challenge, and as a legitimate son of my race I accepted it with honor, since any commentary on his insolent telegram would be excessive. Once more I wished to prove to Coolidge's hired assassin and servant of Wall Street that to be humble does not mean to be a coward.

Immediately afterward, having read the threatening letter before the Army in Defense of National Honor, I saw palpably reflected in the unsettled faces of the leaders, officers, and soldiers an impressive grimace of hatred for the traitors and cowardly invaders.

"Death to the Yankees!" roared my soldiers with all the power of their lungs, and "Death to the Yankees!" responded the wild mountains of Nueva Segovia like an echo.

"To Ocotal, to Ocotal. We swear to die in defense of our national honor!" cried my soldier patriots. "We will not allow an outrage against our sovereignty!"

"At the proper time, my companions," I replied. "If our country needs our blood, we will offer it with pleasure."

The challenge that the adventurer G. D. Hatfield had laid down to us had to be answered with deeds. I ordered a review of my cavalry, and only sixty soldiers were in a condition to fight, since just two days before I had sent the other columns on expeditions in various directions and as far as the outskirts of Jinotega; thus, not able to contain the warlike enthusiasm of my soldiers, I decided to attack the invaders in their magnificent positions in Ocotal, where there were no less than two hundred armed men, exalted with their greatness.

[19, 3 pp.]

1. Emilio Aguinaldo was a nationalist Philippine leader who fought for independence against Spain and the United States in the last years of the nineteenth century and the first years of this century. As president of the Philippines, he declared war on the United States at the beginning of 1899 and began a guerrilla war against the American intervention in his country. Captured in 1901, he abandoned the independence struggle, swore allegiance to the United States, and retired to private life.

2. This reply to Hatfield coincided with Sandino's principal response contained in Doc. 16.

19. A TELEGRAPHIC REPORT
ON THE BATTLE OF OCOTAL,
JULY 17, 1927

San Fernando, 11:50 A.M.
July, 17, 1927

To all the civic and military authorities:

We are writing to make known the motives that brought about the battle that took place yesterday, July 16, 1927.

1. To demonstrate that the force that continues protesting and defending the constitutional rights of Dr. Sacasa is an organized one.

2. To dissolve the idea of those who think we are bandits and not men of ideals.

3. To prove that we would prefer to die than to be slaves, because the peace that Moncada established is not the peace that can give men freedom, but rather the peace enjoyed by the slave, who is not disturbed by any but dominated by all.

4. Anyone might think that, since we lost many men, our army's morale must decline. But today more than ever before we have become impatient because the traitors and invaders of our country have come out in search of us, and so we are eager to confirm our unyielding determination to end our lives if we cannot enjoy the real freedom to which we have a right as men.

In conclusion, I wish to make it known that the only person responsible for everything that happens, now and in the future, is the president of the United States, Calvin Coolidge, because he has persisted in maintaining in power his lackey Adolfo Díaz, a person who enjoys the contempt of every good Nicaraguan.

Patria y Libertad.
A. C. SANDINO

[11, 56]

20. THE BATTLE OF SAN FERNANDO
OF JULY 25, 1927[1]

The first defeat of the Sandinistas was in San Fernando, eight days after the attack on Ocotal, when we were overtaken by an enemy squadron. I was almost killed, and we were forced to flee in disorder. The campesinos who had entered Ocotal were attacked, and to save themselves, once their possessions were destroyed, they asked if they might join our ranks. Three months later we were eight hundred men.

The festering struggle continued and our people served in shifts. We were victorious and we were defeated, but the enemy was hampered by his inability to understand our tactics. Futhermore, our spy system was superior. Thus we were acquiring North American weapons and ammunition, because we were capturing personnel and supplies. It is unfortunate that the pirates are so big, because their uniforms do not fit our people. [. . .]

[6, 15]

1. In the 1984 edition this document was taken from the original source [6, 15], which contains differences from the former version extracted from the book by Alemán Bolaños [1, 47].

21. THE BATTLES OF OCOTAL,
SAN FERNANDO, AND LOS CALPULES,
JULY 1927

We reached Ocotal at a quarter to one on the morning of July 16 and we took fifteen minutes to position ourselves for combat. At exactly one o'clock the first shot was fired against the unit that the invaders and traitors had stationed in the place called El Divisadero, which was taken by assault, and meanwhile there were simultaneous attacks on all the other units based around the town, which were annihilated, while those who managed to flee were pursued.

The battle lasted for fifteen hours, the Yankees and the subordinate constabulary having been besieged and denied a water supply. Fear forced them to remain inside their walls, awaiting the death that we hoped to give them, but our humanitarian heart gave way to self-criticism. To put an end to them, the easiest thing would have been to burn the two districts where the proud and cowardly criminals were concentrated, but the families who owned the two districts begged us with tears in their eyes not to cause them the great misfortune that would be theirs if we resorted to burning, and so, recognizing that they were my compatriots, I sacrificed a total victory. Thus it was that that herd of swine remained alive. I had favored the interests of my fellow citizens over total victory and so was forced to order the retreat of my people and to leave in perfect order. Sadly, we had to mourn the deaths of six of my brave soldiers, among them the valiant Colonel Rufo Marín. History will immortalize their names. From the enemy we captured ninety beasts of burden, some riding horses, and thirty-two Springfield rifles with their corresponding equipment.

On the 25th of the same month the Yankees appeared in the town of San Fernando displaying white flags, and when they reached a point fifty yards from the barracks doors, they opened fire on five soldiers who were standing guard there, one of my patriotic soldiers and three of the invaders being killed. I immediately ordered the cavalry to ride to the area nearest to San Fernando to stop the enemy and to fight them, while the other cavalry units concentrated themselves at our general headquarters so that we might better organize our forces to defeat the enemy. Unfortunately, however, the unit under the command of Colonel Porfirio Sánchez, exhausted by their long marches, camped in Los Calpules, where they were surprised by the invaders. Recovering from that surprise, however, our men fought a two-hour skirmish which was enough to inflict thirty-two casualties upon the filibusters.[1] I should point out that in all my guerrilla units there are outstanding sharpshooters who could compete in championship matches, a fact proved by the five enemy airplanes that we have destroyed when they tried to approach our trenches. It's true that the enemy's advance force is composed of a fleet of mail planes, but this does not intimidate my brave soldiers because the enemy knows that from the altitude they fire their weapons our powerful *concones* can shoot them down no matter how high they fly.[2] Our guerrilla plan is perfectly organized, and moreover, we have faith that God will fortify our spirit so that we may annihilate the invaders and traitors of my country. The entire region of Nueva Segovia belongs to us in body and soul, and this in itself assures our effectiveness in our struggle against the enemy.

With their brutal acts the Yankees sow terror among the peaceful inhabitants. In their punitive expedition they violated sixteen women, nine virgins among them, two of these unfortunate girls dying as a result of the brutal outrage of the northern barbarians. In the towns and villages they destroy houses and furniture as well as provisions and crops. They destroy newly planted fields and domesticated animals.

Finally, what I have stated in this report is based upon the purest truth and set down exactly. For example, in the battle of Los Calpules we lost three of our brave soldiers, twelve Lewis machine gun clips, five rifles, and four animals; for that very reason, we have no interest in hiding the truth because we would have nothing to gain from saying the opposite.

Brothers of my land: In conclusion, I have only to tell you that your companions in arms were terribly bitter when they found among the enemy dead many of our companions who yesterday, defending the same ideal, shared with us in common the warm glow of the camp, but who today, perhaps for a crumb of bread thrown to them, kill our own brothers. Keep in mind above all that you are Nicaraguans and that your attitude will give way to the bitterest self-reproach.

Compatriots: We will remain under arms with complete determination and self-denial for as long as Adolfo Díaz remains in the presidency, since it is well known that this man is the disgrace of our fatherland, and we are fully convinced that no foreigner, however powerful, has the right to impose conditions upon us that only our citizens should determine. Mr. Stimson said to Dr. Sacasa's delegates that the maintenance of the serpent Díaz in the presidency is a matter of honor and prestige for the United States. In this regard, I am in agreement with Dr. Sacasa that a great nation acquires honor and prestige when it respects the sovereignty of weak and small nations instead of oppressing those who fight for the security of their own institutions. We fight for honor and not for prestige, because if we lose our honor we will have lost our right to live.

I am speaking to you, traitors, impostors, toadies, mercenaries, acolytes. Get down on your knees, all of you, because I am going to invoke the blessed names of my companions in arms, who have died in defense of the liberty of Nicaragua: Rufo Antonio Marín and Carlos Fonseca.[3]

El Chipote, August 1, 1927

A. C. SANDINO

[19, 2 pp.]

1. Sandino's frequent references to U.S. forces as *filibusters* or *pirates* may reflect the traditional use of the word *filibuster* in referring to William Walker and his followers, who dominated Nicaragua and other parts of Central America in the period from 1855 until 1860. Even more likely, it was Sandino's reaction to the frequent use of such terms as *bandit*, *pirate King*, or *brigand* by Moncada, U.S. officials, and the American press when referring to him and his followers. RC

2. *Concones* were rifles that the Mexican government supplied to the Constitutionalist revolution of 1926–1927, which reached the Atlantic coast of Nicaragua aboard the steamship *Concón*, from which they take their name.

3. Honduran internationalist, soldier in the ranks of the Army in Defense of National Sovereignty, who had the same name as the leader of the Popular Sandinista Revolution.

22. LETTER TO DR. D. CASTILLO,
AUGUST 26, 1927

El Chipote
August 26, 1927

Dr. D. Castillo
Estelí, Nicaragua

My well-remembered friend:

In these days when the country's traitors are multiplying, it is getting hard to recognize my friends.

The men of Nicaragua have divided themselves into three classes:

1. Puritanical and honorable Liberals.
2. Chicken Liberals (or eunuchs).
3. Sell-outs of their country, in other words, Conservatives.

I beg you to tell me to which of these classes you belong.

Patria y Libertad.

A. C. SANDINO

[19, 1 p.]

23. MANIFESTO TO THE NICARAGUAN PEOPLE, AUGUST 26, 1927

El Chipote
August 26, 1927

The puritanical and honorable Liberals, in other words, those who did not sell their weapons or recognize Adolfo Díaz in exchange for public offices, and who did not join the "machos" to insult Nicaragua—such Liberals will never permit the division of their party in the next elections, because this would mean allowing the triumph of the Conservatives, something every patriot should seek to avoid. We will remain under arms as long as the government is Conservative, and we will surrender our weapons only to a Liberal government, even if we should not be followers of that government, and then in the arena of civil combat we will search for the real patriot who can provide new orientations to the affairs of our afflicted mother, Nicaragua.

A. C. SANDINO

[11, 62]

24. LETTER TO ADÁN MARADIAGA, SEPTEMBER 1927

El Chipote
September [?], 1927

Señor Adán Maradiaga
Teacher of the Castilian Language and Chicken Liberal

Overlooking the perversity of your judgement, I will make reference instead to that thing you reproduced, with great cynicism, in the newspaper, *El Comercio*, no. 8842, on August 21 last, with the title "A Letter from the Rebel Sandino," which you reproduce as an original from my own hand, regretting meanwhile that I must waste my time refuting vulgarisms which, like you yourself, are worth nothing more than the spittle of my contempt. I have never had any pretension of exhibiting myself as an intellectual of great stature, since my humble personality is unacquainted with the tortuosities of the language of Cervantes. But believe this, and listen to it well: however great my lack of culture, the parallel between you and myself before our nation's history, regardless of your great intellect, is entirely different. And so that you may be wiser in your spiteful critique, I must inform you that I have never had a secretary, and that my "official" correspondence is all that I elaborate with my own hand, aside from letters to my confidential friends; the rest is a matter of time, which I cannot afford to waste on trivialities, and for that reason every person who knows how to write applies himself voluntarily to this or that work, without being obliged to do it with "syntax," "prosody," and orthography, because you must remember that the army that marches with me is not an army of schoolteachers, but rather a handful of valiant and self-denying patriots who defend with their blood the liberty and integrity of our country, a country that, with your criminal indifference and perverse intellectuality, you have permitted to be tarnished, since clearly you do not let yourself see that your patriotism reaches down to the level of the umbilical region. Aside from this, I do not recognize you as a Liberal, since your cowardice and your sojourn in Danlí (Honduras) when the country needed you proved you to be a chicken. I can grant you time to vindicate yourself, and for this purpose, if you wish to accept employment in my army as a teacher of the Castilian language, I will accept your services with pleasure, assigning you a salary of 200 córdobas per month. And in the event that you should not be equipped because you sold your rifle, I will give you a Concón or a Springfield so that you may know how to interpret conscientiously our self-denial and sacrifice. And then you will have the right to call yourself a Liberal, not to censure the people, whom with your "wisdom" you are obliged to educate. Concerning the key that you mention in your letter, I can only tell you that never have I constituted myself the guardian of outside interests, and for the same reason you will not be able to justify the originality of the handwriting, and much less the style of the said letter. What I can judge in your perversity is that you have left reflected in it your idiosyncrasies (and the defects of our race), and for this I pity you, miserable person!

Patria y Libertad.
A. C. SANDINO

[19, 2 pp.]

25. GUIDELINES FOR THE ORGANIZATION OF THE ARMY IN DEFENSE OF THE NATIONAL SOVEREIGNTY OF NICARAGUA, SEPTEMBER 2, 1927

The Guidelines for the Organization of the Forces Defending the National Law of Nicaragua are established in the following manner:

1. The Military Institution of the Defenders of the National Law of Nicaragua is composed of Liberal Nicaraguan volunteers and Latin Americans who may wish to join our army and who are ready to defend with their blood the liberty of Nicaragua; and who for the same purpose recognize as their Supreme Commander the patriot General Augusto César Sandino, who, with loyalty and sincerity, has known how to defend with complete self-denial the Nation's honor, as a legitimate Nicaraguan; and who, in that same sprit, will adapt their behavior to the highest level of discipline, subjecting themselves to and recognizing the Military Code of the Republic.

2. The Military Institution of the Defenders of the National Law of Nicaragua totally disavows every act, order or command emanating from the traitor and usurper Adolfo Díaz, as well as from the invaders of the fatherland, who with enormous cynicism are trampling upon our sovereignty, because it is recognized that our country's policies should not originate in a foreign country, but should be based instead upon the most absolute national spirit.

3. The Defenders of the National Law of Nicaragua do not form a partisan faction that intends to divide the Liberal party; on the contrary, they are the heart and soul of the fatherland and of our race, and for that same reason restrict themselves to the defense of our sovereignty and maintenance of the rights of the Liberal party, rights violated by the turncoat and traitor José María Moncada, who with his unbridled ambition did not consider the grave consequences into which he fell by his cowardly acts, betraying the fatherland, his leader, and the party. In the same vein, recognizing that Nicaragua should not be the patrimony of any particular group or party, *we swear before the symbol of the fatherland to die rather than to sell ourselves or to surrender to the offers of the invad-*

ers, oligarchs, and traitors who for so many years have trafficked with the Nation's honor.

4. Every fighter who at a later time takes up arms, joining the Defenders of the National Law of Nicaragua, will be obliged to notify the Supreme Commander, who will provide him with the necessary formalities, choosing the zone where he will operate.

5. The department of Nueva Segovia, where Nicaraguan patriotism has continued to exist, will be divided into the following four zones: Pueblo Nuevo, Somoto, Quilalí, and Ocotal. In each of these there will be a Head of Operations, who will be officially named by the Supreme Commander of the Revolution.

6. Each Head of Operations is strictly prohibited from carrying out hostile acts against the peaceful campesinos, or from taking forced loans unless authorized to do so by the Supreme Commander, and in such event he must duly verify the amounts that he employs for the provisioning of the forces under his command. Disprespect for this provision will result in a trial in conformity with the Military Code.

7. Every leader belonging to the Forces Defending the National Law of Nicaragua is *strictly prohibited* from entering into secret pacts with the enemy or from accepting agreements that may be harmful to the fatherland and the party. Whoever violates this provision will be judged by a Council of War.

8. The powers of the Revolution are constituted at the general encampment on the hill called El Chipote, bastion of the Defenders of the National Law of Nicaragua, which we will continue to defend with loyalty to the symbol of the fatherland and the Liberal party.

9. Every order emanating from the Supreme Commander of the Revolution will be respected with the highest spirit of discipline, and for that reason every leader belonging to the Army in Defense of the National Sovereignty of Nicaragua is obliged to obey that order and to see to it that it is obeyed with the duty that honor and patriotism require.

10. The Army in Defense of the National Sovereignty of Nicaragua, made up of selfless patriots, does not receive a daily wage, since such an act would be judged by the civilized world with the most acrid censure, it being understood that every truly patriotic Nicaraguan is obliged to defend voluntarily the nation's honor; however, the Supreme Commander of the Revolution commits himself to providing everything that is indispensable to the army in the form of equipment and clothing.

11. Every official communication originating from the General Headquarters, or from leaders and officers, will carry subscribed at the end the words *Patria y Libertad*, which will be recognized as official throughout the Army.

12. The Army in Defense of the National Sovereignty of Nicaragua is in active communication with the other Indo-Hispanic nations of the con-

tinent and for this purpose has already named its representatives who are working for the benefit of our cause, in order that our triumph may become a fact, filling with glory those who, setting aside every personal ambition, will know how to accept the sacrifice that the defense of our country's honor demands.

13. The military ranks granted by the General Command will be recognized after the victory of our cause, and each interested individual will receive his corresponding commission.

14. *The Supreme Commander of the Revolution swears before the fatherland and the Army in Defense of the National Sovereignty of Nicaragua that he has no political compromises with anyone, and that for that reason his acts correspond to the highest patriotism, and he will assume the responsibility for them before the fatherland and before history, and, in virtue of what is stated above, we, all the leaders and officers, ratify and sign this.*

El Chipote, Nicaragua, Central America, on the second day of the month of September, nineteen hundred and twenty-seven

Patria y Libertad.

Here all the signatures headed by that of the Supreme Commander of the Revolution, General Augusto César Sandino

[19, 2 pp.]

26. GUIDELINES FOR VISITORS TO SANDINO'S CAMP, SEPTEMBER 2, 1927[1]

GUIDELINES TO WHICH A DELEGATE OR DELEGATES LEADING A MISSION TO THIS CAMP MUST ADAPT THEIR REPRESENTATION

1. The delegates' nationality will be legally affirmed.

2. Credentials justifying the delegation will be duly exhibited.

3. The period of time that he or they must live in the country will be duly verified, along with the class of business or enterprise causing them to remain here, since otherwise the reasons obliging our people to defend their rights cannot be known.

4. If the delegation should represent the usurpist government of Adolfo Díaz, under no circumstances will we permit any conference whatsoever for as long as the invaders are treading upon our soil.

5. If the delegation is not covered by the previous article, this General Headquarters may name a representative of high military rank to receive and hear the wishes of the applicants, choosing the place called Santa Rosa for the said conference, for which purpose the delegate or delegates must raise a flag of truce, that is, a white flag, and present themselves without weapons. The number of persons wishing to be received cannot exceed three.

6. This General Headquarters commits itself to give full and effective guarantees to the person or persons who comply with these guidelines and who come here protected by a high level of good faith.

El Chipote, Nicaragua, September 2, 1927
Patria y Libertad.
A. C. SANDINO

[19, 1 p.]

1. In previous editions, before 1984, this document bore the date January 6, 1928, as mistakenly indicated in the source from which it was taken [11, 15–16]. Recently it was

proved that it was signed on September 2, 1927, the day the "Guidelines for the Organization of the Army in Defense of the National Sovereignty" were established.

27. LETTER TO FROYLÁN TURCIOS, SEPTEMBER 8, 1927

General Encampment of the Liberating
Forces in Defense of the National Integrity of
Nicaragua.
El Chipote, September 8, 1927

To the Director and Editor of the Review *Ariel*
Tegucigalpa, Honduras, Central America

My dear sir:

An issue of your review in which I was able to admire the highest expression of your healthy intellect has arrived at my camp. Clearly you have purified your patriotism, because your mentality knows how to interpret it conscientiously.

The ideas you have put forward regarding my humble person and my opposition to my country's invaders fill my spirit with deep satisfaction, since you are the one, with your impartiality, called upon to give a faithful interpretation to my acts, which are intended to defend my country's honor faithfully and without personal ambition.

Your review has opened broad avenues of thankfulness in our hearts, and, in this respect, please accept our gratitude in the name of the handful of brave men who accompany me, and in my own name.

This occasion gives me an opportunity to assure you personally that Sandino and his forces will not surrender to the traitors, much less to the invaders of my country, and thus may you make it known to your colleagues of the press, to Honduran intellectuals, to the workers and artisans and people in general of Central America, and to the Indo-Hispanic nations.

We wish to prove to pessimists that patriotism is not invoked to gain sinecures and public jobs (*as Moncada did it*). Rather it is demonstrated through tangible deeds, by offering one's life in defense of the nation's sovereignty, since it is better to die than to accept the humiliating freedom of the slave.

I take advantage of this opportunity to subscribe myself to you and at the same time to send you a fraternal and cordial greeting from your attentive and obedient servant.

AUGUSTO C. SANDINO

[19, 1 p.]

28. THE BATTLE OF TELPANECA OF
SEPTEMBER 19, 1927

El Chipote
September 20, 1927

The obstinacy of the President of the United States, Mr. Calvin Coolidge, continues to be the cause of the shedding of blood in Nicaragua. On the 19th of the present month there was a bloody battle in the village of Telpaneca, which came about in the following manner:

I ordered a cavalry unit to the edge of that town under the command of Colonel Francisco Estrada, in order to provide protection to our authorities, because we knew the Yankees were pursuing them pitilessly, and that the constabularies were under orders to murder those same authorities. Our cavalry arrived on the outskirts of the town at twelve o'clock at night and, in accordance with their order and the plan they had been given, they began to encircle the enemy.

At 12:45 the first shot rang out against the enemy barracks, and simultaneously firing began against the other enemy units. An hour later my men had managed to dislodge the enemy from their outer positions, and little by little they were gaining control of the village. But when they had gotten into the town the enemy exploded some mines, though without doing any damage. The struggle became ever more hard-fought, because the enemy had their line of fire in the form of a square in all the village houses with their high windows, and in each house there were four machine guns. The thrust of my people into the village was heroic, and they managed to reduce the invaders to a few houses and to capture three machine guns, forty-two rifles, and about fifty thousand rounds of ammunition for rifles and machine guns, and the number of dead among the machos and the constabularies was reckoned at eighty, aside from one hundred and fifty dead animals belonging to the enemy. Concerning my men, they amused themselves by collecting supplies from the forward barracks. Dawn came, and they had to retire to the sound of the trumpet, or rather before the famous ball that is the sun. The eighty deaths of which I speak were those of the enemy alone.

A. C. SANDINO

[19, 1 p.]

29. THE BATTLES OF SAN FERNANDO, LAS FLORES, AND TELPANECA, JULY AND AUGUST 1927[1]

Before setting ourselves up permanently on El Chipote, we took part in some additional battles, including that of San Fernando of July 25, which was an unexpected clash with a strong body of marines whose number was greater than our own. A terrible battle took place in which I myself was close to death, because they had set up several machine guns aimed in my direction, and I can't myself explain how I was able to get out of there alive. Almost my entire army fled in disorder. But, as a precaution against something of the kind, we had previously decided upon a place where we would regroup, in this case, San Fernando itself, a little village where blond people abound, located about six leagues east of El Ocotal, almost at the base of the enormous hill of El Chipote. After this defeat at San Fernando, an even worse one followed at a road junction not far from El Chipote, which we call the battle of Las Flores, the biggest defeat we suffered in the six years of war against the marines. There my army found itself, greatly damaged and scarcely in a state of reorganization after the defeat at San Fernando, with another main body of marines. Look, Román, the Yankees fought in their own way, with school tactics, and with great confidence and self-control, in squads, and with those squads arranged in geometrical formations. I would have preferred to avoid that encounter, because the system I had decided to use was that of my guerrillas and not that of pitched battles. Still, we were forced to meet them in battle. The fight was dreadful, and our primitive technique of scattering, with each soldier seeking his own way out, wasn't possible this time, because we had been surprised and we were surrounded and of course it's much easier to target a group than an individual who is running away. In spite of everything, we defended ourselves as fiercely as we were attacked. I don't know what would have been the results from between the two techniques. Maybe they would have beaten us, but not in the disastrous way they routed us, because at the most critical moment, the damned airplanes came to protect the marines. They killed a large number of my soldiers and spread total disorder in my ranks. But, airplanes or not, that battle was a total victory for the marines, who, furthermore, captured a large quantity of war equipment and food that we were transporting to El Chipote.

Though for us it was a tremendous defeat, this battle of Las Flores was at the same time a great lesson, because by means of it we learned much more about how we ought to fight in the future. The marines pursued us enthusiastically, but we managed to outwit them and pierce their rear-guard, and ten days after the defeat of Las Flores we surprised them in Telpaneca, where they had set up their quarters.

Telpaneca is a village of more than two thousand inhabitants. The attack was a total success. We occupied the village and provisioned ourselves. The only thing we didn't capture were the marine quarters, because they had surrounded their lines of trenches with barbed wire, and, aside from that, they had an extensive network of intercommunicating trenches, imitating the system of entrenchment used in the European War. In this way they were able to circulate through a good part of the village without endangering their skins. For this reason I distributed part of my people on the nearby heights where we set up our machineguns, with which we kept them bottled up in the trenches while the troops gathered provisions in the village. The situation remained that way all night, until early the next morning when the squadrons of airplanes began to bomb and machine-gun us, for which reason we began our withdrawal to the mountains.

[7, 85–87]

1. Like Doc. 2, 58, 120, 179, and 201, this account of some of Sandino's early battles was told in 1933 to José Román, and published in the latter's book, *Maldito país*. RC

30. LETTER TO FROYLÁN TURCIOS, SEPTEMBER 20, 1927

El Chipote
September 20, 1927[1]

Señor Don Froylán Turcios,
Director of the Review *Ariel*
Tegucigalpa

Esteemed poet:

Previously I wrote a letter to you in which I explained my ideas to you, as well as my thankfulness for the thoughts you expressed about my humble person, and in regard to my attitude, which is guided by my wish to defend my country's sovereignty, even if to do so we must offer our lives on the altar of freedom. Because, even though traitors and pessimistic hypocrites, with their spite and limitless ambition, may look upon me as a candidate for an insane asylum, I hope to prove to the civilized world that there are still people in my beloved Nicaragua who know how to die defending their honor. My obsession is to repel with the dignity and pride of our race every imposition that, with the cynicism derived from strength, the assassins of weak nations are imposing upon our country, and you may be firmly convinced that as long as I possess bullets, I will make them understand that their audacity will cost them dearly. I do not doubt that we are very small to defeat the pirates and Yankee criminals, but those assassins also cannot deny that our decision is based upon the sacred principle of defending our sovereignty.

For my army and for me it would be improper to accept guarantees from the traitors and invaders of my country, because they are not the persons called upon to grant such guarantees to us. We are our country's legitimate sons who should be granting such guarantees to them. I do not want them for myself. I want them for the nation, and they can become effective if the piratical invaders cease their occupation of our territory. There is nothing that justifies their meddling in our internal politics, nor do I believe that the greatness of the "*colossus*" is sufficient cause to employ that greatness to murder Nicaraguans. Because even if this should be their intention, it would in no way benefit them, because even if they should annihilate us, they would find in our bloody remains only the treasure that envelops the hearts of Nicaraguan patriots. This would serve only to humiliate the "*chicken*" that is displayed on their coat of arms in the form of an eagle. You may be certain, and you are authorized to make it known to Central America, to the community of intellectuals, to the workers and artisans, and to the Indo-Hispanic race, that I will be intransigent and that I will not abandon my position until I have thrown the invaders and traitors from my country and from power, those who for so many years have trafficked with the nation's honor.

Nicaragua should not be the patrimony of oligarchs and traitors, and much less should we accept humiliation from the expansionist pirates of the dollar, and it is for this reason that I will fight for as long as my heart shows signs of life. And if through some fateful and unforeseen disaster I should lose my entire army, which I do not think will happen, you may continue to believe, my esteemed friend, that in my arsenal of war I retain some hundredweights of dynamite, which, setting myself in its midst, I will light with my own hand, so that in the cataclysm produced by that explosion the repercussion of that detonation may be heard at a distance of four hundred kilometers, and those who have the good fortune to hear it will be witnesses that Sandino has died, but that he did not allow the profane hands of traitors and invaders to desecrate his remains, because only the *omnipotent God* and true patriots will know how to judge my work. Be persuaded, Señor Turcios, that your pen has vibrated in the heart of my valiant army, as in mine, because you have clearly reflected your love of country, knowing how to interpret it conscientiously. For this same reason, please accept our fraternal thanks.

At the same time, we wish to make known to you our condolences for the death of your sister, and we beg God with all our heart to strengthen your spirit and to permit you to submit yourself to such great sorrow.

I am on the eve of a bloody battle with the invaders and traitors of my country, of which I will give you an extensive and detailed report at the first opportunity; meanwhile, please accept my feelings of great esteem, as well as a fraternal greeting from your friend and admirer.

Your most affectionate and attentive servant,
AUGUSTO C. SANDINO

[19, 2 pp.]

1. This letter and that of September 24, 1927 (Doc. 31) received a reply from Froylán Turcios on October 11 of that same year. The reply is included in the first Nicaraguan edition (174–76). A summary of its content: Froylán Turcios appreciates Sandino's letters and tells him that he has opened an active campaign for his autonomist cause, since *Ariel* is influential not only in Honduras but in every part of Latin America. Sandino's struggle, he says, is most beautiful and is already having repercussions throughout the world. In Nicaragua's situation, only two roads remain: either to win a victory or to die in the struggle.

The fight must be prolonged for six months, because at the end of that time, in a movement of universal conscience, all the world's nations will force imperialism to leave Nicaragua. For Turcios, Sandino is the practical realization of his opposition to U.S. intervention in Latin America. He expresses the pride he feels in the Nicaraguan guerrilla fighter, for whom he declares his enthusiasm, affection, and admiration. Sandino's victories, he concludes, will ultimately pass into history.

31. LETTER TO FROYLÁN TURCIOS, SEPTEMBER 24, 1927[1]

El Chipote
September 24, 1927

Señor Don Froylán Turcios
Tegucigalpa

Esteemed friend:

I have the honor of presenting to you Señor Juan G. Colindres, a special envoy who is carrying private correspondence for you, so that he may be personally identified by you and so that you may exchange impressions with him, according to the instructions that the said messenger is carrying. I do not doubt that as a person familiar with humble individuals you can appreciate the self-denial of this gentleman in carrying out such a delicate mission. The said gentleman may remain on this mission for as long as you think convenient. My desire, dear friend, is to prove to the civilized world that my attitude does not affect any government of our sister republics, and that for that same reason they should not harbor distrust. History will closely examine the responsibility I have assumed for my acts before the fatherland, defining them in any way that seems convenient. Once again you may be assured that my great love for my country and my desire to see it free, as well as my faith in God, will encourage my army and myself to continue fighting against my country's invaders until we have punished them cruelly and dislodged them from our territory.

Sending you my thanks in advance, I remain as always at your disposal, your most affectionate friend and servant.

Patria y Libertad.
A. C. SANDINO

[19, 1 p.]

1. This letter corresponds to a handwritten copy located in the IES archive and replaces the version that appeared in the first Nicaraguan edition. Also excluded is another letter of the same date (addressed to Turcios and taken from *Repertorio Americano* 15 [1927]: 24, since it is only a combination of paragraphs from the present document and Doc. 28.

32. LETTER TO BLANCA DE SANDINO,
OCTOBER 6, 1927

El Chupón
October 6, 1927[1]

Señora Doña Blanca de Sandino
San Rafael del Norte

My sweet wife:

Today I received your letter dated August 15 last, which I answer with the greatest pleasure you can imagine. I don't know how to respond to your complaints. I know that I don't make you happy, but I must tell you that when I proposed marriage to you that proposal was inspired by the greatest wish to love you with all the power of my heart, and I never imagined that circumstances would place me in a position to cause you unhappiness, or that your desperation would become so great that you would consider suicide. Although you say that I don't love you, I want to assure you that despite the great love I have for you, one can make sacrifices such as those we are making now, those of us who with weapons on our shoulders are desperately defending our rights as free men, since we can never accept the yoke of slavery because of cowardice. I prefer to lose your love and to die in open battle against the murderous invader before permitting you, myself, and our children, if we should have them, to survive in the state of infamy that only cowards and the irresolute can accept. I have placed the love of my country above all other forms of love, and you must convince yourself that in order to be happy, in order that we may be happy, it is necessary for the sun of freedom to shine on our country. Not only treachery and gold are triumphant; with greater reason justice will also prevail.

Be optimistic, have faith in God, and he will help to free us, so that tomorrow when we are together and the same God makes us a gift of a child, he may bless the memory of his father, who with unbreakable will prepared for him fatherland and freedom.

I sent you one of the many journals that reach us from the Indo-Hispanic countries; through it you can get some small idea of the work that is being done on our behalf.

I don't want you to come, because the thing is not as easy as you might imagine. Don't talk to me of jealousy, because I have already told you that I know what I'm doing, and besides you must convince yourself that I love you, that you are my wife, and nothing is to be gained from throwing salt into the sea. I am your sea and you must confide in me.

Greetings to my mother-in-law, and tell her that this letter is for you, for her, and for Lucila; and that if I don't write to them it's because time doesn't give me the opportunity to be courteous. Give my mother-in-law an embrace for me and a kiss to Chila.

Earlier I sent you some leaflets that I've distributed throughout the republic, and the question of the election should be based on them.

Greetings to all who ask about me, especially Don Santos Aráuz and Santos Rivera, as well as Colonel Clemente Rodriguez; tell those gentlemen not to get too much involved with the machos, because it would be a pity if tomorrow we were political enemies, since I have begun to consider them men of tomorrow. Let them read this letter, so that they may be convinced that even though I am in the jungles I remember them constantly.

I suppose there can be no doubt about our victory, because God not only has favored our cause, but has also become an interested party. Let's hope that the greatness that the Yankees may attain doesn't dazzle all of you, because God's greatness is our protector. The pirates will leave our territory and later not even they will be able to explain the reasons for their defeat. Our victory will be providential.

Yes, my Blanquita, accept a million kisses and a flood of embraces, until I can give myself the pleasure of taking you personally into my arms.

Yours,

A. C. SANDINO

P.S. Since I want to get the mail out fast I will not revise what I have written. You do it.

Farewell.

[19, 2 p.]

1. In the 1981 edition this letter appears dated 1928 instead of 1927, as is indicated in the typed copy preserved in the IES archive.

33. MANIFESTO TO THE NICARAGUAN PEOPLE CONCERNING THE ELECTIONS, OCTOBER 6, 1927

MANIFESTO TO THE NICARAGUAN PEOPLE CONCERNING THE ELECTIONS

I must respond to the many letters that my coreligionists and compatriots are sending me, asking my opinion concerning the election for the next presidential term, to be carried out under the disgraceful administration of the traitor, Adolfo Díaz, and supervised with complete cynicism by someone who calls himself a representative of a foreign government. I should perhaps remain silent in order not to give the professional politicians an opportunity to distort my thoughts as they may see fit, but the bonds of friendship and my fraternal feelings for the common workers, crystallized in my great love for my country, oblige me to give an opinion about the subject mentioned.

The Army in Defense of the Sovereignty of Nicaragua does not have compromises with anyone. It does not aid or defend tyrants. Its slogan conforms to the most sacred principles of loyalty and honor, and, politically, it recognizes only the legality of the election of Dr. Juan B. Sacasa, emanating from the sovereign will of the people. It does not shirk its responsibilities for the sake of conventionalities or accede to foreign demands, because its acts are defined by its deeds. If my country's constitutional president was thrown out of this land by the imperialist Yankee forces and criminally betrayed by his principal military commander, to whom he confided the leadership of the army, the handful of brave men who defend legality at the cost of their blood bear in one hand the symbol of their country, and in the other the rifle that defends and will continue to defend the rights of this nation, so frequently mocked and humiliated.

The pathetic glory that my fatherland's invaders hope to add to their flag by killing my countrymen bristles the feathers on the symbolic chicken that they display on their coat of arms.

The political orientation of my country should shun every form of caudillismo, because our somber experience requires us to pursue a different path. Concerning the presidential candidate, the nation that has always been the victim of the unbridled ambitions of tyrants ought to consider calmly and without constraint first of all whether that candidate will know how to defend the dignity of the Republic, and, at the same time, whether he knows how to interpret the needs of the people, because it must be kept in mind that every government leader imposed by a foreign power who rises up among us will represent and defend only the interests of foreigners, and never the collective interests of the nation. The leader who feels a true love for his country should detest with pride every humiliating proposal that affects the nation's sovereignty.

Progress and civilization must not be held back, but we do not desire them as the consequence of our subjugation. It is for this reason that the people must think deeply when they elect our leader, because if unhappily they should elect a tyrant, it will be the people themselves who will create a dictatorship, which, in order to sustain itself, must keep the country in a state of slavery and misery. The idealism of the defenders of the national integrity of Nicaragua will continue to uphold the country's honor, and, at the same time, the principle of the constitutionality of Dr. Juan B. Sacasa and his high position as constitutional president, unless he should legally decline that office before the people. For this very reason, I recommend to the liberal public that, before accepting the candidacy of General José María Moncada, they calmly keep in mind that, by this act, they would violate the principle of constitutionality that they have defended with their own blood.

All right, then, upon what is this election based? Is it imposed upon us or is it the result of the popular will? What are its conditions? Is it intended to bring to the presidency the leader who made a secret pact with the invaders? I will speak honestly: If the presidential election is carried out imposed by the murderous invaders of my country, refusing to abandon our national territory, I will continue to fight until I have decimated them and driven them out by force, and God will crown our efforts. If, on the other hand, the election is the result of the popular will, it ought to be carried out in such a way that the civil candidate who will guide the fate of the country is chosen by a legitimate Liberal convention. If our government is constituted in this way, we will aid it in the consolidation of our sovereignty and the independence of our government. However, if it is forced upon us, we must repudiate it with our armed protest, until we have realized our ardent wish to win our independence from Yankee imperialism.

If General Moncada is a real patriot, he should reject the aspiration he demonstrates of winning the presidency as it was won by those who have stained our national honor. In this time of sorrow our country does not need tyrants. I implore him, as a legitimate Nicaraguan and as a man of honor, to control such an ambition if he really wishes to stem the flow of blood from our nation's wounds.

The Army in Defense of the Sovereignty of Nicaragua will be pleased if the names of the civilians Sofonías Salvatierra and Escolástico Lara emerge from the Liberal convention, for they are men of high intellect and the capacity to direct the nation's future, men who have not stained their hands with fraternal blood.

The people are sovereign and their right to elect their leaders must be respected; and for this reason they will struggle untiringly until this right, today trampled upon by the conquerors, has become effective. It doesn't matter that Moncada said that *life ends and the country remains.* I believe the opposite: *Life is offered up for the country's freedom.* At the same time I recommend this idea to those who would call themselves Liberals and who freely squander their money on propaganda to ingratiate themselves with those who tomorrow will increase our country's sorrow. For your sake, to make up for the heavy cost of the banquets and champagne, you should realize that the huge number of lives lost, of orphans, and of those mutilated by war deserve more concern and pity from your hearts. Tyrants do not need your champagne. It is patriotism that should be injected into their veins.

In conclusion, I must say to the people that if the circumstances of this national war should bring a loss of life, and if, because of this, drastic steps are taken so that the legitimate rights of the revolution can be respected, it will not be because we are advocates of the death penalty, because we have a heartfelt dislike for such a procedure, swearing to fight against capital punishment once the government that embodies our ideals has been constituted.

My fellow brothers, you have asked for my opinion and I have given it to you. This is it. Unfortunately, the number of Nicaraguan traitors will grow. Today another man is added and yet another. Who is it that sold out the people's justice and who expects the invaders and assassins of our fatherland to put him into the presidency? Who? José María Moncada.

Patria e Libertad.
A. C. SANDINO
El Chipote, October 6, 1927

[2, 37–39]

34. "LA CHULA" AND THE BATTLE OF LAS CRUCES OF OCTOBER 9, 1927

El Chipote
October 10, 1927

The weapons that defend the National Law of Nicaragua have again covered themselves with glory.

Some days ago in our main encampment, at ten in the morning on the 7th of this month, unusual enthusiasm was observed during the first test firing of an "apparatus," which offered magnificent results. The general staff, convinced of the effectiveness of this weapon, examined the topography of the area, maintaining a strict reserve. Once we had studied the route taken each day by the Yankee airplanes in their task of killing peaceful campesinos, we searched for a dominant height for setting up the apparatus. We didn't have long to wait for a result. At ten in the morning on the 8th, "La Chula," which is what we called the apparatus, was set up in a place where, with its great power, it could reach the enemy planes which, protected in a cowardly manner by their altitude, destroy defenseless villages.[1] At 10:30 two enormous airplanes came over the mountain range where "La Chula" was waiting for them; with the apparatus pivoting from side to side, our men took careful aim. We heard the sound of firing, which was answered by a shower of bullets coming from the second airplane, but our bullets had hit their target, and the latter fell to the ground. The aviators died. From the murderous craft we captured two machine guns and a large supply of ammunition, a powerful telescope, two .45 caliber pistols, and all the other useful things it carried.

Since it was expected that following this act the invading forces, albeit in some fear, might try to send out a few columns in support of the fallen plane, I set up a beautiful trap for them which they stepped into like pigeons.

Indeed, on the second day, the 9th, news came to me that the filibusters were approaching Las Cruces, a place where my people customarily spend the night, and I at once sent out four columns to close off all their exit points. At two that afternoon the columns began firing simultaneously and the enemy was defeated by my forces, not knowing for more than ten minutes where that hail of bullets was coming from. The battle was a bloody one. The enemy force was made up of two hundred men, of whom not ten escaped with their lives. They were almost entirely destroyed, and as a result their whole supply train fell into our hands. It is important to note that we made the greatest progress in regard to machine guns. We captured eight Lewis machine guns from them, with a good supply of ammunition, though we don't need that much ammunition, given the quantity we already possess, which we will never be able to use up. If we mention this, it is to point out the size of our booty. We also took an American flag from them, which we are preserving as a war trophy.

The battle lasted for six hours. We used more than a hundred hand bombs, and fourteen machine guns were employed in the fighting.

The commanders of our column are the following: first commander, Colonel Carlos Quezada; second commander, Colonel Simón Montoya M.; third commander, Captain Ladislao Palacio; fourth commander, Captain Antonio Galeano.

These are the principal leaders who participated in that glorious battle, which after 117 years has many affinities with the battle that the heroic Mexican people endured on the mountain of Las Cruces at the beginning of their struggle for independence.

Patria y Libertad.
A. C. SANDINO

[2, 15–16]

1. *La chula* means a pretty or sassy woman. In Doc. 65 Sandino refers to this device as "artillery," but according to other eyewitnesses it was a large machine gun taken from a warplane shot down near Quilalí, each of its disk-shaped magazines containing a hundred rounds of ammunition. See Instituto de Estudio del Sandinismo, *Ahora sé que Sandino manda* (Managua, 1986), 221–22. RC

35. LETTER TO COLONEL FÉLIX PEDRO ZELEDÓN, OCTOBER 21, 1927

El Chipote
October 21, 1927

Colonel Félix Pedro Zeledón
Yali

My respected Colonel:

Your esteemed letter dated the 11th of this month is in my hands, and I reply to it with the same affection and sincerity as always. At the same time I am happy to inform you that Liberalism will come to power before any such elections, because at the beginning of December or near the end of November we will advance upon the heart of the country, and from now on there will be no more neutral zones; we will advance over the Yankees and the Conservatives, and justice will be imposed. I have been working outside the country to get moral support from the other Spanish American countries, which, however, we will soon no longer need, since recently have come to us the weapons that Dr. Sacasa left in Puerto Cabezas when he evacuated that port. It's a week now since ten artillery pieces arrived here from that port, and they proved themselves on the 9th of the month in the battle of Las Cruces, and thank God our triumph was sensational; so that you may have some impression of that victory, I send you a copy of the report that we sent to Honduras for publication by the press of that country.[1]

Colonel, certainly there will be persons who will think the revolution no longer has any reason to exist because licking the Yankees' feet will suffice to assure the triumph of Liberalism. Those who think this way have no right even to live, because such a way of thinking profanes the memory of our ancestors, who died so that our sovereignty would be respected. Freedom is not won with flowers! It is with bullets that we must drive the enemy from power! The revolution is synonymous with purification! As long as Adolfo Díaz continues to govern the people, whom he has abused with the aid of his supporters, the revolution is a necessity that honor and shame demand of us.

Colonel, when I began my advance into the interior, it was because already then I was prepared, with my bludgeon raised behind my back, to defeat the United States of America in the event they wished to do battle with our forces. Our army does not have political compromises with anybody, and so its acts conform to the highest form of patriotism.

From this day on you may be sure that there will be no elections and that our triumph will become a reality. Once a state of siege has been declared, the chicken Liberals will be forced to support us, because otherwise they will be insulted by the puritans and by those who have suffered.

I have seen a manifesto from Moncada where he says that when we became independent we didn't deserve it, and that for this reason he supports the intervention. What a brute this imbecile is! What can the people expect from a hypocrite who has used the blood of our heroes to get sinecures and public offices? Let the people judge him.

Greetings to your family, and accept the affection of your friend who holds you in esteem.

Patria y Libertad.
AUGUSTO C. SANDINO

[19, 1 p.]

1. This report, which must have been prepared before this letter, has not been found. Since this letter is dated October 21 and the battle of Las Cruces took place on October 9, clearly more than a week had elapsed since the arrival of the weapons. RC

36. LETTER TO BERTA MUNGUÍA, OCTOBER 22, 1927

Fortress of the Defenders of the National
Integrity of Nicaragua
El Chipote
October 22, 1927

Señorita Berta Munguía
Secretary of the Group in Solidarity
with the Nicaraguan Labor Movement
León

Esteemed señorita:

Your letter of the 29th of last month has reached me, and I have the pleasure to refer to it. I greatly appreciate the distinction you have given me by making me honorary president of your powerful organization; at the same time I understand the solidarity that you are seeking to embody, which is justified by the same idealism that moves my own liberating principle, spiritualized in the great love of our country and crystallized in the *redemption* of *Nicaraguan workers and artisans.*

It is certain that cowardice causes persons with the biggest hearts to sink into the depths of pessimism, but it is also true that the people of the Indo-Hispanic continent, mostly humble people, have known the glory of winning their rights with their own blood.

Time has yet to demonstrate to the civilized world and to our brothers, the Central Americans, that, if for so many years the traitors and oligarchs sank our country into the bloodiest despair, the modern Nicaraguan generation will no longer tolerate or allow the enslaving politics that the worm-eaten and decadent Nicaraguan aristocracy, composed of degenerate traitors, has carried out, trafficking with the nation's honor and the people's misery. Nicaragua ought not to be the patrimony of oligarchs and traitors. The cowards who sold the people's justice to turn it over defenseless to our enemies have fallen into the darkest crime of high treason; the people possess the sovereign power to condemn that monstrous crime, and it is for this reason that for me, your servant, a member of the international of workers, the loyalty of my principles, to defend the sovereignty of my country and the people's rights, is based upon the highest spirit of our nation's political life.

In regard to your organization, in a collective sense, you should broaden it as you judge most opportune and fitting to include all the workers' groups of the Republic, so that if you should see that forces, either national or interventionist, are being organized to fight us, you can hold meetings to protest against the traitor Adolfo Díaz and the government of the United States of America, for the cynicism with which they send the people out to slaughter while preaching *peace*! With respect to the military situation, my army is strong and full of enthusiasm, because we have not fought a battle against the invaders and traitors, however bloody it may have been, in which the victory has not been ours. The commanders and officers of my guerrilla units are mostly artisans and workers from all over the country, made competent in the military sense by their self-sacrificing discipline, the loyalty with which they defend our ideal being self-evident. In my heart you will find ample fraternal room to accept you as my idealistic co-believers, and in my sword you will find the loyalty with which we shall defend our principles.

You may offer a fraternal and warm salute to my compatriots of your great organization, accepting from me my tokens of consideration and esteem.

Patria y Libertad.
AUGUSTO C. SANDINO

[19, 1 p.]

37. LETTER TO GENERAL SIMÓN MONTOYA, OCTOBER 30, 1927

El Chipote
October 30, 1927

General Simón Montoya
On the Field of Honor

Esteemed General:

Here there is nothing new, and we wish only to see your triumph completed. General, don't lose heart, because just today I am sending another column under the command of Captain Centeno, who will go where Quezada is, that is, to the hill of Lumbí that you mentioned to me. I am informed that the cachurecos who came from Pantasma are near Los Jabalines, and so I am prepared to reinforce Quezada, with whom I believe you will already be in contact at this time.

I also believe that the traitors and invaders are afraid to come to El Chipote and for this reason don't wish to fight it out with you. It may also be that they want to remove their companions' bones and for this reason aren't resisting. If they are looking for a way for you to let them take away such remains, tell them you have an order from me that, if they want to do such a thing, they should regroup outside our zone and send a committee of civilians, and we will give the remains to them.

But don't put your trust in talk, because they are traitors and it may be that they are only waiting for more personnel, who can't come because of the obstacles in their way. If that should be the case, tell them you will let them leave with their lives if they abandon the supplies they are carrying, but that otherwise they will die.

Which means they can evacuate, but leave everything where it is; otherwise you should go hard on them until you've driven them out. To be righteous it is enough for us to let them live stripped of their possessions.

General, if you are tired, hungry, or a bit afraid, ask God to comfort you, but don't come here, because every day I am sending you more people. You may sleep, some first and others later on, but keep two of your leaders awake, because the soldiers aren't as careful as they should be.

God will grant us this new triumph, which will be the definitive one, because I am certain that after this battle they will not come back, and you and your men will be covered with glory! When we enter Managua, it may be that we won't even be able to take a step because of the many flowers the young girls will thrust upon you. Don't lose heart, and say this to all my men: that they keep in mind that the sacrifice they are making is nothing but the performance of our duty to our country, our race, and our party. May God help me to help you.

Patria y Libertad.
AUGUSTO C. SANDINO

[19, 1 p.]

38. WAR COMMUNIQUÉ, NOVEMBER 2, 1927

During twelve days of light skirmishes in a sector of thirty-two square kilometers, the invaders and traitors have been destroyed by the dreadful power of dynamite, which has made them understand that those who betray their country, or who try to humiliate the weak with punishable invasions, are marked by fate as terrible offenders. Such persons are punished with slow agony to make them more conscious of the need to expiate their enormous guilt.

On October 20 reports were received at this General Headquarters that in Jinotega enemy forces were being organized to attack us in our own positions; and that a strong column was coming from Estelí composed of Moncadistas and cachurecos, commanded by the invaders. Another strong column of Yankees had been detached from Ciudad Sandino (formerly El Jícaro), intending to join those coming from the interior. The moment was right to again punish those who dared to invade our guerrilla zone.

On the 21st of the same month I ordered the departure from this general encampment of four columns of one hundred and fifty soldiers each, with two batteries of Lewis machine guns, for the purpose of locating the enemy force and defeating it. But since the traitors and mercenaries are multiplying, there was no lack of a person to inform them of our troops' plan of action. The man who gave them information about our forces was the traitor and mercenary Pompilio Reyes, whose life has been pardoned on several occasions when he was the perpetrator of other ruinous deeds. The information that Reyes gave saved the traitors and invaders from total isolation.

On that October 22 we had chosen the terrain where we should fight them, but they avoided the encounter with our units. When the enemy altered their route I was obliged to make a general concentration of all the guerrilla units that operated at various points in our zone for the greater success of our defensive and offensive operations. On the 25th, at the place where the roads from Las Cruces and San Juan de Segovia meet, the enemy had a brief skirmish with one of our guerrilla units that was moving toward General Headquarters. This cost them nineteen casualties, and our unit acquired seventeen mules, nine additional animals loaded with ammunition for Springfield rifles, twenty-eight empty sacks, and a pack basket with bologna and hot sausages. The enemy remained camped in the mountains from October 26 to October 30, which damaged them greatly, because there was no better place for us to prepare our attacks and, in the event that they should evade them, to annihilate them completely.

Day by day the guerrilla forces of national integrity are gaining experience and admirable skills, and so it will be very difficult for the enemy to surprise them, since the enemy always endures the first shots, and so is demoralized from the beginning of every encounter. It may be said that the village of Quilalí is the capital where the defensive powers of national integrity are constituted, and for this reason on the surface it appears to be dismantled. But under the surface of the earth its powerful mines are loaded in such a way that a single man is sufficient to blow them up in a moment. Thus, if the enemy should occupy Quilalí and seek to remain there, their destruction will be complete.

On October 30 the Yankees and traitors thought we were unaware of their movements because of the silence they maintained on the march; but our guerrillas, who never lost sight of them, pursued them at a short distance, hoping to find the right terrain and a good opportunity to defeat them. The topography where the traitors and invaders marched didn't assure us of a perfect victory. For this reason we did not consider attacking them and, for this reason too, the enemy concentrated only upon moving from one place to another with no fixed course, since their plan of attack was changed after they recognized that the Army in Defense of the National Sovereignty is now sufficiently organized and better prepared for combat. The invaders were informed that they would suffer the most terrible disaster if they occupied Quilalí, and so they reversed their march, heading toward Ciudad Sandino, moving day and night to get themselves out of the zone that they recognized as dangerous.

As we said, the area they occupied was thirty-two square kilometers, and the enemy could hardly have left there without leaving hundreds of dead behind. Thus it was that as they moved toward Ciudad Sandino, Colonels Juan Gregorio Colindres and Simón González and Major Marcial Salas began a forced march to reach them and to force them to fight, choosing the place called La Conchita to punish them decisively. The force of traitors and invaders was made up of four hundred and fifty men.

On November 1 the sun's first rays lit up La Conchita. The pine trees moved incessantly with the first summer winds.[1] At one o'clock on that day history assigned to its pages one of the great triumphs of the Army in Defense of the Sovereignty of Nicaragua. One of the bloodiest battles, in which the Nicaraguan autonomists would have to offer their lives in high sacrifice for the fatherland, was about to begin. At the stated hour, the defenders of the national integrity were on the line of fire, waiting for the enemy with their feet firmly set. At that moment the advance party came forward, made up of fifty men. Then came the vanguard of one hundred and fifty. The center consisted of a hundred and fifty and in it came the war train and the Yankee general staff, along with sharpshooters. A hundred men, mostly pirate-conquerors, made up the rearguard.

We attacked with a volley of "concón" rifle fire and a rain of bombs that caused the enemy terrible damage, filling them with fear, which we took advantage of to fire upon them with the greatest daring and bravery. The deaths that the traitors and invaders suffered were horrifying. Their bodies were terribly destroyed by the effects of the dynamite. They had no other choice but to flee in shame, because their confusion and demoralization were such that those who did not perish from the gunfire or from the bombs died decapitated by machete blows.

The enemy dead came to ninety-four men. Their general staff was totally annihilated. We took from them a large quantity of ammunition of several kinds, ninety rifles, seventy mules, boxes of medicine, and clothing that they had stolen from the house of Don Antonio López during their stay at the hacienda El Jicarito.

El Chipote, November 2, 1927
Patria y Libertad.
A. C. SANDINO

[9, 297–99]

1. The beginning of the dry season. RC

39. RESOLUTION CONCERNING TRAITORS TO THE FATHERLAND, NOVEMBER 14, 1927[1]

General Headquarters of the Defenders of
the National Law of Nicaragua

DECREE

I, Augusto C. Sandino, General in Chief of the Army in Defense of the Sovereignty of Nicaragua, in use of the faculties granted to me by that same army and in support of the political constitution of the nation, make known to the entire Nicaraguan people the following resolution:

The following are traitors to the Fatherland:

1. Every Nicaraguan who for political purposes traffics with the nation's honor, soliciting official support from the invaders of the fatherland, and from the White House government, as well as anyone who leaves the country to serve as a delegate or representative of the government of the traitor Adolfo Díaz.

2. He who has celebrated secret pacts with the enemy, whether a military or civilian leader.

3. He who lends support to the invaders and traitors to assassinate Nicaraguan patriots who are defending the nation's sovereignty.

4. He who supplies official statements, either verbal or written, declaring opposition to our countrymen.

5. He who solicits protection from the invaders with the pretext of defending his own interests, whether a national or foreigner. To him will be applied the same punishment that the political constitution prescribes for traitors to the nation.

At the same time I make it known to Nicaraguan society, to the people with whom I am joined by the bonds of spirituality in defense of our rights, as well as to the foreigners established in this country, that, since the Army in Defense of the Sovereignty of Nicaragua is a perfectly organized and disciplined institution, it will grant every class of effective guarantees to *nationals* and to *foreigners*, so long as they maintain strict neutrality.

Given in El Chipote, the fourteenth day of the month of November of nineteen hundred and twenty-seven.

Patria y Libertad.
A. C. SANDINO

[19, 1 p.]

1. For this edition this document has been transcribed from a typed copy now located in the IES archive. It has editorial differences from the previous edition's version [10, 302].

40. FORM LETTER TO EXPRESS GRATITUDE, NOVEMBER 17, 1927

El Chipote
November 17, 1927

Señor———
Jinotega

My dear sir:

The good news has reached my camp that you are a sincere friend of ours, and this has allowed me to develop some impression of your healthy judgement. The thoughts you have expressed regarding my attitude toward my country's invaders fill my spirit with deep satisfaction, since you have been called upon to offer a faithful and impartial interpretation of my acts, which are directed toward the loyal defense, without personal ambition, of my country's honor. The favorable opinion you have of us has brought gratitude to our patriotic hearts, and in this sense please accept our thanks, in the name of my army and myself.

To me it does not seem at all excessive to inform you that I and my army are religious Catholics and, therefore, we ask you to recommend us in your prayers, because those prayers will be our principal weapons for defeating the enemy; we do not have any concern for the lives of our enemies, and we fight only for our country's freedom. God will crown our efforts with success.

I use this opportunity to offer you my best wishes and at the same time to send a fraternal and cordial salute from your attentive and respectful servant.

Patria y Libertad.
AUGUSTO C. SANDINO

[19, 1 p.]

41. LETTER TO COLONEL FÉLIX PEDRO ZELEDÓN, NOVEMBER 26, 1927

El Chipote
November 26, 1927.[1]

Colonel Félix Pedro Zeledón
Yalí.

My esteemed Colonel:

Your worthy letter of the 22d is in my hands, and I have the pleasure of responding to it. I appreciate the decision you have taken to support us, and I never had any doubt about that support, since I granted you my confidence, naming you one of my aides in that former time.[2] The information you give me concerning the lapses you say my troops were guilty of in those places I attribute mainly to partisan intrigue, which is always rooted in the human heart, because, Colonel Zeledón, I'm sorry to say that my army is at this time more disciplined than that of the traitors and invaders of this country. Nevertheless, the sacred obligations that my army and I have accepted for ourselves obliged me to open an active investigation so that, without ceremony, the expedition's leaders might answer for their acts and, under given circumstances, indicate their responsibility. The result of that investigation was that in the hacienda belonging to one Señor Calderón, where my force arrived, the enemy had assembled for the purpose of attacking one of our reserve units in El Ojoche, and it was very natural that the owner of that hacienda was not pleased by such an unexpected visit, which is why they surprised you with alarming information, defamatory to my army. Be certain that my orders were complied with in a strictly military sense, because for this I can depend upon the support of the finest leaders who uphold the principles of nobility and morality, and, above all, of high discipline. Attached to your note I found the sum of fifty dollars and, with it, a request for a guarantee for Señor Andrés Reyes, which with pleasure I send to you, because I am pleased that even my enemies themselves are convinced that our purpose is limited to the defense of our country's sovereignty, despite the insulting epithet they give us of "bandits." I am returning the fifty dollars previously mentioned and sadly inform you that we do not sell guarantees, because we give them, full and effective, to anyone who deserves them. Before making such a remittance, you ought to have realized that with such an act you would wound my dignity as a patriot, leaving me in the position of a vile mercenary. If that had been my intention, I would have done it when the mercenary Moncada betrayed our country, our party, and our race. I thought the length of time you were with me would have been enough for you to know me. If you should consider sending me another remittance of that kind, I would be happy if you didn't. God will sustain us and with his infinite power help us defeat the traitors and invaders of our country. Do not think because of what I've said to you so frankly that I bear animosity toward you; no, very much to the contrary, I feel satisfied when I set friendship aside to speak to a Nicaraguan such as you. Greetings to your family and do accept as always the affection of your friend.

Patria y Libertad (not gold).
AUGUSTO C. SANDINO

[19, 2 pp.]

1. Two somewhat different versions of this document, the typed originals of which are in the IES archive, were published in the 1984 edition. To save space, however, only the second and apparently more finished version is included here. RC

2. Sandino refers here to Zeledón's participation in the Constitutionalist campaign that took place in Nicaragua from May 1926 until May 1927.

42. LETTER TO COLONEL POMPILIO REYES, NOVEMBER 27, 1927

El Chipote
November 27, 1927

Colonel Pompilio Reyes
Jinotega

My esteemed Colonel:

I had the pleasure of receiving your greatly appreciated letter of the 17th of this month, to which I reply with the same sincerity as always. In reality, Colonel, your explanation pleased me very much, but you should have done it sooner to avoid the consequences and the bad reports against you that came before me, to the point that last month I had to issue a letter sentencing you.[1] It was said that you were one of the guides who escorted the traitors and invaders, and prior to the start of that battle our people had heard that they were hidden in the mountains, and that one of the constabularies had said, "*Three days ago Pompilio Reyes broke with us.*"

Well, all right, I didn't doubt this, since I had written to you begging you not to take any steps against us, saying that we were not harming you in any way and that therefore you should leave us in peace; since you didn't respond, I thought that maybe you had imagined that I was afraid of you, and that for that reason you didn't want to take a little bit of trouble to honor us with a few words.

All this was what brought about your loss of guarantees with us. Up until today I am aware of what the committee did that went to search for you at your house; that is, I knew only that a little black billy goat, which I knew about because of its color and age, belonged to you, but nobody ever told me anything about any clothing or gold. However, I will try to get to the bottom of anything there may be in this respect, and you can count on keeping your animals, because they must certainly be here in this encampment.

I am very happy that the stories they told me about you were false, and, since you don't fear that they will later be confirmed, you may return to your house and once again enjoy the peace of your home, for which I have had a special liking, as I have had for you. I hope to see you happy because you are a hardworking citizen and have suffered for the cause that I, your servant, still loyally defend. I don't say anything against a Liberal who does not wish to fight until he triumphs or dies, because I have become convinced that many Liberals were fooled by the false promises of the Yankees that they were not to take sides in the campaign recently ended. In this respect, I will tell you that I never stopped believing that first we would defeat the Conservatives and that after that we would have to fight the invaders as well. I remember that when I left for Puerto Cabezas you told me that you didn't think the machos would take part, to which I replied *that they wouldn't*. I said this, of course, because otherwise at that moment the people who were not very dedicated would have left us, and we wouldn't even have beaten the *cachos*.[2]

There is something that isn't very pleasant, but I will mention it to you so that you will have a clear idea of the humble personality of your servant. For almost twenty years I traveled over a good part of the three Americas, and there were many opportunities for me to make some money, but my real wish was to be useful to my country, and, being in Mexico in May 1926, I became aware of the heroic struggle that was being prepared against the illegitimate government, for which I prepared myself and came to take part in, determined to die or triumph. Thus it was that I invited my closest friends to join me, and on October 28, in the early morning hours, we all left the San Albino mine together, full of enthusiasm and *cheering for the Liberal Party*! We shouted calls for *freedom*, and at last had our first battle. After Moncada, because of malice or fear, sold out the people's justice, I looked back and *saw the trail of my companions' bodies*! How could I possibly imitate Moncada's cowardly act? Wouldn't it have been better never to have taken up arms at all if now because of our fear we were made to give them up? No, I and my honored companions did not want to forsake the obligations to which we had previously pledged ourselves until we had finally brought it to an end. Yes, my Colonel, I believe that Moncada has not complied with the duty that a soldier's honor requires of him, and that that man made use of Liberal blood to attain sinecures and public jobs, and it was for this reason that he traded his rifles for dances and banquets. If from the day he made a secret pact with the enemy until the last day of his life, everything this man ate turned to blood at the very moment he ate it, he would never be able to eat the blood of all the heroes he betrayed.

Patria y Libertad.
AUGUSTO CÉSAR SANDINO

P.S. I have sent you guarantees so that you will no longer be afraid and may return to dedicate yourself to your work.
Farewell.

[19, 2 pp.]

1. This letter, dated in El Chipote on October 2, 1927, is not included in this edition. In it Sandino warns Reyes that the campaign against him and his men has become intolerable and that, for this reason, if Reyes failed to stop it, he, Sandino, would take drastic measures, even being obliged to order him shot.

2. Another term for Conservatives. RC

43. JUDGMENT, NOVEMBER 27, 1927

El Chipote,
November 27, 1927

Sentence for the judgement of Sinforiano Maradiaga, a resident of the city of Danlí, Honduras, forty-five years of age, married, his wife Carmen Soto of Sabana Grande; he has no children by her and has been six years in this country, and at the present time he is a defendant in this encampment, from whom statements have been taken; he said that he is innocent of the acts that he is charged with, and this command, taking into account the fact that Señor Maradiaga's acts do not involve complicity, for which reason he might receive capital punishment, I have ordered that he be set free, being obliged to remain peacefully in his house, without damaging the interests of the Counterrevolution.[1] Señor Maradiaga offered a quantity of money so that his life might be saved, but we did not accept it, since we have set him free without any interest in being paid, because we fight "to save the nation," and least of all for money.

If Señor Maradiaga, after being given his freedom, continues causing trouble in one way or another, he will be pursued by my forces and, once captured, I will have him shot, and there will be no other way for him to save himself.

Therefore, this same judgement will serve him as a guarantee so that he may remain in his house without anyone molesting him. All the expeditionary leaders and other officeholders of my command must respect him and, moreover, grant him the aid that he requests from our officeholders.

Patria y Libertad.
A. C. SANDINO

[19, 1 p.]

1. The concept of the "Counterrevolution" (*Contra revolución*), used by Sandino in this sentence, derives from the fact that the autonomist struggle was a movement *against* those such as José María Moncada who betrayed the Constitutionalist revolution. This, and no other, is the sense in which it was used.

44. DECREE, NOVEMBER 1927

General Headquarters of the Defenders of
the National Sovereignty of Nicaragua

Augusto César Sandino, General in Chief of the Army in Defense of the Sovereignty of Nicaragua, making use of the faculties granted to him by that same army, makes known to the commanders, officers, troops and civilians residing in the zone occupied by the Army in Defense of the National Sovereignty that this General Headquarters has information that some commanders aid and protect the stealing of animals from the soldiers themselves, in agreement with civilians to whom every type of guarantee has been granted by recommendation of those same commanders, turning those animals over to private individuals so that the latter may take them out of the zone to sell them in Honduras, violating with this act the irrevocable probity that as commanders and officers they are obliged to possess, having given a pledge of honor and loyalty to defend the cause that we uphold with a legitimate right.[1] Since this culpable act discredits our cause, providing our enemies with an opportunity to label us with the shameful epithet of "bandits," I am prepared to proceed with all my energy, without special considerations or indulgences, severely punishing every commander, officer, or soldier who, desiring to accumulate money, commits the stated abuses, for it is unjust that, owing to the acts of a few disloyal persons, our army should be discredited in the eyes of the public. For the purpose of arranging the best possible supply of animals for the army, the commanders, officers and soldiers must subject themselves to the following orders:

1. No commander, officer, or soldier may have more than two animals for his personal use, and he may not sell them or transfer them to any private individual. If the sale is effected from soldier to soldier, the latter should give the purchaser (of the same army) a statement showing the amount he is to receive, which should be approved by the immediate commander to whom the said soldier pertains; if an officer makes such a sale, the approval must be given by the Supreme Commander, so that he himself has some control over the animals belonging to the army.

2. The General Headquarters will keep a special book where the name of the commander, officer, or soldier who has animals under his control will be recorded.

3. No private person may have in his possession animals belonging to our army, unless some member of the latter has deposited them with him, whether this be because of fatigue, sickness, or the need of care, and in such a case he must give evidence justifying such a deposit. He who does not offer proof in this way shall be regarded as acting in bad faith, and this will be a cause for immediate punishment.

4. Evidence of these misdeeds will be judged by the immediate commanders, named by this Headquarters and chosen from among the most impartial and honorable, for which purpose they will be given their respective nominations in order to form a Council of War.

5. The price of each animal cannot be more than five to ten pesos, and a soldier will not be permitted to engage in more than two sales, since otherwise he could not be regarded as the defender of an ideal, but rather as a merchant disguised as a soldier.

Patria y Libertad.
A. C. SANDINO

[19, 1 p.]

1. The animals in question are probably horses, mules or burros. RC

45. ENGAGEMENTS AND SKIRMISHES DURING THE MONTH OF NOVEMBER 1927

From the 4th of the current month, the Army in Defense of the National Sovereignty of Nicaragua has had the opportunity to defeat the invaders and traitors on every side, causing them to suffer serious reverses. Crimes have never been recorded as treacherous and savage as those that the traitors and filibusters commit, but it can clearly be seen that God is on our side, because the number of the enemy's casualties is devastating. Our forces have filled the enemy with fear, and now they no longer enter into combat in open country, limiting themselves to fortifying themselves inside the churches of Ocotal and Telpaneca.

The expeditionary cavalry units under the command of Colonels José León Díaz, Antonio Maldonado, Sergeant Major Pedro Navarro, and Captain Pastor Ramírez, who are active in the Somoto area, managed to locate the remnant of the Díaz forces who operated on the Honduran border under the command of the patricide and assassin Anastasio Hernández, who received instructions from the illegitimate government of Adolfo Díaz by means of the treasonous and doleful Paguaguas of Ocotal.

It was four o'clock in the afternoon when our cavalry units suddenly made their appearance from several directions at the encampment of the assassin Hernández. Firing broke out at once, and three hours later the murderers fled in desperation, abandoning on the field seventeen dead, ten rifles, three hundred cartridges, eighty animals, some five hundred pesos in cash, and a considerable amount of merchandise that had been stolen by them. Our forces stayed there until the next day to await their reaction, but they did not come back, and we do not think they will be able to reorganize themselves. This place is called El Manzano and is located north of Dipilito Viejo.

A minor engagement on the eleventh of this month: The cavalry unit that operates in the area of Los Planes was able to surprise the enemy, made up of traitors and Yankee filibusters, who, seeing themselves caught in a circle of fire and torn to pieces by dynamite, fled faster than a rabbit and full of fear, leaving behind fragments of flesh that could not be identified. On this occasion Sergeant Major Antonio Galeano demonstrated one of his greatest feats, grappling with one of the invaders hand to hand and managing to send him to a better world.

Skirmishes with the cavalry of Colonel Francisco Estrada: On November 20, 1927, at a place called Las Flores, the cavalry unit of Colonel Francisco Estrada defeated the filibusters and traitors, inflicting twenty-two deaths upon them and pursuing them for twenty-four consecutive hours, so tenaciously that they were again able to inflict some casualties, the greater part of them Yankee pirates. Nineteen rifles, a Lewis machine gun, and abundant ammunition were captured from the enemy.

On November 27 the cowardly buccaneers, convinced of their inability to defeat us in the open field, limited themselves to bombing peaceful villages from the sky, dropping incendiary and asphyxiating bombs on the humble shacks of defenseless campesinos.

Yesterday morning, at ten o'clock, two of the invaders' airplanes amused themselves by dropping incendiary and gas bombs, killing thirty-two women and eleven children, but the finger of providence arranged for one of them to be shot down, and Sergeant Major José Rosas Tejada, with his machine gun, worked miracles, because he was able to reach them, cutting them to pieces and as a result killing one of the murderous and cowardly aviators.

On November 25, 1927, Colonel Juan Gregorio Colindres tenaciously pursued the enemy with his cavalry in the valley of El Bálsamo, managing to exchange shots with them and inflicting nine deaths upon them, roving over a radius of forty-four kilometers until he surrounded them in the town of Telpaneca where we think we can defeat them, because we are determined neither to ask for nor to offer mercy.

We are expecting news of new encounters, which should be taking place in the department of Estelí, possibly in the village called Pueblo Nuevo.

Patria y Libertad.
A. C. SANDINO

[19, 1 p.]

46. LETTER TO COLONEL JOSÉ LÉON DÍAZ, DECEMBER 1, 1927

El Chipote
December 1, 1927

Colonel José León Díaz
Cacaulí

My esteemed Colonel:

I have the pleasure of informing you that today I sent off for publication by the Honduran press an account of the victory achieved by our cavalry under your command against the cachurecos in El Manzano.[1]

I have also seen some letters sent to Colonel Salgado in which it was stated that the Yankees entered Honduran territory, and that those same Yankees intended to attack Honduran forces in their own territory, and that they claimed that the Honduran government is giving us support. Well, you know that in any case, the Hondurans are our brothers, and we would not allow the machos to humiliate our brothers. What we ought to do is to forget all our family grudges and recognize that our legitimate enemies by race and language are the Yankee invaders. And you, if you should see that they are entering Honduran territory by force, wait for them in some suitable place and give them hell in an ambush.

If while traveling on some road you should learn that the enemy is near, you will decide if you have passed by some good place for an ambush and will return there to prepare it. But if there is another place ahead that is closer, hurry there in an organized manner and take possession of it quickly, in order to have the desired result.

You will see to it that our muchachos don't commit any injustice, so that God will protect us; it is for this reason that we have achieved powerful victories over the enemy, because we never stray from the path of justice. Although I may not be there with you, I always pray to God for the welfare of every one of you.

Try to keep me posted about everything that is happening, so that I can send it to the Honduran press.

Greetings to all our muchachos and accept the sincere affection of your friend.

Patria y Libertad.
AUGUSTO CÉSAR SANDINO

[19, 1 p.]

1. For a description of this battle, see Doc. 45.

47. RESOLUTION NUMBER 7, REPUDIATING EVERY UNFAIR ACT OR CONTRACT, DECEMBER 14, 1927

Fortress of
Nicaraguan Sovereignty

RESOLUTION NUMBER 7

Augusto C. Sandino, general in chief of the Army in Defense of the National Sovereignty of Nicaragua, in support of the political constitution of my country, and in virtue of the faculties granted by that same army to nationals and foreigners, makes it known that since Yankee imperialism has intervened militarily in the Republic, assassinating Nicaraguan citizens with barefaced cynicism, without declaring war, and with the single purpose of aiding the country's traitors, led by the illegitimate Emiliano Chamorro and Adolfo Díaz, who to keep themselves in power have requested the protection of the Yankee filibusters, in detriment to our national sovereignty, hiding from the civilized world the monstrousness of the crimes committed by the *patricides and Nordic punitive army* upon the Nicaraguan people—for this reason, the people, being free and sovereign and with rifle in hand heroically defending themselves and making every effort to free their country from the Yankee intervention, resolve that every unfair act or contract celebrated by any national or foreigner that affects national properties, which ought to be sacred and respected, will be repudiated, such properties not being transferable or grantable to any group or enterprise that assists the traitors, for so long as the nation does not reestablish the legality of its government, which should emanate from the people's will without the intrusion of Yankee imperialism. Later a commission will be named to revise every contract that may be considered injurious to the nation.

We suspend the individual guarantees of every national or foreigner who upholds a right derived from a concession granted by the traitors or invaders, whether this be for the cutting of wood or for other activities on the Atlantic littoral, which region is dominated by the forces who defend the sovereignty of Nicaragua.

This provision goes into effect from the moment of its publication.

Make it known and comply with it.

El Chipote, December 14, 1927
Patria y Libertad.
A. C. SANDINO

[19, 1 p.]

48. LETTER TO BERTA MUNGUÍA, DECEMBER 26, 1927

Fortress of the Defenders of the Sovereignty
of Nicaragua
December 26, 1927

Señorita Berta Munguía
Secretary of the Group in Solidarity
with the Nicaraguan Workers' Movement

My dearest sister:

Constancy and loyalty find ample room in the hearts of those of us who preserve undefeated the love of our country and our race. It is for this reason that from this moment on I address you thus and authorize you to address me in the same form. Your letter, dated in León on November 26, has acquainted me with the great events that are about to occur in favor of our cause, by means of which I have always firmly maintained the faith and hope of redeeming my country, even if I should have to offer my life on the altar of freedom. I will not answer all the points of your letter one by one because I have an overload of correspondence from abroad and the enemy is near, on the eve perhaps of the bloodiest fight for freedom that may ever be recorded in the history of Nicaragua.

I am firmly convinced that there is great enthusiasm in my army for fighting the buccaneers. The valor and courage of my race are lodged in the breasts of my patriotic soldiers. We have proved and continue to prove to the traitors and filibusters that Sandino and his army will not waver and that today, more than ever before, we have faith in God that we will make the traitors and invaders eat the dust, and that we wish with all our hearts to fight them hand to hand, as we have done on several occasions.

Our principal glory is to humble the greatness of the powerful, converting them into miserable skeletons in our rustic mountains, since they have persisted in supporting so much infamy and treason, aiding those whom the sun of my country should never have shone upon.

I want to see our Nicaragua free and sovereign; I want to see the imperialist flag of the Stars and Stripes lowered in the Campo de Marte;[1] in brief, I ardently wish to see the blue and white bicolor flag that protects every Nicaraguan waving in total freedom. And do not forget our two official phrases: *Patria y Libertad*.[2] These words embody my beliefs and my spirituality, and there is no money in the world that can make me diminish them. Finally, convinced of your sincerity and loyal adherence to our cause, I advise you to keep our idealism firm. You have with you our sister Dolores Matamoros, whom you may address in the same way. Be, both of you, the heroines of my vanguard, because just as France had its Joan of Arc, Nicaragua will have the glory of displaying your names on its history's pages. Turn yourselves into examples for the youth of Nicaragua; inject the servile and those who would enslave us with your patriotism and enthusiasm; do not lose heart. Go onward! Ever onward! *Vencer o morir*, this is the slogan of the defenders of national sovereignty. Do not fear or reflect too much. If we should die in the struggle for our freedom, our bodies will fall with our faces turned toward the sun, and our martyr blood will quicken the hearts of the true Nicaraguan patriots who will follow our example. Accept, in these phrases, the affection of your brother, because in them is to be found the dignity of our dear country. And make them known as well to our brothers, the workers.

Affectionately,
Patria y Libertad.
A. C. SANDINO

[19, 1 p.]

1. Mars Field, a military base in Managua occupied by U.S. marines during most of the period from 1910 until 1933. RC
2. The other official phrase, *vencer o morir* (win or die), is mentioned later in this paragraph. RC

49. LETTER TO FROYLÁN TURCIOS,
DECEMBER 29, 1927[1]

December 29, 1927

To Froylán Turcios
Tegucigalpa

Dear friend:

Informed by your letter dated the 15th of the current month, I am surprised that you have not received my earlier notes, which were written before the dates you mention in your letter. Perhaps some person interested in reproducing my correspondence took it to someone who is not authorized to receive it, or is engaged in delaying it or hiding it for some mischievous purpose. Besides, I thought that it would have caused you a great deal of work, exhausting your patience. Nobody may reproduce anything I send you, for I do not direct or maintain correspondence (that is to say of an official kind) with anyone, because you are the only one to represent me in the whole Hispanic continent. Since I first made known my sacred protest to the civilized world, you were the first person in Central America who knew how to interpret my idealism, and you were the first to defend me, your disciple, and it was from your spiritual well that I drew the idea of freeing my dear country. For that very reason, I confirm to you full, legal, and adequate power to be my representative in Central America and in the other Indo-Hispanic countries. Once again, you are authorized to accept and deliver statements to the world press, to corporations, and to private persons, and to anyone who, in your opinion, honors and upholds the dignity of my country and my race.

My acts prove the loyalty of my principles, and, in proof of this, I have not wanted to give free reign to the countless letters that reach me from outside this country, because I cannot break my word. I will leave to your healthy judgement and untarnished patriotism the response and resolution of that correspondence, which you will receive along with the present letter. I do not need to make any suggestions to you, because my principles are embodied in your spirit. Continue to claim that there will be no human power to stop Sandino and his army, no gold in the world that will arouse ambition in the hearts of the defenders of the national sovereignty of Nicaragua, and for as long as the sickening boot of the invader tramples upon the sovereignty of my country, we will fight tirelessly until we have turned Nicaragua's freedom into reality.

I long with all my heart to see the imperialist Yankee flag hauled down from the Campo de Marte or eradicated by my army. I desire with all my soul to see the bicolor flag of blue and white that protects all Nicaraguans waving entirely free. And for as long as this is not so, I will continue fighting until I win or die. God and my country's mountains will help us turn our ideal into reality. At this very moment, I am again faced by a powerful enemy, made up of traitors, mercenaries, and invaders, aided as always by cowardly aviators. I am firmly convinced that, as the enemy develop their plan of attack, my army will make them eat the dust, and I am certain that this will be the bloodiest battle ever seen in Nicaragua and Central America. The honor of my country and my race stands above the ambitions of the buccaneers and patricides. We have faith that God will protect us, because until this day my army has never suffered a defeat. Tell this to the civilized world. Strengthened by my belief in the Supreme Being, I will send you an accurate and opportune report of our military operations. My army returns your greetings to you, and for yourself please accept an enduring embrace from your disciple and friend.

Patria y Libertad.
A. C. SANDINO

[19, 1 p.]

1. Two versions of this letter exist: the one reproduced in *Ariel* (vol. 4, no. 57, [January 1928], 1096), and the one published here, transcribed from an original typescript in the IES archive.

50. THE BOMBING OF CIUDAD ANTIGUA, DECEMBER 6, 1927

El Chipote
December 29, 1927

To Froylán Turcios

Esteemed friend:

I send you the enclosed letter in which an account is given of violent acts committed by the macho bandits against unarmed Indians.[1]

Look. This is the Yankee civilization.

So that you can have a better idea of the case, I will describe for you in a few words the town that was bombed. It is twelve kilometers from Ocotal. It possesses a temple that is its greatest pride, for the antiquity of its construction. Its walls are four yards thick. In it there is a Lord of Miracles that is much venerated by all the faithful, and today because the Yankees profaned it, all are weeping in anger. The inhabitants of the town number about ten thousand, but most are very humble and God-fearing people. I think you must expose these human beasts.

Patria y Libertad.
A. C. SANDINO

Copy of the Letter from Florencio López to Sandino

Ciudad Antigua
December 23, 1927

General Augusto C. Sandino
El Chipote

Esteemed General:

After greeting you with true affection, wishing you the happiest success in your work to redeem our unfortunate country, I must go on to inform you of the following: On the sixth of this month this town was attacked by two Yankee airplanes. The attack with machine guns and bombs continued for an hour and a half. The elderly woman Norberta Quinónez was gravely wounded; Paulina Centeno received a fracture of the left forearm; a little girl named Quiñónez received two serious wounds, and another girl a light one. They destroyed the greater part of the houses of this town, and the church suffered fifty-two large ruptures. Only Divine Providence allowed us to stay alive, after the horrors the gringo bandits committed from their goddamned airplanes.

Your subordinate and friend continues to await your orders.

FLORENCIO LÓPEZ

[12, vol. 4, no. 57, (January 1928), 1107]

1. Because of its content and importance, this letter from Florencio López, taken from the same source, is here reproduced in full.

·1928·

51. MAJOR ENCOUNTERS NEAR EL CHIPOTE AT THE END OF 1927 AND ON NEW YEAR'S DAY, 1928[1]

At an opportune moment sympathizers with our cause rushed information to this headquarters relative to the organization that the punitive Nordic army, along with the patricides, prepared some two months ago in Matagalpa for the launching of a general attack upon El Chipote. Our army did not need to make a show of valor, since this has been and continues to be demonstrated whenever the pirates carry out expeditions in our zone.

On last December 30, at eight in the morning, the enemy, made up of three hundred Yankees and two hundred patricides, halted at a place called Trincheras four kilometers from Quilalí, as if to conduct an exploration, and by slow degrees they maneuvered like some loathsome reptile, which couldn't be done in any other way since they were not moving in a straight line. The liberators' irony was reflected in their gaze; their sarcastic smiles accentuated their expressions of hatred for the invaders; the firing sights of the famous "concones" searched eagerly for the hearts of the murderers of our sovereignty. With their feet firmly placed, the mortar operators waited for the enemy to bunch up so that they could exterminate them with the terrible explosions of their bombs.

So it was that at five minutes past eight the chain of Yankee riflemen, made up of sixty men who advanced slowly against our trenches, was completely destroyed by the well-aimed discharges of our musketry, causing tremendous confusion and indescribable panic among the enemy, who in giddy flight trampled down everything in their way, the place we chose to defeat them being called El Paso de la Muerte. Those who miraculously escaped with their lives will remember that place forever. With the enormous number of casualties inflicted upon them over a period of five minutes, the enemy could not reorganize at the same point of combat to effect an orderly retreat. Instead, in total disarray they fled by different trails toward Quilalí, hoping to join another column of blond bandits who had left Telpaneca, aiding the advance of the seventh column of pirates who were defeated at Trincheras. With the violence of a thunderbolt and God's help, in five minutes freedom's defenders destroyed the battle plan that the punitive army had taken two months to prepare.

Exploring the field we affirmed the results of our victory: *sixty-four enemy dead, sixty-nine rifles and a Lewis machine gun, six thousand cartridges of various kinds, and many other items of less importance.*

With our one-day march the enemy's advance in this sector was ended.[2] With the same impetus we hope to confront another column of traitors and invaders who have advanced from Telpaneca to take part in the general attack that the invaders hoped to launch against El Chipote.

On the 31st the enemy had still not been informed about the violent defeat of those who had left Matagalpa full of pride, and so they came determined to do battle with us, but the judge of the village of Varillal and twenty of his companions were sufficient to punish them cruelly, inflicting eleven deaths and several wounds upon them.

On January 1 news reached this headquarters that Yankees numbering some three hundred were marching by way of the Telpaneca road with orders to take part in the general attack upon El Chipote. I at once ordered Colonels Estrada and Colindres to move out with their cavalry to cut off the enemy's advance, and to pursue them until they were eliminated. Our people intensified their action with such good luck that, at 1 P.M. on that same day, they took up positions at the place called Las Cruces, the same place where the bandit conquerors were defeated two months before, awaiting them there with determination.

Fifteen minutes later we let the punitive column advance beyond us, bottling them up and forcing them to fight man to man. In three hours of fighting with rifles and grenades, the enemy was decimated and then almost totally destroyed with machetes. This horrified the surviving pirates, forcing them to flee in a shameful manner, leaving *ninety-seven dead and sixty wounded* on the field of battle, among them two principal officers who were identified by documents taken from them. Also taken from them were their battle plans and the codes used by their aviators. The captured spoils of war were quite considerable: six Lewis machine guns, three Thompson machine guns, two Lewis automatic rifles, forty-six Lewis rifles and sixteen mules loaded with ammunition of various calibers, and a large quantity of provisions.

In this cruel way the foreign assassins and patricides, who for so long have abased the sovereignty of my beloved Nicaragua, have again been punished. We continue to attempt to destroy other columns of buccaneers who are seeking to unite their forces to attack us. We are confident that before long we will destroy the punitive forces and the patricides.

Patria y Libertad.

A. C. SANDINO
Fortress of the National Sovereignty of Nicaragua
El Chipote, January 4, 1928

[12, vol. 4, no. 59 (1928), 1113–14]

1. By its contents, this letter, addressed to Froylán Turcios, is in reality a war communiqué. In 1927 and 1928 most of these were prepared in the form of letters to the director of the review *Ariel*.

2. For a detailed description of this disastrous battle from the American point of view, see "Testimony of the Major General Commandant before the Senate Committee on Foreign Relations," in *The Marine Corps Gazette* 13, no. 1 (March 1928): 53–54. According to General Lejeune, commander of the Marine Corps, only five marines were killed and twenty-three wounded in the encounter. RC

52. THE DESTRUCTION OF QUILALÍ
EARLY IN JANUARY 1928

Fortress of the National
Sovereignty of Nicaragua
El Chipote, January 4, 1928

To Froylán Turcios
Tegucigalpa

Dear friend:

In these very moments, as North American cynicism, masked by hypocrisy, appears before the representatives of the Indo-Hispanic nations in the Cuba conference, the spite of the Yankees due to their shameful defeat at the hands of the liberation forces has left thousands of Nicaraguans homeless, for the sole reason that they are natives of Nueva Segovia.[1]

The town of Quilalí, set on fire by the conquerors, has been burning for three days. One by one the houses of that town have been reduced to ashes. Quilalí has disappeared from the geographical map of Nicaragua, burned by the criminal hand of the adventurers who are destroying our sovereignty.[2]

The autonomist army always puts the interests of our fellow nationals ahead of everything else, even when the foreign enemy, acting without scruples, faces complete destruction at our hands. The Nicaraguan people understood that Quilalí was mined and that blowing up its rich mineral deposits would have turned their homes into fragments. And for this reason, in order not to cause terrible harm to our compatriots, we abstained from exterminating those miserable people who in ignoble flight turned their backs upon us, taking refuge in Quilalí, abandoned by us a short time before, the bandits using this opportunity to satiate their fiercest instincts. Everything that stood in their way was reduced to ashes; the fruits of the labor and deprivations of humble campesinos were eliminated by the conquering horde. Hundreds of young girls and respectable matrons have been violated. Many of them died after their disgrace, murdered by those who are seeking to make the world believe in the unselfishness of their efforts to bring peace to our land.

Because of the tremendous crimes of these human brutes, hatred exists for them, much hatred, the simple hatred of the patriots of Nicaragua. The Yankee savagery will not encounter a single word of pity while Sandino remains alive, and his army will fight fiercely until it has cast these adventurers from our territory. Once again, dear poet, I want you to make the world know that, for as long as the invaders trample upon my country's dignity, I will be inflexible; I will not permit conferences with the conquerors and traitors.

Patria y Libertad is my creed. I want absolute freedom for my country, and I will accomplish this even at the cost of my own blood. My army is strengthened by its faith in the cause of justice, and by its faith in God, who will help us gain our independence from Yankee imperialism.

It will cost those *bandits* a great deal of Anglo-Saxon blood and many millions of dollars to tear down the brilliant and venerated bicolor flag, the emblem of legitimate Nicaraguans that flutters proudly on the high summit of El Chipote.

Receive my army's greetings for the New Year, which in its course will witness the glorious triumphs of our freedoms. And accept from your friend and disciple a warm embrace and best wishes for the New Year along with my offering of patriotic joy for having humbled the brutal power of the savages of the North in three bloody battles.

Patria y Libertad.
A. C. SANDINO

[12, vol. 4, no. 59 (1928), 1123]

1. The sixth Pan-American Congress was held in Havana, Cuba, between January 16 and February 20, 1928. The Nicaraguan delegation was led by Foreign Minister Carlos Cuadra Pasos, a Conservative politician notorious for his openly pro-American positions. In his speech to the delegates, Cuadra Pasos justified and applauded the American intervention in Nicaragua, while calling attention to the "endeavors" of the U.S. government in search of "peace and stability" for that Central American nation.

2. General Lejeune told the Senate Foreign Relations Committee that in order to remove eight or nine wounded marines the American forces "cleared away the centre of the village, they burned the shacks, and Lieutenant Schilt flew a plane in there, down the road, and landed in this little space. It seemed impossible for him to do it, but he made nine trips and took out nine wounded, under fire each time he went in and under fire each time he went out." "Testimony," 56. RC

53. RESOLUTION NUMBER 20:
CONFISCATION OF NORTH AMERICAN
PROPERTIES, JANUARY 8, 1928

Fortress of the Defenders of
the Sovereignty of Nicaragua
El Chipote, January 8, 1928

I, Augusto C. Sandino, general in chief of the Autonomist Nicaraguan Army, using the faculties granted by that same army and upholding the political constitution of my country, make known to my fellow citizens that the piratical invaders, not limiting themselves to fighting the Nicaraguan patriots who with weapons in hand honorably defend their country's sovereignty, but rather in their eagerness for destruction and to exterminate our race, have sown terror, destroying in a cowardly fashion everything they have found in their way, filling the country with mourning and consternation, murdering, violating, robbing, and burning the homes of peaceful campesinos, leaving thousands of children as orphans, and widows and invalids with no help at all, since to commit these acts of savagery they use fleets of airplanes and large-caliber cannon, contrary to all human law, certain of impunity because of their knowledge that our army lacks these elements of combat; considering that in all conscience they have committed tremendous injustices, I resolve:

To confiscate and take control of the North American properties and interests in the Republic and especially in the zone that the Autonomist Army dominates, interests that must serve to indemnify the immense number of victims of the pirates aided by the patricides.

Communicate it and comply with it.

Patria y Libertad.
A. C. SANDINO

[12, vol. 4, no. 50 (February 1928), 1113]

54. MESSAGE TO *THE NEW YORK WORLD*, CIRCA JANUARY 16, 1928

The World
New York

Let our voices be heard in Havana. Let men not lack the moral courage to tell the truth about our misfortune. Let them tell how the people of Nicaragua, who fight and suffer bravely, are determined to make any sacrifice to defend their freedom, even if it should cause their own extermination. The results of Havana will amount to nothing if the ideal of the Spanish-speaking peoples does not crystallize. And if they allow us to be murdered to the last man, we will have the consolation of knowing that we fulfilled our duty.

Patria y Libertad.
A. C. SANDINO

[9, 330]

55. MESSAGE TO THE PAN-AMERICAN CONGRESS, JANUARY 17, 1928

Honorable Sixth Pan-American Congress
Havana, Cuba

From the encampments of the Army in Defense of the Sovereignty of Nicaragua I have observed your proceedings, hopeful of some effective action in support of our sovereignty. Before sessions terminate, protest the presence of illegal delegates of so-called President Adolfo Díaz; protest against the hypocrisy of Coolidge, who speaks of good will and sends an army to murder Nicaraguans. Protest against the indifference and servility of Latin American delegates in the face of United States aggression.

Call on our sister republics to demand immediate withdrawal of the North Americans who are violating the autonomy of my country, repudiating the consequences of President Coolidge's acts before the world.

Patria y Libertad.
A. C. SANDINO

[18, vol. 1, no. 369 (1928), 25]

56. FRAGMENT OF A LETTER,
JANUARY 19, 1928[1]

Our wounded die for lack of adequate medical treatment of their wounds caused by bombs and shrapnel, and also because of malaria. I am speaking not only of the soldiers, but also of the civilians, among whom are many women and children, because the enemy airplanes are causing more damage in the towns than in our trenches. Ciudad Vieja, Guanacaste, and San Albino have been turned into smoking ruins.

Washington is called the father of his country; the same may be said of Bolívar and Hidalgo; but I am only a bandit, according to the yardstick by which the strong and the weak are measured.

[10, 19]

1. Published in *El Universal Gráfico* of Mexico City on January 19, 1928. In the source from which it was taken [10, 19] only these two paragraphs were reproduced.

57. LETTER TO FROYLÁN TURCIOS, JANUARY 23, 1928

Fortress of the Defenders of National Sovereignty

El Chipote, January 23, 1928

To Froylán Turcios
Tegucigalpa

Dear friend:

In these moments, as the roar of foreign cannon thunders through our mountains, seeking to put an end to our country's freedom, I am deeply satisfied by the receipt of your letter, because I see in your sentences your spirit's emotion, founded upon an ample generosity as sublime as the patriot's self-denial.

When we launched the cry *Patria y Libertad*! we did so in humble isolation, separated from all partisan passion and personal ambition. In such circumstances we never believed that our brothers, the people of Central America, would understand our ideal, since corrupting gold has gnawed away at the moral conscience and undermined the intelligentsia of Latin America. More than this: men of courage have grown timid, transmitting to the new generations the virus of cowardliness. We have fought for nine months amidst isolation and the indifference of our brothers of Central America and the Hispanic continent, but we have not for this reason become demoralized, recognizing that our high duty as legitimate sons of Nicaragua obliges us to sacrifice our blood on the altars of freedom. Our deeds, great and tragic, will convince the entire world that in Nicaragua, among thousands of slaves and patricides, there are men who deeply love the land that gave them birth.

I must inform you that the Yankees have landed a thousand more marines who will come to El Chipote, because those they thought were enough to destroy us have been decimated and are now incapable of carrying out their purpose of exterminating us. If the two thousand more marines whom they talk about should come here to attack us, I will have to make a tremendous effort to advance toward the center of the country, to bring my vigorous action against the conqueror to the very heart of the

Republic, proving by bold and bloody deeds how real citizens defend their country's sovereignty.

If this should happen we will be forced to stay out of contact for a while, because if the enemy appears in such overwhelming numbers, I will not be able to offer them decisive battles, but I will defeat them in another way. Do not be concerned, because news of our triumphs will continue to reach you.

I received the issues of *Ariel*, and I am firmly convinced that you will continue to work for our cause, which is the great cause of the freedom of Central America.

My companions salute you, as does my army.

Receive an enduring embrace from your true friend.

Patria y Libertad.
A. C. SANDINO

[12, vol. 4, (1928), 119]

58. EL CHIPOTÓN, OR THE SIEGE OF EL CHIPOTE, 1927–1928[1]

Very well, the lesson of the battle of El Ocotal convinced me that it was a foolish thing for us to die in pitched battles against the United States, and that it was preferable to maintain our protest for as long as possible, and so I decided we would quarter ourselves on an immense hill that I knew about, thanks to Colonel Coronado Maradiaga. It's a mountain covered with pastures and possessing several springs. Part of that precipitous and isolated peak is cultivated, and there, separated from its base by vertical cliffs of craggy rocks and hidden by perpetual clouds, we would establish ourselves like condors high above the plains, where we would descend only to prepare ambushes. This hill is El Chipote, then still an unnamed peak of the Andes. [. . .]

Finally we were able to establish our quarters on El Chipote, and, not long after that, large forces of marines and detachments of renegade Nicaraguans were constantly sent out to capture us. All of them, however, without exception, fell into ambushes. As long as the siege of El Chipote lasted, we were able to launch surprise attacks against them on various occasions, and these turned into real battles. For example, that of Las Cruces, which was the first of these, and where we captured the first United States flag. Afterward, in several other battles, we captured so many flags that by then they were no longer novelties. In the battle of Las Cruces we also captured maps and documents, and several officers and soldiers died, among them Captain Bruce and Captain Livingston and other officers whose names at the moment I don't remember, but which are duly registered in our archives. And besides, they were fully published in the newspapers of that time. Captain Bruce I remember very well, because he had published a statement that before January 1 he promised to have Sandino's head. Well, before that date he lost his own, which we sent to the marines, telling them, however, that I had kept his field glasses, which are the same ones I use today. Excellent, in a beautiful leather case and with a small compass. One of the captured flags I gave as a gift to the Mexican National Museum along with some other objects such as a set of surgical instruments, medals, insignias, orders of the day, codes, programs of attack, and so forth.

On El Chipote [. . .] little by little the situation was becoming more difficult, while at the same time they were squeezing us and closing in upon us, but we never lacked people or weapons or stores of supplies and ammunition. The bombing attacks and the massive destruction of the crops and cattle that belonged to the local people, carried out for the purpose of denying us provisions, caused many, many men to come to us to swell our ranks. And women as well. The latter came mainly from Honduras and El Salvador, endangering their lives and offering their services as nurses, washerwomen, cooks, barbers, and some simply to accompany and amuse the muchachos between one ambush and another. At that time, I believe, a third of my army was made up of Hondurans and Salvadorans, but there were never any localistic national sentiments, and we were all united by a mortal hatred of the marines who had made shit out of the countryside with their damned airplanes.

As far as weapons are concerned, we captured brand-new ones from the marines. More than we needed, because we were no longer fighting pitched battles, but rather surprise attacks, ambushes, and assaults. Here today, tomorrow at the mines, the next day a hundred or two hundred kilometers farther on. Besides, from across the Honduran border, which is almost in the immediate vicinity of El Chipote, we obtained everything we needed. Medicines, dynamite, provisions, and so on, so that the destruction of the countryside by the marine airplanes was ridiculous and brutal. I can assure you that during the entire siege of El Chipote, which lasted for nine months, several squadrons of airplanes attacked us every day. In the beginning two or three times a day and at any hour. Later they came systematically. At exactly six in the morning the first four airplanes appeared followed by four more, and they occupied themselves with bombing and machine-gunning, and so it continued all day long, every two hours. Four planes, eight planes, four planes, eight planes. Until about five in the afternoon. Of course we fired at them, and we managed to shoot some down. In truth, those airplanes caused us very little personal injury, though it's a fact that in the beginning they shocked and worried us a great deal. But later we looked upon them as not much worse than a thunder storm, and we knew very well how to dig ourselves in. But they killed large numbers of cattle and horses. [. . .]

I have to laugh because this never stops being funny. It's the story of the flowers of El Chipote, as the muchachos called them. Before the siege of El Chipote, at the San Albino mine, I had provided myself with more than a ton of compressed dynamite sticks, the ones we later used to make bombs. Our bombs were made of a certain amount of dynamite wrapped in several layers of lightly dampened rawhide with inserted nuts, nails, staples, pieces of metal from unserviceable rifles and pistols or any other metal objects we could find. These bombs were very effective, because once placed on the tip of a double rocket they were fired from the peak of El Chipote. It was for this reason that the muchachos called them the flowers of El Chipote, and they were weapons of a unique originality, like everything else in this war, but, most importantly, they had excellent practical results. In all the encounters it was observed that the fragments of the marines' hand grenades went very high up into the air only a few meters from the explosion. They weren't dangerous to the man who threw them, or to the man they were intended for. Our bombs, on the other hand, could have a deadly effect thirty meters from the explosion, because the fragments fanned out in all directions at ground level. Those that were shot off by rockets were called the flowers of El Chipote, because the flora of that hill is exuberant, and since they generally shot them off at night toward places where we were told the marines were on patrol, they blossomed down there below like a huge flower of fire.

We had mechanics' shops, carpentry shops, tailor shops, barber shops, and a bakery, all operated almost entirely by volunteer women who, as I've said, came from the Segovias, from Honduras, and from El Salvador, and all of them placed themselves in danger. In those shops of El Chipote marvels of unimagineable inventiveness were created, and also some impossibly ridiculous things, considering the materials we had to depend upon. According to Cabrerita, the wise Solomon said that when necessity makes demands, the mind responds. And even after El Chipote, those heroic women followed us into the mountains, taking charge of our encampments.

The situation of El Chipote worsened day by day because of the animals that were dying, which made life unbearable because of the decomposition of the corpses and the nauseous stench, and, although we boiled our water, I feared an epidemic. The buzzards and vultures filled the skies, to the point that on one occasion we machine-gunned them, mistaking them for the airplanes. Our lives became harder with every passing day and, though we continued ambushing and fighting fiercely, because of the hygienic problems I mentioned, I decided to abandon our invincible Chipote.

With some advance planning, we made some straw puppets dressed in clothes and hats of the kind used by our army and armed with wooden rifles, and we set them up in suitable places where they could be seen, and we even arranged replacements for the "dead." One moonless night we quietly abandoned our maternal Chipote en masse. It was an operation so well executed that for several days the planes continued their attacks, devastating that place and the territory all around for many kilometers, where in fact nobody any longer remained. Finally they noticed our trick and when they tried to pursue us they had no idea where we might be. We were far away where we could just make out the peak of El Chipote with its honor guard of clouds.

After that the struggle continued, hard and always more intense, and with constantly changing scenes. American money gets things done, and it tried to vilify us in the whole world by calling us bandits and altering the facts in its reports. There was always one dead marine for every hundred bandits, as they liked to call us. The airplanes of the marines, they said, didn't kill people or destroy the cattle and crops of campesino families, they cleansed the country of bandits. But to me it seems like a lie that our worst enemies were our national press, most of the public employees, and the National Guard. History will give an account of this.

Now that I'm thinking about it, let me tell you something very funny. Another trick of the same kind, ridiculous but effective, was the report of my own funeral. Through the campesinos we made this known to the marines, and later, after many reconnaissance flights, the planes confirmed it. The report was announced officially by the State Department and the Navy Department in Washington, and many newspapers and magazines in the United States described the burial of *the bandit Sandino, exterminated at last by the pacifying airplanes of the U.S. Marines.*[2] Practically all over the world my death was commented upon, and it was also of great literary interest to poets and journalists who favored our cause. The virile sentiments expressed in their prayers and odes to my death even made me cry. So because of this we quickly revealed the truth. Concerning the Nicaraguan press, with the glorious exception of some small magazines, it's better not to talk about it. To me it's a pity that many would-be intellectuals have treated me that way. . . .

All right, now listen, because this is important. In fact, it's a key point for a good understanding of my war, and pardon me for again interrupting the chronological order, but to tell you the truth I don't expect you to write the history of my campaign. The historians will do that. What I want is for you to absorb and describe the spirit of that war and its meaning for Nicaragua and all the nations that value freedom.

To use the vulgar expression, on El Chipote we turned the tables on them.[3] In fact, El Chipote was our real "Nicaraguan Guerrilla Academy." During the siege of El Chipote, as we fought, we also organized a well-designed guerrilla system based on the experiences of countless clashes, favorable and unfavorable, which, after being summed up were commented upon by each officer, all of them analyzing them thoroughly in order to draw conclusions and to learn how to perform better under various circumstances. Some soldiers also took part in this work. During that siege, which lasted a little more than nine months, there were many clashes and ambushes that we don't have to enumerate and that among ourselves we called "El Chipotón" or the "Siege of El Chipote."

During that siege we managed to recuperate our forces and expand and organize the army, to the point that we turned it into a war machine that was precise and unique in the way it did things, and almost infallible in the way it prepared ambushes, retreats, counterattacks, assaults, surprise moves, communications systems, dispersions, and the transportation of the wounded and the dead, because only when it was absolutely impossible to do anything else did we leave a wounded or a dead man behind. In short, an organization the way I like things done, carried out with thoroughness while trying not to leave the smallest detail to chance, so that all, absolutely all the officers, were well informed about what they were to do and how to take command in the event of an emergency involving their superiors, and therefore able to bring the operation to a conclusion, even in the most unexpected circumstances. I must say that this organization and the almost perfect functioning of my army was not just my own doing. It was the result of the collaboration of every officer and soldier who knew how to do his bit, and how to risk his life stoically and heroically so that the plan could be carried out and brought to a conclusion with steady but constant progress. Here I'm merely giving you a general idea, because you don't need more for your book, but in our archives we have everything minutely documented.

You can imagine what the hill of El Chipote was like when the marine commander in that area, a certain Major Young, as I learned from my information service, convinced that I had been eliminated by the airplanes, decided to advance toward the encampment at the peak. Cautiously and always protected by the airplanes, he advanced, sweeping the area with mortar fire, machine guns, and grenade-launching rifles, until at last he reached a thicket that was waving in the wind. Of course Young never encountered any resistance at all, but even so it took him several days with his batallion of marines to ascend the six kilometers from the foot of the mountain on the Murra River to the peak. When Major Young finally captured our glorious encampment near the end of January 1928, besides the pestilence and the corpses of rotten animals, he found some of the straw puppets that had somehow managed to escape the bombs. As might be expected, he stated in his official report, which received a lot of publicity, "We have at last brought an end to the banditry of Sandino."[4]

[7, 85, 87–94]

1. Like Docs. 2, 29, 120, 179, and 201, this account of the siege of El Chipote in 1927 and 1928 was told by Sandino in 1933 to José Román, and published in his book, *Maldito país*. RC

2. In an article published in *The New York Times* on January 19, 1928, Harold N. Denny, author of *Dollars for Bullets*, describes Sandino's "death" and "funeral" as follows:

According to [credible reports reaching Marine Corps headquarters], Sandino was a victim of the intensive bombing and machine-gunning which Major R. F. Rowell's

squadron of fighting planes gave El Chipote on Saturday. First word of the reported ending of Sandino's bloody and spectacular career reached Managua from Nicaraguans coming in from Jinotega, the one-time Sandino capital, where, they said, they had picked up the news by the 'grapevine telegraph' system which carries information swiftly throughout the wilderness in which the marines and rebels are fighting. . . . Yesterday marine aviators flying over San Rafael saw what was evidently a large funeral procession. Colonel L. M. Gulick, the commanding officer, considered the reports a sufficient basis and sent orders for the marines at Jinotega to investigate the supposed funeral in the hope of finding and identifying the body. . . . Since Major Rowell's air raid, observers have flown down close to the ground at El Chipote and have seen doors swinging as if the huts were unoccupied and no signs of life, except two men and a mule, where formerly the place was swarming with men.
RC

3. Sandino's expression: "le dimos vuelta a la tortilla." RC
4. In another article in *The New York Times* on January 27, 1928, Denny describes Major Young's occupation of El Chipote:

White stripes of cloth spread out on the summit of El Chipote today (January 26) formed a signal code which told Marine aviators that Major Archibald Young's column of 400 men had completed the occupation of the mountain stronghold from which General Augustino (*sic*) Sandino was recently driven and that the marines there were 'O.K.' . . . The aviators saw Major Young's men destroying what was left of Sandino's fortifications—after the terrific bombing of a week ago. . . . The airplanes have been constantly hovering over the mountain while Major Young's column moved up it to get signals and to drop more bombs if the ground troops encountered serious resistance. Apparently only casual opposition was offered, but the aviators several times in the past few days saw evidence that the rebels were firing on the marines. The marines' advance today carried them above the cloudline and the aviators frequently lost sight of them. The top of El Chipote is at an elevation of more than 5,000 feet, and Sandino boasted for eight months that it could not be taken. Major Young's advance has been slow, methodical and cautious. His column marched from San Albino to reach the mountain top at 10 A.M. today.
RC

59. LETTER TO FROYLÁN TURCIOS,
JANUARY 1928

To Froylán Turcios

Esteemed Teacher:

With great pleasure I again send you my communications so that, as always, you may continue informing our sympathizers of the movements of the Army in Defense of the National Law of Nicaragua.

I remit to you this clipping from the newspaper *Diario Moderno*, in which there is a cable referring to the fundamental principles that I set out for the disarming of my forces. I regret not being able to send you a copy of these principles, because on the day that I announced them, owing to special circumstances, it wasn't possible for me to preserve a copy. Briefly, however, they are the following:

1. The withdrawal of the invasion forces from our territory and the removal of Adolfo Díaz from power, and his replacement with a national government made up of members without regard to political tendency; and

2. Elections to be supervised by representatives of the Hispanic-American republics.

Once these principles are firmly accepted, we will lay down our arms, retiring to private life.

The Yankees, having been defeated in the multiple battles that took place in the neighborhood of El Chipote, and convinced of the impossibility of capturing that hill, availed themselves of every possible means to block the arrival of our supplies, burning all the valley settlements and isolated houses and the deposits of corn; pitilessly killing the inhabitants, of both sexes and all ages; eliminating every live animal, both horses and cattle; and leaving the zone in a state of terrible desolation. The reporter Carleton Beals was a personal witness to all these things.

Having understood their campaign plan, without firing a single shot, we abandoned that hill by way of a narrow forest trail known only to us, leaving behind for them at intervals straw puppets dressed as soldiers and set up in firing positions; by the time they had achieved their intentions, preceded by an enormous bombardment with rifle and machine-gun fire, along with that of the airplanes that cooperated in that famous battle, I and all my organized forces were at the gates of Matagalpa, challenging the Yankee leader in that town. Today I am camped on another hill called El Chipotón,[1] and since it isn't possible, and much less convenient, to make our future plans known, we merely say to our sympathizers that they shouldn't be worried or discouraged by our abandonment of the hill, El Chipote, because our army is well prepared and certain that our triumph does not consist of possessing one place or another, but rather in keeping alive our armed resolve against the invaders. A big part of our triumph we have placed in the hands of the generous moral force of the democracy of our continent.

In order that our sympathizers may understand that it is impossible for the invaders to conquer us, I should tell you that for the Yankee imperialists it would be easier to defeat a conventional world power than to conquer Sandino and his columns. Therefore, we confront them or we don't, depending on whether or not it is to our advantage, it being well understood that our mission is to kill the invader in any way or place we can. And if tomorrow, or some other day, I should see the need to evacuate this hill called El Chipotón, I have another better hill called El Chipotazo.

I would like all of you to know that I detest and condemn the abuses that are being committed in my name during this campaign. And I protest against those who wish to make unjust accusations against me for acts that I am far from approving.

Patria y Libertad.
A. C. SANDINO

[19, 2 pp.]

---

1. From this time on Sandino often referred to his camps or headquarters as El *Chipotón*—El Chipote with the augmentative suffix *ón*—or even as *El Chipotazo*, as may be seen in this same letter. RC

60. LETTER TO REAR ADMIRAL DAVID F. SELLERS, FEBRUARY 1928

Mr. D. F. Sellers
Representative of Imperialism in Nicaragua
Managua

I had planned to write a letter in which I would reply to yours of January 20 concretely and point by point, but special circumstances do not allow me to do so directly at this time.

I refer to the final point of your communication. Do not believe that the origin or basis of this struggle is the past revolution. Today it is the Nicaraguan people in general who drive the foreign invasion from my country.

As to the Stimson-Moncada agreements, we have repeated a thousand times that we do not recognize them.

The only way this struggle can come to an end is through the immediate withdrawal of the invading forces from our territory, at the same time replacing the current president by a Nicaraguan citizen who has not made himself a candidate for the presidency, the forthcoming elections to be supervised by representatives from Latin America instead of U.S. Marines.

Patria y Libertad.
A. C. SANDINO

ADMIRAL SELLERS'S LETTER

> Commander U.S. Special
> Service Squadron
> U.S.S. *Rochester* Flagship.
> Managua, Nicaragua
> January 20, 1928

General Sandino:

As you know, the Government of the United States, according to the so-called Stimson agreements, signed last May, is obligated to protect the lives and properties of American citizens and foreigners, and to maintain order in Nicaragua until the regular Presidential election of next November has been held.

In the days and months just past the task intrusted to the forces of the United States resident in Nicaragua has been hampered in the Department of Nueva Segovia by the hostile activities of a certain part of the inhabitants, under your command. Your refusal and that of your companions to accept and consent to the provisions of the Stimson agreements, reinforced by the illegal operations of your men, have caused considerable harm, spilling much unnecessary blood, and creating an intolerable situation in that department.

In view of the full implications of the solemn obligation contracted by the United States of keeping order in Nicaragua and disarming the inhabitants of the country, the forces at my command have within the last few days been considerably increased by reinforcements of men and munitions, which we intend to use to the full, as also the vast resources our Government has placed at our disposal.

It is unnecessary for me to assure you that the only end we have in view is the reestablishment of order in Nueva Segovia, to insure complete peace under conditions that will enable the peaceful citizens of Nicaragua to enjoy for their families and properties the measure of security they have a right to expect.

It is equally superfluous for me to state emphatically that the energetic and intensive campaign which our forces will open very soon can have but one ultimate result.

The unnecessary sacrifice of human lives is so serious a matter that I have thought that although you have refused to disarm before, now, in view of subsequent events, you may wish to consider the desirability of putting an end to the present armed resistance to the forces of the United States, and that you might follow the example of your fellow-citizens of both political parties who, last May, agreed to settle their difficulties in lofty and patriotic spirit, avoiding further bloodshed.

In carrying out the policy of my Government for the reestablishment of order as expeditiously as possible, I do not feel justified at this moment in limiting any of our preparations which are energetically being made, unless you consider it opportune to signify immediately and in writing your willingness to discuss the ways and means of your acceptance, and that of your companions, of the Stimson agreements!

I shall be gratified to receive any communication you may send me, addressed care of the Legation of the United States in Managua.

D. F. SELLERS.
Rear Admiral of the United States Navy
Commander of the Special Service Squadron

[18, vol. 1, no. 569 (1928), 58]

61. SANDINO IN THE JOURNAL ARTICLES OF CARLETON BEALS, FEBRUARY–MARCH 1928

WITH SANDINO IN THE HEART OF THE MOUNTAIN

San José, Costa Rica, March 4
(Via Tropical Radio Telegraph Company)
[. . .]

Sandino was born on May 9, 1893, in the village of Niquinohomo.[1] He is short, not more than five feet five. When I saw him he was dressed in a uniform of dark brown with almost black puttees, immaculately polished; a silk red-and-black handkerchief knotted about his throat; and a broad-brimmed Texas Stetson hat, pulled low over his forehead and pinched shovel-shaped. Occasionally, as we conversed, he shoved his sombrero to the back of his head and hitched his chair forward. This gesture revealed straight lines from the temple to the jaw-bone. His jawbone makes a sharp angle with the rest of his face, slanting to an even, firm jaw. His regular, curved eyebrows are arched high above liquid black eyes without visible pupils. His eyes are of remarkable mobility and refraction to light—quick, intense eyes. He is utterly without vices, has an unequivocal sense of personal justice and a keen eye for the welfare of the humblest soldiers. "Many battles have made our hearts hard, but our souls strong," is one of his pet sayings. I am not sure of the first part of the epigram, for in all the soldiers and all of the officers I talked to he has stimulated a fierce affection and a blind loyalty and has instilled his own burning hatred of the invader.

"Death is but a tiny moment of discomfort not to be taken seriously," he repeats over and over to his soldiers. Or he will say: "Death most quickly singles out him who fears death."

There is a religious note in his thinking. He frequently mentions God— "God the ultimate arbiter of our battles;" or "God willing, we go on to victory;" or "God and our mountains fight for us." His sayings run from tongue to tongue through his little army.

In our interview with Sandino he first mentioned some battles fought near Chipote. He claimed that all told nearly four hundred marines had lost their lives. This, of course, was an obvious exaggeration. General

Feland insisted that only seventeen have died, but I am convinced after talking with many marine officers that the American casualties total between forty and sixty.

After describing the manner in which several American airplanes were brought down, Sandino in rapid fire gave me the basis of his demands in the present struggle: first, evacuation of Nicaraguan territory by the marines; second, the appointment of an impartial civilian President chosen by the notables of the three parties—one who has never been president and never a candidate for the Presidency; third, supervision of the elections by Latin America.

"The day these conditions are carried out," declared Sandino, "I will immediately cease all hostilities and disband my forces. In addition I shall never accept a government position, elective or otherwise. I shall not accept any government salary or pension. No position, no salary—this I swear. I will not accept any personal reward either today or tomorrow, or at any time in the future."

He left his chair and paced to and fro to emphasize this point. He stated vehemently: "Never, never will I accept public office. I am fully capable of gaining a livelihood for myself and my wife in some humble, happy pursuit. By trade I am a mechanic and if necessary I will return to my trade. Nor will I ever take up arms again in any struggle between the Liberals and Conservatives, nor, indeed, in any other domestic struggle— only in case of a new foreign invasion. We have taken up arms from the love of our country because all other leaders have betrayed it and have sold themselves out to the foreigner or have bent the neck in cowardice. We, in our own house, are fighting for our inalienable rights. What right have foreign troops to call us outlaws and bandits and to say that we are the aggressors? I repeat that we are in our own house. We declare that we will never live in cowardly peace under a government installed by a foreign Power. Is this patriotism or is it not? And when the invader is vanquished, as some day he must be, my men will be content with their plots of ground, their tools, their mules, and their families."

Managua, February 20

San Rafael del Norte, General Augusto C. Sandino's headquarters when I saw him, is a small town of adobe walls and red tiles situated just over the Nueva Segovia line in the Department of Jinotega on the high flank of the Yalí Range. It lies in a narrow pass, through which flows a sparkling mountain stream. On the other side of the watershed, past the high crown of Mount Yucapuca and a smiling populous valley, lies Jinotega, capital of the department. To the southwest the range stretches toward the departments of Estelí and León; and all of this region is suitable for effective guerrilla warfare and is fanatically Liberal. With the slightest show of success on Sandino's part, it would flame into open revolt. Here and there through all of this country are isolated Sandino bands, and further toward the Honduras frontier, near Chinandega, the local unit of the National Constabulary a month ago suddenly took to the hills for Sandino. Thus San Rafael is a point of departure west into this region or south toward Jinotega, Matagalpa, and the much-disputed Muymuy, where the combined Díaz forces and resident American marines were—before the Stimson-Moncada agreement—unable to stay the Liberal arms. Sandino has chosen the latter route. And this is all known country to him—the third time his course has led over this ground. Near San Rafael are still signs of the rifle-pits his forces dug for previous combats, and near Yucapuca are the stone bulwarks along the ridge. San Rafael itself is strongly pro-Sandino and has known him of yore. Here it was that a year ago in the little white church on the main plaza he married Blanca Aráuz, the local telegraph operator.

As I told in last week's dispatch, I was finally brought in to see Sandino at 4 A.M., after an exhausting ride to the camp. While we talked his most frequent gesture was the shaking of his forefinger with a full-armed movement; he invariably leaned forward as he spoke; and once or twice he took to his feet, emphasizing a point with his whole body.

His utterance is remarkably fluent, precise, evenly modulated; his enunciation is absolutely clear, his voice rarely changes pitch, even when he is visibly intent upon the subject matter. Not once during the four and a half hours, during which he talked almost continuously without prompting from me, did he fumble for the form of expression or indicate any hesitancy regarding the themes he intended to discuss. His ideas are precisely, epigrammatically ordered. There was not a major problem in the whole Nicaraguan question that he dodged or that I needed to raise. In military matters I found him most assured; a bit flamboyant and boastful and with a tendency to exaggerate his successes. However, he is exceedingly astute, knows the country well, and, with luck breaking even, can remain in the field indefinitely. By keeping the mountainous country north and east at his back, he cannot be cut off by 2,500 marines or 5,000; and he can shuttle back and forth along the line where these mountains meet with more settled areas, from Muymuy clear to the Honduras frontier, or more than half way across Nicaragua, enjoying a fairly adequate food supply, tapping rich agricultural sectors, and passing rapidly from point to point; whereas the American troops, to cover this same region, and maintain intact their line of communications with Managua and León, must swing over an arc half again as long. Sandino's soldiers, inured to hardship and a hit-or-miss food supply, as my previous articles demonstrated, will have a still greater advantage this rainy season. The American troops, operating in an unfavorable climate, will then be completely isolated from Managua, León, and the coast cities, for the roads become two feet deep with mud—utterly impassable; even ox carts are blocked. The marine mobilization route, the long arc from Matagalpa around through Estelí to Ocotal, will become even more difficult and roundabout than now, whereas Sandino will be comfortably enjoying what is, contrarily, the dry season in the mountains, every inch of which he and his men know perfectly. As he puts it to me, "I waited in Chipote. The marines concentrated, shipped up supplies, laid month-long plans to oust me, crept gradually up and around my position. They are still there. I am here near Jinotega, half way into the heart of the country. I shall go further into the heart of the country. When they have remobilized here and shipped in troops and more troops and get all set to come out and catch me, I shall be north again—or somewhere else."

And indeed, it must be admitted that while the marines were massed in Nueva Segovia, to have Sandino calmly march into the more-thickly populated regions of the center of the republic, through coffee finca after coffee finca, across two departments, has made the marines a bit ridiculous with all their machinery of war, their science, and their airplanes.

The espionage system of Sandino is excellent. When we neared Jinotega Colonel Colindres ordered two soldiers to take off their red and black hat-bands, remove their leggings, tie bundles over their shoulders, and report on the activities of the marines in the town of Jinotega and elsewhere. There was nothing whatever to identify them as Sandino soldiers. In contrast, an outsider in a Sandino encampment must explain his presence.

The present rather plodding tactics of the marines to suffocate Sandino will, I predict, prove unsuccessful. The Sandino troops have learned the habits of the airplanes. The Sandinistas travel early in the morning, late in the afternoon, or at night; at other times, only in the jungles, where they are invisible from above.

Both General Emiliano Chamorro and President Adolfo Díaz, whom I interviewed today, are pessimistic regarding the early capture of Sandino and predicted that he could only be captured by arming further native troops, without the elaborate supply trains, the extensive equipment, and the careful preparation for combat required by the American forces. At present the United States has armed six hundred native constabulary. This, however, is not a unified force, but is largely used for garrison purposes and is scattered in small detachments throughout the republic. But the United States, now apparently favoring Moncada, the Liberal candidate, is afraid to arm native troops, which will be controlled by a Conservative Party administration. The alternative, President Díaz told me, is to send down three or four times the present number of marines. Thus the only hope for a prompt capture of Sandino would seem to be in the organization of light flying columns, disposed to face great odds, for Sandino has already demonstrated his cleverness in ambushing such columns. Hence, I repeat, given an even break of luck, Sandino will last out until the rainy season, which means that he will not be taken before next December, making satisfactory elections impossible and hence upsetting the whole American program in Nicaragua.

Sandino discussed the campaign. "We have learned many things from the invader. Formerly we used to camp in the open fields, but we saw that our enemy seized the homes of Nicaraguan citizens for his barracks, ruthlessly shoving the occupants out into the streets. So we had to care equally for the welfare of our soldiers; only we have always tried to utilize the homes of those known to sympathize with the invader, and this with the minimum of inconvenience to the occupants. In general, though, the people have offered their homes to us voluntarily, their homes and their all, for they are with us and they know we are fighting for the independence of our country.

"Yes, we owe all to our enemy. If he had never attacked us, then, indeed, our condition would be miserable. From him we have taken everything we possess. If we had not been attacked, we would have no clothing and no ammunition and we would have perished, for we are incapable of living by banditry. We have taken nothing from the peasantry, save that which has been tendered to us voluntarily. In El Chipote the entire countryside used to toil up to the heights with food and animals for our soldiers, laying what we needed at our feet. In the way of food, we have had plenty, for the countryside is with us, to almost a man. Do you think we could have existed in one fortified place for half a year with all the might of the United States against us, if we had been merely bandits? If we were bandits every man's hand would be against us; every man would be a secret enemy. Instead every home harbors a friend. The enemy said: 'He must finish soon. He has no food supply, no ammunition, no guns.' But the enemy forgot that the people would feed us; he forgot that he himself had guns and ammunition."

At this point Sandino ordered brought into me the various weapons taken from the American forces: Browning, Lewis, and Thompson rifles, airplane machine guns, etc. "We now have thirty machine guns," he declared. "Does a bandit travel around with thirty machine-guns, except in Chicago? In the battle of Ocotal we sustained fifteen hours of combat featured by constant firing. In the main battle of Las Cruces we fired twenty thousand shots. Not so bad for a mere bandit."

Sandino's first order on his arrival in San Rafael was that the first soldier touching anything not belonging to him would be shot. My conversations with the shopkeepers of the town bore out the conclusion that

Sandino troops were absolutely orderly and paid for everything they wanted.

General Sandino himself touched upon one instance of forced assessments. "One Colonel Porfirio Sanchez arrived ahead of me in Yalí and levied forced contributions on a number of private citizens. He was thrown out of the Army of Defense of the Sovereignty of Nicaragua, and if I lay my hands on him he will be shot. The money he exacted has all been made good—here is a receipt for $2,000 from Elvira Rodríguez for the amount he forced her to pay him and which we refunded.

"My record is absolutely clear. Any man can examine every step I have taken. He will never find that Sandino his life long has ever taken anything that has not belonged to him, that he has ever broken a promise, that he has ever left any place owing any man a cent. My parents were landed proprietors. When but a boy I handled fifteen to twenty thousand dollars and never touched a cent not mine. I have worked honestly for a living in many places, in Bluefields, in Honduras, in Guatemala, for the Huasteca Petroleum Company in Mexico, in the San Albino mines, and on occasion in most responsible positions."

He showed me the ledger of army expenditures. "Everything we take in and spend is faithfully recorded here. Today, for instance, I gave Colonel Colindres fifteen dollars, all I had at the moment to buy clothes for five of his soldiers who escorted you from El Remango and who came in dirty and ragged. I suggested to him that he tell the shopkeeper we are poor and that we make the money go as far as possible, and if it didn't quite stretch to send the bill to President Coolidge, who is to blame for this violation of my country."

SANDINO—BANDIT OR PATRIOT?

Managua, February 29

All those joining the Sandino forces are obliged to sign a pledge, or *pauta*, which was drawn up by General Sandino himself in El Chipote in September, 1927, and which, among other things, embodies the following conditions:[2]

Those who join the Army for the Defense of the Sovereignty of Nicaragua agree to:

1. Defend the sovereignty of Nicaragua and obey its military code.

2. Refuse to obey every order of Adolfo Díaz and the foreigner and always act in the highest and noblest spirit.

3. Defend not only Liberals, but all Nicaraguans, since all are betrayed by the present Government.

4. Submit themselves unquestioningly to all the orders of the Supreme Chief of the Army.

5. Respect all the rights of the civilian.

7. Make no secret pacts with the enemy.

9. Maintain proper discipline.

10. Expect no salary, only necessary equipment such as clothes, ammunition, and food.

14. The Supreme Chief of the Army in turn promises to make no political compromises with anybody or with any political group.

After reading me the pledge Sandino said: "We are working, as you see, for all of Nicaragua, Conservatives and Liberals alike. Colonel X, here, for instance, is a Conservative, convinced of the righteousness of our cause. Our one aim is to throw out the foreign invader."

"But since you are not strong enough to do so, does not opposition merely result in the sending of more and more marines, the intensification of intervention?"

"We are not protesting against the size of the invasion, but against invasion. The United States has meddled in Nicaragua for many years. We cannot merely depend upon her promise that she will some day get out. Every day intervention is more pronounced. The United States promised to give the Philippines their independence; they are still a subject people.

"You tell me that the governments of Honduras and El Salvador are hostile to me. Tomorrow they will regret such an attitude. All of Central America is morally obliged to help us in this struggle. Central America should stand together against the invader instead of with the governments that ally themselves with the foreigner."

"Is it true, as has been charged, that most of your army is made up of adventurers from other Central-American countries and from Mexico?"

"Quite the contrary. It is true, I have with me men and officers from Costa Rica, Guatemala, El Salvador, Honduras, even one or two from Mexico, who have been attracted by the righteousness of my cause, but they are in a decided minority. The backbone of my army is Nicaraguan, and the officers who have been with me longest are Nicaraguans. I have received many offers from outside troops, but in most cases I have turned them down.

"Our army," Sandino told me, "is tried and true. It is composed of workers and peasants who love their country. The intellectuals have betrayed us, and so we have had to take up arms. What we have done has been through our own unaided efforts."

"How about the story," I put in, "that two captured Americans taught you how to make bombs?"

"A lie of the marine officers to hide their discomfort at our successes. It is comforting to the American ego to think that we were taught what we know by the marines. . . . Call in our bomb maker," he ordered an aide.

An elderly, sparse, smiling man appeared, who explained to me that the bombs were made by wrapping dynamite tightly in rawhide along with stones, nails, pieces of steel, glass, etc. A heavy bomb, wrapped in the skin of some animal, was placed in my hand. It was tied with rawhide thongs and looked more like a child's Teddy-bear than a bomb. But I was told that it could wipe out the better part of a company if advantageously thrown. The bomb-maker also explained the technique of the dynamite rockets used to bring down airplanes.

Sandino gave me a list of battles fought in the environs of El Chipote during the past six months. His conclusions are as exaggerated as those of the marines, perhaps more so:

1. El Chipote	20 American dead
2. Ocotal	80 American dead
3. San Fernando	Sandinista defeat
4. Santa Clara	Sandinista defeat
5. Murra	18 American dead; one American suicide; two wounded. A Thompson machine-gun and eleven rifles captured.
6. Telpaneca	Much arms and ammunition taken
7. Las Cruces (five battles)	250 to 300 American dead. In one battle an American flag captured. "The bearer refused to release his grasp. My men had to cut off his hand with a machete. He was a brave man and deserves praise."
8. San Pedro de Susucayán	15 American dead. Four automatic rifles seized
9. Zapotillal	Airplane brought down
10. La Conchita	60 to 80 American dead
11. San Pedro de Hule	Uncommented
12. Plan Grande	Uncommented
13. Buena Vista	Sandinista defeat
14. Las Delicias	American defeat
15. Amucayán	Uncommented
16. Barellal	Uncommented
17. Santa Rosa	36 American dead
18. El Mantiado	Uncommented

I asked Sandino his reasons for leaving El Chipote.

"We left El Chipote without firing a shot, without losing a single soldier, or a single gun or cartridge. The marines bombarded the place a whole day after we left. We left because the marines were devastating the countryside and destroying the homes of our friends. They were destroying our food supply, not by attacking us but by terrorizing the *campesinos* who had previously brought us provisions, And it takes a lot of provisions to feed a thousand men, stationed in one place, day in and day out for months on end. We determined to carry the war into the enemy's territory. It was a hollow victory the marines gained at El Chipote. I called upon the most resolute and tried of my soldiers to stake all on a march into the populated interior of Nicaragua, as a signal to the civilized world to take note of the savagery being practiced against a free and independent nation. I said we should risk all, and our slogan should be: 'Victory or Death.'

"The gain thus far has been all on our side. After spending months in attempting to take Chipote, after concentrating men, ammunition, and supplies in Ocotal, Nueva Segovia, preparatory to a general attack, the marines learn that I am here in Jinotega, half-way across Nicaragua. Now let them bring marines and more marines into Jinotega, supplies and more supplies. When they have their base well established and are ready to come after me, I'll cut it off by taking Matagalpa or Trinidad, or I will move back to Nueva Segovia, or down to Muymuy, or to León, or somewhere else."

"What," I asked Sandino, "do you consider the motives of the American government?"

"The American Government," he said with a lurking smile, "desires to protect American lives and property. But I can say that I have never touched a pin belonging to an American. I have had respect for the property of everybody. And no American who has come to Nicaragua without arms in his hands has been injured by us."

"Then protecting American lives and property, you imply, must be a pretext?"

"The truth of the matter is that the American Government has made so many arrangements of not too savory a character with the regime now in power that it is afraid of any other government. But if I had been in the shoes of the American Government and had forced the present Nicaraguan regime to give away the rights of my brother Nicaraguans, and then had seen justice coming down the straightway, I would have known that the moment to accede gradually had come. I would have retraced my steps, rather than drown a nation in blood."

"What kind of agreements do you refer to?"

One of Sandino's officers spoke up. "There is a concession to a certain New York banking-house to construct a railway to the north coast. This concession has a clause which killed the traffic on the San Juan River. Greytown is now a deserted hole from which a ruined population has fled like rats from a drowning ship. Those who could burned down their homes to get the insurance. This concession and the previous management of the railroad also ruined many coffee-growers of central Nicaragua who have all these years been forced to ship to the Pacific, thence by the roundabout route of Panama in order that this same banking concern could profit by the shipments over the railway already in existence. The transportation costs became prohibitive, and so this same house and its friends, and the bank which it also controlled, busily bought out the ruined coffee-growers. Too, coffee from the fincas of this financial clique was given preference over the railway; that of independent growers had to pay graft or rot in the rain. Independent growers, ruined, were obliged to sell out their holdings at great loss. The regime of this banking-house and of those which succeeded it beggared the entire country, placed a chain of debt about our neck which for years prevented every sort of internal improvement. This successive economic spoliation of our country cannot possibly benefit the broader commercial interests of the United States itself. The presence of American marines in Nicaragua in support of such iniquitous practices is a betrayal of the people of the United States."

"And the canal?"

Sandino smiled: "Already we have been robbed of our rights in the canal. Presumably we were paid $3,000,000. As a matter of fact, Nicaragua, or rather the bandits in control of our government at that time, thanks to Washington, received but paltry thousands, not enough for each Nicaraguan citizen to buy a soda-cracker and a sardine; for such a bargain, signed by four traitors, we lost our sovereign rights in the canal. The deliberations regarding this sale were made by a fake congress behind closed doors guarded by Conservative Party troops backed up by Yankee bayonets. My own father was arrested for protesting the Bryan-Chamorro Treaty and the granting of improper military and naval rights to the United States. It would have been far better had each Nicaraguan received a cracker and a sardine. A few starving stomachs would have known at least one nibble of luxury. Personally, I should hope to see the Nicaraguan canal built by a private stock company, part of the shares to be held by the Nicaraguan goverment in return for rights granted, in order that we might have a future income not provided by bankers at ruinous rates, with which to build roads, railways, schools, and improve the economic conditions of the country. As it is, the eighteen years of American meddling in Nicaragua have plunged the country deeper into economic misery.

"Let me repeat," declared the General, "we are no more bandits than was Washington. If the American public had not become calloused to justice and to the elemental rights of mankind, it would not so easily forget its own past when a handful of ragged soldiers marched through the snow leaving blood-tracks behind them to win liberty and independence. If their consciences had not become dulled by their scramble for wealth, Americans would not so easily forget the lesson that, sooner or later, every nation, however weak, achieves freedom, and that every abuse of power hastens the destruction of the one who wields it."

[13, vol. 126, nos. 3270–73 (1928), 289, 314–17, 340–41]

1. The actual date was May 18, 1895.
2. See Doc. 25.

62. MESSAGE TO SENATOR WILLIAM E. BORAH, FEBRUARY 1928[1]

The only way to bring an end to the present struggle is to withdraw the United States Marines from our territory, replace the current president by some Nicaraguan citizen who is not a candidate for the presidency, and have the coming elections supervised by ministers of the governments of Latin America, and not by United States soldiers.

In the name of the Nicaraguan people, I protest against the prolonged barbarism of your forces in my country, which has culminated in the recent total destruction of Quilalí. I will never recognize a government that has been imposed upon us by a foreign power. I demand the immediate withdrawal of the invasion forces; otherwise, from this date forward I will not be responsible for the life of any North American public official who resides in Nicaraguan territory.

Patria y Libertad.
A. C. SANDINO

[9, 282–83]

1. According to the source from which this document was taken, this message was transmitted to Senator Borah through Carleton Beals, who was with Sandino in January 1928. Nevertheless, Beals makes no mention of it in his articles.

63. THE BATTLE OF EL BRAMADERO,
FEBRUARY 27, 1928

El Chipotón
February 28, 1928

To Froylán Turcios
Tegucigalpa

Dear Teacher:

I have the honor of informing you that the weapons defending the sovereignty of Nicaragua continue to cover themselves with undying glory.

Yesterday, the 27th of the current month, there was a bloody battle between our forces and the punitive army and the patricides in a place called El Bramadero, in the department of Estelí. After our evacuation of the fortress of El Chipote and after we had traversed the greater part of the departments of Jinotega and Matagalpa, we decided to set up camp in the new fortress, El Chipotón, a place absolutely unknown to the punitive forces, and from here with very great success I began to carry out the plans that we had drawn up. On the 26th I ordered out the infantry column under the command of General Simón Montoya, aided by the cavalry units of General Luis Espinosa Z. and Colonel Carlos Quezada, as well as the batteries of Lewis machine guns commanded by Lieutenant Colonels José Rosas Tejada and José Lagos. This entire force was expected to overtake a regiment of eight hundred pirates who had left the village of Yalí in the direction of Condega. The moment was not long in coming. On the 27th, at two in the afternoon, as our army reached the juncture of the highways that lead from Telpaneca to Estelí, they were informed by Sergeants Major Leopoldo Telléz and Lorenzo Blandón, leaders of the advance guard, that the previously mentioned regiment was located less than a kilometer away on that same road. Our army immediately took up positions, and we had hardly gotten into place when the great pirate procession began to enter the ambush, moving slowly, unwinding like some wretched snake. When the pirates' advance guard reached our infantry's extreme forward position, the latter began to fire their weapons and, simultaneously, our two cavalry units attacked the enemy's flanks, both rear and forward; in this way the pirates were herded into a circle of riflemen and machine gunners, being almost completely wiped out. We are certain that their losses have not been less than seven hundred. We think this is the first time the Yankees have suffered a massacre of this kind in Central America.

The battle lasted five and a half hours. We took from them four hundred Lewis rifles, sixteen machine guns, one hundred and eighty mules loaded with provisions and ammunition, eleven cameras, four pairs of binoculars, two cases of surgical instruments, sixty 45-caliber pistols, and a large quantity of kitchen utensils. All this was collected and taken to our main encampment. Divine Providence protects us. With our war arsenal enriched in this way, we can be certain that at this time we are stronger in war equipment than that ridiculous Adolfo Díaz himself.

This month there have also been clashes of little importance, the biggest being the one that took place on the outskirts of San Juan de Segovia, where twenty-seven casulaties were inflicted upon the conquerors and some rifles were taken from them.

Soon we will give you additional news about our new operations.

Please receive, in my name and that of my Army, a fraternal embrace.

Patria y Libertad.

A. C. SANDINO

P.S. Our army is mourning the death of our brother, General Luis Espinoza Z., and the grave wound inflicted upon Colonel Carlos Quezada.

[12, vol. 4 (1928), 1177]

64. LETTER TO FROYLÁN TURCIOS, MARCH 14, 1928

Fortress of the Defenders of the
National Sovereignty of Nicaragua
El Chipotón, March 14, 1928

To Froylán Turcios

Admired teacher and friend:

Because you are the only person who has known how to make a conscientious interpretation of our patriotism and loyalty to our creed, I have decided to send you an extract of my ideas regarding the usefulness of a national government in our country, so that you can explain those ideas in such a way that they may be understood by the democrats of our continent.

Above all else, it should be recognized and understood who is truly responsible for all the blood that has been spilled during the years of civil war in our unfortunate Nicaragua. The man who governs the United States of America, Mr. Calvin Coolidge, is the one responsible for this bloody catastrophe.

According to the Tacoma treaties, no Central American government originating from a coup d'état was to be recognized as legal,[1] and yet, in spite of this, Emiliano Chamorro, in league with his intimate comrade, Adolfo Díaz, carried out the *Lomazo* of 1925, thus achieving power in an illegal manner; and, although he was not recognized by the Yankee government, since this would have constituted the height of political immorality, his accomplice, Adolfo Díaz, was indeed recognized, even though the civil war was in full swing at the time of that recognition.[2] The White House politicians revealed their partiality to the Conservatives, using absurd pretexts to declare neutral zones, and yet, in spite of those injustices, we Liberals were victorious, and when we reached Managua's doors, the United States government imposed its authority upon our army in an arbitrary and cruel way, threatening us so that we would lay down our victorious weapons at the feet of the conquered murderers of our fatherland. The Liberal army was made up of members of the working and campesino classes, with the exception of a few leaders who were true political hucksters with aristocratic affectations. For his personal convenience, José María Moncada (*a recognized traitor*) persuaded most of the military leaders to lay down their arms, offering the people free elections so that they might choose the government they desired.

Although the greater part of the army opposed Moncada's position, it was forced to suspend hostilities with the enemy, because it could not at that moment recognize who the leader might be who could take revenge in defense of our nation's honor. At that moment, the turncoat, José María Moncada, caused the military leaders to forget that the United States of America had no right to intervene in our internal affairs, and persuaded them to overlook the irony of being offered free elections to choose a government of our desire, when in fact the United States had just disavowed the government of Dr. Juan B. Sacasa, who had been elected by an overwhelming majority, in order to recognize the organizer of the *Lomazo* himself, the ridiculous Adolfo Díaz. In previous months Dr. Sacasa had been recognized by the Yankee government but later was disavowed because he was not to Mr. Coolidge's liking, for which reason it may be supposed that Chamorro's *Lomazo* had been secretly authorized by the aforesaid Coolidge. The result of this outrage against our sovereignty is that this merciless struggle continues to ravage Nicaragua.

Yes, and now Coolidge, not satisfied with all the blood he has shed, continues to intensify our afflictions, supporting the murderer of his fatherland, José María Moncada, under the pretext that he offers free elections, but in reality, from the very moment that the United States gave support to a candidate and failed to heed the true will of the people, who are demanding a national government, no such freedom existed. If the Yankee government wishes to offer freedom to the Nicaraguan people, let it remove its troops from our territory and allow us to elect a national government, but if it promised to help Moncada to win the presidency, let it keep its promise, and meanwhile the war will continue until the people have won their independence.

If it is absolutely essential that our elections be supervised by foreigners, let representatives from the Latin American countries be summoned, because they do not constitute a threat to our sovereignty and they are bound to us by ties of race, religion, and language, but we will never accept as mediators the pirate hypocrites who stain our country's autonomy with their filthy boots.

To put a stop once and for all to dictatorship, and thus to bring about an effective peace, a national government is now indispensable in Nicaragua. Supervision of elections in our country by the United States will not aid in the establishment of public peace, because their twisted, unjust, and subterranean policies are well known to us—policies always biased in favor of wicked Conservatives or wicked Liberals, bringing revolutions as their consequence, which for our small countries result in retrogression and disaster.

I have seen some of the official articles of the venal press of Nicaragua, in which the writers seek to convince the people of the impossibility of a national government, but these altar boys of Yankee power create such propaganda as a business, and the people can expect nothing from such Machiavellisms.

The supreme ideal of our army is to throw the conquerors out of our territory and to promote the formation of a purely national government. We have already said that once this has been accomplished we will retire to private life. But at the moment, in view of the impossibility of the Liberal and Conservative parties arriving at an honorable understanding in support of a national government, which is the kind of government that all legitimate sons of Nicaragua should support, I have concluded that our army, which has known how to distinguish itself by its patriotism, can find a solution to this problem that the others look upon as impossible.

In view of the difficulties that the parties of caudillismo have in coming to an arrangement that can benefit the nation, from this moment on, and with complete loyalty, the Army in Defense of the National Sovereignty of Nicaragua offers its unconditional and devoted support for the consolidation of the national government to which all good sons of Nicaragua aspire. At the same time it commits itself to contain, with a powerful hand, any acts of aggression against the national government that may be planned by the spiteful patricidal caudillos, who deserve nothing but the absolute contempt of the Nicaraguan people.

Patria y Libertad.
AUGUSTO C. SANDINO

[12, vol. 4 (1928), 1176]

1. In 1922 the republics of Nicaragua, El Salvador, and Honduras, at the request of the United States, and under the supervision of the American ambassadors to those countries, held a series of conferences aboard the warship USS *Tacoma*, anchored in the Gulf of Fonseca. Several Central American political problems, particularly those involving those three nations, were dealt with, and the bases were established for the Second Central American conference held a year later. The first conference had taken place in Washington in 1907.

2. The term *Lomazo* in Nicaragua signifies a military coup d'etat, that is the illegal acquisition of power through seizure of strategic La Loma Fortress on the peak of the Tiscapa volcano in Managua. Sandino here refers specifically to the coup that brought Chamorro to power in 1925. The "civil war" is the Constitutionalist War of 1926–1927. RC

65. LETTER TO FROYLÁN TURCIOS, MARCH 25, 1928

El Chipotón
March 25, 1928

To Froylán Turcios
Tegucigalpa

Dear friend:

I have the honor of informing you of the new victories achieved by the Army in Defense of the National Sovereignty of Nicaragua, which I will do briefly, given the little time at my disposal in these moments.

Since I told you in my previous letter that I would not allow the enemy to unite in order to carry out their plans to attack me, and that instead I would take the offensive whenever we had a ninety-nine percent likelihood of success, this we have done, *and all the Yankee schemes have come to nought.*

Because the piratical infantry have become aware of the terrible punishment that we have inflicted upon them and so are now avoiding every encounter with our army, we have actively dedicated ourselves to setting up ambushes for their airplanes, which have now brought us excellent results.

On March 8 General Manuel María Girón Ruano left this General Headquarters with a cavalry unit, taking along the famous "Chula," for the purpose of ambushing their airplanes on the route which they have been seen flying over daily.[1] A few minutes before ten on the morning of that same day the murderous aviators appeared, breaking through the sky with their soaring machines in the direction of the force led by General Girón, who personally manned the "Chula" with such wonderful success that one of the perforated airplanes fell to the ground in the outskirts of Estelí, killing the two aviators whose names are Captain William C. Bird and Sergeant Rudolph A. Frankforter, as our friends who happily witnessed the fall of the apparatus have informed us.

On the 18th of the same month we had a chance to suprise the airplanes again, at the very moment that they were mercilessly bombing the modest huts of honored campesinos who live in the mountains of Murra. As long as they were certain that there was nobody in those huts who could respond to their aggression, the cowardly aviators appeared very intrepid, but it pleased God that at that moment the cavalry under the command of Colonel Ferdinando Quintero arrived on the scene, and with the fifteen automatic rifles that that unit possessed, wasting no time, they responded to the miserable aviators, who suddenly shot skyward and with lightning speed fled from our view.

Colonel Quintero accompanied by other gunners occupied the positions decided upon by this command to await the arrival of the airplanes on the second day. What we had expected happened. On the 19th there was a formidable bombardment by a flotilla of airplanes that passed over four times, dropping a great quantity of explosives, asphyxiating gases, and incendiary bombs upon the Indian huts. But the finger of destiny made the conquerors' proud machines fly over our artillery, which functioned brilliantly. The result of this bombing was that the two airplanes crashed, and we have been informed that the aviators perished.

Soon we will give you new information about our operations.

Patria y Libertad.
A. C. SANDINO

[12, vol. 4, no. 64 (15 April 1928), 1175]

1. For the "Chula," see Doc. 34. RC

66. A PROTEST AGAINST U.S. INTERVENTION: LETTER TO H. J. AMPHLETT, APRIL 29, 1928[1]

La Luz, April 29, 1928

H. J. Amphlett
Manager of La Luz Mine

I have the honor to inform you that on this day your mine has been reduced to ashes by disposition of this command to make more tangible our protest against the warlike invasion that your Government has made in our territory without any right other than that of brute force.

As long as the Government of the United States of North America does not order retirement of its pirates from our territory there will be no guarantee in this country for North Americans residing in Nicaragua.

In the beginning I was confident that the people of North America would not be in accord with the abuses committed in Nicaragua by the Government of Mr. Calvin Coolidge, but I am now convinced that North Americans in general uphold the attitude of Coolidge in my country; and it is for this reason that all that is North American that falls into our hands assuredly will have come to its end.

The losses which you have sustained in the aforementioned mine you may collect from the Government of the United States and Mr. Calvin Coolidge, who is truly responsible for the horrible and disastrous situation through which Nicaragua is passing at present.

The pretext advanced by Mr. Coolidge for his intervention in Nicaragua is to protect life and property of North Americans and other foreigners resident in this country, which is tremendous hypocrisy. We Nicaraguans are respectable men, and never in our history have there been registered such happenings as have presently occurred. And that is the harvest reaped by the insensate policy of your Government in our country.

The most honorable resolution which your Government should adopt in the conflict with Nicaragua is to retire its forces from our territory, thus permitting us, the Nicaraguans, to elect our national Government, which is the only means of pacifying our country.

With your Government rests the conservation of good or bad friendship with our Government, and you, the capitalists, will be appreciated and respected by us according as you treat us as equals and not in the mistaken manner which now obtains, believing yourselves lords and masters of our lives and property.

[14, 18 May 1928]

1. This letter was given to Henry Amphlett, a British subject who acted as administrator of La Luz Mine, property of the American La Luz and Los Angeles Mining Company, where Adolfo Díaz had once worked. The more complete English-language version that appeared in *The New York Times* on May 18, 1928 replaces the brief extract used in the 1984 edition. RC

67. LETTER TO THE PATRIOTIC LEAGUE
OF NATIONAL DEFENSE
OF QUETZALTENANGO, GUATEMALA,
MAY 4, 1928

El Chipotón
May 4, 1928

Messrs. Don Oscar A. Sandoval, Ernesto Carrera, Don Ricardo Barrientos, Don Gumercindo Lucas Blanco, Don Luis Gerardo Barrios, Don M. Rodas B., Don Jacobo H. Sánchez, Don Antonio Escoto, Don Carlos de León, Don Manfredo L. de León, Don Salvador Pacheco Mayorquín, and Don Remigio Mérida, members of the Directing Committee of the Patriotic League of National Defense of Quetzaltenango

Most distinguished companions:

In my hands the kind and important communication from the Directing Committee, worthily presided over by yourselves.

It is not strange that the noble sons of Quetzaltenango should faithfully and enthusiastically reveal their concern for the triumph of justice in Nicaragua, which is the triumph of justice of all the Latin American peoples against the imperialist policies of the Anglo-Saxon colossus. I have the honor to express my personal gratitude and that of my army for your displays of flattering sympathy for our cause, which is also the cause of Latin America.

As long as our hearts continue to beat in our breasts you may be certain, noble companions, that the perverse imperialist plans will have only one result: that of precipitating the people of the United States into the chaos that the imperialism of the White House is carving out for itself in Latin America. Respect for morality and the practice of justice are the only foundations of stability and prosperity of nations. A powerful people who strike down the rights of weaker peoples will succeed only in raising the arm of vengeance of those peoples, who, confronting the reality of their misfortunes, possess only one road to salvation: their unity.

A united Latin America will save itself; divided it will die.

Let us work, companions, for that unity; to assure the true independence of our peoples and to pass on to our children a name worthy of our forefathers, who knew how to struggle and die heroically to make us free, a freedom that today would be snatched away from us by evil intentions.

My general representative abroad, Señor Don Froylán Turcios, is the authorized person to whom you may send the assistance that may permit you to cooperate in this work of salvation of our beloved Central American fatherland.

Receive in the name of my army and of myself a fraternal embrace.

Patria y Libertad.
AUGUSTO C. SANDINO

[19, 1 p.]

68. LETTER TO FROYLÁN TURCIOS, MAY 8, 1928

El Chipotón
May 8, 1928

To Froylán Turcios
Tegucigalpa

My greatly esteemed friend:

It pleases me to inform you of my army's recently completed operations, so that through you they may be made known to the independent nations of our continent.

It was one in the morning on April 29; the moon was darkened by the smoke produced by the burning of the four main buildings of the American mining enterprise of La Luz and Los Angeles in the department of Bluefields, which was carried out by order of this command. A note was left for the manager of the company explaining to him the reasons that induced us to carry out such a drastic but necessary measure;[1] in this same letter, of which I attach a copy, I will give an explanation through you to those who could be shocked by my new actions.

The civilized countries are fully aware of the countless burnings and other crimes that the invading Yankees commit every day in our territory, and they know that, despite the indifference of the Latin American governments in the face of this outrage against our weak nation, we have succeeded in defending ourselves heroically for over a year, and that during this time we have never imitated the pirates in their brutal role as incendiaries. But today, having completed a year of tremendous struggle, we have recognized that our worst mistake would be to allow the Yankee companies to continue peacefully exploiting our soil, because to a large extent they are the main cause of the bellicose invasion that is destroying us, under the pretext of defending the interests that they possess in our country.

The Yankee pirates are murdering us in the full light of day and in the presence of all the nations that in every epoch have distinguished themselves as conquerors and enslavers, countries such as England, Germany, France, and Italy. It would appear that all these nations, and Spain as well, have some secret pact to remain deaf to the groans of the weak countries when they find themselves under the brutal boot of any one of them.

It was for this reason that this command sent out a circular to all the consuls of the nations referred to, making them aware that in this second year of war against the American pirates all the foreigners referred to will face the same fate until they unanimously request that our sovereignty be respected, forcing the invaders to end their occupation of our territory, so that we may freely choose our own national government. When this happens all foreigners will possess guarantees in our land, so long as they subject themselves to our laws and do not impose themselves upon us as they do in Africa and in some pariah countries that remain in Latin America.

My dear teacher, it is necessary to assure ourselves that to win our victory we can rely for effective support only upon our unbreakable will to win or to die, and that all the other proposals we have received are but trivial songs. [. . .] And if this cannot be achieved, do not contact anyone else, because with my four heroes I will manage with God's help to tear down the Yankee imperialist sway; it is certain that faced with our victory the cowardly governments of Latin America will hold their hands over their faces in shame.

[. . .] I hope that because of the frank way this letter has been conceived it will not seem strange to you, because you are the one I must speak to with total sincerity, since you are my hope and the powerful arm of my cause.

In the last few days there have been some military operations of little importance and I am awaiting the coming of the rainy season to begin a great plan of hostile actions against the invaders. Possibly with this plan that I have prepared I will be able to put a large part of the enemy forces out of action during the entire month of August. What I can promise you is that if the conquerors do not leave our territory there will be no elections in November, because I have better ways ready to destroy the Yankees at that time.

Receive in my name and in that of my army a long and fraternal embrace.

Patria y Libertad.
A. C. SANDINO

[12, vol. 4 (1928), 1254]

1. This note corresponds to Doc. 66 of the present edition.

69. LETTER TO FROYLÁN TURCIOS, MAY 15, 1928

El Chipote
May 15, 1928

To Froylán Turcios
Tegucigalpa

Honored teacher and friend:

I communicate to you with pleasure the new victory won by our army against the punitive forces.

After conducting a long march along the Atlantic coast, one of our cavalry units commanded by General Manuel María Girón Ruano ambushed a column of buccaneers who were en route from Jinotega to the port of Bocay. The battle took place on the 13th of this month in the place called El Zapote, ninety kilometers east of Jinotega. Our cavalry were camped on the same road that runs from Jinotega to Bocay in a place called La Chuscada, through which the blond beasts of the North intended to pass.[1] I was informed of the enemy's movements and with no loss of time ordered General Girón's cavalry to march to Bocaycito, for the purpose of impeding the pirates' advance, but upon reaching the place called Los Cedros, General Girón was informed by one of our campesinos that the bandits were not far away. As that same commander was beginning to deploy the forces under his command into guerrilla units, the first shots from the advance guard were heard, and thus, almost without delay, a brutal battle unfolded. Our bombs, rifles, and artillery were used effectively by our companions, but the enemy's power was formidable, and despite their vigorous efforts our column retreated, and the enemy remained in control of the disputed hill.

The next day, at four in the afternoon, we had surrounded that same hill, and with the fierce bravery of the defenders of the national law of Nicaragua, a sudden attack was launched against the Yankee trenches, the latter finding it impossible to contain the power of our brave soldiers. The hill fell under our control and the pirates fled in shame, leaving the field covered with bodies, among them, the first and second leaders of the punitive column. We captured from them ammunition, rifles, animals and provisions. The dead Yankee officers previously mentioned died at the start of the first clash of the afternoon of the 13th, and they had aleady been buried, but our muchachos, eager to know those whom Justice had punished, disinterred them, finding in the grave a tightly closed bottle containing a small piece of paper that said,

Cpt. William L. Williamson, USMC
Killed in action.
Bocay Trail Along Bocaycito River.
4 P.M. May 13, 1928.
Nearest Relative: Mother, address not known.
Cousin's Address:
Pfc. Clyde O. Daniel, USMC; Mr. B. (*sic*) Coco Solo, Canal Zone

The graves of the bodies referred to were changed and their bones will be sent to their families only when the latter offer proof that they have tried to achieve the withdrawal of the invaders from our nation's territory.

This same Captain William Williamson left a large packet of correspondence, including letters of great interest that in respect for morality will not be made public, except if this should be agreed upon at a later time. Also found were his commission papers containing his regimental register and rank, a photograph of a boy named Phill, his nephew, and his address, which was not known to his companions in arms. We learned this through his correspondence: Mrs. Florence McGee, 1213 Mason St., St. Louis, Mo.

(I attach the photograph of the boy Phill so that it may be used as an illustration in your review *Ariel*.)

Soon I will send you new details of our operations.

With feelings of highest esteem and the warm greetings of the leaders, officers, and soldiers of the Army in Defense of the National Sovereignty of Nicaragua, I remain yours as always.

Patria y Libertad.
A. C. SANDINO

[12, vol. 4 (1928), 1255]

1. This disparaging term, which Sandino used in a number of documents during this period, was an aftereffect of the American military intervention of 1912 and is a further indication of how much Sandino and other Nicaraguans were angered by such events. In the city of León, after that intervention, an unnamed poet wrote of "the blond pigs of Pennsylvania advancing on our gardens of beauty," and of the trembling of the Latin soul at "the pawing of Nietzsche's blond beast." See Denny, *Dollars for Bullets*, 122. RC

70. LETTER TO THE U.S. SECTION OF THE ALL-AMERICA ANTI-IMPERIALIST LEAGUE, MAY 20, 1928

El Chipote
May 20, 1928

Members of the United States Section
of the All-America Anti-Imperialist League

39 Union Square, Room 40

New York City

Sirs:

I am glad to inform you that I have received from the hands of Dr. Gustave Machado (who came to our encampment as a representative of the Central Committee of the Hands-Off-Nicaragua Association) a package containing cotton, bandages and other medicines to cure the wounds of our soldiers.

We are especially delighted that you, honest North Americans, manifest in this manner your protest and disapproval of the policies of aggression that the existing Government of the United States is carrying on in Nicaragua.

We know that the majority of the North American people is not directly responsible for the ferocious crimes that the marines commit every day in our country. Even to us came notice of the news of the meetings and public manifestations against sending the marines to Nicaragua. We well know the situation of the working class in your country, as victims of the oppression of the exploiters, exploited by the same interests that are now fighting to enslave the peoples of Latin America.

But it is our conviction that if all the citizens would make heard their voice of protest, the opinion of the majority would be carried out, the opinion against the criminal plans of the Washington Government.

We want to transmit through you the feeling of gratitude of the army of liberation of Nicaragua to the anti-imperialist fighters of the United States for the sending of medicines, asking them at the same time that they should make known our opinion of the indifference of the North American people who permit the systematic extermination of a defenseless people by a country that is not officially at war, in violation of the Constitution of the United States.

With cordial greetings, I am yours for country and liberty.

A. C. SANDINO
(Seal) "Patria y Libertad."

[14, 24 June 1928]

El Chipotón
June 10, 1928

To Froylán Turcios
Tegucigalpa

Great esteemed teacher and friend:

With deep surprise I read in the May 1 issue of *Ariel* your editorial about the danger that exists in regard to the territorial integrity of Honduras because of the border question with Guatemala. Your words, as well as those you reproduce from the editorial from *El Cronista*, of that city, for a moment made my blood freeze. I quickly realized that persons associated with the imperialist Yankee policy are the inciters of this Central American bonfire.

At this moment I am more worried about the serious problems that exist among yourselves, the leaders of Central America, that is to say of the Great Fatherland, than I am about the cause that I myself defend with my few hundred brave men, because I am convinced that with our firmness of spirit and the terror we have succeeded in sowing in the hearts of the pirates, the outcome of our efforts will be clear, while you meanwhile are surrounded by patricides who always pursue the scent of great causes, to leave the seeds of treachery behind.

My dear friend, in the name of Nicaragua, of Honduras, of Guatemala, and in the name of God, I beg you and all men of understanding and clear Central American patriotism to try to avoid in every possible way the heating up of spirits and conflict among ourselves. You have the obligation to make the people of Latin America understand that among us there should be no frontiers, and that all of us have the clear duty to be concerned with the fate of each of the Hispanic American nations, because all of us face the same danger before the colonizing and absorbing policy of the Yankee imperialists. The blond beasts are located at one of the extremes of Latin America, and from there they avidly observe our political and economic movements; they know our weakness of character and seek to keep unresolved the serious problems that exist in a latent state between our countries. For example, the border question between Guatemala and Honduras, between Honduras and Nicaragua; the canal question between Nicaragua and Costa Rica; the question of the Gulf of Fonseca between El Salvador, Honduras, and Nicaragua; and the question of Tacna and Arica between Peru and Chile. And so in this way, there is a chain of serious problems among us that need to be resolved. The Yankees have studied us well and they take advantage of our state of culture and of the weakness of our characters to place us in danger whenever it serves their interests.

The Yankees are our peoples' worst enemies, and when they observe us in moments of patriotic inspiration and see that we are experiencing sincere impulses leading toward unification, they rake up our unsettled questions, and thereby incite hatred among us, and so we remain divided and weak and thus easy to colonize.

Living as we do in the twentieth century, the time has come for us to demonstrate to the whole world that until today the Yankees have succeeded in distorting their slogan. Speaking of the Monroe Doctrine they say: *America for the Americans.* Good, this is well put. All of us who are born in America are Americans. The mistake the imperialists have made, however, is that they have interpreted the Monroe Doctrine as follows: *America for the Yankees.* All right then, so that the blond beasts don't continue to be confused, I will re-write the sentence in the following terms: *The United States of North America for the Yankees. Latin America for the Indo-Latins.*

Accepting these phrases, as one should, as slogans, the Yankees can only come to our Latin America as guests, but never as lords and masters, as they are prone to do. It will not be strange if I and my army are found in any Latin American country where the murderous invader treads in a posture of conquest.

Sandino is Indo-Hispanic and he has no frontiers in Latin America.

With nothing else to ask of you, dear teacher, I send you my heart, with which I have spoken to you in this letter.

Patria y Libertad.
A. C. SANDINO

[10, 27–28]

72. A LETTER TO THE RULERS
OF LATIN AMERICA,
AUGUST 4, 1928

El Chipotón
August 4, 1928

Señores presidentes:[1]

In view of the fact that your fifteen countries would be those most affected if Nicaragua were allowed to become a colony of Uncle Sam, I am taking the liberty of sending you this letter, inspired not by hypocrisy or by false diplomatic courtesies, but by the rough frankness of a soldier.

With such shame as they may still possess, the Yankees wish to mask their intentions behind a project for the construction of an interoceanic canal across Nicaraguan territory, which would cause the isolation of the Indo-Hispanic republics. The Yankees, who do not pass up any opportunity, would take advantage of the estrangement of our peoples to bring to reality the dream that they inculcate into their children in their primary schools, that is, that when all of Latin America has become an Anglo-Saxon colony, the blue field of their flag will have only one star.

Before the cold indifference of the Latin American governments, and left to its own resources, the Army in Defense of the National Sovereignty of Nicaragua has for fifteen months honorably and brilliantly faced the terrible blond beasts and the pack of traitorous Nicaraguan renegades who support the invaders in their sinister designs.

During this time, señores presidentes, you have not carried out your duty, because as the representatives that you are of free and sovereign peoples, you are obliged to protest diplomatically or, if necessary, with the weapons that the people have placed in your trust, against the nameless crimes that the White House government orders carried out in cold blood in our unhappy Nicaragua, without any right and with our country blameless except for its unwillingness to kiss the whip that lashes it, or the fist that strikes it.

Do the Latin American governments think perhaps that the Yankees would be content with the conquest of Nicaragua alone? Have these governments perhaps forgotten that among twenty-one American republics six have already lost their sovereignty? Panama, Puerto Rico, Cuba,

Haiti, Santo Domingo, and Nicaragua are the six unfortunate republics that have lost their independence and become colonies of Yankee imperialism. The governments of those six nations do not defend the collective interests of their compatriots, because they came to power, not as a result of the popular will, but imposed instead by imperialism, and so it happens that those who rise to the presidency backed by Wall Street magnates defend the interests of U.S. bankers. In those six unfortunate Spanish-American nations, all that remains to the people is the memory of their independence and the distant hope of reconquering their freedom through the formidable efforts of a few native sons, who fight tirelessly to rescue their country from the infamy into which the renegades have sunk them. The Yankee colonization advances swiftly over our nations without encountering a wall of bayonets in its path, and therefore when its turn comes each of our countries is overwhelmed by the conqueror with little effort on its part, because, until now, each has defended itself alone. If the governments of the principal nations of Latin America were led by a Simón Bolívar, a Benito Juárez, or a San Martín, our fate would be other than it is, because they would know that once Central America had been dominated by the blond pirates, Mexico, Colombia, Venezuela, etc., would follow.

What would become of Mexico if the Yankees succeeded in their dastardly designs to colonize Central America? The heroic people of Mexico could do nothing, despite their manly qualities, because they would be crushed beforehand in Uncle Sam's grip, and the help they might hope to receive from sister nations could not reach them because the Nicaraguan canal and the naval base on the Gulf of Fonseca would stand in the way. And so Mexico would be destined to struggle against Yankee imperialism isolated from the other nations of Latin America, using its own resources, which is exactly what is happening to us now.

The celebrated Carranza doctrine proclaims that Mexico, because of its geographic position, must be—and in fact is—the advance guard of Hispanism in America. Then what might be the opinion of the present Mexican government with respect to the policy the Yankees are carrying out in Central America? Have the Ibero-American governments not seen that the Yankees are amused by the prudent policy adopted in situations like that of Nicaragua? It is true that, for the moment, Brazil, Venezuela, and Peru have no intervention problem, as their representatives declared this year at the Pan-American Conference in Havana during the discussion of the right to intervene, but if those governments were more conscious of their historic responsibility, they would not wait for the conquest to unleash its havoc on their own soil, but would come instead to the defense of a brother nation that struggles with a bravery and tenacity born of despair against a criminal enemy a hundred times larger and armed with every kind of modern weapon. At such a tragic and decisive moment in history, can governments that express themselves as Brazil, Venezuela, Peru, and Cuba did retain sufficient moral authority over their sister nations? Will they have a right to be heard?

Today it is with the peoples of Spanish America that I speak. When a government does not reflect the aspirations of its citizens, the latter, who gave it power, have the right to be represented by virile men with concepts of effective democracy, and not by useless satraps whose lack of moral valor and patriotism are a disgrace to a nation's pride.

We are ninety million Spanish Americans, and we should think only about our unity, recognizing that Yankee imperialism is the most brutal enemy that now threatens us and the only one that intends to put an end to our racial honor and our peoples' freedom through conquest.

Tyrants do not represent nations, and freedom is not won with flowers.

To form, then, a united front and to stop the conqueror's advance over our lands, we must begin by respecting ourselves in our own house, and not allow bloodthirsty despots like Juan Vicente Gómez and degenerates like Leguía, Machado, and others to make us look ridiculous before the world as they did in the pantomime in Havana.[2]

The honorable men of Latin America should imitate Bolívar, Hidalgo, San Martín, and the Mexican lads who on September 13, 1847, fell at Chapultepec, pierced by Yankee bullets, dying in defense of their country and their race, rather than surrendering to a life of disgrace and shame into which Yankee imperialism would cause us to sink.

Patria y Libertad.
AUGUSTO C. SANDINO

[10, 34–37]

1. Sandino evidently sent copies of this letter to fifteen Latin American presidents. RC
2. Juan Vicente Gómez, Augusto Leguía, and Gerardo Machado were contemporary dictators of Venezuela, Peru, and Cuba respectively. RC

73. A BATTLE ON THE COCO RIVER, AUGUST 1928

Rio Coco Encampment
August 10

Our arms have just covered themselves with glory by entirely exterminating a column of one hundred and fifty marines who tried to reach our redoubts above the currents of the Coco River.

The action began when we spotted the two enormous launches that transported the enemy, which we attacked in spite of their numerical superiority and the better weapons at their disposal. General Manuel M. Girón Ruano commanded one of the units of our troops during the attack that distinguished itself under the direct rifle and machine gun fire of the "machos."

The battle lasted for several hours, we having to fight against the marines who by then had come ashore and were advancing along the river bank. First we defeated these, killing sixty-eight of them and wounding another twenty-eight.

The launches were sunk at last, and all of the crew members who had survived the battle were drowned. Concerning the twenty-eight wounded whom we had captured, these also died because of an epidemic that developed among them, which is known here by the name "remoral." Only our own men, accustomed by now to life in these inhospitable regions, were able to survive this illness.

In recognition of the services to the country given by our leaders, Manuel M. Girón Ruano was promoted to the rank of major general, and Carlos Aponte Hernández and Francisco Altamirano were elevated to the rank of colonel.

The supreme commander,

A. C. SANDINO

[19, 1 p.]

74. A BOY-MAN, SEPTEMBER 1928[1]

1. Sent to Latin America

Two years ago, in the month of November, my unit was in the line of fire in the Quilalí mountains, waiting for four Conservative generals who, with machine guns, had assassinated with impunity men of Liberal affiliation, not even sparing their families during their cowardly assassination.

By way of a path of the kind we call *picadas*, inextricable roads that only the *chanes* or *baquianos* (guides) know, a nine-year-old boy reached our lines, asking to speak with the person who writes these words. When he reached my presence I saluted him, and he, returning my salute, offered me a maguey-rope saddlebag containing Guinea hens and boiled yuccas with chilied *chicharrones*.

Like so many children of our America, this child of pure Indian race, in whose eyes glowed the indomitable pride of our ancestors, was wearing something that looked like an undershirt, which could be made out in the form of two little rolls of rags twisted around his biceps, hanging from a few bits of a child's button-shirt still clinging to his shoulders, along with underpants, also in a tattered condition, hanging from his waist. Everything about the boy cried out in protest against the present civilization, and my memory of the surprise he showed on his face still brings uncontrollable emotion to my throat.

When I returned the saddlebag to him, thanking him and asking him to greet his parents for me, he replied, "I want to be one of your soldiers. I want you to give me a rifle and some bullets to fight against the bandits who are killing us in our homes. In my own house," he added, "we knew you were here in the mountains, and I've come bringing these things for you to eat."

He was incorporated into our forces because there was no way to convince him that because of his age he couldn't stand the harshness of the war. He has taken part in thirty-six battles and today, instead of his rags, he displays a beautiful uniform, and an understanding of reading and writing that he has acquired in our army. He is a *boy-man*.

The following dialogue was carried on by this boy and another only a few months different in age, who was taken into the army in that same period under those same moral and physical conditions. The first *boy-man* speaks: "It seems to me that a mountain has been removed from my mind. I have a wish to travel through the twenty republics of Latin America, because the companions who are with us and who have come from those republics to fight alongside us against the machos say that there are ninety million of us Latin Americans, and, as you know, these revolutions are intended to unite our race against the Yankee imperialists."

"It's good that you want to travel, brother," the other boy replies, "and we mustn't lose hope that more than once we will go as delegates from our country to those beautiful lands."

Could these children have reasoned as they do now if they had continued to live unknown and ignored in their shacks?

2. A Forty-Five-Year-Old

A man, his wife, and their son are seated at a little table. The wife strips the leaves from some hot green corn tamales, which, along with milk curd and other country dishes, bring pleasure to their home. The husband smiles at the dish of food, talking in a lively way about the events that the anti-imperialist war has brought about. The boy takes big sips from his *café con leche* while he scolds the cat, which just then scampers up the display case where they keep their merchandise.

The husband: "Old woman, it's a terrible shame that the war against the Yankee invaders will end and that I haven't taken part in a single battle. What will people say when our troops get to Managua and people ask me to tell them something about this great campaign?"

The wife: "It's true, my boy, it would make me very unhappy if you didn't have anything to say. And besides you shouldn't go just to have something to say, but also because you have an obligation to serve this cause, which is the cause of all of us. I will get some provisions ready and you will go to fight the machos."

3. Two Boys Playing

Two boys from six to seven years of age, the sons of soldiers, play war in the middle of the house, while a torrential rain is causing the rivers to spill over their banks. One of them has a little toy car and the other a cap. The one with the cap says to his friend, "I'll buy your little car from you."

"And what will you give me in return?" replies the other.

"This cap and some buttons."

"Ah," says the one with the cap, putting the great importance of the phrases he speaks into his facial expression, "for this we will need fifteen days of conferences and a meeting of the entire army to see if this business can be carried out." And they continue playing war.

These dialogues between campesinos and the men of the army make me recognize that the struggle we have undertaken will bear abundant fruits for the moral and intellectual betterment of our peoples. And yet, in spite of the abject traitors, nobody can erase the hatred that today exists against the Yankees among the inhabitants of the Segovias.

Patria y Libertad.
A. C. SANDINO

[9, 335–37]

1. These three short tales, "A Boy-Man," "A Forty-Five-Year-Old," and "Two Boys Playing," were included in a letter from Sandino to Froylán Turcios.

75. LETTER TO FROYLÁN TURCIOS, NOVEMBER 20, 1928

El Chipotón
Nicaragua, C.A.
November 20, 1928

Señor Froylán Turcios
Tegucigalpa, Honduras, C.A.

My dear teacher:

I have the honor of informing you that, face to face with the results of the Yankee interference in the presidential elections of the 4th of this month, which imposed the traitor José María Moncada as president of the Republic for the period from 1929 to 1932, I have decided to invite the Liberal Republican and Laborite parties and the Solidarity Group to unite their activities with those of our army. In a previous letter I informed you of the position of the parties mentioned regarding the elections, and, concerning the Solidarity Group, it is one of the organizations that have opposed the interventionist policy and its harmful effects upon our national sovereignty. To achieve such a unification, a delegate from our army will appear before those groups to offer them the clauses of the agreement, a copy of which I am sending you today. In the same manner I am sending you a copy of the army's manifesto mentioned in the agreement.

Conforming to what is stipulated in this document, I have named Dr. Domingo Mairena Hernández as our special delegate to Dr. Pedro José Zepeda, resident in Mexico, D.F., for the purposes indicated, and to take steps concerning matters about which I have given him precise and positive instructions. In regard to the instructions that I have given Dr. Mairena, his trip should not be delayed at any transit point, and I am confident that he will make every effort to reach Mexico quickly, even to the extent of making a forced march. If, as I strongly hope, the unification takes place and the governing junta is installed, presided over by Dr. Zepeda, I hope to learn if he would be willing to accept the governing junta's representation abroad, since in that case our army will not have the honor of being represented by you.

From the clauses themselves of the agreement it can be seen that the unification would only go into effect if the buccaneers do not evacuate Nicaraguan territory. If they do evacuate, I would like to ask you to take steps with the Hands-Off-Nicaragua Committee of Mexico, D.F., and with other organizations that sympathize with our cause, in your role as my personal representative on the continent, so that I may be given the opportunity to remove myself with my general staff to a sister republic— Mexico, for example—for the purpose of supplying myself with *elements*, putting myself in better contact with the Nicaraguan people, and presenting a united front to the turncoat José María Moncada. These same activities will be worked upon by our special delegate, Dr. Mairena, before the same groups. From Mexico he will inform you of the results of the efforts leading to unification, and, given the opportunity, and in case the pirates evacuate the country, he will send you information about the efforts being made to effect my departure, with my general staff, in the manner I have stated.

For the best results of your efforts in regard to this final matter, I ask you to inform Dr. Mairena and Dr. Zepeda about what you are doing to make this effort more harmonious. From me you will receive the best possible information about all the work we are doing both inside and outside the Republic. I do not believe it would be excessive to inform you that if the buccaneers do not withdraw and the efforts toward unification do not succeed, because the groups in question do not respond to the call that I have made to them, I will continue with my army to fight the invaders and the sell-outs of their country. And furthermore, if the army itself should not want to pursue its liberating role, for any reason that it may deem valid, I will "go off on my own," firing off a shot at the buccaneers here, and another there, never giving them quarter. God is with us in these supreme hours, you have said, and this phrase that I daily repeat will take us to our final victory. With the affectionate greeting of the army, I have the honor to send you an expression of my admiring affection.

Your disciple.
Patria y Libertad.
A. C. SANDINO

[11, 109–10]

·1929·

76. REPLIES TO GENERAL LOGAN FELAND
AND ADMIRAL DAVID F. SELLERS,
JANUARY 1, 1929[1]

El Chipotón
Nicaragua, C.A.
January 1, 1929
General Headquarters of the Army in
Defense of National Sovereignty

Mr. Logan Feland, Brigadier General, U. S. Marine Corps, Commanding U. S. Naval
Forces, Ashore in Nicaragua, Managua

I hereby acknowledge receipt of your communication, and that of Rear
Admiral U.S. Navy Commander Special Service Squadron, D. F. Sellers,
sent to me by you and dated December 4 of last year in Managua and
Corinto respectively. Attached to the present letter you will find the reply
that I am giving to Mr. Sellers, and this reply will also serve as my response to your communication.

Patria y Libertad.

A. C. SANDINO

El Chipotón
Nicaragua
January 1, 1929
General Headquarters of the Army in
Defense of the National Sovereignty of
Nicaragua

Mr. D. F. Sellers, Rear Admiral U.S. Navy,
Commander Special Service Squadron
Corinto, Nicaragua, C.A.

Sir:

I have in my possession your communication, signed in that city
on December 4 of last year, in which you state that, although your
earlier attempts to communicate with me by peaceful means have
failed, you are again appealing to my patriotism in order that I might
end my armed resistance against the forces under your command,

who, at the bidding of the Nicaraguan government of the usurper Díaz, are attempting to restore order throughout the country.

The patriotism to which you appeal is the same that has sustained me in my efforts to repel force by force, while absolutely refusing to accept your government's meddling in the internal affairs of our country, and demonstrating that the sovereignty of a people will not be discussed, but rather defended with weapons in hand. And it is this same sentiment that today moves me to inform you that only with General José M. Moncada could I enter into an agreement to reach an effective peace in our country, since he, being a member of the Liberal party, which he betrayed, could rectify his errors through a commitment that he might agree to with us, on behalf of the Nicaraguan people and the Liberal party itself, to respect the conditions that at the proper opportunity will be proposed by our liberating army.[2] Based upon the above, I must explain to you that in order for us to arrive at an effective peace with the government of General José M. Moncada, our first and absolutely indispensable condition is the withdrawal from our territory of the North American forces under your command.

As to acceptance of this condition, you will begin by evacuating your forces from the four northern departments of our republic: Nueva Segovia, Jinotega, Estelí, and Matagalpa, Nicaraguan civil and military authorities being allowed to remain in those departments, but under no circumstances any commanding officer or subordinate personnel of the United States.

In the event of your acceptance, the peace conferences for arriving at an understanding with General José M. Moncada will take place in the town of San Rafael del Norte between five representatives of our army and five representatives of General Moncada. The five representatives of our army will travel under the guarantee of the Nicaraguan authorities, it being necessary, however, to point out that the individuals so commissioned will carry their own weapons.

In your reply you will inform us of the date for the evacuation of the said departments and the date you wish to designate for the beginning of the conferences.

Without the conditions referred to above, *there will be no peace*, and, though you say in your letter that the continuation of my armed resistance serves no purpose, I say to you that only the continuation of my armed resistance will bring the benefits to which you allude.

I do not deem it useless to inform you that foreign lives and properties will be better guaranteed by us, the people of Nicaragua, than by the forces of a foreign government, because all foreign meddling in our affairs will bring only the loss of peace and the anger of our people.

Patria y Libertad.

A. C. SANDINO

[11, 118–19; 19, 2 pp.]

1. On December 4, 1928, Brigadier General Logan Feland (USMC) sent a letter to Sandino asking for a conference to discuss proposals for returning the country to full peace, indicating that if the invitation were accepted, Sandino was to suggest the place, date, number of escorts, and route to follow, so that Sandino could be guaranteed protection through the suspension of military activities in a sufficiently large area. The letters of Sellers and Feland were included in the 1981 edition but are omitted here. The contents of Sellers's letter may be deduced from General Sandino's reply.

2. These conditions were subscribed to by Sandino on January 6, 1929 and correspond to Doc. 79 of the present edition.

77. LETTER TO JOSÉ MARÍA MONCADA, JANUARY 1, 1929[1]

El Chipotón
Nicaragua
January 1, 1929

General José María Moncada
Presidential House
Managua

Sir:

As you will see from the copy of the reply that I am giving to the messages that I have received from D. F. Sellers, Rear Admiral U.S. Navy, Commander Special Service Squadron, and Logan Feland, Brigadier General U.S. Marine Corps, Commanding U.S. Naval Forces Ashore Nicaragua, copies of which I also attach, it is solely with you that I wish to arrive at an understanding in order to obtain an effective peace in our internal affairs.

If you disregard this patriotic call which I am making, the responsibility for the Nicaraguan lives that are lost will rest on your shoulders.

The reply you give me in this respect, taking into account the formula of the reply that I am sending to the gentlemen alluded to, may be sent to me at San Rafael del Norte, where my wife, Blanca de Sandino, has instructions regarding the matter.

As I turn to you for the achievement of a settlement, do not make the mistake of regarding this as a sign of weakness on our part; what motivates us in this case is the hope that the Yankee does not find a pretext to trample upon our country's soil, and, at the same time, to prove to the civilized world that we Nicaraguans are capable by ourselves of arranging our internal affairs as a free and sovereign nation.

Patria y Libertad.
A. C. SANDINO

[19, 1 p.]

1. The text of this letter, taken from a copy in the IES archive, presents some differences from that published in the 1981 edition (253).

78. MANIFESTO TO THE NICARAGUAN LIBERALS, JANUARY 1, 1929

Coreligionists and companions:

I come before you after three years of intrepid struggle to invite you once again to continue the liberating action that our army has sustained since the treason that José María Moncada committed against our Liberal party, entering into agreements with the Yankee invaders on May 4, 1927. The result of that betrayal of the Liberal party by Moncada was that the Yankee invaders have imposed him as president of the Republic for the period from 1929 to 1932.

With Moncada's imposition it appears as if the Liberal party is willing to accept the sell-out of Nicaragua to the Yankees made by the Conservatives, but this is not true, because what distinguishes Liberals from Conservatives is that we Liberals have always opposed and will always continue to oppose the Yankee intervention, and we have condemned and will always condemn the selling of our country to the filibusters that has been carried out by the Conservatives.

The thrusting of Moncada, so often a traitor to our Liberal party, into the presidency of the Republic gives him the opportunity to satisfy his ambitions for personal profit. Proof of this is that on May 5, 1927, in La Cruz de Teustepe, Moncada told me in the presence of my general staff that I should not commit the insane act of sacrificing myself for the people, that the people are not grateful, that he was speaking from experience, that the duty of every man is to make money, to acquire comfort and personal well-being, without any concern for others, that life ends and the country remains, and it was for this reason that he felt no remorse when he sold his rifles at a moment when our cause had triumphed. This is Moncada; this is the traitor who makes promises to the people, and who calls himself a Liberal. If what Moncada said to me is not enough evidence to brand him as an opportunist, history shows that he has never been a Liberal. On several occasions he has stated that he is not a Liberal, that "Liberal" signifies robbery, assassination, infamy. It was he who as minister of the interior in 1910 ordered the machine-gunning of the people of León. As a result of this act by Moncada against the freedom of the people of León, the young Luis Somarriba died, clutching the Liberal banner, which he did not release from his grip until Moncada's myrmidons had cut off his hands with machetes. Moncada's whole life has been one of treachery toward our party, and to put things simply, Moncada is Adolfo Díaz himself with a red sash.

For the good of the country our army has preserved the honor and dignity of the nation and of the Liberal party in the face of the invaders, the Conservative sell-outs of their country, and the traitor José María Moncada.

Faced by the Yankee pirates' imposition of Moncada, we are ready to drive him from power with bullets, until we have again established our own national government. Like the Conservatives, Moncada will concern himself only with the Yankees' interests because they have given him power. The national government that we proclaim today will look out for the interests of the nation's sons, and not the interests of the pirates. We will not fire a single shot against Liberalism, and we do not think there is a Liberal who will fire upon us. We will use our weapons of liberation only against the traitor Moncada and against those who follow him, because they are not Liberals, but traitors to their country and to their party. Our weapons of liberation are ready to drive Moncada from the power that the invaders have given him as a reward for his treason. The traitor Moncada will not be able to resist our army's power, and he will not hesitate to ask for Yankee intervention. With everything I have said I have defined my position regarding the traitor Moncada, and that position will not change for as long as we do not see our nation free of invaders and sell-outs of their country.

El Chipotón, January 1, 1929
Patria y Libertad.
A. C. SANDINO

[19, 2 pp.]

79. PROPOSALS FOR AN AGREEMENT WITH JOSÉ MARÍA MONCADA, JANUARY 6, 1929

FUNDAMENTAL PRINCIPLES OF AN AGREEMENT PROPOSED TO GENERAL JOSÉ MARÍA MONCADA SO THAT HIS POSITION AS PRESIDENT OF THE REPUBLIC IN THE PERIOD FROM 1929 TO 1932 MAY CONFORM TO THE CONSTITUTION

General José María Moncada is not a constitutional ruler of Nicaragua, because when his election as president of our Republic took place, a large part of the Nicaraguan people were up in arms against the Yankee invasion of our country and against the usurper Adolfo Díaz. However, General José María Moncada could indeed become a constitutional leader by rendering himself accountable to the Nicaraguan people by means of a document, and to the liberating army by complying with the fundamental principles that this agreement outlines below. In this case General José María Moncada will be a constitutional ruler because the law will favor him for having obtained, because of his honesty and integrity, the votes of a large part of the Nicaraguans who found themselves with weapons in hand at the time the presidential election of the said General Moncada took place, repelling the Yankee invader and fighting the usurper Adolfo Díaz.

Without the acceptance of the fundamental principles of this agreement he will not be a ruler of the people of Nicaragua and so will in fact be disregarded.

The *fundamental principles* appearing below are those which a president of the Republic of Nicaragua who is elected by the people and for the people should regard as basic in his governmental program; in virtue of this, they are the same which the Army in Defense of the National Sovereignty of Nicaragua is offering through its supreme leader, who accepts them for the advancement of our country, so terribly scourged by the bad governments that have succeeded one another from 1909 until the present date; or, in other words, since the Wall Street bankers loaned $800,000—eight hundred thousand *dollars*—to Adolfo Díaz, so that he could overthrow the government of General José Santos Zelaya, constitutional president of Nicaragua in that epoch, such a loan being inadmissible because at that time that same Díaz was a simple bookkeeper, with a daily salary of $2.65—two pesos and sixty-five centavos—in the North American-owned mines of La Luz and Los Angeles, Pis-Pis, Atlantic Coast of Nicaragua, a man who could not have guaranteed a loan of that amount, and because it is not possible that that amount would have been loaned as a result of naiveté on the part of the mining company, or because of the great affection it felt for the renegade sell-out of his country, Adolfo Díaz.

It is well known that the rebellion against General José Santos Zelaya encouraged the treason of Juan J. Estrada, who at that time was governor of the department of Bluefields, and that that treason was committed by Estrada in connivance with Adolfo Díaz and Emiliano Chamorro.

In the same manner, it is known to the Nicaraguan people that the direct pressure of the government of the United States of America made itself felt in Nicaragua when President José Santos Zelaya ordered the execution of the Yankee adventurers, the one named Cannon, the other Groce, who had been paid by the leaders of the revolt to set off a bomb in the San Juan River against ships carrying the soldiers of President José Santos Zelaya.

The Nicaraguan people know that since that time Nicaragua has never had a constitutional government, and that all those who have thrust their way into national power were imposed by Yankee bayonets, with the exception of the free election carried out in the period of the honorable ex-President Bartolomé Martínez, as a result of which Carlos Solórzano and Dr. Juan Bautista Sacasa were elected president and vice president respectively; a constitutionality cut short by the famous *Lomazo*, carried out on October 24, 1925, by the spurious sons of Nicaragua, Emiliano Chamorro and Adolfo Díaz, which, we have no doubt, was in response to instructions of the same Yankee octopus.

Note that not even the presidency of Bartolomé Martinez was legal, but that he nevertheless supported a constitutional election.

In such a situation it is obvious that all the treaties, pacts, or conventions celebrated between the governments of the United States of America and the individuals imposed upon Nicaragua by those same governments, from 1909 until the present, possess no legality because they have not been recognized by the Nicaraguan people, and that they are indecent as well and therefore ought to be entirely nullified by a government that is of the people and is expected to defend the nation's interests.

With these basic considerations established, the fundamental principles that we propose are the following:

1. To demand of the government of the United States of America the immediate and total withdrawal of their invasion forces from our territory, and if to accomplish this it becomes necessary to use force, the gov-

ernment of Nicaragua that commits itself to follow these fundamental principles may rely in advance upon our brave and patriotic assistance.

2. Not to accept during his administration any Yankee loan, and if for the requirements of that administration a loan becomes necessary, it must be done through Nicaraguan capitalists, giving them the same rights that would be given to the Yankees, with the condition that the debt cannot be transferred to foreign capitalists.

3. *To consider null and void* the Chamorro-Bryan Treaty and any treaties, pacts, or conventions that have been celebrated by the governments that have held power from 1909 until the present date, which impair our national sovereignty.

4. To reject in a most manly fashion any interference that governments of the United States of America may wish to attempt in the internal and external affairs of our free people, and much less to allow those governments in the future to supervise presidential elections, or elections of any kind, since we ourselves are capable of carrying out free elections.

5. To recognize the status of "town" which we have granted to the place named San Juan de Segovia, with the boundaries that we have marked out, it having formerly been called Valle de San Juan de Telpaneca, this town having more than two thousand inhabitants and possessing its own economic life, producing within its jurisdiction more than fifteen thousand hundredweights of coffee.

6. That through the initiative of the executive before the national Congress the cultivation and sale of tobacco in the Republic be declared free, abolishing all laws obstructing that freedom, the government being allowed to collect moderate taxes on its cultivation, and with the right of exportation when production expands to the point that that product may be sent abroad with the likelihood of advancing the country. This proposal is being made in view of the fact that in the regions where our army has operated, the use of tobacco is indispensable to the inhabitants, owing to the climate and the harmful insects, and at the same time because the plant is nearly wild and so is one of the country's principal forms of natural wealth, which, if its cultivation and sale are declared free, will bring great benefits to the nation.

7. That through the initiative of the executive the national Congress issue laws dealing with labor accidents and a maximum of eight hours of work daily in industrial and agricultural enterprises belonging to both national and foreign owners, task-work excluded, such laws to be suitably regulated. By the law of the eight-hour day, overtime should be recognized in cases of more than eight hours of labor.

8. That through the initiative of the executive the national Congress issue the laws required so that industrial or agricultural enterprises, of either national or foreign ownership, will pay their workers in cash and not with "coupons" or "vouchers" or in any of the other ways that such

enterprises presently adopt; such payments should be made every ten days and not every two weeks or monthly, or after even longer periods of time.

9. That through the initiative of the executive the national Congress issue a law requiring industrial or agricultural enterprises, national or foreign, where more than fifteen workers or families are employed, to maintain schools at the expense of their owners, in which workers of both sexes will receive primary instruction.

10. That through the initiative of the executive the national Congress issue a law as a result of which the right of women to receive the same salary as men for equal work performed will be recognized, women's work being duly regulated in accordance with the particular physical condition of women.

11. That through the initiative of the executive the national Congress issue laws and regulations to regulate the labor of children in industrial and agricultural enterprises belonging to national or foreign owners, in such a way that the children may attend school and their work may be performed under moral and hygienic conditions.

12. That through the initiative of the executive the national Congress recognize the right of workers of both sexes to organize unions or any other kind of association, establishing a national department of labor, that is, an office to regulate relations between employers and workers; the same national Congress should recognize the right to strike of all workers, both industrial or agricultural, through the initiative of the executive himself.

13. That the first government of Nicaragua ever to be legal should not agree to pay one cent of the expenses that the government of the United States of America has incurred since its forces invaded our territory in a bellicose fashion, under the pretext of being summoned by the usurper Adolfo Díaz. Our nation is not required to expend its resources for the experiments with modern war machines that the U.S. government has ordered carried out against our courageous Nicaraguan patriots.

14. That the first Nicaraguan government that is of the people and for the people should deal at once with the matter of Central American union, with the obligation *to declare it and to proclaim it* if the chancelleries of the Central American states try to delay it with compendious expedients or the twisted nomenclature of diplomatic protocol; with all the power it possesses the government of Nicaragua should support this declaration and proclamation, effectively aiding those who advocate union, who in the respective Central American states have supported this initiative against their governments' opposition and all other opponents of the Great Ideal, these being not only the Central American who may oppose its realization, but also the foreigner who would like to continue

the separation, as more favorable to his way of thinking and his own interests.

The case of Nicaragua having been one of the many which have caused the Indo-Latin peoples to consider the need for establishing a united front against Yankee imperialism and possible acts of aggression on the part of some other imperialism, and our liberation army being that which, by its posture, has made that need imperative, the government that agrees to carry out these fundamental principles should, consecutively or simultaneously with its declaration of Central American union—whichever is more convenient—invite an assembly of representatives of the countries of Indo-Latin America, continental and Antillean, to take steps leading to a continental and Antillean Indo-Latin confederation, placing it on solid and immutable foundations, so that its system of governance and administration may be established straightforwardly upon those fundamental principles, and therefore easily carried out.

15. That the government of Nicaragua that accepts the fundamental principles of this agreement, numbers one through fourteen as well as this one, commits itself to provide the greatest guarantees to the campesinos in general of the departments of Nueva Segovia, Jinotega, Estelí, and Matagalpa, because they are the people who have made common cause with our army in defense of our national law.

We propose that the laws expressed in this document be issued, because some of them might have been issued in a similar form by earlier governments, but since those governments have changed the laws as they would change their shirt, the Nicaraguan people do not know which are the actual laws that govern them, since they are not enforced even if they do exist. Upon being issued, the laws that we propose should be rigorously enforced, because the Nicaraguan people do not need laws that exist only in the government's archives.

We have not seen the government program that General José María Moncada has offered to the Nicaraguan people, but we know that what is offered in it as attractive to our citizens is the construction of highways and railroads, which surely would not be of any importance to the Nicaraguan people, even if they were built, if their beneficiaries were to be only the foreign companies, the only real gainers from such constructions, because we are not unaware that the government of Nicaragua has pledged to the Yankees even the benches in our public buildings. What the Nicaraguan people need is to restore their rights lost from 1909 until the present.

The Nicaraguan people will not recognize any government of Nicaragua as legal, much less this one, if it continues to make itself the handservant of the government of the United States of America.

From what is contained in the fundamental principles in this document, it can be seen that there is not one that asks for amnesty for the members of the Army in Defense of the National Sovereignty of Nicaragua.

The reason for this is that no individual who has been called to government as was the usurper Adolfo Díaz can place "outside the law" the citizens who are defending the nation's honor, and if he did so at the request of the invaders, they had no right to label as "bandits" those of us who have known and will always know how to do our duty. As we understand it, *bandits* are those people who would like to deny us our rights as citizens of a free, sovereign, and independent nation.

Two broad solutions remain for General José María Moncada:

1. If General José María Moncada does not have secret pacts with the bankers of the United States of America and with Adolfo Díaz, he will not find it inconvenient to accept the fundamental principles of this agreement.

2. If General José María Moncada is not prepared to sacrifice his life, as he told me in La Cruz de Teustepe, to restore the rights that have been taken from the Nicaraguan people from 1909 until the present date, he should renounce the position he now holds in favor of a citizen whom he regards as capable of sacrificing himself for Nicaragua.

If these fundamental principles should be accepted in all their points, the weapons of the army of liberation will be set aside, in the manner agreed to in the conferences, and after this document is signed by the representatives of General José María Moncada, it will be turned over to the Nicaraguan people in an appropriate manner. Then this ex-leader of the army of liberation will withdraw to some region of our republic to dedicate himself to work in the fields.

Las Segovias, General Headquarters El Chipotón, Nicaragua, Central America, the sixth of January of nineteen hundred and twenty-nine.

Patria y Libertad.
AUGUSTO CÉSAR SANDINO

[19, 5 pp.]

80. LETTER TO THE PRESIDENT OF MEXICO, EMILIO PORTES GIL, JANUARY 6, 1929

El Chipotón
Nicaragua, C.A.
January 6, 1929

Señor licenciado Emilio Portes Gil
Provisional President of the United States of Mexico
Mexico, D.F.

My dear sir:

With the assurance derived from the fact that you are the representative of the heroic and virile Mexican people, I do not hesitate to solicit from your government the needed protection to obtain and enjoy the high honor of being accepted with my general staff in the midst of your exemplary people.

It is not possible to state in writing the far-reaching projects contained in my imagination for the guarantee of the future of our great Latin America.

Captain José de Paredes, the bearer of this letter, will reveal to you verbally, in part, the present political situation in Nicaragua, along with our calculations. The same young captain will be able to explain to you in what form we wish to have the support of your government.

In the hope of greeting you personally, with the aid of your treasured cooperation, and offering you my gratitude in advance, I have the honor to attest that I am your attentive and reliable servant.

Patria y Libertad.
A. C. SANDINO.

[11, p. 122]

81. LETTER TO FROYLÁN TURCIOS, JANUARY 7, 1929[1]

General Headquarters of the Army in
Defense of the National Sovereignty of
Nicaragua
January 7, 1929

Señor Froylán Turcios
Tegucigalpa, Honduras

I am in possession of your note dated in that city on the 28th of last December, in which you are pleased to present to this Supreme Headquarters your resignation as the representative of our army on the continent.

On this date I have the honor of informing you that that resignation has been accepted, and simultaneously to state that you are prohibited from negotiating with the army's documents that you have in your possession, of which you will give the necessary account to the agent whom this general command will appoint for that purpose.

Meanwhile, communications from you are not desired in this camp. When I look upon cases like yours, I am reminded of Diogenes, the philosopher. You forgot that the puppets are in the bazaars, and that those who fight in the Segovias have their own ideas.

Please communicate this arrangement by radio to the press of the world.

Patria y Libertad.
AUGUSTO C. SANDINO

LETTER OF FROYLÁN TURCIOS TO GENERAL SANDINO

Tegucigalpa
December 28, 1928

General A. C. Sandino
Wherever he may be

My dear friend:

Yesterday I belatedly received your letter of the 18th of this month, and after again and again reading the part that refers to the grave point that sums up the liberation struggle, I have become entirely convinced that calamity looms over our cause, and that with the new ideology that you present to me, you are taking rapid steps toward your certain failure.

I gave my greatest efforts to this magnificent campaign, and I was determined to offer my blood for it. For the war of independence that you are leading there is no sacrifice I wouldn't make. But I understand that now we are no longer in agreement about the ends to be pursued in the struggle, which as I see it no longer tends to retain the single pursuit of sovereignty in your action against the pirate, but rather now seeks to find ways to change an internal political regime, using civil war to attain this end, and upon this road I cannot follow you.

If you persist in the plan that today you affirm to me, we will separate like two brothers who cannot understand each other.

In my letter of the 17th of this month, which by this time should be in your hands, I clearly expressed my opinion, taking the points of your last letter into account.

I am and will continue to be with you in body and soul, in the epic endeavor to cast out the Yankee, the invader and conqueror of Nicaragua: but never to carry out fratricidal struggles, though these may have the most justified reasons as their foundation.

You may be certain—and do not forget my words—that the Yankee will never leave your country by a decision of the northern government of imperialism or the traitorous governments of Nicaragua. He will only leave under fire, through the superhuman perseverance of Sandino, and this enterprise of titans was the one that God entrusted to you. And no other. To plan projects of a regional order, for the fantastic purpose of compelling the pirates to withdraw, is to build castles in air and to diminish your legendary epic. Your name is blessed and admired in every corner of the world, because you sustain a war like that of Bolívar and Washington; because, being the brilliant champion of liberty, you are the symbol of the race[. . . .]

But I see that I am tragically mistaken to think that you would pay any attention to me, or that I could achieve anything by writing pages and pages to you about this. You have made your decision, and my voice will be useless. Your *teacher*, as you call me, no longer has any influence over your soul.

I only beg you to send me the form that I should use to make my separation from you known to America, because I would never forgive myself if in my explanation there were one word which didn't please you.

I was determined not to leave this country as long as I could be useful to you, but I understand that my presence here will not serve you in any way, and that on the contrary I am an obstacle to your plans.

An intense salute to the Sacred Legion.
Patria y Libertad.
FROYLÁN TURCIOS

[11, 114–16]

1. For a better understanding of the position Sandino adopts in this letter, the message Turcios sent to Sandino on December 28, 1928 is also reproduced here.

82. REPRESENTATION TO
THE HANDS-OFF-NICARAGUA COMMITTEE,
JANUARY 18, 1929

General Headquarters of the Army in
Defense of the National Sovereignty of
Nicaragua

The undersigned, General and supreme leader of the Army in Defense of the National Sovereignty of Nicaragua, using the powers conferred by that same army, considering that Señor Froylán Turcios presented to this general command his resignation as general representative of our army on the continent, which was accepted on the 7th of the present month, agrees:

To confide that general representation on the continent to the Hands-Off-Nicaragua Committee, with its headquarters in Mexico, D.F., empowering that same committee to appoint the representatives it deems necessary to the world in general, but always in a collective character, like that which is conferred upon itself, to prevent a monopolization of the notices coming from our General Headquarters, it being so vital to our cause that this information be known by the civilized world.

El Chipotón, Nicaragua, Central America, the eighteenth of February of nineteen hundred and twenty-nine and seventeenth year of the anti-imperialist struggle in Nicaragua.

Patria y Libertad.
AUGUSTO CÉSAR SANDINO

[19, 1 p.]

83. THE BATTLE OF GUANACASTE
OF JANUARY 1929

Sixty-two horses and twenty-eight mules were counted as dead, and two enemy machine guns were completely destroyed by our bombs.

On the now-famous tree of Guanacaste, site of the battle on a precious little stretch of sandy ground, were found bits of brain and intestines of one of the buccaneer artillerymen who waged the most intense resistance sheltered by the base of the tree.

Included among the captured items were two deteriorated mountain cannon, one hundred and eighteen saddle mounts, one hundred and eighteen coats, one hundred and eighteen cashmere blankets, one hundred and eighteen knapsacks with many useful items, sixty Lewis rifles, forty-six Springfield rifles with a great deal of ammunition, forty hand grenades, twelve Lewis magazines, two Thompson magazines, four automatic rifle magazines, nine 45-caliber pistols, two hundred Thompson rounds, six boxes of ammunition for the cannon, each containing twelve shells, and many insignias attached to the clothing of the pirate soldiers of Wall Street, among them two for captains, one for a second lieutenant, and one for a sergeant. All the insignias taken from the hats of the dead filled up a small half-*arroba* flour sack and weigh seven pounds, five ounces. The insignias are those of bronze that represent the Yankee eagle and the America that loves to devour.

Those who distinguished themselves in the battle: first of all, the seventeen-year-old soldier José Santos López, the sergeant, also seventeen, José Luis Mariona, bugler of the column and formerly of the Salvadoran army and of Salvadoran nationality. It is worth observing that Mariona grappled hand to hand in a continuous action with two enemy soldiers until he defeated them, then continued fighting with weapons seized by his own hands. For this action Captain Arturo Fernández, a Guatemalan, will be promoted in the order of the day.

Also fighting brilliantly were Sergeant Major Desiderio Aguilera and the fourteen-year-old soldier Ricardo Obando, the soldier Aquilino López, Lieutenant Gregorio S. López, and the soldiers Valentín Múñoz, José María Paz, and Toribio Sánchez, who was the one who opened fire and destroyed by means of a bomb the enemy's largest cannon. Information is expected from the other columns, which will be made known when opportunity permits.

With such a brilliant victory our liberation army has begun its struggle in the new year against the enemies of the peoples' freedom.

General Headquarters of El Chipotón, Nicaragua, Central America, January 18, 1929, Seventeenth Year of the Anti-Imperialist Struggle in Nicaragua.

Patria y Libertad.
AUGUSTO CÉSAR SANDINO

[19, 1 p.]

84. A DENIAL, FEBRUARY 24, 1929

For the honored press of the world in general:

The surprising news has reached our camp that General José María Moncada, current agent of the Wall Street bankers in Nicaragua, imposed by Yankee bayonets, has resorted to a most outrageous lie. He has altered the meaning of the note sent to him last January 1 by this Supreme Command of the Army of Liberation, which, as the world now knows, limited itself to informing General Moncada that only with him, without the involvement of Yankee intermediaries, were we prepared to make agreements, by virtue of the compact that he was to make with the Nicaraguan people in the presence of our army and the Liberal party, to respect the fundamental principles to be proposed to him in conferences that would take place in San Rafael del Norte.[1]

The fundamental principles referred to are absolutely unknown to anybody, because they remain in our General Headquarters and will continue to remain there as long as this supreme command does not make some other arrangement.

Thus General Moncada lied in a stupid and vicious way when he said that we proposed to him the division of Nicaragua into two parts: one governed by me and the other by him. There is no one who will believe this.[2]

It is well known to the civilized world that I fervently wish that not only Central America should be unified morally and materially for its defense against Yankee imperialism, but also continental and West Indian America, and so I could not possibly consider breaking up Nicaragua, and, though our position is known abroad, I think it is useful to make these statements, because in this way they will become known to the Nicaraguan people, who are kept in the dark by the mercenary press of Nicaragua about events in our own country.

Upon releasing that base, dirty, and cynical lie, to charm the people General Moncada declares that this is "an insane thing to do" and a "betrayal of the fatherland of our elders." The insanity and betrayal to which he alludes are his, since I would be incapable of such a crime.

Nobody would resort to such measures except someone hoping to confuse the Nicaraguan people, to the benefit of the masters who have granted him power in our country: the slave carrying out the instructions that those same masters have given him. This is the puppet the Nicaraguan people have as their president, and the lowness of his acts should make our fellow citizens understand how much more he may yet be capable of, this man who has recourse to measures unworthy of an honorable person, and much more so from one who calls himself president of the Republic.

As a reward to the people who helped him in other times, General Moncada has ordered the bombing and strafing of the peaceful inhabitants of our Segovian mountains in these first months of his administration. Anyone who would like to convince himself of the savagery of General Moncada and of his masters, the Yankee pirates, could at this moment approach the Honduran border through which caravans of Nicaraguan campesino families are passing, dragging their misery along with them, fleeing the bombings and strafings inflicted by the pirate aviators with the same hatred as ever for the Nicaraguan people. Those who approach them may witness scenes of great sorrow in which elderly people, children and women, some of them sick, hungry and clad in rags, in the greatest state of desperation before the inhumanity of the cruel underling Moncada and the buccaneers whom he serves. Hundreds of campesinos, unable to endure the fatigue of the road because of poor health, have died on the trails that lead from the Segovias to Honduras.

The Yankee pirates took a deep plunge when they intruded into the internal affairs of our nation, and today, having no decent way out, they make Moncada attribute ideas to me that I am far from imagining, in order to supply themselves with a pretext for staying in Nicaragua.

They see me as a little enemy and they never believed that in the land where there are some who lick their feet there are also some who could spit upon them and slap them in the face. We have buried many thousands of pirates in our mountains and there are many more for us to kill.

For the forces newly enlisted by Moncada I also have some new plans. I am prepared to tire them out, and when they have exhausted their resources and their physical powers, they will surely be demoralized as well, and then I will attack them with greater force than ever before. The war will continue for as long as invading forces tread upon our land.

I have said countless times that I will not rest as long as the buccaneers are in Nicaragua, and in respect to General Moncada, who resorts to the bloodiest lies to make an exhibit of me before the Nicaraguan people and the civilized world, I understand that he does this because as a pirate he fears me. And that fear is justified, because sooner or later he will fall into my hands so that I may bring him to justice.

General Headquarters El Chipotón, Nicaragua, C.A.
February 24, 1929
Patria y Libertad.
A. C. SANDINO

[19, 3 pp.]

1. See Doc. 77.
2. Soon after taking office as president, Moncada issued a proclamation that in effect accused Sandino of wanting to divide the national territory. The full text of that proclamation, in which a summons is also made to those who might wish to enlist "voluntarily" in the fight against Sandino, appears in 11, 123.

85. A SEGOVIAN ANECDOTE[1]

For the honored press of the world in general:

The day dawns brightly. The mountains seem bluer than at other times, with the rays of the sun that bathe them. The calendar marks January 15, 1929. My watch tells me it is twenty minutes past nine in the morning. The airplanes are discovering the dry hills of El Pedregal.

"Tell the committee leaders who are about to leave to stay where they are for a moment so we can observe the planes that we can hear out there, because we shouldn't let them discover us." This was my order to one of my aides.

El Pedregal is two kilometers north of my encampment. Today the airplanes are launching a major bombing and strafing attack.

"Four planes have arrived three times today at those places," said one of the muchachos.

"I managed to count fifty-four bomb explosions," said another, "and forty flashes from the machine guns, but later I went to bathe your mule, and I confused the count."

"General, it is three in the afternoon," my aide Alejandro told me. "The committee has left to carry out your new order. If you request it, I can go to see what that flotilla of airplanes was shooting at so much today."

"Go on, then," I replied, "have a look and let me know what you see."

"I'm back, my general. Nobody does more ridiculous things than those damned Yankees."

"What did you find out?" I asked him.

"Well, really nothing, sir. They saw a grizzled old mare that because of its age and poor condition had been abandoned. The whole hill is pitted by bombs and bullets from the airplanes, and the poor guys didn't even touch the animal. I took her over to the other side of the hill, because she was black from so much smoke and might have gotten sick from it."

It seems unbelievable that wherever the pirates go in the Segovias they provide an opportunity to make themselves appear ridiculous, and to show themselves to the civilized world as incompetent soldiers and boasters of a prestige they don't possess. I have heard reports, constantly told to me, that North American soldiers are good for carrying out mock battles on July 4, the anniversary of their independence, or at other exhibitions or festivals. It may be that they do this because they are eager to terrorize with noise the nations that have fewer resources than they have.

They say they put an orange on a man's head and shoot at it from a certain distance, piercing the orange without touching the man. But the calm they demonstrate at those times isn't easily maintained in the Segovias. Here I don't have men with oranges on their heads.

Many thousands of Yankee pirates are buried in our virgin mountains. In other times when they killed a Yankee in our country they brought him back weighted down with gold, but today we kill thousands, and instead of bringing them back the people hide them.

General Headquarters El Chipotón, Nicaragua, Central America, March 4, 1929, and Seventeenth Year of the Anti-Imperialist Struggle in Nicaragua.

Patria y Libertad.
A. C. SANDINO

[10, 67–68]

1. Sandino sent this document along with Doc. 86 to the Mexico City newspaper, *El Universal*.

86. AN OPEN LETTER TO
PRESIDENT HERBERT HOOVER,
MARCH 6, 1929

To Herbert Clark Hoover
President of the United States of America

Sir:

I am pleased to inform you that through the efforts of our soldiers we have managed to remove from action the ex-leader of the United States, Calvin Coolidge, and his secretary of state, Frank B. Kellogg. This is the pair of insolent individuals who brazenly ordered the massacre of my countrymen, desolating our fields with fire, violating our women, and pretending to deny us our sacred rights to freedom.

As always our army of liberation is firm and victorious and eagerly awaits the orientation that you will give to the macabre and conspiratorial policy that Coolidge and Kellogg left behind them in Nicaragua. We wish to inform you as well that we are ready to punish implacably every abuse of the United States of America in the affairs of our country.

Nicaragua does not owe a single penny to the United States, but you owe us the peace lost in our country since 1909, when the Wall Street bankers introduced the corrupting vice of the dollar in Nicaragua. For every thousand dollars that the Yankee bankers have introduced into my country, a Nicaraguan has died, and our mothers, sisters, wives, and sons have shed tears of sorrow.

In August, 1909, the spurious Adolfo Díaz was a simple fourth-class employee with a daily salary of $2.65—two dollars and sixty-five cents—at the North American mining company La Luz and Los Angeles, located in Pis-Pis, the department of Bluefields, the Atlantic coast of Nicaragua. From that mine Adolfo Díaz was taken to be the instrument in Nicaragua of the Wall Street bankers, who encouraged him to join the rebellion that had begun with the treason of Juan J. Estrada against the constitutional government. At that time Juan J. Estrada held the post of governor of Bluefields.

The Wall Street bankers supplied $800,000—eight hundred thousand dollars—to Adolfo Díaz for the support of that unfortunate rebellion, and since that tragic moment mourning and grief have spread across my country. If all the blood spilled and all the Nicaraguan corpses produced by Wall Street dollars from that time until the present could be brought together in one place, so that on July 4 the U.S. imperialists in Washington and New York could consume those corpses and drink the blood of my compatriots, together they could not eat and drink everything on that holiday on which the independence of the United States is celebrated. All Nicaraguans are fully aware of the truth of the words I have expressed.

The Wall Street bankers with their high and mighty dollar looked upon Adolfo Díaz and other corrupt Nicaraguans as instruments that they themselves created to make Nicaragua accept loans which we did not need. Those bankers chose those corrupt turncoats to give an appearance of legality to the treaties and pacts that would allow them to take possession of Nicaragua. The Yankee pirates understood that the vast majority of the Nicaraguan people angrily rejected the treaties and pacts celebrated between the bankers and some four Nicaraguan sell-outs. This recognition has caused the U.S. government to employ every trick to keep in power in our country the Nicaraguans who offered themselves as their hand-servants to wield power over their own brothers.

For this reason in 1923, at the behest of the Yankee government, the Central American governments celebrated treaties aboard the United States cruiser *Tacoma* in the Gulf of Fonseca, and the same Yankee government proposed the terms to be agreed to by those governments. Among the terms of those treaties, it was established that no government of Central America coming to power through a coup d'état was to be recognized by the other Central American governments, or by the government of the United States.

What the Yankees hoped to achieve by this was to secure power to those persons who had sold them Nicaragua's sovereignty, because the treaties they had made with the sell-outs were to last for *ninety-nine* years and could be prolonged at the will of the United States. At that time the Wall Street bankers saw themselves as lords and masters of Nicaragua. They knelt down before their strong boxes full of metal, their hands and eyes lifted toward heaven, giving thanks to the god *Gold* for the great miracle he had granted them (the accursed dollar, the wood-borer that weakens the foundations of Yankee imperialism, and will cause its downfall)!

Rejoicing in the same manner were the hypocritical Nicaraguan sell-outs who were kept in power at that time, as they are today, with the support of Yankee bayonets.

Divine Justice brought an end to the life of Don Diego Manuel Chamorro, president of Nicaragua at the time the *Tacoma* treaties were agreed to. The Nicaraguan people, who had thought their right to freedom had been forever lost, saw an improvement in the prospects for Nicaraguan sovereignty with the death of Diego Manuel Chamorro. The citizen Bartolomé Martínez assumed the presidency and supported a just and honorable election, as a result of which Carlos Sólorzano and Dr. Juan Bautista Sacasa were elected president and vice president respectively, assuming the duties granted to them by the Nicaraguan people.

Too much pride disturbed the hearts of the ex-president of the United States, Calvin Coolidge, and of the secretary of state, Frank B. Kellogg, when they saw that justice had placed itself on the side of our people; an *evil purpose* disturbed the minds of Adolfo Díaz, Emiliano Chamorro, and their followers, and thus it was that on the night of October 24, 1925, they carried out their famous *Lomazo*, now well known to the civilized world.[1]

They then demanded that Don Carlos renounce the presidency of the Republic, declaring him insane. They disavowed the legality of Dr. Sacasa's vice presidency, persecuted him, and forced him to leave the country.

Chamorro made himself president of Nicaragua. The United States of America, making a display of political decency for the civilized world, did not recognize Chamorro. Instead, however, it recognized his accomplice, Adolfo Díaz. There is no doubt in our minds that all of this was the work of Coolidge and Kellogg, responding to the orders of Wall Street.

Mr. Hoover: If you have eyes to see, see. If you have ears to hear, hear. Consider, if not yourself, the people you represent.

Coolidge and Kellogg are two North American politicians whose policies have come to naught. Their activities in Nicaragua have brought an enormous loss of prestige to the land of Washington. They have caused torrents of blood and tears to flow in my country, and they have brought sorrow and tears to many American homes. With a tiny bit of intelligence on their part, none of this would have happened, and the United States would have continued to conceal the true nature of its policies. Today the democracy of the United States finds itself at the edge of an abyss, and either you can stop it or you can push it over. Your government's acts are now a matter of life or death for your country.

Until six years ago you had been able to maintain *an appearance of legality* in your treaties and in your intrusions into Nicaragua, but after the death of Don Diego Manuel Chamorro, our good friend Fate unmasked the Yankee policy in my country.

By the actions that kept Coolidge and Kellogg in my country, they have produced an enormous wave of hatred and distrust for you which is almost worldwide in scope. In Nicaragua you have no friends except a small group of evil men who do not represent the genuine feelings of the Nicaraguan people. I, on the other hand, represent with my army the true feelings of our countrymen. Though they have not taken up a rifle in my army, the vast majority of Nicaraguans are with me in spirit.

I am not unaware of the material resources that your nation has at its disposal. In fact, you have everything, but "what you lack is *God*."[2]

Among those who were intimidated in Tipitapa on May 4, 1927, only the spiteful, the weak, and the irresolute allowed themselves to be humiliated by the noisy demands of Yankee power. Dr. Sacasa was the man whose task it was to reject Coolidge's abuses against Nicaragua's sovereignty with force, but he failed to do so. He was afraid, and so you have him there, humiliated and down on his knees before you.[3]

Perhaps you are mistaken when you think that you will humiliate everybody, as you did Sacasa. As long as you continue the policies of Coolidge and Kellogg, you will continue encountering Sandinos.

It must be seen that there exists a divine breath of justice that sustains us but is a tempest for those who would perform evil acts.

It is upon reason, justice, and right that I have made my stand in opposition to the policies that you have unleashed against my country.

Patria y Libertad.
AUGUSTO CÉSAR SANDINO

[19, 4 pp.]

1. In fact, the *Lomazo*, the seizure of La Loma Fortress in Managua, occurred on October 25.

2. This is a paraphrased quotation from the last line of the poem "Oda a Roosevelt" (Ode to Roosevelt) by the major Nicaraguan poet, Rubén Darío (1867–1916): "Y, pues contáis todo, falta una cosa: ¡Dios!" (You can count on everything, but you lack one thing: God). RC

3. After a period of protest and indecision about the agreement made at Tipitapa, Sacasa had agreed to become Moncada's minister in Washington. RC

87. A SEGOVIAN STORY,
MARCH 10, 1929

For the children and young people of Latin America, both Continental and West Indian:

A thousand years ago two men came into the world. They were from the same country, but they didn't know each other. In their childhood the two enjoyed the opportunity to live in comfort.

The one had a calm and perceptive personality. He liked to suffer for the good of others. The other was evil, a hoarder of money, contemptuous of his brothers but generous with those who were alien to his race.

The latter in his eagerness to store up wealth made an alliance with his brothers' enemies in order to kill them and to take possession of their properties after their deaths.

One of them was named Rin and the other Roff.

Rin dedicated the greater part of his life to preaching morality and patriotism to his fellow-citizens, whereas Roff frequented banquets and dances, constructed palaces by the dozen, and eventually possessed more than a thousand of them, all built of marble and gold.

Despite his wealth, Roff was not satisfied, and so he decided that he might increase his money by selling his country. For this purpose he used some tricks. He traveled to a faraway kingdom and offered to sell his country to the king, telling him that it was a great farm that belonged to him, that it was for sale, and that the people who lived there were his slaves.

The king bought his country, not because he believed what Roff had told him, but because it was a useful way to expand his dominions. When the king went to receive his new property, which he had purchased along with everything in it, the people were surprised by Roff's shameful behavior, but more still by the buyer's contempt for them.

The people of the country rose up in arms against those who would deprive them of their rights as free men, and they fought desperately for twenty years because the king was very powerful. But in the end they were victorious, regaining their independence. So much blood was spilled in that terrible war that it never went away, but stayed forever fresh.

The inhabitants of that country wanted coming generations to know what had happened in their land, so they collected the spilled blood and with it they filled up, one by one, the castles of Roff. And when they had finished filling up the last of them, all the castles collapsed at the same moment and the places where they had been built were turned into seas of blood.

Rin was one of those men who defended freedom, and he made the people understand that they were citizens, and not animals to be parceled out and sold.

And yet, during the war that had been fought to establish justice, some persons had abandoned their camps to offer their services to the king, humbly accepting the mark of slavery that was branded on their faces.

They renounced their status as men.

After the war that had been won for the sake of freedom, the years passed, and Rin died, murdered by one of those who preferred to be a slave, a man whom Rin had criticized to his face for such a wicked desire.

Roff continued to live for many years in the midst of dances and banquets. Although his castles had been doused in a sea of blood, his seat of power was now a city of many millions.

But he became ill with leprosy, and his tongue became infested with worms. The people regarded him as filthy, and he was thrown out of all the towns. No one went near him again, and the man who had sold his country died of hunger and thirst among the crows, and it was never known what became of his remains.

•

For a long span of time the people remembered the twenty-year war. The generations that followed cursed the enemies of freedom and blessed those who had defended it and achieved its triumph.

The curses were disappearing but the blessings remained. The new generations, every day more zealous in defense of their freedom, prepared to defend it, and today that nation is one of the most admirable in the entire world.

•

A thousand years have passed, and neither Rin nor Roff now lives. The sea of blood (History) remains, always fresh as an example to all the ages.

Rin took his riches with him because he kept them in his heart. Roff could not take them with him, because his wealth was of a very heavy kind.

Search in Latin America, continental and West Indian, and if in any of those countries you should find a new Roff, search, I implore you, until you have found a new Rin.

•

And now that my story is finished, I will deliver to you another fantastic revelation: the thirty pieces of silver of Judas, the man who betrayed Christ, about whom you must have heard people speak, exist today as they did then, marvelously reproduced in the strong boxes of Wall Street's bankers.

And for this reason, my little friends, I beg you with all my heart that when you have grown to manhood you must not permit or accept any loans from the United States of America.

Because behind every dollar a Yankee soldier marches, armed to the teeth, as dangerous as a wolf that is eager to swallow you up. And woe unto the country that accepts or requests the aid of their accursed thirty pieces of silver!

If by chance you do not find in my words enough moral force, ask your parents. They, who know, will speak for me.

General Headquarters
El Chipotón
Nicaragua, C.A.
March 10, 1929
Patria y Libertad.
A. C. SANDINO

[19, 4 pp.]

88. LETTER TO THE CENTRAL AMERICAN PRESIDENTS, MARCH 12, 1929

El Chipotón
Nicaragua, C.A.
March 12, 1929[1]

My dear sir:

With my great desire to achieve the liberation of my country I am impelled to address the four governments that still remain in Central America. In the same form in which I have the honor of writing to you today, I am also writing to the other three. Not being able to approach you personally, I do so symbolically. Enclosed you will find a leaf from the Segovian forests where Nicaragua's honor still resists. The name of the tree it comes from is *palanca*, lever. At this moment Nicaragua has a lever like that which Archimedes had, and it needs a fulcrum just as he did.

I ask you to consult with your people as to whether the fulcrum for which this portion of the great fatherland is searching through me may exist in your country. Archimedes could turn the world upside down; we together could stop being humiliated by the Yankee. If Nicaragua finds in your brother-nation the fulcrum it is searching for, perhaps this note will attain a place in your history.

With my best wishes for the collective progress of Central America during your term in office, I am your most affectionate servant.

Patria y Libertad.
AUGUSTO CÉSAR SANDINO

[19, 1 p.]

1. The Central American presidents to whom General Sandino sent this letter are Vicente Mejía Colindres (Honduras), Pío Romero Bosque (El Salvador), Lázaro Chacón (Guatemala), and Cleto González Víquez (Costa Rica).

89. DECLARATIONS TO THE WORLD PRESS, MARCH 18, 1929

DECLARATIONS TO THE WORLD PRESS OF THE SUPREME
COMMAND OF THE ARMY IN DEFENSE OF THE NATIONAL
SOVEREIGNTY OF NICARAGUA

Taking into account the statements made by Moncada and the Yankee pirates who are trampling our country under foot, to the effect that they will take the offensive against our army of liberation, we have decided to assume a defensive posture and to attack only when that will be to our advantage.

We understand that the enemy is taking the offensive because he hopes to cause us serious problems during the remaining month and a half of summer.[1] When the first rains start in the coming winter, we will take the offensive, and we will give new lessons to the assassins of freedom.

We are preparing a new type of incendiary bomb made of various ingredients, which, after they explode, allow them to keep on burning for fifteen minutes, and with them we will burn down the barracks in the towns where the blond beasts are corralled.

The Segovian Forests, El Chipotón, C.A.
March 18, 1929
Patria y Libertad.
AUGUSTO CÉSAR SANDINO

[19, 1 p.]

---

1. In Central America *summer* may refer to the dry season and *winter* to the rainy season.
RC

90. A LETTER TO THE LEADERS
OF THE AMERICAS: PROPOSAL FOR
A CONTINENTAL CONGRESS,
MARCH 20, 1929[1]

Las Segovias, El Chipotón,
Nicaragua, C.A.
March 20, 1929
General Headquarters of the Army in
Defense of the National Sovereignty of
Nicaragua

To the President of the United States of Mexico
Mexico, D.F.

My dear sir:

In the name of the Army in Defense of the National Sovereignty of Nicaragua, and of myself, I am privileged to inform you that our army will have the honor to propose to the Latin America governments, continental and West Indian, as well as to that of the United States, the holding of a conference in the capital city of the Argentine Republic, between representatives of the respective American governments and myself, representing our autonomist army.

For the same purpose I am writing today to the governments of Guatemala, El Salvador, Honduras, Costa Rica, Panama, Colombia, Venezuela, Ecuador, Peru, Brazil, Bolivia, Paraguay, Uruguay, Chile, Argentina, Cuba, the Dominican Republic, Haiti, Puerto Rico, and the United States of America.

As I have said, Nicaragua will be represented by myself, and separately by representatives of the government of our Republic that the governments of the Americas now recognize, if it agrees to accept the invitation.

The purpose of the conference will be to present an original project from our army, which, if it should go into effect, will assure the sovereignty and independence of our twenty-one Indo-Hispanic republics and friendship between the America of our race and the United States of America, upon a basis of equality.

The project to be presented by our army through me will be a test of the right of the Indo-Hispanic peoples to express their opinion regarding the freedom and independence of the Latin American republics, which today suffer intervention from the United States; it will consider as well the magnificent natural advantages with which God has endowed these countries, and which are the reason for the attempts to oppress them.

This project will also deal with matters relating to the construction of Nicaragua's interoceanic canal. It was written in the destiny of our peoples that our humble and outraged Nicaragua was to be the country chosen to summon us to unity with a brotherly embrace. She is the one who has sacrificed herself and would gladly give all she has if by this means she might achieve the freedom and absolute independence of our Latin American nations, both continental and West Indian.

Our project is conceived in such a way that Nicaragua will not sell her right to the interoceanic canal that is to be constructed in our territory. The Nicaraguan canal should be opened in order to advance our civilization, but this cannot be undertaken by Nicaragua and the United States alone, because a work of this kind is of far-reaching importance to the people of the entire globe. To carry out such a project all of our America, continental and West Indian, needs to be consulted, because the America of our race is also advancing in industry and commerce. We cannot deny to ninety million Latin Americans their right to express an opinion regarding the circumstances in which the Nicaraguan canal should be constructed. Our Indo-Hispanic America already committed its first mistake not to have been consulted about the opening of the Panama Canal, but we can avoid yet another mistake in regard to the Nicaraguan canal.

At the conference to which we are inviting all the American governments, we will consider whether or not it would be desirable for American capital to construct the Nicaraguan canal alone. If the conference should decide to grant this privilege to the United States, in return for that privilege the United States must sign a solemn pledge in the presence of the representatives of the twenty-one Latin American republics that it will terminate every North American intervention in our republics and cease all meddling in their internal affairs, committing itself as well not to foment rebellions against the governments of Latin America, continental and West Indian, which do not wish to become hand-servants of governments of the United States of America. With a pledge of that kind we can avoid the contagion of servility in our governments and at last will become free, sovereign, and independent.

If we should allow the United States to construct our Nicaraguan canal without pledging to respect the sovereignty and independence of our nations, we would be doing a disservice even to the United States. Possessing the Nicaraguan canal they would feel more powerful than God Himself and so would defy the entire world, which would bring as its consequence the destruction of that great North American nation.

Mr. President, it will be a great honor for me if your government accepts the invitation that our army is making to you today to appoint representatives to the conference that we are proposing, communicating this by radiogram to your representative in the Republic of Honduras, so that he may notify the special mail service of our army, which will be quickly informed of your government's decision.

If we should have the honor of your government's attendance at that conference, I am happy to inform you that the president of the Argentine Republic, the citizen Hipólito Irigoyen, will notify you of the date on which the meeting will take place, our army's delegation having conferred upon him the task of fixing that date and of notifying the American governments. I have the honor to be the affectionate and obedient servant of yourself and of the Mexican people.

Patria y Libertad.
A. C. SANDINO

[19, 2 pp.]

1. This letter was sent to all the governments of Latin America and to that of the United States. RC

91. PLAN FOR THE REALIZATION
OF BOLÍVAR'S HIGHEST DREAM,
MARCH 20, 1929

ORIGINAL PROJECT THAT THE ARMY IN DEFENSE OF THE
NATIONAL SOVEREIGNTY OF NICARAGUA PRESENTS TO THE
REPRESENTATIVES OF THE GOVERNMENTS OF THE TWENTY-ONE
LATIN AMERICAN STATES

PREAMBLE

Various and diverse are the theories that have been conceived to accomplish, at one time an approachment, at another an *alliance*, and at yet another a federation, which, embracing the twenty-one divisions of our America, would integrate us into one *nationality*. But never before as much as today has that unification, unanimously longed for by the Latin American people, become so essential, nor have there been the urgent conditions or the facilities that now exist for the fulfillment of such a high purpose, historically prescribed as the maximum task to be accomplished by the citizens of Latin America.

We have had the opportunity to state that our first mistake was "not to have been consulted about the opening of the Panama Canal, but we can avoid yet another mistake in regard to the Nicaraguan canal."

Profoundly convinced, as we are, that North American capitalism has arrived at its last stage of development, transforming itself as a result into imperialism; and that it now no longer has any respect for theories of right and justice, ignoring the inexorable principles of independence of the divisions of the Latin American nationality, we view as indispensable, and even more so, undelayable, the Alliance of our Latin American states as a way to maintain that independence before the designs of U.S. imperialism, or before that of any other power that may wish to subject us to its interests.

Before entering into facts, I wish to be allowed to outline how, why, and in what circumstances we conceived the idea of the absolute need for an Alliance among our Latin American states, which we are proposing in the present project.

The conditions under which our armed struggle against the forces of invasion of the United States and their allies have taken place have convinced us that our firm and prolonged resistance of three years could continue for another two, three, or four years, or who knows how many more, but at the end of our campaign the enemy, who possesses every kind of weapon and every type of resource, would necessarily record his victory, because we have found ourselves alone in our efforts, unable to rely upon the essential cooperation, official or extra-official, of any Latin American government, or of any other country. And it was this dark vision of the future which forced us to devise the best means to prevent the enemy from achieving victory. Our mind worked with the regularity of a clock, elaborating the optimistic panorama of our own America, triumphant on some future tomorrow.

We also agreed that the government of the United States would never abandon its inclination to succeed in its ambitious projects in this part of our America, violating Central American sovereignty, projects upon which the future maintenance of North American power largely depends, even though in order to accomplish this it must destroy a civilization and sacrifice countless lives.

On the other hand, an isolated Central America, even less, an abandoned Nicaragua, relying solely upon the anguish and collective suffering of the Latin American people, might possibly stop imperialist greed from constructing the interoceanic canal and from establishing their proposed naval base, tearing apart the lands of Central America. At the same time, however, we clearly understood that the silence with which the Latin American governments looked upon the Central American tragedy implied their tacit approval of the aggressive and insolent attitude assumed by the United States against a huge part of this continent; an aggression which at the same time signified the collective decline of the right of self-determination of the Latin American states.

Laboring under the influence of these considerations, we have come to realize that it is absolutely essential that the intense drama experienced by Central American mothers, wives and orphans, deprived of those whom they loved most on the Segovian battlefields by North American soldiers of imperialism, should not be sterile or betrayed, but rather put to use in support of the Latin American nationality, by rejecting all the treaties, pacts, or conventions that have been entered into with an appearance of legality, which in one way or another impair the absolute sovereignty not only of Nicaragua but of the other Latin American states. To accomplish this, there is nothing more logical, nothing more decisive or vital, than the fusion of the twenty-one states of our America into one unique Latin American nationality, thereby making it possible to consider, as an immediate consequence, our rights over the canal route through Central American territory as well as our rights over the Gulf of Fonseca, also in Central American waters, as well as over all those other enclosed areas in the vast territory between the Rio Bravo in the north and the Strait of Magellan in the south, including the islands of Latin American heritage, which could be used as strategic points or as avenues of communication of common concern to the Latin American community. But, in association with other grave problems affecting the independence and stability of the Latin American states, what we hope to preserve for ourselves, without further delay, are the naval base in the Gulf of Fonseca and the interoceanic canal route across Nicaragua: places that one day not very distant will become the world's magnet as well as its key and therefore, finding themselves under Latin American sovereignty, will be bastions for the defense of its unrestricted independence, and a marvelous engine for the development of its full material and spiritual progress.

For these reasons the project presented to this great assembly confronts straightforwardly the solution to the problems stated in the following basic points:

PROJECT

1. The Congress of Representatives of the twenty-one states comprising the Latin American nationality declares the abolition of the Monroe Doctrine and, consequently, annuls the right that that doctrine pretends to confer to interfere in the internal and external politics of the Latin American states.

2. The Congress of Representatives of the twenty-one states comprising the Latin American nationality expressly declares its recognition of the right to form an alliance that belongs to the twenty-one states of continental and insular Latin America, and therefore the establishment of one nationality, to be called the Latin American nationality, thereby making effective Latin American citizenship.

3. The Congress of Representatives of the twenty-one states comprising the Latin American nationality announces its agreement to hold periodic congresses of representatives drawn exclusively from the twenty-one states of the Latin American nationality, without interference of any kind by other nationalities.

4. The Congress of Representatives of the twenty-one states comprising the Latin American nationality declares the establishment of the Latin American Court of Justice, a body that will decide in the last instance all cases that in any way affect or may affect the Latin American states, as well as those cases in which the so-called Monroe Doctrine has sought to exercise its influence.

5. The Congress of Representatives of the twenty-one states comprising the Latin American nationality resolves that the Latin American Court of Justice will have as its seat the Central American territory between the interoceanic canal route across Nicaragua and the naval base that may be

established on the Gulf of Fonseca, without this implying any special privilege for the Central American states, since by assigning the seat of the Latin American Court of Justice to that region of America, an attempt is made to demonstrate to the world the vigilance being exercised by the twenty-one Latin American states as a group over that geographic area, which, more than any other, is a strategic point for defending the complete sovereignty of the Latin American nationality.

6. The Congress of Representatives of the twenty-one states comprising the Latin American nationality declares its recognition of the Latin American Court of Justice as the supreme and only arbitrating authority in cases of reclamations, border litigations, and every other cause that, one way or another, affects or may affect the intimate and solid harmony that should be characteristic of the relations of the twenty-one Latin American states.

7. The Congress of Representatives of the twenty-one states comprising the Latin American nationality agrees to proceed to the immediate organization of an army composed of 5,250 citizens belonging to the student class, between eighteen and twenty-five years of age, including teachers of law and the social sciences. These teachers, as well as the totality of the members of that army, must be physically capable of military service. An essential requirement for membership in the proposed army is the possession of Latin American citizenship. This Army does not constitute the entire strength of the sea and land forces of the Latin American Alliance, but rather the basic foundation of the full force upon which the Latin American nationality may rely for the defense and maintenance of its sovereignty. At the same time this basic foundation of the total sea and land forces of the Latin American Alliance constitutes a symbolic representation of the compact existing among the twenty-one Latin American states, as well as of their decision to cooperate for the defense of the interests of that same Latin American nationality.

8. The Congress of Representatives of the twenty-one states comprising the Latin American nationality agrees that each of the twenty-one states accredited to it will appoint 250 of its citizens for the establishment of that Army.

9. The Congress of Representatives of the twenty-one states comprising the Latin American nationality agrees that each of the constituent governments will contribute from its public treasury a fixed and proportionate amount for the maintenance of the basic foundation of the sea and land forces of the Latin American Alliance.

10. The Congress of Representatives of the twenty-one states comprising the Latin American nationality agrees to confer upon the citizen president of the Latin American Court of Justice the role of commander in chief of the sea and land forces of the Latin American Alliance.

11. The Congress of Representatives of the twenty-one states compris-

ing the Latin American nationality agrees that the term of office of the citizen president of the Latin American Court of Justice, as well as the commander in chief of the sea and land forces of the Latin American Alliance shall be for six years, with the understanding that by the express agreement of the representatives of the twenty-one Latin American states, before the Latin American Court of Justice, his mandate may be revoked, if by remaining in that high office he may constitute a threat to the proper execution of the functions for which that highest court is responsible.

12. The Congress of Representatives of the twenty-one states comprising the Latin American nationality agrees that the election of the president of the Latin American Court of Justice is to take place in the following order: Argentina, Bolivia, Brazil, Colombia, Costa Rica, Cuba, Chile, Ecuador, El Salvador, Guatemala, Honduras, Haiti, Mexico, Nicaragua, Paraguay, Peru, Panama, Puerto Rico, the Dominican Republic, Uruguay, and Venezuela.

13. The Congress of Representatives of the twenty-one states comprising the Latin American nationality ordains that the election of the president of the Latin American Court of Justice and thus the commander of the sea and land forces of the Latin American Alliance will be carried out exclusively by the citizens of the state to which the designation of that official corresponds, since it is recognized that the Latin American citizens of each state are those most qualified to know the public and private virtues of the citizen whom they may decide to elect to that high office.

14. The Congress of Representatives of the twenty-one states comprising the Latin American nationality invests the representatives of the twenty-one Latin American states, before the Latin American Court of Justice, with the right of veto in the event that acceptance of the president elect into this highest court may imply some harm or prejudice to the better realization of its aims.

15. The Congress of Representatives of the twenty-one states comprising the Latin American nationality agrees that the election of the 250 citizens who will represent each of the said states in the sea and land forces of the Latin American Alliance should be accomplished by means of special competitions invoked for that purpose by the governments of the twenty-one Latin American states. The 250 students who in each state are the winners of the competitions, thereby proving their physical and intellectual aptitudes, will be those whom each of the twenty-one states sends as their authentic representatives to the sea and land forces of the Latin American Alliance.

16. The Congress of Representatives of the twenty-one states comprising the Latin American nationality agrees that each of the constituent governments will appoint a determined number of professors of law and social sciences to exercise their functions in accordance with basic point number 7. The 250 citizens who are the winners of the competitions in

each state will be those who will elect, from among the members of the corps of professors of their own state, the individual who is to represent that state in the Latin American Court of Justice.

17. The Congress of Representatives of the twenty-one states comprising the Latin American nationality declares that one of the fundamental obligations of the members of the Latin American Court of Justice as well as those of the sea and land forces of the Latin American Alliance is that of rendering a detailed account of their activities during the term of their administration before the Congress of Representatives of the twenty-one Latin American states, which account this same Congress has decided should be made periodically and without delegation.

18. The Congress of Representatives of the twenty-one states comprising the Latin American nationality agrees that the members of the Latin American Court of Justice and those of the sea and land forces of the Latin American Alliance will swear their loyalty before the Congress of Representatives of the twenty-one Latin American states to the constitutive principles of Latin American nationality and to the organic law and regulations established for their functioning, committing themselves with absolute loyalty to assure the preservation of the sovereignty and inalienable independence of the Latin American nationality, which has been placed in their charge.

19. The Congress of Representatives of the twenty-one states comprising the Latin American nationality agrees that the ranks and titles conferred by the sea and land forces of the Latin American Alliance upon its members will be recognized as fully valid in each and every one of the Latin American states.

20. The Congress of Representatives of the twenty-one states comprising the Latin American nationality agrees that each of the governments of the respective states accredited to it accepts the permanent membership on their general staff of a member of the sea and land forces of the Latin American Alliance, thus manifesting with one additional proof the existing bond between each of the governments of the twenty-one Latin American states and the sea and land forces of the Latin American Alliance.

21. The Congress of Representatives of the twenty-one states comprising the Latin American nationality advises that all members of the sea and land forces of the Latin American Alliance are positively prohibited, from the day of their entrance into that organ, from belonging to any political party or carrying out activities of a political nature, within or outside the Latin American nationality.

22. The Congress of Representatives of the twenty-one states comprising the Latin American nationality agrees to grant the power to the president of the Latin American Court of Justice and to the commander of the sea and land forces of the Latin American Alliance to recommend to the

governments of the twenty-one states the diplomats, specialists in international politics, and experts whose ability has been demonstrated in practice in the previously mentioned bodies.

23. The Congress of Representatives of the twenty-one states comprising the Latin American nationality appoints a committee charged with the responsibility of elaborating the organic law and regulations that will guide the functioning of the Latin American Court of Justice as well as the sea and land forces of the Latin American Alliance, and these will be put into effect after their approval by the representatives of the governments of the twenty-one Latin American states.

24. The Congress of Representatives of the twenty-one states comprising the Latin American nationality declares that the Latin American Court of Justice and the sea and land forces of the Latin American Alliance recognize and will make every effort to maintain the absolute sovereignty of the twenty-one Latin American states, and that the steps they will take in the utilization of their powers will not involve any limitation upon the sovereignty of any of the Latin American states, since any act regarded as a limitation of expressed absolute sovereignty is to be done in accordance with the principle of Latin American nationality, for the formation of which each Latin American state cedes to this idea of defense and the common welfare everything that, without in any case damaging the norms of the internal life of each state, tends to strengthen and assure the said Latin American nationality.

25. The Congress of Representatives of the twenty-one states comprising the Latin American nationality declares that in the event of civil war originating in any of the signatory states of the Pact of Alliance, the belligerent parties have the right, if they deem it convenient, to request armed contingents of the sea and land forces of the Latin American Alliance; which, given their neutral character, will constitute an effective guarantee to all those who may wish to remove the belligerent parties from power, there being a justifiable reason for this in the view of the Latin American Court of Justice.

26. The Congress of Representatives of the twenty-one states comprising the Latin American nationality positively declares that the only entity qualified to carry out works leading to the opening of the canal and the construction of a naval base on the Gulf of Fonseca, in Central American territory, as well as every project involving common use by the twenty-one Latin American states, is the Latin American nationality, for their direct benefit and without in any way compromising the complete sovereignty of one or more of the signatories of the Pact of Alliance.

27. The Congress of Representatives of the twenty-one states comprising the Latin American nationality wishes to clarify that if the material development and the present economic resources are not, at the moment, sufficient to realize the opening of the interoceanic route through Central

American territory and a naval base on the Gulf of Fonseca, or in any other place strategic to the defense of the sovereignty and independence of the Latin American nationality, the signatory states of the Pact of Alliance will reserve all their customs duties for the construction or establishment of the works referred to, promising that in no case whatever will the Latin American nationality permit the alienation, sale, transfer, or rental of the works in question, or of any others that would compromise the stability of Latin American sovereignty and independence, to the benefit of a power or powers extraneous to the Latin American nationality.

28. The Congress of Representatives of the twenty-one states comprising the Latin American nationality agrees that, for the construction of any of these works, either the interoceanic canal or the naval base, the Latin American nationality commits itself to requiring that the company or companies charged with bringing those works into being must indemify the citizens of the states concerned if during their construction those citizens should be harmed in their lives or properties.

29. The Congress of Representatives of the twenty-one states comprising the Latin American nationality agrees that, in cases of aggression by one or several powers against one or several states of the Latin American nationality, the Latin American states will act unanimously to express their official protest against the aggressive power or powers, with the threat that they will effect the immediate and joint withdrawal of their diplomatic representatives accredited to the aggressive power or powers.

30. The Congress of Representatives of the twenty-one states comprising the Latin American nationality agrees that, after the communications referred to in the previous basic point have been made and the satisfaction demanded of the aggressive power or powers has not been obtained, the governments of the twenty-one Latin American states will proceed to the automatic confiscation of the properties and investments that the aggressive power or powers may possess within the boundaries of the Latin American nationality, using the product of that expropriation to support the war brought about by the aggression of the foreign power or powers.

31. The Congress of Representatives of the twenty-one states comprising the Latin American nationality declares that the governments of the twenty-one states will use for the defense of Latin American sovereignty, in the event that an international conflict does not warrant an outbreak of hostilities, the economic boycott against the power or powers initiating the discord, cancelling both the acquisition and the sale of products with the power or powers that provoked the employment of this measure.

32. The Congress of Representatives of the twenty-one states comprising the Latin American nationality agrees to adopt, as an immediate measure following the signing of the Pact of Alliance, the constitution of a committee of Latin American bankers, officially supported, which has as its purpose the preparation and realization of a plan by means of which

the Latin American nationality will achieve, through the use of its own funds, the cancellation of the contracts that exist between the Latin American states and the United States of America, the said committee of bankers taking charge of the construction of material works and lines of communication and transport, as well as the floating of loans that, in virtue of the treaties now existing between the Latin American states and the United States of America, the governments of the former require.

33. The Congress of Representatives of the twenty-one states comprising the Latin American nationality agrees that the Latin American nationality should use all the diplomatic and peaceful means that circumstances advise for the purpose of acquiring, through the agency of the committee of Latin American bankers, the rights that the United States of America seeks to retain over the Panama Canal, the latter thereby coming under the authority of the absolute sovereignty of the Latin American nationality.

34. The Congress of Representatives of the twenty-one states comprising the Latin American nationality entrusts to the Latin American Court of Justice the mission of carrying out a thorough investigation in the states of Puerto Rico, Cuba, the Dominican Republic, Haiti, Panama, Mexico, Honduras, and Nicaragua regarding the loss of lives and possessions suffered by Latin American citizens in those states during the occupations and invasions ordered by several governments of the United States of America.

35. The Congress of Representatives of the twenty-one states comprising the Latin American nationality resolves that, in accordance with the report rendered by the Latin American Court of Justice, the Latin American nationality should proceed to demand the immediate and total withdrawal from the states where an intervention has taken place, automatically recovering the territories used by the United States of America as naval bases, provisioning centers, or other structures intended for possible acts of aggression, which impair the sovereignty of the Latin American states.

36. The Congress of Representatives of the twenty-one states comprising the Latin American nationality declares that, during the process of the aforesaid investigation, neither the Latin American Court of Justice nor any individual state will take into consideration the supposed responsibility contracted by the Latin American states with the government of the United States when the former were defending themselves, with their sovereignty trampled underfoot, during invasions or occupations carried out by forces of the United States, since losses of lives and North American properties resulting from those acts of aggression constitute nothing more than the results of the exercise of the right of self-defense, inherent to any people under attack.

37. The Congress of Representatives of the twenty-one states compris-

ing the Latin American nationality agrees to adopt measures that may prevent the ingress of citizens of the United States of America into Latin American territory from resulting in any threat to interests of any kind of the Latin American nationality, preventing as well the penetration of North American finance capital into the Latin American states in the form of investments or other forms, thus eliminating the use by the Yankee government of the handy recourse of "protecting the lives and interests of North Americans" in order to violate the sovereignty of the Latin American states.

38. The Congress of Representatives of the twenty-one states comprising the Latin American nationality agrees to unify the customs duties of the twenty-one states, establishing furthermore upon that unified tariff a discount of twenty-five per cent on the exportation and importation of the products of the twenty-one states in the markets of the Latin American nationality. Cultural expression, books, journals, pictures, and other works needed for the development of the arts and sciences will enjoy absolute freedom from duties in the twenty-one Latin American states.

39. The Congress of Representatives of the twenty-one states comprising the Latin American nationality agrees that the accredited governments should effect a systematic exchange of students in the economic and social sciences of the twenty-one Latin American states, so that each state may establish scholarships corresponding to a determined number of students for each state.

40. The Congress of Representatives of the twenty-one states comprising the Latin American nationality agrees that the governments accredited to it should develop Latin American tourism in a special manner, as a way to promote a coming together and a mutual awareness among the citizens of the twenty-one Latin American states, giving tourists, among other advantages, a ten per cent rebate on railroads, steamships, airplanes and other means of communication and transportation that exist or will be established in the twenty-one states of our America.

41. The Congress of Representatives of the twenty-one states comprising the Latin American nationality agrees to appoint a special committee for the purpose of preparing the rules and invoking the assemblies that would have to be held in order to provide an opportunity for Latin American intellectuals and scientists to offer the formulas upon which the committee of Latin American bankers should be constituted, to find the best means to promote mutual knowledge among the twenty-one Latin American states, the means of reincorporating the Panama Canal into the Latin American nationality, and, in general, to make the necessary preparations for each of the initiatives included in this project, of which it is in need.

42. The Congress of Representatives of the twenty-one states comprising the Latin American nationality declares recognized under the designation of "Flag of the Latin American Nationality," the emblem that the

Army in Defense of the National Sovereignty of Nicaragua has the honor to present to this same Congress. It expresses, with a harmonious combination of colors, the symbolic fusion of all of the flags of the twenty-one Latin American states, brought together today into one strong and glorious nationality.

43. The Congress of Representatives of the twenty-one states comprising the Latin American nationality adopts as the official motto of the Latin American Alliance, embodied in the Latin American Court of Justice and in the sea and land forces of the Latin American Alliance, that which the vibrant new Mexican generation has chosen as the motto of its deep creative restlessness, interpreting therewith the fruitful destiny of our nationality surging into world history and charting new paths: *Let courage speak for my race.*

44. The Congress of Representatives of the twenty-one states comprising the Latin American nationality, which meets in a fraternal mingling of governments and peoples of the twenty-one states, acclaims as the name of the place where the Latin American Court of Justice will have its seat, that of Simón Bolívar, raising in the Hall of Honor of the Latin American Court of Justice, as homage of admiration to the memory of that eminent architect of Latin American independence, a monument crowned by the lofty figure of the greatest forger of free peoples.

CONCLUSION

Citizen representatives of the twenty-one Latin American states:

Having revealed the original project that the Army in Defense of the National Sovereignty of Nicaragua is presenting to this great assembly with the high purpose of establishing an Alliance of undeferrable urgency among the twenty-one separate states of the Latin American nationality, we find ourselves fully aware of the enormous historic responsibility that we take upon ourselves with our America and with the world. For this reason, we have not intended to set forth a vain and risky plan, but rather, by interpreting our reality, we have tried to make of this project something effective and capable of finding solutions to our most immediate problems, facing above all else the imperative necessity of achieving the unanimously desired Latin American Alliance, which can be opposed only by theories of an unfortunate skepticism and of small value to the domestic and foreign policies of our states.

Basing our acts upon reality, we are proposing an alliance and not a confederation of the twenty-one states of our America. We understand that to reach this great goal, what is needed more than anything else is the establishment of a primary foundation, which the Alliance gives us. This is not, then, the culmination of our aspirations. It constitutes only the first definitive step toward new and fruitful endeavors of our nationality in times to come.

Perhaps men possessing advanced and universalist ideas will think that our dreams have collided with too many frontiers in the geographic expanse bordered by the Rio Bravo in the north of our America and the Strait of Magellan in the south. But they must also ponder the vital necessity for our Latin America to establish an alliance prior to a confederation of the twenty-one states that compose it, thereby assuring our domestic freedom and independence, now theatened by the most voracious of all imperialisms, to fulfill in time the great destiny of the Latin American nationality, now already consummated, as a land of promise for people of every nation and race.

El Chipotón, the Segovias, Nicaragua, Central America, the twentieth day of the month of March of nineteen hundred and twenty-nine.

Patria y Libertad.
AUGUSTO CÉSAR SANDINO

[19, 24 pp.]

92. LETTER TO ERCILIA PEPÍN, APRIL 15, 1929

General Headquarters of the Army in
Defense of the National Sovereignty of
Nicaragua, the Segovias, El Chipotón,
Nicaragua, C.A.
April 15, 1929

Señorita Ercilia Pepín
Director of the Colegio de Señoritas "México"
Santiago de los Caballeros, Dominican Republic

Distinguished señorita:

I have the privilege to inform you that on January 2 of this year we had the honor to receive at our General Headquarters, through the Hands-Off-Nicaragua Committee with its headquarters in Mexico, D.F., your worthy and intelligent letter, dated May 15 of last year in that historic and a thousand times heroic city, and with it the exact replica of our beautifully made national flag, which through your worthy agency was presented to our liberation army by the noble students of the Colegio de Señoritas "México" of that same city, of which you are the wise director.

Aware of the great value of your solidarity with our vindicating cause, we greatly appreciate the making of our national flag by the distinguished students of that illustrious school, and with the same deep emotion with which we received our immortal flag, from whose folds the free winds of our mountains absorb your patriotic prayers, our highest gratitude goes to you and to them. Your glorious gift will continue to make the swarms of Yankee invaders draw away from our country's soil, as it has done during these last three months.

May it please the God of free nations for our flag to attain the symbolic importance that you predict for it, so that it may be hoisted by the people of the Americas and bring a happy conclusion to the efforts that it fell to our generations to undertake in this period of human development, which will establish the principles of universal brotherhood and the absolute condemnation of the conquest and domination of one nation by another. Our army will have cause for deep satisfaction if that symbolism should become widespread, because we have always believed that our liberating action in Nicaragua is merely an episode in the combined effort that the people of this continent must carry out against Yankee imperialism.

The valuable Latin American contingents that are now forming in the ranks of our liberation army offer encouraging signs of a unity of thought among the people of the Americas against Yankee imperialism, and in fact everywhere on our continent the Yankee policy in Latin America is condemned. The attitude of our people could not be otherwise. The desire to achieve self-determination that gave life to the nationalities of the Americas was a united desire, and united too is our recognition of the threat that our liberty faces from northern imperialism.

May your firm solidarity and that of your distinguished students always be with us so that our dreams of continental freedom may soon become a reality, and may you and they and the Dominican people accept the expression of our highest consideration.

Patria y Libertad.
A. C. SANDINO

[19, 1 p.]

93. LETTER TO HIS LIEUTENANTS REGARDING THE MILITARY COMMAND DURING HIS ABSENCE, JULY 1, 1929[1]

El Chipotón
the Segovias
July 1, 1929

Generals Pedro Altamirano, Ismael Peralta,
and Carlos Quezada

Esteemed companions and friends:

I have the honor to greet you, confirming my note sent to you and dated last May 20.[2] Allow me also to inform you that on this date Generals Francisco Estrada, Pedro Antonio Irías, and José León Díaz are appointed commanders of our autonomist forces, in the following manner: first commander, General Estrada, second commander, General Irías, and third commander, General Díaz. The generals referred to are those who will explain to you the plan that we are developing, in accordance with our aspirations to see our country entirely free.

The decisions made by them will be looked upon as if I myself had made them. The plan we are developing is in accordance with everything we have accomplished toward the advancement of our nation's sovereignty, and you will understand that I cannot be explicit in a written form, but Generals Estrada and Díaz will explain to you everything that is to be done.

Fraternally.
Patria y Libertad.
A. C. SANDINO

[10, 75]

1. The fact that this letter appears signed in El Chipotón on July 1, 1929, when Sandino was already in Mexico, suggests that it was postdated for reasons of security and, in any case, to mislead the enemy.
2. Not included in this edition. RC

94. LETTER TO THE PRESIDENT OF MEXICO, EMILIO PORTES GIL, JUNE 30, 1929

Veracruz, Ver.
June 30, 1929

To the President of the Mexican Republic
Licenciado Don Emilio Portes Gil
Mexico, D.F.

Mr. President:

Upon returning to this noble Mexican land, sacred and loved by me and by the Army in Defense of the National Sovereignty of Nicaragua, after three and a half years of struggle for the freedom of my country, punished by Yankee imperialism, my ardent desire has been, distinguished ruler of this great brother country, to send you a greeting from my Army and from myself: a greeting that sums up our hopes and distinctly expresses my sincere recognition of your generous attitude toward me and those associated with me.

If some governmental responsibilities and international commitments force you, for the good of the present and future of Mexico, to work with the greatest discretion when dealing with my country's affairs, I am certain, Mr. President, that your feelings as a Mexican and your ideas as a patriot do not conflict with your role as first magistrate of this great nation, that those feelings have encouraged you to grant me and those associated with me your brotherly hospitality in this land so sacred to my heart. It is in this way that I have been able to see that my efforts of the last three and a half years to free my country have not been without some effect, since the generous welcome of the government over which you preside and of the people whom you govern fill my heart with satisfaction and hope.

I say to you, Mr. President, that in assuming my attitude against the North American invaders, I have done nothing other than to follow the example of the Mexican patriots, in whose glorious deeds my spirit and my ideal have always found an inexhaustible source of strength and an abundance of powerful inspiration for my struggle. And I have even begun to think that the radiant spirit of Benito Juárez, the father of the Americas, has illuminated my steps through the mountains and over the rugged terrain of the Segovias, and that his voice, which free America one day heard clamoring for justice and freedom against the invaders, has said to me: "Have faith and continue."

I also declare to you that, having adopted the Liberator's phrases as my own, I will not give peace to my spirit or rest to my bones for as long as one invading soldier treads upon the sacred soil of my ancestors.

Mr. President, with the rough sincerity of a soldier, I express to you my deep appreciation for the protection that Mexico has offered to me to travel here from the fields of battle, and I will transmit this to my army so that everyone there may know the lasting impression your generosity has left on my spirit, so that you may be venerated in their hearts as well.

The representative of our army on this and on other continents has the responsibility of providing you with a detailed and exact report of the situation existing in my camps, and of the deplorable conditions to be found in that region of my country where we are fighting the Yankee invaders without letup and without rest.

Our representative, Dr. Pedro José Zepeda, is responsible for delivering to you the trophies that we have taken from the invaders, in accordance with the notarized statement that he will place in your hands, as well as a rifle that our representative, Dr. Zepeda, will be happy to give you along with our reasons for sending it to you.

With my great respect and gratitude to the citizen president, whose patriotism guides the fate of this great nation and safeguards the dignity of the race, I am your very attentive servant.

Patria y Libertad.
AUGUSTO CÉSAR SANDINO

[19, 2 pp.]

95. MESSAGE TO THE SECOND WORLD ANTI-IMPERIALIST CONGRESS MEETING IN FRANKFURT, GERMANY, CIRCA JULY 1929[1]

Distinguished Congress Members:

In the name of the Army in Defense of the National Sovereignty of Nicaragua, I come before your organization, which we consider the first moral authority of oppressed peoples, to call your attention to the abominable deeds committed by the imperialist policy of the United States in Nicaragua, a sovereign state of Central America. The entire civilized world knows that since 1909, when Yankee imperialism announced its project for construction of an interoceanic canal via the Rivas Isthmus and the San Juan River in Nicaraguan territory, and the establishment of a naval base on the Gulf of Fonseca, over which the republics of El Salvador, Honduras, and Nicaragua possess joint ownership, there has persisted in our country a condition of constant struggle for the maintenance of our territorial integrity, threatened by that imperialism.

That project, conceived by Yankee imperialism, has cost the Nicaraguan nation approximately forty thousand human lives of both sexes, and more than a hundred million córdobas in damages to the property of our fellow citizens.

Yankee imperialism in Nicaragua, as in every country of our racial America where it has intervened contrary to all international decency, set out to establish a small and wretched oligarchy, made up of submissive men who could never represent the opinion of the Nicaraguan people, including among its principal leaders Adolfo Díaz, Emiliano Chamorro, and José María Moncada. This oligarchy was created in order to enter into offensive treaties that have brought great injury to our fundamental rights as a free people.

The Nicaraguan people absolutely disown and have rejected with every ounce of dignity, and at the cost of their own blood, the treaties, pacts, and conventions celebrated between the United States government and the oligarchs imposed by that government in Nicaragua. The people of Nicaragua do not recognize as constitutional any of those regimes which have come to power in our country from 1909 until the present, since those regimes have achieved power supported by the bayonets of U.S. imperialism.

With the announcement in 1909 of the Bryan-Chamorro Treaty, which was signed in 1916, a bloody rebellion broke out, resulting in a drastic armed intervention by the regular army of the United States, and, as a result of that intervention, the autonomist Nicaraguan, General Benjamín Zeledón, was killed by bullets of Yankee soldiers serving the interests of Wall Street.[2] In 1922, in order to retain in power the Nicaraguan renegades who have imperiled our sovereignty, the U.S. government, docile servant of Wall Street bankers, called upon the governments of El Salvador, Guatemala, Honduras, and Costa Rica, and the regime it had itself forced upon Nicaragua, to hold a conference, in which, at the initiative of the American state department, it was stipulated, among other points, that the signers of the pact resulting from that conference could not recognize any government of the Central American republics coming to power through a coup d'état, the U.S. government being obliged to follow this same line of conduct.[3]

Justice put itself on the side of our people when the so-called president of Nicaragua at that time, Diego Manuel Chamorro, a blind instrument of imperialist interests as were the oligarchs before him, died while holding the power he had usurped, and the vice president, Don Bartolomé Martínez, respecting the popular will, turned power over to those who were chosen in a free election: Carlos Solórzano and Dr. Juan Bautista Sacasa, president and vice president of the Republic, respectively.

In recognition of the high civic conduct with which Bartolomé Martínez governed Nicaragua, it is our duty to state that, despite the illegality of his vice presidency, like the presidency of his predecessor, Diego Manuel Chamorro, he acknowledged the people's right to exercise their vote and for this reason we regard him as among those honorable men who merit the respect of their fellow citizens.

Yankee imperialism, recognizing that justice had come to the aid of the Nicaraguan people, urged the spurious sons of Nicaragua, Adolfo Díaz and Emiliano Chamorro, in league with the interventionist power, to carry out the military coup of October 24, 1925, known to the civilized world as the *Lomazo*, which had as its consequence the mangling of the constitutionality of the presidency of Don Carlos Solórzano and the vice presidency of Dr. Juan Bautista Sacasa.[4] Emiliano Chamorro then made himself president of the Republic.

The people of Nicaragua rose up in arms and fought for a year against the despicable oligarchy, but as our Constitutionalist Army, already victorious, was approaching the gates of Managua, it received a most insolent and unprecedented demand from the United States government through President Coolidge's personal representative, Colonel Henry L. Stimson, the present secretary of state in the Yankee government, to the effect that our army of vindication was to lay down the weapons with which it had the right to gain our country's freedom.

Our Constitutionalist army had established as a basic tenet the repudiation of the Bryan-Chamorro Treaty and all other treaties, pacts, and conventions entered into by the government of the United States and the governments it had imposed with its bayonets on Nicaragua, but José María Moncada, the man who then served as commander of our Constitutionalist army, failing to perform his most basic duties to the Nicaraguan people, who were eager for honor and freedom, abandoned his principles to the Yankees, tempted by his secret ambition to be offered the presidency of the Republic of Nicaragua, which was done for him by the invaders.

The unit of that Constitutionalist army that the undersigned commanded at that time vigorously rejected the demand made by Colonel Stimson, the personal representative of Coolidge, as we have said, and hence the agent of the Wall Street bankers. Our column accepted the challenge of the unprincipled invader, and to the undersigned fell the honor of being elected leader of that group of patriots who for two and a half years have fought with enormous bravery against the greatest imperialist power on earth.

Our army continues to uphold the principle of absolute sovereignty and therefore disavows all the treaties, pacts, and conventions celebrated between the governments of the United States and those of Nicaragua, which prejudice the principle of absolute sovereignty proclaimed and upheld by our combatants. Once again we must state that those treaties, pacts, and conventions have been entered into against the better judgement of the Nicaraguan people. Our army believes that during the two years and three months that it has pursued its tenacious struggle against Yankee imperialism, it has attained sufficient moral authority to urge all free men and all free nations on this earth to regard as null and void the indecent treaties agreed to by the United States and the spurious sons of Nicaragua.

The Nicaraguan people, of whom we deem ourselves legitimate representatives, would allow the construction of an interoceanic canal across their territory, as well as the establishment of a naval base on the Gulf of Fonseca, through an agreement with the other joint owners of that gulf, El Salvador and Honduras, if those projects were carried out with the resources of the twenty-one Latin American republics, and for the benefit of all the nations of the earth, but they do not believe that those projects should become the exclusive property of Yankee imperialism. Our army believes that by retaining these projects within the Latin American nationality, Nicaragua will not have limitations imposed upon its independence, since our army's basic beliefs derive from the principle of absolute sovereignty.

Our army believes in its urgent duty to declare to the world that it regards the Latin American peoples as a racial unity possessing unbreakable ties. It is not, therefore, only Nicaragua which must solve the problems raised by the projects in question. All of Latin America, both continental and West Indian, has the right to express its opinions in this respect. In everything touching upon its fundamental rights as a free people, the Latin American nationality, with its racial unity and its unbreakable ties, as we have said, has the right to be consulted.

Members of this Congress, let this opportunity serve to extend to you, the greatest moral authority of oppressed peoples and the purest representation of their wishes, a passionate and cordial greeting, and to present our respects and our solidarity to the men who make up this great World Anti-Imperialist Assembly, with our best hopes for the greatest success of your humanitarian labors.

In the Thrice Heroic City of Veracruz, Mexico, 1929
Patria y Libertad.
A. C. SANDINO

Resolution of the Second World Anti-Imperialist and Pro-National Independence Congress, meeting in the city of Frankfurt, Germany, in favor of the Army in Defense of the National Sovereignty of Nicaragua and the freedom of that country.

Supported unanimously by the twenty delegates who have represented the countries of Latin America in the Second World Anti-Imperialist Congress, which met in the city of Frankfurt am Main on July 22 of this year, the said Congress, which was the most powerful expression of moral force of the oppressed peoples of the earth, approved the following resolution:

The Second World Anti-Imperialist and Pro-National-Independence Congress, considering:

That the armed intervention of the United States in Nicaragua, aside from being a brutal offense against the autonomy and independence of a small nation, violates the most fundamental human rights, with the destruction of undefended towns (Murra, Yalí, Telpaneca, and Quilalí, among others); the heartless killing of women, children and the elderly; the destruction of property in the zones where the Army of General Augusto César Sandino operates; the cynical outrage against the feminine sex; the desecration of cemeteries (an example of this unusual occurrence being the destruction of the mausoleums, monuments, and gravestones in the San Pedro Cemetery in Managua on the night of June 5 of this year); and other reprehensible and punishable acts, resolves:

1. To condemn energetically these acts of barbarism carried out by the forces of the Army of the United States at the service of imperialism in

Nicaragua, and to deem them as worthy of universal reprobation, being contrary to every principle of Justice and Law that the governments of Washington falsely proclaim to the world in order to hide their savage and barbarous designs against the weak nations of Latin America.

2. To agree to the full and effective support of the Army in Defense of the National Sovereignty of Nicaragua which General Augusto César Sandino commands, and which for more than two years has defended the territorial integrity of Nicaragua, resolutely opposing the imperialist armies of the United States, which have carried out the savage and barbarous acts which motivate this resolution.

Frankfurt am Main, the twenty-fourth of July of nineteen hundred and twenty-nine.

[6, 5–8; 19, 1 p.]

1. The Second World Anti-Imperialist Congress met in Frankfurt, Germany, in July 1929. José Constantino González was delegated by Sandino to represent him there. At its conclusion, a resolution favoring the Army in Defense of the National Sovereignty was edited and approved, and its text appears at the end of this document.

2. The Bryan-Chamorro Treaty was signed on August 5, 1914. Two years later, in 1916, it was ratified by Nicaragua and the United States, on April 12 and February 18 respectively.

3. This was the *Tacoma* Conference. See Doc. 64, n. 15.

4. The date was actually October 25.

96. LETTER TO GUSTAVO ALEMÁN BOLAÑOS, SEPTEMBER 9, 1929[1]

Mérida, Yucatán.

I have held the opinion that the sincere direction of our struggle will allow us to reorient the disoriented, the mistaken, and the confused, and it is indeed important, as you say, not to lose contact with the nearsighted patriots, and the manifesto I have issued will help in this direction.[2]

There has been no intention on my part to leave, as reported by the press, nor have I resorted to anything like a disguise. I am always in the public view.

I don't concern myself with insinuations about who might become president. Both in public and in private we deal prudently with the smallest details of our orientation, and I am pleased that you should recognize that we have known how to keep ourselves in a state of mind consistent with the moment through which we are passing.

Neither extreme right nor extreme left, but rather "United Front" is our slogan. This being the case, it isn't illogical for us to seek the cooperation of all social classes in our struggle, without ideological classifications or "isms." This being the case, I regard it as very logical that we should incorporate the organizations of the extreme left, since they are the ones that might make some people believe that we preach decided social doctrines. You may be entirely confident that this is the orientation we will follow.

About the principles that have been presented to the traitor Moncada, of which I sent you a copy, you will see that we have offered a program that we think appropriate to Nicaragua with its social problems, and also so that workers who are inept enough to be tricked by the ambitious may understand their position in the nationalist struggle. Without this orientation toward their true problems, they will always provide rich pasturelands for backward politicians. By conducting our activities correctly, we will always be able to distinguish between patriotism and false patriotism.

I am sending you *Sandino ante el coloso*.[3] It is a pamphlet that contains in essence all our activities. It suffers from two mistakes: that of saying that Sócrates Sandino and I are brothers of the same father and mother, and that the sell-out Díaz is Nicaragua's minister in Washington. Regarding the first mistake, I should explain that I am my father's first son and that my mother is Margarita Calderón, Socrates's mother being Doña América de Sandino. Concerning the second mistake, you already know who represents the traitors in Washington, the puppet Sacasa. Aside from these two errors, everything else is authentic.

Regarding the thoughts that Dr. Francisco J. Medina has expressed about Moncada, I had the good fortune to recognize this from the moment we arrived to rescue him from the siege that the Conservatives had imposed upon him in Las Mercedes. Please tell people like Dr. Medina that the moment of rectifications has come, and that those who are mistaken should join those who saw things clearly from the start, in order to work for the restoration of our right to national sovereignty.

It will not be Colonel Martí who will be commissioned now to go to Central America, because he is sick at the moment in a hospital in this city. Possibly my second adjutant, the young Rubén Ardila Gómez, of Colombian nationality, will arrive here, and he will leave within ten days at the latest.

I congratulate you for having written to the poet Turcios, and the true causes that brought about our rupture are to be found in a pamphlet that I recently sent you. I retain a deep sympathy for him, and if he accepts his mistake, I will be very happy to count him among my friends.

We are dealing with the Nicaraguan cause from the two points of view that it presents. First, considering it within the framework of Latin American nationality, and from this point of view matters relative to the canal and to construction of the naval base planned by the North American piracy in Nicaraguan territory must be dealt with; and second, matters relating to the country's domestic politics.

[1, 82–85]

1. This document and the others that follow are fragments of letters that Sandino sent to Gustavo Alemán Bolaños in 1929. They are presented here as published.

2. The manifesto referred to was published as Doc. 123 in the 1984 edition. However, it is omitted in this edition because, in the opinion of Sergio Ramírez, it was probably written not by Sandino but by Gustavo Alemán Bolaños, and also because it repeats many concepts expressed elsewhere by Sandino. RC

3. "Sandino before the colossus," a report by Emigdio Maraboto published in Veracruz, Mexico, in August 1929. RC

97. LETTER TO GUSTAVO ALEMÁN BOLAÑOS, SEPTEMBER 26, 1929

Mérida, Yucatán

Every day that God gives us light we have even greater probabilities of success in the enterprise that we have begun, because important correspondence is coming in from various places. I understand the need to be in contact with the people you mentioned to me, and in this matter as in many others I agree with you. Regarding the distance of the moment, we are not worried because everything is going well too, and when the time comes we will find quick ways to deal with it. We are to be congratulated that Moncada's Machiavellian maneuver has failed because of the subtle efforts he tried to develop here in Mexico to gain recognition, and for this a character at Moncada's service in this country will pay, and I think his name is Hernán Robleto.

The clipping you attached to the back of your letter brought an involuntary smile to my lips. The hermit's life that I'm leading, according to our enemies, is something I must explain to you. By nature I have a retiring character, and I only talk a lot when I'm touched by the gland of acute Latin-Americanitis that I have. Surely I almost never go out, but it's because I don't need to go out and I prefer to stay in my observatory, and I don't want people to think I'm going about exploiting my popularity.

[1, 85–86]

Our army's success is the result of our espionage service. The enemy doesn't carry out a maneuver that we don't know about at once. From this result the ambushes in which the Yankees have lost so many men, aside from those who have died from the diseases of that climate, because our bullets and machetes have cost them ten thousand men.

Froylán Turcios has not disposed of one cent belonging to the Army of Nicaragua. It's true that we have moved away from each other, and that he doesn't represent us now in America, but to his honor we can't say anything against him and we continue to respect him. I had already admired Froylán because of his newspaper articles. When we needed to communicate with the peoples of America during the most intense period of our struggle we saw an article by Froylán in which we saw that he sympathized with our cause; because of this he became our representative. The separation was sought more by him. The pretext was that we were looking for a person to carry on the Liberal party's presidential struggle.

Dr. Pedro José Zepeda, who is located in this capital (Mexico City), was to have received some documents that we sent to him through Domingo Mairena Hernández, but the latter got drunk in Honduras and sold the documents. He is now chief clerk of the Interior Ministry in Managua (Nicaragua). Froylán Turcios had copies of those documents, and he took advantage of the opportunity to write to us to propose that we stop what we were doing.

Then came a whole list of proposals that Adolfo Díaz was supposed to offer us. Froylán agreed to all this, and he suggested that we give up our weapons in Costa Rica and that, if we recognized the leadership, it would grant us an amnesty. Unworthy proposals, because Moncada is a bandit and we can't recognize him, and even less can we accept an amnesty from him. From this came the chilly atmosphere, and Froylán, who knew how important it was for him to serve us as intercessor between America and our army, asked us to tell him how we would accept his resignation, and then we accepted it.

What we lacked was not weapons, or money, or bullets, but moral support, the sympathy that we have always had from all the countries of

America. We were overwhelmed by the silence, by the isolation. The desperation of being ignored. We missed the world knowing that we were still in the fight; it was for this reason that I left Nicaragua.

Froylán's resignation brought this isolation. We have agents, but unfortunately many of them have been selfish, and others, frankly, traitors; some merely inactive. When Turcios was our representative in Honduras, we were in contact with the world. That is, the world knew about us. We were communicating with our American brothers. But Turcios was gone and we were left isolated. The struggle has continued in Nicaragua as intensively as before, but North American money has imposed silence upon us.

Some of our agents receive letters and reports from us, for the purpose of making them known, and they selfishly hold onto them. They keep them without publishing them, in order to make use of them later for their books, utilizing for personal advantage the nobility and the sympathy for our cause.

When we no longer had Turcios, we considered Machado as our representative in Mexico, and we placed our greatest hopes in him, asking him to represent us. He hasn't even responded to accept. He had accepted the responsibility to prepare a pamphlet to make known something of what we are doing in Nicaragua and he asked me for a receipt for a thousand dollars for his pay. Then after nine months he informed us that he didn't have the money and that he had asked for the receipt in order to petition for the money. As it turned out, the pamphlet was never produced. Our cause has been getting weaker abroad because of the lack of communication, because of the lack of that spiritual interchange which animates us in the struggle. North American money, on the other hand, buys people and injects influence in order to restrict news about us abroad, and that isolation causes us to waste away.

But now I have found my general representative. He is Dr. Pedro José Zepeda. I have the most complete confidence in him, and he will do the work that needs to be done. Then, tranquil insofar as that is concerned, we will return to the struggle. Of course the struggle has not ended. I am in the midst of things even when I'm outside Nicaragua.

I'm exposed at all times, and when I left Nicaragua I did so surrounded by a ring of machine guns, a total of twenty-four; and here, as in any other place the hand of our enemies can reach me.

I'm paying for this journey of my aides and myself with my own money. In Nicaragua I have invested money in the struggle we are pursuing, and this trip is paid for from the fruit of my savings. This struggle is completely unassociated with any economic interest, and the deepest contempt for money is felt in the camps of our army.

[11, 135–37]

99. LETTER TO GUSTAVO ALEMÁN BOLAÑOS, OCTOBER 8, 1929

Mérida, Yucatán

With the arrival in Mérida the day before yesterday of the Lone Eagle, Lindbergh, we consider it opportune to publish in the local press my dedicatory remarks to you upon giving you the typewriter that accompanied me during the first campaign.

Keep in mind that when we captured that machine, the Pan-American pantomime in Havana was taking place, and not long after came the so-called "goodwill" flight. And what a beautiful and opportune coincidence: the very day Lindbergh landed in Managua, the armed airplanes of the United States flew desperately day and night, carrying dead and wounded pirates from Quilalí to Managua. The same "messenger of goodwill" is a witness to what I'm saying, because he, Lindbergh, helped to lower those dead and wounded from the airplanes. Surely it was for this reason that the aviator did not mention Nicaragua in the accounts of his tour. Well done.[1]

[1, 76]

1. For reports of the "fierce fighting" at Quilalí and Lindbergh's landing at Managua, see *The New York Times*, 3 and 4 January 1928. RC

100. AN ANECDOTE, OCTOBER 1929

The morning was foggy and cold. The houses of the port appeared saddened by the torrential downpour of the previous night. The big barge on which I was traveling with my five aides arrived at the customs pier. We jumped out onto the dock, and in the fog we came upon some men armed with new carbines and an abundance of cartridges. They were not dressed as soldiers and to me they looked like Mexican agrarianists.

That day was December 1, 1926, and for the first time I had landed in the city of Puerto Cabezas on the Atlantic coast of Nicaragua, where Dr. Juan Bautista Sacasa, constitutional president of Nicaragua in that period, had established his cabinet.

A young man of thirty-five years of age, dark, with black eyes and eyebrows close together, of normal height, thin beard closely shaved, dressed in a khaki riding habit, a broad-brimmed hat, high dark-colored boots, and a black-bordered red kerchief at the neck, was walking with slow steps along the dock, his gaze turned downward, from time to time giving himself little slaps on his boot with a horsewhip. The young soldier spoke to me, asking if we had come on some military mission.

I informed him that I was the leader of a revolutionary column that operated in the Segovias and that I wished to have an interview with Dr. Juan Bautista Sacasa. He accompanied us to the presidential house. The young man was a colonel in Sacasa's army and a resident of the city of Diriamba. His name was Salvador Bosque.

On February 2, 1927, we left again for the Segovias with some weapons and some new companions, and among them was Colonel Salvador Bosque. Like one single soldier we proceeded to take control of those regions of northern Nicaragua, and before the formidable thrust of our soldiers the enemy was terrified and barely resisted. Colonel Salvador Bosque was the first officer of the Second Company of our famous cavalry which spread so much fear among the enemy. Our column marched from victory to victory, controlling valleys, towns, and cities.

Those regions where our column operated are very rich places, and our forces enjoyed an unusual sympathy, because all the inhabitants are revolutionaries and make common cause with us. There is one of those villages that is a true garden of humanity. The women there are uncommonly beautiful and generous. Our cavalry was made up of young men who, furthermore, were for the most part romantic, and so that village was visited constantly by the several units that made up our column.

Colonel Bosque, who distinguished himself as a brave man and as one of our cavalry's boldest horsemen, won the heart of one of our beautiful young Segovian girls. The girl was of the peasant class, but very pretty and educated. The wedding was to take place at the end of the war.

Our struggle constantly grew in intensity, and our young men crowned themselves with glory on the battlefields. We left those regions to move on to others farther away, where the enemy had managed to corner the future traitor, José María Moncada. Our cavalry marched up there and brilliantly defeated the enemy forces that were besieging Moncada. The last battle of that Constitutionalist War took place in Teustepe on May 1, 1927. In that battle Colonel Salvador Bosque died.

On May 4 of that same year the traitor José María Moncada deserted our ranks to go to Tipitapa to make a secret pact with the enemy. I returned to the Segovias with all the men I was able to take with me, and when I arrived at the village where Colonel Bosque had left his heart we were received with the customary enthusiasm.

The bride was in mourning and weeping inconsolably. The young men of our cavalry who had been inseparable friends of Colonel Bosque tried to console her with the same songs and sounds of guitars that in other days had offered happy moments to that romantic pair, but the girl cried and cried, and she wasn't soothed. . . .

The situation became more complicated for us, and our struggle brought greater dangers and sacrifices. The Yankee invaders of our territory and their allies, the Conservative sell-outs and the cowardly Moncadista Liberals, attacked us furiously. That awful pressure from the enemies of the national sovereignty of Nicaragua forced me to take refuge in the Segovian jungles, where we have upheld our country's honor and perhaps that of our race with strength and inflexibility. . . .

For more than a year I did not know the names of the unfortunate young girls who were violated by murderous Yankee invaders during their movements through those inoffensive and undefended towns, and so the impression I felt was a terrible one . . . when I came to know that that virgin bride of the late Colonel Bosque of my cavalry had been cruelly violated by miserable Yankee invaders and that as a result of that savage and humiliating act the young girl was wasting away, pale, shocked, and the mother of a son with blue eyes and a ruddy skin, and nobody even knew who his father might be. . . .

How terrible! Do my readers not see that that child is the fruit of the indifference of the governments of our Latin America, before the sorrow of my beloved and many times blessed Nicaragua?

Mérida, Yucatán, Mexico, October 1929
Patria y Libertad.
AUGUSTO CÉSAR SANDINO

[2, 25–27]

101. LETTER TO THE PRESIDENT OF MEXICO, EMILIO PORTES GIL, DECEMBER 4, 1929

Mérida, Yucatán, Mexico
December 4, 1929

Most Excellent President of the United States of Mexico,
Licenciado Emilio Portes Gil
Mexico, D.F.

Mr. President:

Despite my recognition of Mexico's great problems which you must deal with every day, allow me to invite you in the name of Nicaragua's freedom to inform me explicitly of your decisions regarding the conduct that the government of Mexico should adopt in the present circumstances, in which the spirit of the Nicaraguan people entrusts to your patriotism the upholding of their national sovereignty.

I am putting my modesty aside to inform you with all my heart that it is myself, your humble servant, who is most absorbed in the patriotic feelings of my people who for four years have fought bravely against the North American piratical assassins, against the traffickers in our national honor, and against the indifference and near-complicity of the governments of our Latin America, with the single honorable exception of those of Mexico.

Our departure from the Segovias to come here to Mexico has been a matter of life or death for the cause of maintaining the national sovereignty of Nicaragua.

Our powers of observation are reasonably good, and before we assembled our troops in the Segovias those powers permitted us to imagine that our trip to Mexico would suffer a deluge of false accusations, which, though lacking any basis in fact, would have to be refuted with the immediate resumption of our armed struggle in Nicaragua. Furthermore, we were correct when we foresaw that with my departure from the Segovias the Yankee assassins would have to reduce in large part the number of outlaw hordes who were devastating my dear country.

Very well. Even now, Mr. President, I have not seen the smallest sign of the fulfillment of the expectations that motivated us to travel to Mexico, and I have been most thoughtful since I realized that you are secretly denying me an interview. I am aware of the consequences for Mexico that would be inflicted upon you by the United States as the result of an interview with me, but I am also conscious of Mexico's ability, now and in the past, to remain firm in the face of the lordly pretensions of the United States, particularly when fulfilling a duty, such as not allowing the Yankee piracy to colonize Central America.

It's natural to think that a man who for years has been obliged by certain circumstances to oversee an important matter cannot feel satisfied to travel to a place in search of support and then be removed far from the centers of activity, to wait for something that he hasn't even had an opportunity to explain with any degree of thoroughness. I'm that man, and even if fulfillment of our request should be dependent upon the Mexican government's plans, we should not be kept ignorant of those plans, because this would be to display contempt and even to question our mental faculties.

There are, then, reasons enough to be not only pensive, but also concerned, because it seems that no plans of any kind exist regarding me, since I haven't even been granted the honor of an interview with you. I have doubts about one thing, and that is that the messenger we used for the exchange of communications with you, Captain José de Paredes, might have committed some offenses in addition to those I have been aware of until now, such as those expressed in some letters that the same Captain de Paredes left behind in Tegucigalpa, Honduras, which were recently published in that capital's newspapers, letters addressed to Captain de Paredes's mother, to General José María Tapia, to Dr. Pedro José Zepeda, and to me.

Captain de Paredes wrote the letters in question and then abandoned them in Tegucigalpa as he was returning from the mission he came to carry out with you in my name, and before he had returned to our camps. Those letters are written with a fantastic imagination and are totally lacking in truth. This same Captain de Paredes sent a telegram to me from Tegucigalpa dated last November 30, which states verbatim: "Papa to make me responsible for damnable papers. My twenty-two years to blame. Terribly saddened. José de Paredes."

Captain de Paredes's fantasy now makes me believe that he altered the meaning of the oral instructions that I gave him in the Segovias to pass on to you, with the idea that you would then agree to our request, and I believe he surely did much the same thing with me, so that if this is in fact the case, as I have recently begun to imagine, I deeply regret all the problems we might have caused you during these hard times which the politics of Mexico are passing through.

In any case, Mr. President, though my trip may have been the offspring of a misconception, this proves to us that our cause's victory is certain, for the same reasons that I revealed to you in earlier paragraphs, that is, that with my departure from the Segovias the Yankee pirate assassins have reduced their bandit horde in Nicaragua.

(I am not accustomed to keeping up illusions, and so I always hope that deeds will be the basis for my action. "Deeds, not words," is a fine slogan for those of us who rely on action alone.)

With this letter, Mr. President, I intend to reveal myself completely to you, and I am confident that, after you have read it, you will understand me and will be the person best able to determine whether my journey has been the offspring of a misconception or not, as I say in an earlier paragraph. If what I have expressed above should be affirmed by you, there will be no reason for me to insist upon my request for an interview with you, unless for reasons of patriotism you should have something to offer us.

If our business is to end with this letter, in the name of the blood spilled in Mexico in 1847 and in 1914, of that spilled in Nicaragua from 1909 until the present, and of that spilled in the other Latin American nations by the Yankee piracy, I wish to thank you for not placing obstacles in my way or in the way of the men who accompany me in our efforts to return to the Segovias.[1] In no way will any of this lessen our gratitude for the services you were good enough to grant us, and much less will it reduce our recognition of the high patriotism of the Mexican people.

I commend you, Mr. President, for your quick reply, so that we may carry out our journey before slander brings more harm to our poor humanity.

With our sincere consideration and respect, we remain your attentive and loyal servant.

Patria y Libertad.
A. C. SANDINO
Calle 87, No. 492

[17, 4 pp.]

1. The references are to the U.S. war with Mexico in 1847 and the shelling and military occupation of Veracruz in 1914 during the Wilson administration. RC

·1930·

102. LETTER TO GENERAL PEDRO ALTAMIRANO, JANUARY 2, 1930

My very dear brother:

I am sending you four small boxes of .38 special ammunition and two .38 Smith and Wessons for those who accompany you with total devotion. I am also sending you some leaflets in which the complete triumph of our cause is prophesied. General Pedro Antonio Irías knows about the prognostications of Father Reyes, and you should let him tell you about them.[1]

My dear brother, bear in mind, you and the other brothers who find themselves in this struggle, that I am nothing but an instrument of divine justice to redeem this nation, and that if I am in need of some of the miseries existing on this earth it's because I had to come before you also born of a woman and to offer myself to you full of the human miseries common to all of us in this earthly world, because otherwise you would not have been able to believe me if I had not spoken and been the same as you.

Bear in mind, General Pedro Altamirano, that I admire you sincerely and that you and those who are with you have been in other lives with me. May you, your worthy family, and General Pedro Antonio Irías receive the affection of your brother who honors you. And may you also have a felicitous 1930.

Patria y Libertad.

A. C. SANDINO

[11, 147–48]

1. As Sandino reveals in Doc. 1, early in life, in search of "spiritual consolation," he had read mythological books and sought out teachers of religion, one of whom was Justino Barbiaux of the town of Álamo, Veracruz, Mexico. In the present letter his mysticism and interest in spiritualism are revealed decisively. This tendency toward spiritual escape became even more pronounced in the last years of his life. See especially Docs. 130, 132, 133, and 184. RC

103. LETTER TO HERNÁN LABORDE, JANUARY 8, 1930

Mérida, Yucatán, Mexico
January 8, 1930

FOR THE WORLD PRESS

Secretary General of the Communist Party of Mexico
(Section of the Communist International)
Apartado 20–31, México, D.F.

It is an honor for me to send you this letter, which is the result of having read in clippings from *La Prensa* and *The New York Times*, both of last December 26, and from other Central American newspapers that were sent to us, the notice that according to those papers was published in *El Universal*, of that federal capital, to the effect that our departure from the Segovias was initiated by the sum of $60,000, which was offered to us as the price of that departure.

The notice in question states that your party, as well as the "Anti-Imperialist League of the Americas" and the "Hands-Off-Nicaragua Committee" are carrying on an investigation regarding that information, which we have immediately termed slanderous, and that "a prominent member of those groups"—the reports referred to are quoted verbatim—told a reporter of *El Universal* that the photograph of the check paid to Sandino was in the investigators' hands, but that, because the investigation is secret, permission to see the copy of the check had been denied.

We don't know what the "Hands-Off-Nicaragua Committee" has finally decided about the agreement we made in Veracruz with the citizens Federico Bach and Salvador de la Plaza, for that committee to reorganize its activities in the Anti-Imperialist League of the Americas to avoid a dispersion of energies, but we do not believe that the notice that now concerns us originated with any of those three organizations.[1] Rather, we wish to think that that allegation is the infamous work of agents of the Yankee piracy, and so we beg you to let us know what those three organizations are doing to demand responsibility from whoever released that slander which the reporter of *El Universal* picked up in the form of news.

The way this insult was released shows us that the author is totally unaware of our integrity and the clear understanding we have of the responsibility weighing upon us, or that Sandino and the men who accompany him are all campesinos or members of the working class, that they never debase themselves to gain advantages at the cost of the blood of the martyrs who have died in the struggle to free the oppressed. That slander the wicked use to stain the honor of free men is the work of impotent men, of scraps of humanity, of parasites who would destroy humanity, who are not apostles or fighters but spongers and frauds, incapable of sacrificing their lives on the altars of a noble cause, much less of having enough moral value to sign their names to their allegations.

We repeat that we cannot allow those organizations to be indifferent to the matter we here reveal, and we ask your immediate response because some last measures of a strategic nature will keep us in this sister republic for a few days, and because a committee of ours must leave for that capital in days to come with instructions to start an investigation of the matter and, no less important, to reach a clear understanding with the anti-imperialist organizations in respect to their attitude toward our struggle in defense of the national sovereignty of Nicaragua, which, we repeat, is mobilized and ready.

In the name of our army and my own name, I am yours most affectionately.

Patria y Libertad.
AUGUSTO CÉSAR SANDINO

Copy for the "Anti-Imperialist League of the Americas" and for the "Hands-Off-Nicaragua Committee."

[19, 2 pp.]

1. The agreement was signed at Sandino's request on July 8, 1929. Nine months later, in February 1930, another was signed to complement the first.

To reduce the effects of press attacks that have been made against the idealism of the Army in Defense of the National Sovereignty of Nicaragua, and to protect our army from spiteful people who attack us without justification, I have decided to publish documents that will prove the morality of our acts and our loyalty to the principles of Latin American brotherhood, as well as other documents from persons who have tried to present us to the people as incapable of upholding any principles at all.

No one will dare to deny that it was only the recognition of my duties as a Nicaraguan citizen and my love of my country which inspired me on May 6, 1926, to resign the position I held with the Huasteca Petroleum Company in the oil fields of Cerro Azul, Veracruz, Mexico, when the world press revealed news of an armed rebellion on the Atlantic coast of Nicaragua, led by Luis Beltrán Sandoval, against the usurpers of national power, Emiliano Chamorro and Adolfo Díaz. On October 26 of that same year I managed to launch an armed rebellion in the Segovias.

My resignation having been accepted on the 15th of that month, I left for Nicaragua, where I arrived on June 1, and although the revolutionary movement had been smothered by the sell-outs Díaz and Chamorro, I did not lose hope of being able to cooperate in the support of my country's independence against the Nicaraguan sell-outs, seriously threatened, then as now, by the Wall Street bankers. With the moral and financial support of some Segovian Liberals, I assembled a powerful column that later prevented the certain downfall of the rest of the Constitutionalist Army that had been organized by Dr. Juan Bautista Sacasa in Puerto Cabezas, Nicaragua, which was then situated in Chontales under the command of José María Moncada.

Very well, in support of historic truth and with the aid of documents signed by that same José María Moncada, which he sent to me and which are still in my possession, I can show the importance of the column under my command in placing Moncada in a position of prestige, which made it possible for him alone to decide the victory or defeat of the Liberal party. In effect, on May 4, 1927, the victory of the Nicaraguan people or the victory of José María Moncada's personal ambitions depended upon the decision of Moncada himself, and yet, with a disgusting attitude, ignoring the sacred duties of a soldier and of a citizen of Nicaragua, as well as his duty to support my country's sovereignty, he decided in favor of his own personal well-being, surrendering the defenseless Nicaraguan people to the annihilating bullets of the pirates of North America.

Until then the unprincipled governments of the United States had been able to conceal their policies in Nicaragua behind a mask of hypocrisy that permitted them to make those policies appear, at first glance, to possess an aspect of legality before the world, in this way covering up the true nature of their intervention in our internal affairs.

We in Nicaragua also believed in the famous democracy of the Yankee people, as there are still some who do, and we believed that the abuses committed by the White House governments were not looked upon with approval by the North American people. Later, however, we convinced ourselves of the contrary, but because of this same attitude in the first manifesto which I issued in the Segovias, on July 1, 1927, still believing in a remnant of virtue among the avalanche of Walker's descendants, I said in the section referring to construction of the Nicaraguan canal that the three million dollars with which they aspired and still aspire—contrary to all international decency—to possess the right to intervene in our internal and external affairs could be looked upon as shares of stock in the construction of that project.[1] Although my earlier statement attributing to the North American people the same imperialist attitude held by their leaders has provoked statements in opposition to what I am maintaining, I am entirely convinced that the North American people support and will always support the expansionist policies of their unprincipled governments.

When I wrote the Manifesto to which I refer, Nicaragua, my adored country, stood on the eve of one of the greatest epics of its history, which would hold the world in suspense. Who might have told Mr. Coolidge, on the day I wrote that manifesto, that as a result of the abuses committed by him, the Segovian jungles would witness the deaths of thousands of North American pirates, policemen of the Wall Street bankers? The Segovias are sad, desolate, full of sorrow and veiled in mourning, because this is what Mr. Coolidge's stupid policy has brought us to, but in spite of the White House, our Segovian jungles will be immortalized, and they have given our brother countries a chance to witness once again a repetition of the deeds so natural to our race.

Undoubtedly the four years of our war of liberation have also given me more experience, and the opportunity better to understand the need of all our Hispanic American countries to entirely expel from their national soil the citizens and capital of the United States, which in fact present nothing less than an imminent threat to the country that innocently receives them into its bosom; as well as the need to develop our industries and commerce, and to make every effort to establish an alliance with our Hispanic American brothers, together demanding for our America that the work of constructing the Nicaraguan canal and the establishment of a naval base on the Gulf of Fonseca, projected by the Wall Street bankers, will be the exclusive property of the Indo-Hispanic nationality, because only in this way can we defend our racial America from the voracity of the Yankee piracy.

For that purpose, on March 20 of last year, our army proposed to the governments of the Americas the celebration of a conference in the capital city of the Argentine republic, so that, as the representative of our army, I might present to the representatives of the Americas an original project that has as its fundamental purpose the preservation of the absolute sovereignty of the Hispanic American states.[2]

It was at the San Albino Mine, Nueva Segovia, Nicaragua, Central America, when no one dreamed of the surprise that Nicaragua would present to the world, that I set the course of our idealism, to which we have been and will remain faithful for as long as our heart continues to beat, having written this first manifesto with the same ardor and enthusiasm with which we have done everything else associated with our struggle.

January 9, 1930
Patria y Libertad.
A. C. SANDINO

[10, 92–95]

1. The manifesto is Doc. 15 in this collection; William Walker was an American from Nashville, Tennessee, who in the 1850s established himself in Nicaragua, had himself elected president, reestablished slavery, and made English the official language. He died before a Honduran firing squad in 1860. RC
2. See Docs. 90 and 91.

105. LETTER TO MAX F. VIANA, JANUARY 22, 1930

Mérida, Yucatán, Mexico
January 22, 1930

Señor Max F. Viana
Editor of *Mi Revista*
c/o Garcés y Cia., Puerto Cortés, Honduras, C.A.

My distinguished friend:

We are pleased to reply to your worthy letter of December 31 last, sending you our affectionate greeting and our best hopes that this year may be one of brilliant journalistic achievements favoring the noble causes to which you so vigorously dedicate your talents, thereby adding to the victories you have won as an active fighter.

With due punctuality we have received the important publication *Mi Revista*, of which you are the distinguished editor, giving us an opportunity to congratulate you cordially for what it owes to your efforts. Indeed you are right to complain to us for not having sent you our correspondence with complete regularity, but we don't doubt that you will be good enough to forgive us, keeping in mind that our failure to write to you has been the result of a decision made for the benefit of the activities in which we are involved in support of Nicaragua's national sovereignty, which, as you know, is intimately linked to the sovereignty of Latin America. For you as much as for the rest of the Latin Americans it will be more satisfying to see us taking part in activities that will give you an opportunity to lend your valuable cooperation to the struggle of our America to uphold our absolute sovereignty.

Perhaps even today I would deny myself the pleasure of writing to you, so that I might later do so with all the details, if it were not for two questions that you were kind enough to ask us in respect to our present position relative to our struggle against Yankee imperialism.

I am referring to what you say is common public opinion in that region: that we find ourselves in this peninsula in a state of benign incarceration and watched over by the Mexican government, etc., etc., and whether it is true or not that we have received offers from a North American company to enter into a contract to produce some films in Nicaragua, "in the theater of events."

When your letter reached us, I was thinking about some matters related to our anti-imperialist activity, and the questions contained in it gave me a moment of good humor. Among the countless stories going around about us, these are not the least malicious. I am happy to inform you that in respect to the first, we have no knowledge that the Mexican government is keeping watch over us, because Mexico is Mexico, and we don't think any government of this sister republic would lend itself to being our enemy's instrument against us. About the second matter—totally false— because the public is aware that Sandino and the members of his Army in Defense of the National Sovereignty of Nicaragua are not about to make people laugh or to create dramatic scenes even for the movies, but rather our work is to rein in the many unbridled individuals of unmentionable character in addition to those who would enslave the nations.

I was pleased that you note in your letter that you know my character too well to give credence to the story that we would enter into contracts of which even to dream that such a thing should be done would bring eternal dishonor to him who possessed such a wicked imagination.

We are taking very much into account the news you give us about what is said to have happened to Don Froylán Turcios in Paris. We have also seen that Señor Turcios denied the report, and we were really greatly pleased that it was not true that he and a Peruvian student were said to have had the principal role, since we consider Señor Turcios to be sincere though mistaken and not a traitor to our anti-imperialist struggle. The traitors are those who should suffer the penalties which justice determines.

We have many documents that will serve you in your future journalistic labors. Although for the moment it isn't possible to send them to you, we will do so presently, because I think they will always serve to clarify many points that at first glance appear obscure.

About our activities, we must limit ourselves to informing you that they are coming along satisfactorily, it being a question of only a few days until, as I have said, your valuable cooperation will be felt in other ways. In regard to these activities of ours, you will soon know, by what is reported in the press, that they are moving in the right direction.

For our part, you will also receive reports by faster methods, and with them we will again offer proof to you of the fraternal respect with which we regard you.

With an expression of our great respect we remain yours affectionately.

Patria y Libertad.
AUGUSTO CÉSAR SANDINO

[19, 2 pp.]

106. LETTER TO PEDRO JOSÉ ZEPEDA, JANUARY 25, 1930

Mérida, Yucatán
January 25, 1930

Dr. Pedro José Zepeda
General Representative of the Army in Defense of the National Sovereignty of Nicaragua
3a de Balderas No. 24
Mexico, D.F.

My very dear sir and distinguished friend:

Allow us to send you this letter to acquaint you with the concerns and doubts that events associated with our action in defense of the national sovereignty of Nicaragua have given us since our entrance into Mexican territory. Let me hurry along to tell you that we first felt some doubt in El Suchiate, Mexico, and it was this doubt that made me reenter Guatemalan territory, later returning to Mexico after receiving some apologies. In Veracruz I revealed to you twenty-five per cent of our intentions in the struggle we are carrying on in Nicaragua against the Yankee piracy, having reserved the other seventy-five per cent for a time when we might have the opportunity of an interview with our friend and with you. We reached the port of Progreso, Yucatán, Mexico, where upon our arrival an attempt was made to create confusion for a purpose we can't even imagine. Already in Mérida, Yucatán, Mexico, we couldn't find anyone with whom we could reach an understanding, and it isn't necessary to say that such a situation surprised us, because we thought that upon arriving in this city there would already be some instructions about these matters. We sent several messages to you in that capital city. You were rather sensible not to reply to us, and we found ourselves forced to undergo an economic siege in this city's "Grand Hotel," to the extent that when the director of that hotel presented us with the bill, we were forced to reveal our problem to an artist lady by the name of Ignacia Veratiguí, and this lady was good enough to advance us some money with which the hotel bill was settled. During those days Señor Manuel M. Arriaga, a representative of the Federal Executive to the Henequen Cooperative of Yucatán, introduced himself to us, and that same gentleman told us that he had instructions from the President of the Republic, *Licenciado* Emilio Portes Gil, to give us the sum of one thousand Mexican pesos per month.[1]

Señor Arriaga's words were a big surprise to us, and, taking advantage of the two thousand Mexican pesos he gave us, we decided to leave that region for the little port called El Cuyo, in this same state of Yucatán, from where we had intended to leave Mexican territory with the resources that had been presented to us.

As all this was happening, a telegram arrived for us from General José León Díaz, a member of our army, in which he informed us that the forces under his command, which were also under the command of General Francisco Estrada, had left the Segovian mountains, arriving in Tegucigalpa, Honduras, Central America, on August 2, 1929. Our forces, which today are in Tegucigalpa, Honduras, went there in obedience to our instructions, which we had put in writing, and in those instructions we indicated to them that one month after our departure from the Segovias they were to turn their weapons over to General Altamirano, demobilizing a part of our army, and that thirty men, including leaders and officers, were to make their way to this Republic.[2]

We did this because of our confidence in the verbal offers that the President of this republic, *Licenciado* Emilio Portes Gil, had made to us through Captain José de Paredes. Much influenced by this confidence, I had informed my secretary, the citizen Colonel Agustín Farabundo Martí, and we said this as well to that same Captain de Paredes, that we had accepted the loan of ten thousand dollars, an amount we thought sufficient for the thirty leaders and officers of our army to arrive, as we have said above, and also to provide some help to the members of our army who were awaiting our return to continue the struggle in defense of the national sovereignty of Nicaragua against the Yankee piracy. We were not given the full amount we had agreed to, and we received a loan of only five thousand dollars, and this caused a great deal of difficulty for our comrades' trip to this city, the last three having arrived yesterday, the 10th of that month. The telegram from General José León Díaz informing us of his arrival with other members of our army on August 2, 1929, in Tegucigalpa, Honduras, C.A., along with your silence and the instructions to turn over to us the sum of two thousand Mexican pesos per month, and our enemies claiming, on the other hand, that we had sold ourselves to the Yankee pirates produced a great disturbance in my mind, but at last I reached a decision. I sent a telegram to General José León Díaz, telling him that he and the other comrades should remain in Tegucigalpa, Honduras, C.A., until receiving a new order. I also sent a long letter to President Portes Gil, attaching a copy of that letter with the present one to you, along with the last one that I sent to President Portes Gil. I also sent you a letter of instructions.

One of those nights, having already gone to bed in the rooming house at the port of El Cuyo, Yucatán, a messenger arrived with a telegram from you. In that telegram you asked us for an interview, and after our customary meditation, I thought to myself that it was best to accept the interview with you instead of leaving for Nicaragua, since I supposed that you must be bringing something good to us and that we were obliged to choose the lesser evil from a bad situation. We returned from El Cuyo to Tizimín, Yucatán, where we had the pleasure of a meeting with you. During that interview I constantly expected that you would tell us of President Portes Gil's decision, and during the entire exchange of words between you and me I didn't find anything solid, and I heard you say that everything had been prepared in Espita, Yucatán, for us to go to see a farm. This was the way you informed me of the idea that then existed that my companions and I were to remain at a property in a provisional manner until it became possible for President E. Portes Gil to resolve the matter, that is to say, the cooperation that this government might provide in the struggle we were undertaking against the Yankee piracy in Nicaragua. From the conversation with you, I deduced that this government had found it impossible to settle the matter before this republic's presidential elections took place in November 1929. I found the offer very offensive, and I tried to be agreeable with you and with our friend President Portes. We kept in mind that, in order to be agreeable, often it is not enough to possess things in order to offer them, but that it is also essential to salvage some responsibilities. I also kept in mind that Captain de Paredes had told me in the Segovias that when he had come on his mission to this republic you had told him that you thought that before the month of November 1929, we would have been able to resume our activities in the Segovias. I expressed the wisdom of this to you, and it appeared to me that everything you said to me during the interview was in regard to what you said to Captain de Paredes about our quick return to the struggle. We arrived with you at Espita, Yucatán, and were cared for by the family of Señor Alfonso Peniche, in the house of that gentleman. It was through that family that we learned a few minutes after our arrival that it was Señor Peniche who was interested in selling the Santa Cruz farm, which clearly you were going to propose to us. I went with you to the Santa Cruz farm, and all that gave me an odor of disaster, as I told you later in one of our many letters. A correspondent of *El Diario de Yucatán* who resided in Espita, Yucatán, came to interview us, and I realized that it was necessary to say something to him. I told him that, in effect, in accordance with our army's plans, we would dedicate ourselves to agricultural work until we resumed our armed action in Nicaragua against the Yankee piracy.

With those words I sacrificed my own intention, but it was essential to do it that way to achieve the purpose we had proposed, which was the resumption of the struggle upon a solid international foundation, therefore certain to benefit our Indo-Hispanic peoples. The day of our visit to the Santa Cruz farm we left with you for this city and again we stayed about a month in the same hotel.

Luckily for our cause our companions were late in arriving and being without a cent we found ourselves obliged to ask for lodging from the labor leader of this state, Don Anacleto Solís. This same comrade Solís provided us with food on credit for a month, and in his house we have reunited all the members of our army who came from the Segovias.

The order that Señor Manuel M. Arriaga had been given began to be complied with again two months after our return from Tizimín, Yucatán, and since then the two thousand pesos in national currency have been presented to us punctually. With this sum even in the Segovian mountains themselves we have supplied those who have arrived here with clothing and food, all because of the lack of responsibility on the part of the persons assigned to remedy this. What occurred? Why so many dissimulations? Are we, in effect, victims of treachery? We don't know, and we think that not even you yourself know, though you have been and are now required to know. You must not regard this as a direct complaint against you, but rather as a necessary provision. Allow me to inform you, Dr. Zepeda, that today at five P.M. we called an extraordinary session attended by all the leaders and officials of our army who are present here, and at that session it was agreed to declare to you the following:

1. That you should continue being the representative of our Army in Defense of the National Sovereignty of Nicaragua because you enjoy the absolute confidence of that same army.

2. That the powers that our army conferred upon you to represent it in the efforts undertaken before the Mexican government are here repeated.

3. That you should be informed that our army is not in solidarity with the international policy that the president-elect of this republic, engineer Pascual Ortiz Rubio, will put into effect upon assuming the presidency of this country, according to his latest declarations to the press, since this gentleman has been seen flirting with the Yankee government, the common enemy of our Indo-Hispanic nations. The attitude of engineer Ortiz Rubio is considered unworthy.

4. That our army suspects that upon assuming the presidency of the republic Ortiz Rubio will recognize Moncada and that such a recognition would be a slap in the face to the emblem of our army.

5. To inform you that, in your character of general representative of our army and as a citizen of Nicaragua, you have been and are now obliged to understand this policy.

6. That our army in this republic, not having any means to obtain resources to return to the Segovian mountains, having convinced itself of the supposed betrayal of the present moments, orders you to take the necessary steps in the name of our army with persons or institutions sympathetic to our cause, and let them be Indo-Hispanics, to obtain the

amount of ten thousand Mexican pesos so that all of us here present may return to the Segovias, the only place suitable to us as free men and men of honor.

7. That if, upon receiving the present note, because of some displeasure it may cause you, you should decide to offer your resignation of the position which has been conferred upon you, the said resignation will not be accepted as long as a single member of our army, who in a Machiavellian way have been made to come here, exists in Mexican territory.

8. That responsibility is cast upon the Mexican government for what may have happened to our army since June 1, 1929, until the day when the exiled supreme leader of the Army in Defense of the National Sovereignty of Nicaragua reenters the encampments of the Segovias.

9. To render to you the most expressive thanks for the attentions you may offer to our army in the future in your position as general representative of the same and as an honored Nicaraguan citizen.

With demonstrations of our greatest consideration for you and in expectation of your important response, we remain yours fraternally.

Patria y Libertad.
A. C. SANDINO

[7, 104–5]

1. Later in this document Sandino puts the amount at two thousand pesos. RC
2. The instructions have not been found.

107. DECLARATIONS TO *THE NEW YORK WORLD*, JANUARY 28, 1930

The motives for the maintenance of our armed resistance to the North American invasion are the following:

To restore the rights of the Nicaraguan people who since 1909 have found themselves oppressed by the Yankee bankers. The Nicaraguan people do not owe one cent to the government of the United States of America, and all the treaties, pacts, concessions, and conventions that have been celebrated since that epoch until the present, and that may now be celebrated, between the U.S. government and the governments of Nicaragua, imposed by Yankee bayonets, do not possess any validity whatsoever, since they have been entered into and are now entered into behind the backs of the Nicaraguan people. If before signing the onerous and unfair treaties to which we refer the opinion of the Nicaraguan people had been consulted, such documents would have been rejected without further consideration because of the infamy from which they suffer.

We have understood that the principal intention of the United States of America in Nicaragua is that of appropriating to itself that portion of Central American territory where there exist possibilities for the opening of the interoceanic canal route, aside from the Gulf of Fonseca for a naval base. And for that reason our army, along with all the Nicaraguan people not corrupted or contaminated, have concluded that both the interoceanic canal and the naval base alluded to should be regarded as within the sovereignty of the Latin American nationality, for its progress and its own defense. Because, effectively, the region that has aroused the greed of imperialism, though it is situated in the Central American isthmus, must be controlled by our Latin America, since the interoceanic canal route as well as the Gulf of Fonseca have been summoned by natural law to fulfill a historic and decisive role in the life and the future of the nations of the globe, but above all those of Latin America.

The concept I have of the North American people is:

The North American people are as imperialistic as their own leaders. If in the United States there exist some anti-imperialist organizations, it is not precisely because they are clearly integrated by North Americans, but rather in the majority they are Russians, Lithuanians, Germans, Spaniards, Italians, Latin Americans, from all parts of the world, without the

North Americans. Rare will be the exceptions who break this general rule.

If the United States of America wishes to avoid a catastrophe and its imminent collapse, it should have greater respect for the weak nations and those of fewer resources.

Ex-President Coolidge and ex-Secretary of State Kellogg, despite their imperialist adventures, are a couple of failures whom the North American people ought not to blame, since the fact that their names have passed into history enveloped in crimes and blood weighs also, in brief, upon the shoulders of all the North American people, accomplices in their crimes. Those two moral wretches thought at the outset of the armed struggle in Nicaragua that Sandino was a leader of a cheap patriotism. But with the passage of time the justice of our cause has demonstrated to them that we have been sent to serve as a restraint and as a punishment for their own unbridled crimes and those of their successors.

Declarations authorized with our signature.

Patria y Libertad.
A. C. SANDINO
Mexico, D.F.
January 28, 1930

[19, 2 pp.]

108. REPLIES TO A QUESTIONNAIRE FROM *EL UNIVERSAL* OF MEXICO, JANUARY 28, 1930

The purpose of your journey to Mexico?

To fulfill certain agreements with our general representative, Dr. Pedro José Zepeda, related to the struggle we are upholding to maintain the national sovereignty of Nicaragua.

Your opinion of our country's situation with respect to social and political matters and your impression of the Mexican Army?

Concerning social organization it has been demonstrated that Mexico is at the vanguard of the nations of our continent, and this is because in Mexico popular revolutions have been more frequent than in any other country of our America. This same recognition that Mexico is a revolutionary nation inspired us with sufficient confidence to come here, where we find the fundamental basis for the prosecution of our struggle in Nicaragua, which is nothing other than the daughter of the Mexican revolution. Concerning Mexico's internal political condition, any opinion belongs to the Mexican people alone.

The Mexican Army possesses a clear awareness of its mission; for example, there may be seen in its evolution a constant tendency to democratize itself.

It has been said here that you had decided to abandon your activities in support of the total freedom of Nicaragua, and it has even been claimed that you would make a visit to the United States. What truth is there in this? This same report adds that they gave you sixty thousand dollars.

We abstain from responding to that question because its content is tendentious and the work of the enemies of the cause of Nicaraguan sovereignty. In regard to the slanderous claim that we received the sum of sixty thousand dollars, this must originate in the wicked mind of some poor devil who perhaps has never had the opportunity to hold such a sum in his hands, however much he may be inclined to use any means to acquire it, however unworthy it may be. In his low thoughts it looks to the slanderer as if Sandino is made of the same spoiled material that individuals of that species are made of. At an opportune time we sent *El Universal* a copy of the letter we had sent to Comrade Hernán Laborde, secretary general of the Communist party of Mexico.[1] We have in our hands that comrade's reply, which states verbatim:

"Our Central Committee has acquainted itself with your letter of the eighth of this month regarding the notice published by the bourgeois press of this country and that of the United States dealing with your departure from Nicaragua and the cause to which it has been attributed. Our C.C. has agreed to inform you that our Party is entirely without responsibility for publication of that notice; and that, concerning the Continental Committee of the Anti-Imperialist League of the Americas, we can state that they also have had nothing to do with the matter. With full attention, etc. (Signed) H. Laborde."

If it had been our intention to abandon the struggle in Nicaragua, we would not have chosen Mexico for that purpose, as we have pointed out in the course of your questions, because Mexico is a hospitable country for revolutionaries and for free men, never for those who shirk their duty or who have failed. The United States has always been the favorite place of attraction for the Judases. Therefore your question, as the Mexican that you are, brings out resentment in me, because we expect everything noble from Mexico.

You have not abandoned your position, despite your being in Mexican territory? Do you intend to return to the struggle in Nicaragua? What groups continue to fight? What is the situation existing now in your country? How do the revolutionaries carry out their hostilities against the enemy?

In these moments our struggle is limited to the preservation of the war materials which we have fought with, for the time when we resume our activities. At the head of the forces still in the region of the Segovias are Generals Pedro Altamirano and Miguel Ángel Ortez, Colonel Coronado Maradiaga, and Lieutenant Colonel Rafael N. Altamirano. You might have heard all kinds of stories about us, but never one saying that our weapons have fallen into the enemy's hands.

The politicians of Nicaragua have created a condition of servility in their relations with the United States that is without precedent in our history. And the impudent Moncada is constantly stating in the press that he is very concerned for the progress of the country, constructing new railroad lines, highways, etc., seeking in this way to lull to sleep the conscience of the Nicaraguans. But no. They will not achieve this, because our activity there has now penetrated the spirit of our fellow countrymen, and everyone knows that what the Nicaraguan people desire is to disavow the treaties, pacts, and conventions made with the United States of America against their will by the Nicaraguan sell-outs of their country.

We consider the Yankees our enemies, and to them, when they fall into our power, is applied what our young men call a "waistcoat cut," that is to say, automatic decapitation.

Will you visit Señores Portes Gil, Calles, Ortiz Rubio, and Amaro?
In an official character, no. But if I should have an opportunity to do so in private, possibly I would visit them.

Patria y Libertad.
A. C. SANDINO
Mexico, January 28, 1930

[19, 2 pp.]

1. This letter, signed in Mérida, Yucatan, on January 8, 1930, is included in the present edition as Doc. 103.

109. LETTER TO HENRI BARBUSSE,[1]
FEBRUARY 6, 1930

Mexico, D.F.
February 6, 1930

Comrade Henri Barbusse
144 Rue Montmartre
Paris (2ème.)

Very esteemed comrade:

This is the second letter that we have the pleasure of sending you, the first having been sent from our fields of anti-imperialist armed struggle in the Segovias, Nicaragua, in response to the one you sent us there, dated in July, 1928.[2]

From the Segovias as well as from the city of Mérida, Yucatán, where we are residing temporarily in order to establish our anti-imperialist activity upon a firm basis of continental action, we have not stopped mailing you the press items that our struggle has occasioned, without having written to you directly, because we have judged these press items sufficient for you to understand the various phases that our activities against Yankee imperialism have been passing.

The last expression of our work against Yankee imperialism and its agents was sent to you from the city of Mérida, Yucatán, last January, and it consists of a letter that we sent to the Communist party of Mexico in order that it, the Anti-Imperialist League of the Americas, and the Hands-Off-Nicaragua Committee might together undertake their investigation to discover who had released the news item claiming that we had received the sum of $60,000 to leave the Segovias, an item in which it was said that the three named organizations were making an investigation to find out whether or not we had received that amount. The Communist party of Mexico replied informing us that neither it nor the other organizations knew anything about what had been asserted by the bourgeois press. Upon arriving in this capital last January 28, it was confirmed to us by the Communist party of Mexico and by the other two organizations mentioned that the slanderous story about us must have originated from sources of Yankee imperialism or from those of its agents.

Having made clear before the Continental Committee of the Anti-Imperialist League of the Americas and the Communist party of Mexico the position of anti-imperialist struggle that our army upholds, on the 4th of this month we accepted the invitation made to us by the World League against Imperialism and repeated by the Continental Committee of the Anti-Imperialist League of the Americas, according to a letter that we received from it on last January 31, to make a tour in support of anti-imperialist action through Europe and Latin America.

Since accepting the invitation to make the proposed tour, we have reserved the right to inform the Council of the World Anti-Imperialist League of our need to return to Nicaragua to resume our struggle against Yankee imperialism once that tour has been completed.

We have, then, the best intentions that our fight against Yankee imperialism in Nicaragua will acquire the character of anti-imperialist struggle in a firm revolutionary action of the masses on a continental and world-wide scale, in accordance with the resolutions of the World Anti-Imperialist Congress of Frankfurt, an aspect of that position being the unmasking of the Latin American governments, including that of this republic.

Assured of soon having the pleasure of greeting you personally, I remain yours fraternally against imperialism and its agents.

Patria y Libertad.
AUGUSTO CÉSAR SANDINO

[19, 2 pp.]

1. French novelist and peace advocate, author of *Le Feu*, a bitter novel depicting the brutality of World War I, and editor of *L'Humanité*. RC
2. Sandino's first letter to Henri Barbusse has not been found.

110. MESSAGE TO THE SEVENTH MEXICAN STUDENT CONGRESS MEETING IN MONTERREY, NUEVO LEÓN, FEBRUARY 17, 1930

Through me the Army in Defense of the National Sovereignty of Nicaragua has the honor to greet you, young Mexicans, who are in the vanguard of the continental student youth movement, and it congratulates you for having convened the Seventh National Student Congress to resolve the problems that this historic hour has placed before you. Your problems are also our problems, ours on all occasions, and today more than ever before you have made them your own, because we are motivated by the situation in which we have been placed by events, in confrontation with Yankee imperialism, the assassin of free peoples.

We Latin Americans form a single nationality: the Latin American nationality. It is thus the Latin American people and not their governments who in the final analysis are called upon to determine the fate of that same nationality. A government is the servant of the people and not its master.

History informs us that in some regions of our globe, according to the law's solemn dictates, when a citizen came to power he heard these words spoken: "Each of us is like you, but all of us are more than you." Do not forget that times are always the same.

You know all too well that imperialism looks differently upon the contradictions brought about by their own organization, which is founded upon the exploitation of the colonial and semi-colonial countries, and which depends for this exploitation upon certain governments of those countries and, concerning Latin America, upon the abjectness of many Latin American governments. It is not, then, because you have seen us fighting Yankee imperialism in the Segovias that we come before you today to discuss imperialism in these few lines, but rather because of the circumstance that this is a student congress that will study, along with cultural problems, the relations between those problems and Yankee imperialism, because the several ways in which imperialism seeks to infiltrate the educational centers of our continent are not unknown to you.

Nothing will be as important for us as knowing, when the work of your congress has ended, that you have defined concretely the problems that you will study, in order to possess a firm basis for struggle in the future.

Mexico, D.F., February 17, 1930
Patria y Libertad.
AUGUSTO CÉSAR SANDINO

[19, 1 p.]

III. MESSAGE TO THE URBAN AND RURAL WORKERS OF NICARAGUA AND OF ALL LATIN AMERICA, FEBRUARY 26, 1930[1]

Comrades:

The working class of all Latin America today suffers a double exploitation: that of imperialism, mainly that of the Yankee, and that of the native bourgeoisie or the national capitalists and exploiters, who in their eagerness to obtain the favors of the insatiable invader are constantly intensifying the destruction of the revolutionary movement, the persecutions of its directors, imprisonments, and banishments.

To accomplish this criminal work imperialism depends not only upon the open support of the Latin American dictators, but upon an agency even more opprobrious: the organisms and "leaders," that is to say, labor leaders who are bought with crumbs soaked in the blood of the colonial peoples, "leaders" who seek to gain control of the labor movement to infect it with their microbe collaborationists, causing it to abandon the road of revolutionary struggle, the only effective way to fight against imperialism and its continental lackeys. Aside from these enemies of the working class, there exist the nationalist charlatans of the left, who with gestures and demagogic phrases retard the crystallization of a genuine anti-imperialist movement based on the exploited workers and campesinos of America.

In Latin America imperialism has skillfully taken advantage of *Pan-Americanism* to mask its penetration, and it became the task of the heroic soldiers who at my side defend the sovereignty of Nicaragua to reveal this macabre farce represented by the latest congresses of the Pan-American organizations: the Pan-American Labor Confederation and the Pan-American Union.

The first of these held its Fifth Congress in Washington in July 1927, and during its sessions occurred the most cowardly and criminal slaughter of Nicaraguan workers and campesinos, killed by Yankee planes. This congress, which included false representatives of the Nicaraguan workers, lacked the courage to call the bullying marines by their true name, accepting the formula of "foreign forces," imposed by the imperialist Mathew Woll, vice president of the Pan-American Labor Confederation and its mother organization, the American Confederation of Labor. The sole resolution calling for the urgent withdrawal of the Yankee pirates from wherever they might be found, the freedom of Puerto Rico and the Philippines, and the absolute rejection of the other forms of domination of Yankee imperialism in Latin America received the vote of its author alone, the latter having suffered the censure of the entire congress, the Nicaraguan delegation making common cause with the syndicalist Monroeism ratified by William Green.

The second organization, the Pan-American Union, held its last congress in Havana in January 1928. As President Coolidge was delivering expressions of unity and Pan-American brotherhood, his soldiers were violating Nicaraguan women, his airplanes were burning villages and murdering defenseless men, women, and children. At that congress all the dictators, semi-dictators, and future dictators of the continent were present. As was the case at the congress of their syndicalist agents, the above-mentioned Pan-American Labor Confederation, the congress of the Pan-American Union did not proceed beyond a pusillanimous pronouncement against the "interventions." The word "Nicaragua" was not uttered by any of the accomplices of the crimes being committed against her.

Before all this betrayal and abuse, the reply of the working class in Latin America has been: *organization*. In the last two years revolutionary labor unions have been created in Brazil, Uruguay, Mexico, Honduras, Panama, and other countries, which together held a great conference at which they created the Latin American Labor Confederation, one of the pillars needed to support future anti-imperialist struggles.[2]

At this congress, among the very few countries not represented were Nicaragua, Santo Domingo, Haiti, and Puerto Rico, countries that have suffered most from invading imperialism. This is not an accident. The reason may be explained by what was said before, that is, that in each of these countries, for a period which in the name of the struggles of the Nicaraguan people we hope has ended, the poison of the Pan-American Labor Confederation removed the labor movement from its basic foundation, which is the irreconcilable conflict between the exploiting agents of imperialism and of the exploited, the only guarantee of the victory of our cause.

Comrades: Our depature from Nicaraguan territory has not meant a truce in our struggle against the common enemy, Yankee imperialism, but rather the prolongation of our struggle in the sense of acquiring new contingents to strengthen it, which we hope will include the Latin American Labor Confederation.

Until now our Army has recognized the support that sincere revolutionaries have given to our arduous struggle, but with the sharpening of that struggle, with growing pressure on the part of the Yankee bankers, and because of the character that that struggle is acquiring, the vacillators, the timid, are abandoning us, because only the workers and campesinos will go on until the end. Only their organized force will win the victory.

Nicaraguan comrades and all those who are still disorganized and outside the Latin American Labor Confederation, in the name of the heroic soldiers of the Army in Defense of the National Sovereignty of Nicaragua, we cry out to you: organize, your place is in the ranks of the Latin American Labor Confederation, the only labor organization that defends the interests of the working class.

H. Veracruz, Veracruz, Mexico
February 26, 1930
Patria y Libertad.
AUGUSTO CÉSAR SANDINO

[19, 2 pp.]

1. The 1980 edition contains this document in the incomplete form found in source 11, 95. In the 1984 edition the entire text, now preserved in the IES archive, is reproduced.

2 This was a revolutionary labor organization of communist inspiration, established in Montevideo in 1929. It was the response of the revolutionary workers of Latin America to the efforts made by North American imperialists to control the continental labor movement.

112. LETTER TO ERNESTINA DE MÜLLER, MARCH 3, 1930

Mérida, Yuc.
March 3, 1930

Señora Ernestina de Müller
Guatemala

Dear Tina:

I received your letter dated January 20 of the current year and through it have learned that you are returning to Guatemala, leaving Colombia.

Because of the uncertainty of your address and the great amount of work caused by the struggle to which I am dedicated, I had not written to you as I would have liked. But I'm taking advantage of your return to Guatemala to do so, promising to write more often in days to come. I have not had any news of your mother. I have received various letters from home in which they have informed me that my old parents are well, which fills me with happiness.

It's true that a lady and a boy are accompanying me, as the newspapers have said. But it is appropriate to explain that she is not my wife Blanca, but rather Teresa, who has accompanied me through the mountains of the Segovias in my struggle against the invader, and the boy, an adoptive son of mine.[1] Teresa has been the companion of my struggle, and I feel affection for her and acknowledge her. She is my wife because of the love I feel for her in my heart.

I am making preparations to resume the struggle with greater vigor, because there has not been a halt but rather a pause in the thick of the duel between the invader and ourselves. I have faith that in the end we will be able to cleanse Nicaragua of the pirates, with the help of our rifles and of the people of the land who sympathize with our cause and grant us their moral and material support. Nicaragua must be free, in spite of the doubters or cowards.

I return your husband's greeting, and may you accept the invariable and sincere affection of

Patria y Libertad.
AUGUSTO CÉSAR SANDINO

[19, 1 p.]

1. This was Teresa Villatoro, a native of El Salvador whom Sandino had met at the San Albino Mine in 1926, and who rejoined him soon after his marriage to Blanca, traveling with him to Mexico in 1929. The boy was probably her son, who in 1926 was already five years old. RC

113. LETTER TO CAMILO J. GUILLÉN, MARCH 3, 1930

Mérida, Yuc.
March 3, 1930

Señor Camilo J. Guillén
La Ceiba, Honduras

Dear companion:

I have had the greatest pleasure of receiving your worthy letter dated January 15 of this year, to which I refer with the affection and fondness of one who never forgets his old companions in arms.[1]

Your letter fills me with satisfaction, because it shows that in your spirit there still exists a feeling of camaraderie worthy of the patriot and of the soldier. You may be sure that neither in happiness nor in adversity do I ever forget those who first accompanied me in the hard crusade for the freedom of our country, and that you are included among them. Full of hope and faith in the final triumph of our holy cause, if someday we should see realized our dreams of redeeming Nicaragua and of saving our peoples from shame and dishonor, part of that glory will also belong to you, you who still breathe life, and also to our beloved dead, among whom I can do no less than to evoke the gallant figure of Rufo Marín.[2] And if you should wish it so, I will accept you with open arms if you return to our mountains to fight against the wretched invaders. Tell this to the young men whom you say are there with you and who belonged to our army.

It seems useless for me to tell you that the struggle will continue with greater vigor and that neither today nor at any other time while the Yankee treads upon the land of our elders will I be prepared to compromise with traitors and invaders. The struggle to which we find ourselves dedicated is one of life or death for the dignity of our peoples, and, aware of this as I am, I will know how to go on without dishonor until the final act. Neither promises of gold nor the temptation of other offers have affected my spirit in any way. The old comrades will always find me at the post that duty and honor assign to me, firm in my determination to drive out the Yankee invader.

With a handshake for you and the companions of battle you say are there, I have great pleasure to subscribe myself your attentive and faithful servant.

Patria y Libertad.
AUGUSTO CÉSAR SANDINO

[19, 1 p.]

1. Camilo Guillén was a fellow-employee at the San Albino Mine and one of the first men to join Sandino's rebellion in the Segovias in 1926, but he abandoned the struggle soon after Sandino's attack on Ocotal in June 1927. RC

2. An employee at San Albino and one of Sandino's first followers, who was killed in the attack on Ocotal. RC

114. LETTER TO C. SEGURA, MARCH 6, 1930

Mérida, Yuc.
March 6, 1930

Señor Don C. Segura
San José, Costa Rica

My very worthy compatriot:

With the greatest pleasure I acknowledge receipt of your letter dated last February 2, to which I have given the attention it deserves because of the interesting facts it contains. Likewise I acknowledge receipt of the code, which we can't use because we suspect that our correspondence is being read.

We have made broad declarations about our activity in the face of the enemy's low machinations and the wicked slander you refer to, that is to say, that which concerns the sixty thousand dollars. The latter has been given a death blow by the evidence of our conduct, which in every way conforms with duty and honor. For that reason it's useless to go on denying slanderous statements, because our background allows no place for the idea that we can be bribed by the enemy, in exchange for a sum of money. We have been able to refute the slanderers, leaving the dignity of our cause without any blot or stain.

You will have news eventually of our return to the fight in the Segovias, exactly as we have promised, and it will then be indispensable to defend ourselves by all means and with all the resources at your disposal. The more blows you strike against the enemy, the better it will be. It's essential to make them desperate, creating problems for them everywhere and causing the outbreak of small rebellions in the places that have remained quiet until today, which suggested an apparent conformity with the invaders' presence.

If you think it's time to carry out an invasion on that side, don't waste any time and launch it as soon as possible. As far as we are concerned, we have everything prepared for our plans to succeed. When the opportunity arrives, the invader will receive very cruel blows.

I have received your other letters, and if I haven't answered them it's because we've been much occupied by other matters that have deserved our immediate attention.

With a cordial greeting for all your compatriots who are concerned about the success of our cause, I have the pleasure to subscribe myself your attentive and faithful servant.

Patria y Libertad.
AUGUSTO CÉSAR SANDINO

[19, 2 pp.]

115. LETTER TO JUAN J. COLINDRES, MARCH 7, 1930

Mérida, Yuc.
March 7, 1930

Señor Don Juan J. Colindres
Danlí, Honduras

Dear companion and friend:

With great pleasure we are responding to your letter of last January 22, returning to you and yours the affectionate greetings and regards that you sent us. If we haven't complied before with this pleasant duty to our friend and companion, it's because we were absent, inasmuch as we have just returned from Mexico City, where we remained for about a month.

We heartily regret the adverse situation you find yourself in, according to your letter, and we are even sorrier we can't help our companions, since we also aren't in a bed of flowers, despite the vicious slanders that our enemies have made against us, which unfortunately have caused an echo among certain elements who do not know our character and the idealism that so strongly reinforces our struggle for the rights of the peoples of America. By now you must know about those slanders and the vigorous way we have eliminated them.

With real enthusiasm we have learned about General Ortez's energetic activities and his victories against the common enemy, contained in that leader's letter that you copied for us in yours. We had already had news through other channels of General Ortez's activities, but we are always grateful for your reports, which reveal the interest you take in our sacred cause.

Things are going well for us. We hope very soon to be in our free mountains of the Segovias, overcoming all obstacles that may stand in the way of our march, and when this occurs, our enemies who knew we wouldn't sell ourselves for a fistful of filthy gold will issue another sovereign denial. Whatever the obstacles, our cause must proceed on to victory. We must have faith, enthusiasm, and perseverance and not waste any opportunity to upset the plans of the enemy, whether they be Yankees or traitors.

With regards for you and family, I am your attentive servant, companion and friend.

Patria y Libertad.
AUGUSTO CÉSAR SANDINO

[19, 1 p.]

116. LETTER TO ENRIQUE RIVERA BERTRAND, MARCH 13, 1930

Mérida, Yuc., Mexico
March 13, 1930

Señor Don Enrique Rivera Bertrand
Primero de Mayo 14
Veracruz, Ver.

Very esteemed friend:

We have had the pleasure of receiving your last letter, dated the 10th of this month. We accept the greeting you sent therein and return it to you most fraternally.

I am informed that you received a letter from Comrade Jolibois, who was thought to be insane or dead. I also received a letter from that same comrade, which has given us great satisfaction. I am returning the letter of Comrade Jolibois, as you ask us to do. Thanks for your attention.

You were already aware of the fervor reigning in this state and the people's restlessness. The press has permitted something to seep through, and what you tell me is always of interest. I think everything can be reduced to simple maneuvers without any significance for the anti-imperialist struggle. Taking positions on one side or the other would have no real importance for the masses. A tempest in a glass of water, in our opinion.

I'm pleased to learn that you were with Comrade Epigmenio Guzmán, who has been so loyal and sincere toward our side. I hope to write to him, since I didn't have the pleasure of speaking to him personally, which was my wish, as you know. We will take good note of his offer. Patriotic and resolute men are the kind we need for the struggle or for points of support in the conflict. If you should see him again, say hello to friend Guzmán for me.

That fellow Manuel Salvador Sandino is known to me only through letters. I don't have any family relationship with him and he makes a mistake when he uses my name or the cause to exploit the good companions. Once and for all, it's necessary to deny every kind of help to such types, true exploiters and pilferers of the struggle. That sort abounds in the world, and one has to be careful. You shouldn't fall into the grip of such individuals again. I appreciate your good will, but you shouldn't let yourselves be surprised.

To avoid such things, it's good to deal only with those individuals who arrive with good credentials or have authorization from us, written and never verbal. In this way every bit of support will go to its true destination and not into the hands of crooks.

It seems time for me to inform you that in a few days the ex-members of our army Carlos Quezada, Pedro Espinoza, and Carmelo Torres, who have been dismissed as unworthy of belonging to our glorious institution, will arrive aboard the steamship *Superior*. These fellows have been guilty of disgraceful conduct, and this was why we took extreme measures against their activities. Just as we have praise for those who bring nobility to our struggle, we don't spare our insults for scoundrels. Those fellows have made themselves worthy of stern measures. We have already sent instructions to the fighting zones and alerted the friends of Central America, whom they would like to take by surprise.

Since we don't want to abandon anybody, even the unworthy, to their fate here, we provisioned them with what they needed to reach their destination. As a result they won't need help, and if they ask for it, it's a swindle. It will be appropriate to give them the cold shoulder. We must be inflexible with the unworthy. Take note of this and don't let yourself be taken by surprise.

Ardila Gómez is going to Colombia. We have also given him everything he needs, again making sacrifices. As you well know, we are not lying in a bed of flowers.

Don't hesitate to inform us of anything. Whatever you have to say interests us because yours is a sincere and loyal voice.

I received a letter from Anita, which I'm answering.

The matter of the twenty Nicaraguans is a farce. Nobody has received any authorization from me to enter Nicaraguan territory. One must be on the alert against impostors, who are swarming all around us.

Your dream could be realized. Everything is a matter of time. One must have faith and persevere.

My companions and I return your greetings to you most affectionately. You already know how much we remember and respect you.

Patria y Libertad.
AUGUSTO CÉSAR SANDINO

[19, 2 pp.]

117. LETTER TO EPIGMENIO GUZMÁN, MARCH 15, 1930

Mérida, Yuc., Mexico
March 15, 1930

Señor Don Epigmenio Guzmán
Villa Cardel, Veracruz, Mexico

Esteemed comrade:

Even if personally we have not had the pleasure of exchanging impressions with you upon our arrival in Veracruz in July of last year, our good comrade, Enrique Rivera Bertrand, had already had the opportunity to acquaint us fully with your activities in favor of our cause and the purely anti-imperialist spirit that motivates you. This by itself has sufficed for us to take an interest in your reports, and we regard you as a good element in the struggle against Yankee piracy.

On the past occasion to which we refer, it was not possible for us to speak with you because of our fatigue after many days of arduous travel, even when we knew later that you wanted to see us. The occasion was not propitious, and we regret not having seen you, but Comrade Rivera Bertrand always kept us posted about your activities.

Now when we were in Mexico City, we told Comrade Rivera Bertrand about our wish to see you, since he accompanied us on the journey, but our wishes weren't realized. While passing through Villa Cardel, where we knew you resided, we sent our best compliments to you, and we commissioned Comrade Rivera Bertrand to carry our fraternal greeting to you. We know from a letter recently received that he has satisfactorily complied with that commission and has spoken with you.

As we have said on many occasions, we have complete confidence in the Mexican people, and we hope that on every occasion their attitude will correspond to the hopes that the Latin Americans have placed in them. Because that nation is the repository of our hopes, and we don't think it will falter before the maneuvers of imperialism. And just as the nation is a complete aggregate, you are the good individual fighters.

Our position before the common enemy must be clear and defined. Reasons of dignity and respect oblige us not to enter into agreements nor to misrepresent the mission that fate assigned to us, at the moment when imperialism attacks brazenly as in Nicaragua, or in a sly fashion as in other countries where its infiltration has alarming characteristics. To fight, to fight, and only to fight, this is our only mission, our highest duty. Submission and calm can only bring discredit and the disappearance of our autonomous nations.

We hope, esteemed comrade, that you and all Mexicans will know how to comply with your duty, keeping to the straight and honorable line, not allowing the stealthy advances of imperialism.

With a very affectionate greeting for you and the other comrades of that region, we are attentive and faithful servants.

Patria y Libertad.
AUGUSTO CÉSAR SANDINO

[19, 2 pp.]

118. LETTER TO HERNÁN LABORDE, MARCH 29, 1930

Mérida, Yucatán, Mexico
March 29, 1930

Comrade Hernán Laborde
General Secretary of the Communist Party of Mexico
(Section of the Communist International)
Apartado 20-31, México, D.F.

Esteemed comrade:

Your letter of the 22d of this month is in our hands, and what you tell us in respect to the mission that Comrade Contreras will carry out in Berlin is understood in all its details.

In our letter of the 12th of this month we told you of our plan in the event the reply from Berlin was too long delayed. In ours of the 15th of this month, we asked you to inform us by telegram to this city of the results of Comrade Contreras's mission, once you had knowledge of it by cable from Berlin.[1] We repeat our request. We have in view our journey to the Segovias, and I will inform you if it is possible for me to leave for Europe from there, taking events into account.

You will receive our correspondence from Central America, and for this purpose we will inform you of the representation we have there (outside of Nicaragua) so that we can remain in contact with you. We will establish rapid means of communication in convenient places as required, and therefore it will be the same appointed companions who will provide you with the way to write to us.

With our departure for the Segovias the plan we formulated with you will change, but when we receive the decision from Berlin we will let you know how it appears to us most convenient to develop continental and worldwide anti-imperialist activity, upon the basis of the cooperation that has been offered.

We continue preparing the statements. You will have them shortly.

Our intention to leave for the Segovias will not prevent you from writing to me in this city until further notice; we will maintain a system of communications that is set up here for the time when we reestablish contact with you from Central America. As always, then, we ask you to write to the address we gave you in this city.

We continue mobilizing for Central America, despite the financial difficulties we are facing.

We have had the pleasure of reading the letter of credentials that the Central Committee of the Communist party of Mexico has given to Comrade Colonel Agustin F. Martí, as a representative of that Central Committee to our army and in particular to me, in my role as leader of that army. In this regard, I think it would be convenient for the credentials to be extended to represent the Central Committee before the leadership of the Army in Defense of the National Sovereignty of Nicaragua and not the army itself.

The reasons that the Central Committee may adduce for this decision should be "the relations that exist between the Leader," etc. (omitting the word "cooperation"). Concerning all the rest, we are in agreement, and the representation will be recognized when it arrives in the form I'm recommending to you.

Always awaiting your communications, we subscribe ourselves to you fraternally.

Patria y Libertad.
AUGUSTO CÉSAR SANDINO

[19, 1 p.]

1. These letters are not included in this edition. RC

119. LETTER TO ESTEBAN PAVLETICH, MARCH 30, 1930

Mérida, Yuc., Mexico
March 30, 1930

Señor Esteban Pavletich
Mexico, D.F.

Worthy companion and friend:

I have had the pleasure of receiving your esteemed letters of the 23rd and 25th of this month, one written in the penitentiary, a place that brings honor to those who go there because of their efforts on behalf of freedom, as has happened to you, and the other written when you were already outside it. I have read them with real interest, and their contents have caused me sorrow and satisfaction at the same time. Those letters strongly reflect your temperament as an indestructible and tireless fighter, and more than anything else the purity of your idealism. Young men like yourself are those our America needs in the arenas of ideas and action, to deliver her from her internal torments and the dangers from outside.

You mustn't think I was indifferent to your misfortune at the time of the difficult test to which you were subjected by this country's authorities, a test that has served to reveal your spirit as a fighter. From the moment you disappeared from our side we used every resource to find out what had happened to you, without stopping to think that you were held by the enemies of freedom; even if the first investigations were negative, already when we came to Veracruz we knew they were holding you at the city barracks. I was ready to go there to see you, but with Dr. Zepeda's suggestion that that might worsen your situation and with the promise he made to us to take steps to arrange your release, we decided to leave at once and then see what might happen. Still, we wrote from Veracruz to Dr. Zepeda urging him not to forget his promise to arrange your freedom, and, furthermore, aboard the *Coahuila* we sent him a message with the following words: "Urgent to learn fate of Comrade Pavletich. Inform us without delay." Not having had a reply, we repeated several times to Dr. Zepeda our wish that he ask for your release.[1]

Since our friend González was leaving on a mission to Mexico City, he was given the job of finding out what had been done for you, which he

faithfully did. He informed us of the smallest details of your imprisonment and that you would probably go into exile. Therefore all doubts
about our attitude are dispelled. It's partly the way we are and partly our
duty as soldiers to look after good companions such as yourself. Obvi-
ously, to obtain your freedom we weren't about to ask for it on our knees,
or to beg for it as a favor. Our total isolation from the present regime for
basic reasons of idealism and principles makes it impossible to request the
freedom of a companion, even when that freedom is a right usurped by
those who could grant it. For which reason we prefer to leave this matter
in Dr. Zepeda's hands. Whether he did anything or not, this is now beyond our control. We have a message in our possession in which he tells
us that you were released because of his influence.

You should give up every doubt and be certain that we have done what
we could for you within the limits of our difficult situation.

Your attitude in the face of the offers they made to you when you were
taken before Señor Vadillo was logical and dignified. It's never necessary
to wear a golden padlock over one's mouth to remain silent, nor a bow
of flowers on one's hands to bind them up. This would be a vulgar denial
of all character, of all firm idealism. Something more: it would be your
suicide. Our America is plagued by scoundrels, and these are the ones
who have sowed doubt and distrust among the masses. Those with the
noblest intentions have been the worst enemies because by exploiting the
people's good faith and their ardent wish for freedom, they have brought
them frustration, leaving them to learn from painful experience.

I congratulate you sincerely for your attitude. You have placed yourself
at the height of your obligation.

There's no need for you to say that you remain firm and loyal to the
cause we defend, not even to me. I count you among those who neither
yield nor surrender. Comrade González will have an opportunity to bring
you instructions. At this very moment, with our hands and our conscience
clean, we have arranged our return to the Segovias, even if, as you know,
our enemies have tried to crucify us on the ignoble timber of defamation.
We will overcome any obstacle that stands in the way of our march, and
we will reach our beloved battlegrounds in the Segovias to give new demonstrations of love to Latin America, and of resistance and self-respect to
the invader. We repeat today the phrases of Bolívar: *If the elements are
against us, we will be against the elements, and if God is against us, we
will be against God.* (If God is Justice, He will be on our side.)

I believe I will never again leave the battlefields of the Segovias for as
long as a miserable Yankee invader remains on Nicaraguan soil, not even
as a dead man. A formidable duel is about to take place between them
and us, which must free the timid from their indifference and strengthen
the spirit of struggle of continental and West Indian America. Time will
speak for us.

I regret not being able to offer you assistance. They have just finished dismantling the house we lived in because its owner is leaving. Our cash on hand amounts to only a few pennies. If you are not in a bed of flowers, friend Pavletich, neither are we, even though slander eats into our hearts cruelly and tries to leave its poison there. Accept this apology as trustworthy and fair.

With all the respect of your companion and friend,
Patria y Libertad.
AUGUSTO CÉSAR SANDINO

[19, 3 pp.]

1. Preserved in the IES archive, Pedro José Zepeda Collection, is a telegram from Sandino to Dr. Pedro José Zepeda, dated February 28, 1930, on board the *Coahuila*. It reads, "Would appreciate immediate information fate Pavletich. A. C. Sandino." This must have been one of the messages Sandino sent to Zepeda about this matter.

120. THE JOURNEY TO MEXICO AS
TOLD TO JOSÉ ROMÁN IN 1933

I'm pleased that you've studied all that documentation, because you will have noticed that, to put it briefly, the trip to Mexico was a mess I got myself into and for which I alone am to blame. The main reason for the trip was the urgent need we had for war supplies and substantial economic support especially. Very well, a young man from Guadalajara, Mexico, José de Paredes, who came here voluntarily and was a good adjutant because he understood office work and spoke English, having lived in California, eventually told me that he had been well acquainted with President Portes Gil before he was appointed to complete General Álvaro Obregón's presidential term and that, aside from that, he had relatives who had worked very close to Portes Gil. He suggested to me that I let him go and see if it might be possible to get help in Mexico. I thought nothing would be lost by trying. He left and eventually came back with the most flattering offers from President Portes Gil, which naturally couldn't be written down for reasons of security, according to what he told me, but he brought with him the passports and safe-conducts for everyone we had wanted to accompany me. We prepared ourselves as fast as we could and left. I repeat this, I know the blame was all mine. As shrewd as I am, and to trust a stupid ass like Paredes! The passports and safe-conducts were legitimate. And so early in June 1929, we left for Mexico by way of Honduras, El Salvador, and Guatemala. Those who accompanied me among others of my general staff were the following officers of the Latin American legion: Rubén Ardila Gómez of Colombia, Agustín Farabundo Martí of El Salvador, Gregorio Gilbert of the Dominican Republic, Esteban Pavletich of Peru, and José de Paredes of Mexico.[1]

Very well, with an interminable series of pretexts and double-dealing they made me wait in Yucatán. I found myself in Mérida almost without resources and totally ignorant of the plans they might have for me. It had been hinted to me that the U.S. Ambassador, Mr. Morrow, in a murky plot with Portes Gil and some members of my entourage, was simply trying to keep me as a prisoner and discredit me.

Meanwhile the press did its best to convert the matter of my representation into a question of dogs and cats. On one side, Farabundo Martí, with the Communists; on the other, Pavletich, with the Apristas, who turned out to be a drone and a liar, though I give him the benefit of the doubt because it's possible that he had acted out of error because of his youthful enthusiasm.[2] But, however it happened, he was the direct cause of the muddle.

The fact is they didn't tell President Portes Gil that I was seeking military and economic support from Mexico, but rather asylum, and this was not stated to Paredes himself, who never saw Portes Gil, but was passed on instead by intermediaries.[3] Such was my desperation because of the slanderous charges that had been brought against me, because of the intrigues of the Communists, Apristas, and other revolutionary groups, that I expelled Martí, Pavletich, and de Paredes from my ranks, telling them I never wanted to see them again. Then I immediately wrote a long and detailed letter to President Portes Gil asking him for his final reply, and that he permit me to return to my mountains. You saw a copy of that letter, dated in Yucatán on December 4, 1929, and received by the president near the end of that same month.[4] To keep the story brief and to come straight to the point, early in February 1930, the president of Mexico, Emilio Portes Gil, received me in a special interview in Chapultepec Castle. He very pleasantly informed me that the Mexican government had never had, nor could have had, any intention of helping us in our war, because to intervene in the internal politics of another country was a very delicate international problem, that just as Mexico, to the extent of its power, would not allow others to interfere in its affairs, it also wouldn't interfere in those of others, and that it had been his understanding that I had only been asking for hospitable asylum for myself. This is the pure truth. Nothing more and nothing less.

I must also point out that all my travel expenses and the costs of my stay in Mexico were recognized and were paid for by the Mexican government. And let it be understood that this was without our asking for it or committing ourselves to any political arrangements.

Dr. Pedro José Zepeda took me to greet General Plutarco Elías Calles at his retreat in Cuernavaca. I should mention as well that during my short stay in the Mexican capital, I was received and attended to with the rank of a general. They assigned me six aides from national security, aside from two of my own. That was my entourage. And I considered staying a few days longer in that enchanting city, where they also gave me every type of medical examination. But one of those rare things occurred of the kind that so often happen to me. I wanted to see a great bullfight, and so naturally the colonel of Mexican Security who accompanied me ordered the best tickets, next to the ring and next to an exit. The great plaza was fully packed, as they say. We deliberately arrived at about the middle of the first bullfight, in order not to attract attention. I was dressed in civilian clothes and wore dark glasses, but at the end of the third bull, while the band was playing a musical salute, someone with a megaphone cried out,

"Mexicans, General Sandino is with us in the plaza. Viva General Sandino!" And this has to be believed, everyone in the plaza rose to his feet, as if pulled up by a string, crying out, "Viva Sandino!" [. . .]

Back in Mérida, on April 1 I sent several of my men back to the Segovias, I myself staying hidden away in a friend's country house with only four of my aides. We knew that spies of the U.S. government were keeping very close track on us. For what reasons, I don't know. With the help of the Mexican Secret Service, on April 24 I departed by sea for Veracruz, which I left by rail, passing through Guatemala, El Salvador, and Honduras. Early in May I was back in the Segovias, and on the following June 10, exactly a year after my departure, on the hill called Tamalaque, today La Reunión, department of Jinotega, I gave a report of my trip to our army. The war, which during my absence had been kept alive in the Segovias by our army under the command of Generals Pedro Altamirano and Miguel Ángel Ortez, was reactivated in a fierce manner upon my return.

[7, 103–7]

1. Gregorio Gilbert was author of an account of his experiences as a member of Sandino's army entitled *Junto a Sandino*, published by the Universidad Autónoma de Santo Domingo in 1979. RC

2. The Aprista party (*Alianza Popular Revolucionaria Americana*) was a radical political party of Peru, of which Pavletich was a member. RC

3. According to President Portes Gil, writing in his autobiography, he did receive Paredes, who gave him a silk handkerchief on which Sandino had written his letter of January 6, 1929 (see Doc. 80). Paredes told him of Sandino's difficult situation in Nicaragua, Portes Gil wrote, and asked him to grant Sandino asylum in Mexico and to supply him with the weapons needed to continue his struggle. The president agreed to grant asylum, according to his version of events, but refused to give him weapons on the grounds that he could not betray the improved relationship that Mexico had established with the United States some two years before. See Emilio Portes Gil, *Autobiografía de la Revolución Mexicana* (Mexico, D.F., 1964), 596–97. RC

4. See Doc. 101.

121. RETURNING TO THE SEGOVIAS: LETTER TO PEDRO JOSÉ ZEPEDA, MAY 13, 1930

Danlí, Honduras
May 13, 1930

Dr. Pedro José Zepeda
General Representative of the Army in Defense of the National Sovereignty of Nicaragua
Mexico, D.F.

Distinguished doctor and godfather:

I am pleased to inform you that today I am leaving here for the Segovias and that I will be with my muchachos on the 16th, as I communicated to you in a telegram that I left predated in San Salvador.

All my people mobilized themselves when they got news of my return to the Segovias. Thus I have confidence in the most sensational success.

Doctor, try to send the buttons that I entrusted to you as soon as possible to Don José Idiáquez in Danlí, and also a quantity of money so that Don José can transfer his mail to my camps and send me some things that are absolutely essential.

My respects to my godfather and kisses and embraces for the children, and especially César Augusto. Accept the esteem of your friend and godfather.

Patria y Libertad.

A. C. SANDINO

[19, 1 p.]

122. THE BATTLE OF SARAGUAZCA,
JUNE 19, 1930

For the honored press of the world in general:

In the Segovian plains and mountains our salvoes of protest and vigilance against the hordes of outlaws and insolent criminals have not ceased, nor will they cease.

On the broad plateaus of the Segovias may be found two imposing heights, among others: El Saraguazca and El Yucapuca, places that served as our centers of operations in the war against Chamorro and Díaz in 1927.[1]

With the intention of carrying out our army's new plans, which we accomplished with total success on the 18th of this month, I took possession of El Saraguazca with four hundred men and ten machine guns, leaving other columns placed strategically in several locations with more than six hundred men, all these forces completely equipped.

At dawn on the 19th I was informed by the guard officers that on the heights of El Chirinagua and the rock of La Cruz suspicious lights were seen moving slowly down over the lower parts of El Saraguazca as if they were trying to approach our first outposts. As always a cold wind whipped those heights. No doubt remained that the lights we watched belonged to the enemy.

Through the fog General Altamirano, who was officer of the day, arrived with ten men on horseback, bringing me the same news about the enemy's approach. Three mortar shots were ordered as an immediate warning signal to our reserves who were spread out over El Saraguazca. During the first daylight hours of the 19th the battle began in the area of the San Marcos lowlands. By twelve the enemy had been beaten on all sides, the Yankee leader of the attackers having been killed in the first assault. The enemy continued firing almost without letup until six in the afternoon when they were *almost totally annihilated* by our brave soldiers. A flotilla of six airplanes took part in the battle, furiously bombing and machine-gunning us on two occasions. That day was an awful one for the Yankee pirates and Nicaraguan renegades!

At that tragic moment in our history some amazing and odd scenes were observed. The enemy's casualties were uncountable, as were the desertions from their ranks. On our part, we had to mourn the death of

Captain Encarnación Lumbí and the wounding of a young soldier, Roque Matey of Telpaneca.

At four in the afternoon when the aerial attack seemed to have stopped, an enemy bomb exploded, lightly wounding me in one of the joints of my left leg. I haven't given any importance to my small wound, nor have I stopped directing matters concerning our army, because it hasn't even prevented me from mounting my horse.

At six in the afternoon some shots were heard from the enemy who fled desperately through those plains, unaware even of where they had come from. Four hours later we left the heights of El Saraguazca because this was the plan we had decided upon earlier. Thus ended that armed engagement in which two races fought, the one for supremacy, the other for the right to fatherland and freedom.

All our forces are spread strategically throughout the Segovias, and we also possess forces in the departments of León and Chinandega.

The desolation and sorrow of the Nicaraguan people is the exclusive work of the murderous governments of the United States of America.

José María Moncada is the most dangerous man in Nicaragua because he speaks of the accumulation of money in the national coffers, of the construction of new railroad lines and roads, etc., etc., and, with all this, this evil man has brought confusion to our people and to our Liberal party. For us, the Nicaraguans, the best things Moncada talks about are like sweet candies in our Nicaraguan hell.

The people of Nicaragua know full well that from 1909 until the present, all the governments that have come to power in our republic have been illegal, with the exception of the "puppet," Juan Bautista Sacasa, and that, for that same reason, from that date until the present all the treaties, pacts, and conventions celebrated between the Yankee governments and those individuals whom they themselves imposed upon Nicaragua with the thrust of a bayonet have no legal validity, because they have been made at the expense of our people. This is what interests the people of Nicaragua, to nullify those famous treaties, and only in this way can we be free, sovereign, and independent.

The funds that Moncada accumulated don't mean a thing to us Nicaraguans, because he needs that money to pay the salaries of the mercenary army that the Yankee has created in Nicaragua. Nor are we interested in the railroad lines that Moncada has constructed, because we know he needs them for the rapid mobilization of military units and mercenary troops who murder legitimate Nicaraguans. All the construction works and economic measures that Moncada has carried out during his administration are Machiavellian; all have the smell of death, sorrow, and calamity, because everything is done maliciously by the Yankees. José María Moncada says whatever he can to create confusion among the Nicaraguan people, but he never says a word about the illegality of the treaties I have mentioned, because these are matters that concern the Nicaraguan people and jeopardize Yankee interests. Our army fights bravely to free Nicaragua from all those ignominious treaties and from the slavish posture that the Nicaraguan politicians have pursued with the Yankee government.

The North American piracy organized an army of young Nicaraguans which they call the National Guard. The majority of those men were with us, shoulder to shoulder, fighting the Yankee intervention. But the enemy has put a blindfold in the form of a dollar over their eyes, and so they don't see who it is that they are fighting against.

Oh, dear Fatherland, how much sorrow, pain, sadness, and bitterness have the Conservatives burdened you with by imposing so much illiteracy upon our people, so that today a large part of the youthful energies born and nourished on your soil have turned against you and against those who defend you! Will it be possible for those Nicaraguans at the service of the Yankee intervention, rifle in hand, to accept that slavery that we reject with holy rage? What will bring such stupid men to their senses? Have they not understood that to defend the honor of the Fatherland is to seek the freedom of all Nicaraguans? Is it possible that a military uniform, three scant meals a day, and the ten pesos these men are paid each month can give them such a happy life that they forget the dear country that embraces all of us under the same blue sky?

Who are the men truly responsible for so much infamy? *José María Moncada, Adolfo Díaz, and Emiliano Chamorro*, the unholy trinity of miserable sell-outs of their country! You are the three sorry ones, representative of the school of backsliders, cowards, and traitors, who have established in our country the murderous governments of the United States of America!

It isn't important that the traitors are multiplying in Nicaragua. Our army is strongly aware of its high historic role to sweep away all this corruption with the broom of its bayonets!

General Headquarters of the Defenders of the National Sovereignty, the Segovias, June 26, 1930.

Patria y Libertad.
AUGUSTO CÉSAR SANDINO

[19, 3 pp.]

1. The Constitutionalist War of 1926–1927.

123. LETTER TO PEDRO JOSÉ ZEPEDA, JULY 16, 1930

General Headquarters of the Defenders of
the National Honor of Nicaragua

The Segovias

July 16, 1930

Dr. Pedro José Zepeda

General Representative of the Army in Defense of the National Sovereignty of Nicaragua

Mexico, D.F.

Very distinguished Dr. Zepeda:

By means of the report that I'm preparing with a great deal of effort you may understand my state of health. The military operations are going very well, and only I am a bit sick, but Estrada is doing what he can to cure me. He's the only doctor I have.

I encouraged myself to send you these lines simply because I didn't want to neglect writing to you. I don't have a secretary, and I prepared this for the press about as well as I could. One copy is going to you and the other to González in El Salvador.

Try to dress it up nicely and give it as much publicity as possible. I have very little faith in what you can achieve there, but don't lose heart because here we have everything. The gold is where I left it, and as soon as I think I can remove it without danger of losing it, I will send it to you in the manner we talked about.

Now that I'm sick I would like to have you near to cure me quickly. General Pedro Altamirano is very much a soldier, and whenever he comes he has given me a complete report of his activities. Among other things, he brought me a piece of smelted gold, about six to eight pounds, which I will send possibly to be sold in Honduras to buy ammunition for pistols. The war requires money and for lack of it we lose a lot of time in sending out our communications. If nobody offers you anything, don't ask for it, because as soon as I go a bit into the interior there won't be any need for anything.

All the people of these regions are prepared to die with rifle in hand, and it is a pity we can't equip them quickly. Nobody refused the concentration I ordered. On the 9th of this month I organized more than twelve hundred men. All of them have been spread out in various places since the battle of El Saraguazca, where I was wounded.

Everything is going well, and I work the same as I did before leaving Mexico.

My respects to my godmother Helda and the other boys, my pet especially. Accept the sincere friendship of your friend and brother in patriotism.

Patria y Libertad.
AUGUSTO CÉSAR SANDINO

[19, 2 pp.]

124. HOW THE FIGHTING WAS CARRIED ON WHILE SANDINO WAS AWAY: A REPORT TO THE SUPREME COMMANDER, JULY 20, 1930

Report to the supreme commander of the Army in Defense of the National Sovereignty of Nicaragua, General Augusto César Sandino, from Generals Pedro Altamirano, Carlos Salgado, and Miguel Angel Ortez y Guillén, of their activities carried out with the authority of the same supreme commander, during his stay abroad on a special mission of our army:

Battles engaged in by General Pedro Altamirano: six battles (6) in the following places: El Malacate, El Quebradón, two battles in Los Cedros, La Colonia, and El Huate.

Battles engaged in by General Carlos Salgado: three battles (3) in the following places: Rio Negro, Los Robles, and El Limón.

Battles engaged in by General Miguel Angel Ortez y Guillén: fifteen battles (15) in the following places: El Cerco de Piedra, Quebrada El Guineo, El Bramadero, Rio Negro, La Cabulla, Los Limones, Arado Quemado, San Francisco de Coajiniquilapa, Los Robles de Somoto Grande, La Rica, Yalí, El Bálsamo, El Cajón, El Limón, and El Ojoche.

Total of twenty-four battles (24).

Casualties suffered in the expeditionary forces of General Pedro Altamirano:

Dead: Captain Francisco Centeno, Lieutenant Sebastián Montenegro, Sergeant Santos Ramos, Private Guillermo Contreras, Private Francisco Galeano, Private Ramón García, Private Crisanto Acuña, Private Francisco Navarette.

Wounded: Private Pedro López.

Total casualties: eight dead and one wounded (9).

Casualties suffered in the expeditionary forces of General Carlos Salgado:

Dead: Private Santos Pérez, Private Lorenzo Rivera, Private Domingo Múñoz, Private Matías Medina, Private Ramón Granado, Private Fermín

Ruiz, Private Bartolo Díaz, Private Ramón Mejía, and Private Cruz Méndez.

Wounded: Colonel Daniel Ríos, Private Nicolás Sánchez, Private Leocadio González, Private Narciso Vásquez, and Private Moisés Lira.

Total casualties: nine dead and five wounded (14).

The three battles of General Salgado were very hard fought.

Casualties suffered in the expeditionary forces commanded by General Miguel Angel Ortez y Guillén:

Dead: Sergeant Major Juan Noguera Zelaya, Sergeant Major Félix Pedro García, Captain Benjamín Gutiérrez, Lieutenant Prudencio Vásquez, Sergeant Lucío López, Private Jorge Hernández, Private Macario Gómez, Private José Zamora, Private Demetrio Gutiérrez, Private Basilio Gómez, Private Pío Melgara, Private Francisco Moncada, Private Dámaso Ponce, Private Encarnación Olivas, and Private Tránsito Talavera.

Wounded: Lieutenant Colonel José Perfecto Chavarría, Sergeant Major Felícito Gómez, Private Leocadio González, Private Socorro Mejía, Private Ildefonso Mejía, Private Tomás Múñoz, Private Isaías Sánchez, Private Guadalupe Vargas, Private José María Pérez Maldonado, Private Gregorio Hernández, Private Valentín Maradiaga, Private José Polanco, Private Erasmo Marín, Private José Santos López, and Private Ricardo Obando.

Total casualties: fifteen dead and seventeen wounded (32).

Total dead and wounded of the three mentioned Expeditionary Leaders:

Dead: thirty-two (32).

Wounded: twenty-three (23).

General total of casualties: fifty-five (55).

Equipment captured from the enemy by General Pedro Altamirano: one Lewis machine gun, two Thompson machine guns, one Browning machine gun, thirty Springfield rifles; all the machine guns and rifles were captured with their corresponding supplies of ammunition.

Captured by General Carlos Salgado: eleven Springfield rifles, fairly well equipped with ammunition, and a signal flag for the airplanes.

Captured by General Miguel Angel Ortez y Guillén: two Thompson machine guns and fifteen Springfield rifles, machine guns and rifles completely equipped, and a quantity of important documents belonging to the enemy.

Money collected and other interests:

By General Pedro Altamirano: five hundred dollars ($500.00) in cash, a quantity of gold, wholesale value of three thousand dollars ($3,000.00), one hundred (100) mules with complete gear and two hundred and sixty

(260) pistols of various calibers completely equipped, and ten (10) hundredweights of dynamite powder, with its corresponding equipment.

By General Carlos Salgado, nothing.

By General Miguel Angel Ortez y Guillén, nothing.

General Pedro Altamirano was chosen to be Supreme Commander to care for the total supply of war equipment in the possession of the Army in Defense of the National Sovereignty of Nicaragua for the period of time that the supreme commander of our army was absent.

Generals Carlos Salgado and Miguel Angel Ortez y Guillén remained with their corresponding columns in regions remote from the war supplies, with instructions from the supreme commander to keep latent the fires of patriotism among the Nicaraguan people during the time General Sandino remained abroad arranging certain special affairs of our army.

In virtue of what was revealed to the supreme leader and the three leaders mentioned, ratified and signed in the General Headquarters of the Army in Defense of the National Sovereignty of Nicaragua, on the twentieth day of the month of July of nineteen hundred and thirty. Las Segovias, Nicaragua, C.A.

Patria y Libertad.
AUGUSTO CÉSAR SANDINO
Signed by
Pedro Altamirano
Carlos Salgado
Miguel Angel Ortez y Guillén

[19, 3 pp.]

125. LETTER TO PEDRO JOSÉ ZEPEDA, JULY 21, 1930

General Headquarters of the Army in
Defense of the National Sovereignty of
Nicaragua

Dr. Pedro José Zepeda
General Representative of the Army in Defense of the National Sovereignty of Nicaragua
3a de Balderas, D.F.

Very distinguished doctor and godfather:

Without having any letter from you that I can refer to, allow me to write you the present one for the purpose of sending you the report that the expeditionary leaders of our army have given to this supreme command of that army.[1] You will proceed to give it the greatest possible publicity in the entire civilized world.

In this General Headquarters the absence of correspondence from you is beginning to be felt. I don't want to think that the absence referred to is because of you, but you should communicate with us as soon as possible, for the better development of our military operations. We have sent four notes to you since my arrival at this General Headquarters and we have had no response. The last two communications, like the present one, we have sent through the Mexican legation, for which reason I have no doubt that they are in your possession.

Among the many things that are urgent for us here is the ammunition for the Con-Con rifles, and I suppose that by this time you will already have sent us the twelve Thompson machine guns in some form to the place agreed upon.

The expeditionary leaders who will sweep through the places along the border, and to whom new credentials have been given so that they may be identified by any special envoy you may send there, are the following: General Pedro Altamirano, General Carlos Salgado, General Ismael Peralta, General Simón González, General Francisco Estrada, General Miguel Angel Ortez y Guillén, Colonel Pedro Blandón, Colonel Abraham Rivera, and Colonel Domitilo Ledezma.

All the leaders mentioned above, after having conferred with me at this General Headquarters for several days, have left with ample powers, and they are to be found spread out from the shores of Cape Gracias a Dios to the mountains of León and Chinandega.

No special envoy of yours to me should trust any leaders of forces who are not vested with the proper credentials by this supreme command, because he could fall into an enemy snare.

Tell me what the purpose was for the ten thousand dollars, so that it may be understood.

At the moment I write the present letter, I am surrounded by some of the highest leaders of our army, Generals Pedro Altamirano, Carlos Salgado, and Miguel Angel Ortez y Guillén, who have been very busy arranging their affairs relative to the ample report they gave of their activities carried out during the sojourn of this supreme commander abroad.

I have been commissioned by the three leaders in question to give to you through me an attentive and fraternal greeting.

My best caresses for your children and for you the affection of your sincere friend.

Kisses and embraces for César Augusto.

Nicaragua, the Segovias, C.A.
July 21, 1930
Patria y Libertad.
A. C. SANDINO

P.S. There is fighting almost every day in these regions, the enemy getting the worst of it. It costs a lot of money to send letters to Honduras, and for this reason I don't want to occupy myself sending them out for publication.

[16, 2 pp.]

1. Doc. 124.

126. LETTER TO PEDRO JOSÉ ZEPEDA, AUGUST 15, 1930

General Headquarters, the Segovias,
Nicaragua, C.A.
August 15, 1930

Dr. Pedro José Zepeda
General Representative of the Army in Defense of the National Sovereignty of Nicaragua
3a de Balderas No. 24
Mexico, D.F.

Very esteemed Dr. Zepeda:

Your worthy letter of last June 16 is in my possession. I am informed of your opinions.

About your repeated offer in regard to the expedition, I must inform you that I have fully prepared the spirit of all the people of our Atlantic coast, having named General Adán Gómez as expeditionary leader of the Rio Grande zone, and for the Puerto Cabezas zone General Adolfo Covans was named expeditionary leader, and Colonel Abraham Rivera was appointed as that of the Rio Coco.

These three leaders have had interviews with me and we are only awaiting the arrival of the expedition at the place we spoke about, and for that it has been arranged that a unit of four men will remain there without equipment, giving the appearance of civilians. I am not saying anything more to you about this because you will already know what to do to carry it out.

The idea that Colonel Rivera Bertrand should lead the expedition seems very good to me, and in this case the landing place would be Calansanún, in those same waters of the Caratasca.

In that case you should make your appointment to Colonel Enrique Rivera Bertrand, so that he can be identified by our expeditionary leaders, who will have their respective credentials issued by this supreme command.

We are satisfied with all the work performed by you in favor of the cause we defend.

The note sent by Colonel Enrique Rivera Bertrand to you I am accepting as my own to the extent that it agrees, as it does, with the absolute truth.

For me it's hard to enter into debates with people who are so awfully stupid, such as those who have attacked me behind my back at the very time that they knew I couldn't defend myself from their slander because of my involvement with more important activities against the common enemy.

It isn't true that Laborde and the little clique that surrounds him are Communists. By my observations of them I saw that they are enraged conservatives, and that they appear to have orders from the common enemy of our peoples to block every patriotic effort in favor of the nations of our Indo-Hispanic America, because this is the only way we can explain so many insults and so much slander from those individuals against people who deserve respect and consideration from conscientious groups because of their sacrificial involvement in humanitarian struggles.

In the archive of our army, of which this supreme command left you in charge, may be found the first letter I sent to Laborde from Mérida.[1] This letter is long and explanatory, and I wrote it after reading a letter that Laborde sent to Martí, believing at the time that Laborde was the general representative of Mexican Communism, which I esteem and respect, but of which I have never been a member. In what way could Laborde have been a traitor to our Army in Defense of the National Sovereignty of Nicaragua, if he has never belonged to it?

In what way, then, could I be a traitor to a party to which I have never belonged?[2]

We have had correspondence with all the continent's anti-imperialist groups, but with none of them have we made any political compromises because our own army guidelines prohibit this.

The Anti-Imperialist League of the Americas invited us to make a propaganda tour through Europe and to pay our expenses, since I didn't have a cent then and don't now. The invitation was made in writing, and it was also accepted in writing, we having said that if our trip to Europe was of general benefit to the world proletarian cause we would carry it out with pleasure and that afterward we would return to the Segovias. A copy of that reply and the original invitation are in our army's archive, which is in your possession.

Through its members the Anti-Imperialist League promised to contribute the necessary funds for our trip within a week. The week passed, a month passed, and then two, and the funds never arrived, and for that reason the tour never took place. I didn't ask the Anti-Imperialist League to invite us to travel to Europe, because they themselves made the invitation, and at their own free will. But they didn't follow through. Where then is the betrayal of the Communist party? Isn't it possible that the Anti-Imperialist League was trying to make a mockery of our army? We would also have the right, if, as in the case of Laborde, we acted hastily and said that the Anti-Imperialist League had betrayed us for not complying with their spontaneous offer to us.

We are aware that the Anti-Imperialist League's failure to comply resulted from a lack of resources and not because they bore any ill will against us, and their mistake was not to inform us in time so that we would not have thought that we had been deceived by them. And yet I don't blame them for anything, and I continue to respect them because of what they defend.

When the time that we could spare for our trip to Europe had passed, we began to prepare for our return to the Segovias, and at that same time Laborde wrote to us in Mérida, stupidly demanding of us, as if we had been members of his party, the publication of documents belonging to our army during our stay in Mexico, since they clearly considered them of great importance for the work of agitation that they were carrying on inside the Mexican republic itself.

In that case I used the same wisdom with which we had opposed them at the time of their first slanders.

The documents in question are traveling along with me and remain undisturbed, wrapped in our national flag, which is kept unstained as we move from peak to peak in the Segovian mountains, defended by the true sons of Nicaragua before the cruel indifference of most of the governments of our dear Indo-Hispanic America, and they will be published in a book that I will attempt to write at the conclusion of our war of liberation.

Where, then, is the betrayal that the enraged conservative Laborde says was committed against the Communist party of Mexico?

If Laborde could be put on trial as a slanderer, I think he could easily be sent to prison as an example for false apostles who may wish to follow his line.

Yours with complete respect, your very attentive and faithful servant.

Patria y Libertad.

A. C. SANDINO

[19, 3 pp.]

1. Not included in this edition. RC
2. On May 26, 1930, the Central Committee of the Communist party of Mexico issued a long declaration in which Sandino was accused of having "betrayed the world revolutionary movement." The same was reproduced in full in *El Machete*, central organ of the Communist party of Mexico, in June 1930.

127. LETTER TO PEDRO JOSÉ ZEPEDA, AUGUST 18, 1930

General Headquarters
August 18, 1930

Señor Pedro José Zepeda
General Representative of the Army in Defense of the National Sovereignty of Nicaragua
Mexico, D.F.
3a de Balderas, No. 24

Let's hope this paper will suffice to inform you in a general way of our military operations.

Our forces are spread out from the shores of Cape Gracias a Dios to the departments of León and Chinandega. In those two last departments Colonel Domitilo Ledezma is operating as expeditionary leader of our forces. Colonel Ledezma is an old soldier of our army, and it was by him that we sent to León and Managua the copies of the documents that I sent to you for the first time in 1929, relative to the proclamation of the provisional government that our army proposed to you.

The most recent battles taking place between our forces and the mercenary armies have been very bloody but sensational. There are four.

At three in the morning on the 9th at a place named Cosmate, jurisdiction of Jalapa, for the first time in the history of our army, forces made up of a hundred men commanded by General Simón González fell into an ambush. General González was gravely wounded and hangs between life and death, as so often happens to the soldiers defending the honor and freedom of the nations oppressed by the magnates. General González's column was dispersed by the enemy, but they didn't lose any of their war supplies.

Two days later in the place called Las Cruces, jurisdiction of Jinotega, an enemy force made up of four hundred men fell into an ambush. The leaders of our army who commanded the ambush into which the North American mercenary forces fell were Lieutenant Colonels Juan Pablo Umanzor and Dionisio Centeno.

The enemy left more than eight hundred dead in their camp, among whom were nine Yankees, but the one who made himself most conspicuous did so because of his age. This was an old Yankee who wore finer clothes than the others, and it appeared that he was a highly regarded man, though a bandit like the rest. In his saddlebags were found documents and fine objects of the kind used only by men of comfortable means and of great authority. But surely casualties of this kind are concealed and not revealed to the world. I am sending you some of the captured documents, so that with them you may be able to convince the incredulous.

In the place called Las Cuatro Esquinas, jurisdiction of Matagalpa, the enemy, numbering one hundred men, tried to attack the expeditionary forces of our army that were under the command of Pedro Antonio Irías and Miguel Angel Ortez. Our forces had secretly abandoned the field fifteen minutes before. The enemy force, made up of a hundred men, took possession of the field and occupied the same positions that our army had held. Five minutes later three strong enemy columns entered from different flanks and, not recognizing one another, they engaged in a hard-fought battle amongst themselves. When our forces learned what had happened among the enemy, they headed back and fell upon them riding their horses bareback. The enemy was dispersed on all his flanks, leaving the field covered with bodies and with all their equipment in our possession.

In the place called Rancho Grande, on the trail that leads from Matagalpa to the department of Bluefields, an enemy column made up of three hundred men was routed, annihilated, and deprived of all their military supplies by the forces under the command of the expeditionary generals of our army, Carlos Salgado and Francisco Estrada. The victory was decisive because even the wife of one of the mercenary Yankee officers was captured following the enemy disaster.

At the very moment I'm sending you this news, the enemy is preparing a joint attack against our General Headquarters, which is called "Joaquín Trincado." Fleets of enemy airplanes are passing over our regions, trying to approach the columns of buccaneers.

With the help of the Creator we are certain of wrecking the ugly plans the enemy may try to carry out against our army.

Yours attentively.
Patria y Libertad.
A. C. SANDINO

P.S. Dr. Zepeda: I beg you to show the attached documents to those who do not believe in the triumph of Justice.
Farewell.

[19, 3 pp.]

128. LETTER TO PEDRO JOSÉ ZEPEDA, AUGUST 20, 1930

General Headquarters
August 20, 1930

Dr. Pedro José Zepeda
3a Balderas No. 21
Mexico, D.F.

Very esteemed Dr. Zepeda:

I suppose you will know that Teresa remained behind in El Salvador, because I thought I wouldn't miss her.[1] But lately, and especially in the days when I was getting worse from the wound I received in El Saraguazca, I understood the need for her to take care of the small details of our General Headquarters, which because of their minor nature I find it painful to involve myself with, but which in the end are the cause of great things.

So Teresa must not be separated from me for as long as the war continues, since she is very much involved with the management of the camps, and this even Santa Blanca can't do, even if I wished she could.[2]

With this same shipment of mail I'm writing to her to come. If you know that something might have happened to her during her trip through Honduras, I beg you to write to me about it.

Teresa followed me as far as Danlí, but because I didn't give orders to our friends to help her, nobody took care of her, and the Honduran government ordered her removed from the country.

Today the poor woman has reentered Honduras, but she is in San Lorenzo where she is asking me for help to come to these camps. Just today I have taken the necessary measures for her transfer.

I have very much regretted what has happened to you concerning your little house in Chapultepec, but there is no danger. There are ways to get it back.

Please greet Sócrates for me, and tell him I have his letter, and that he can come here whenever he likes.[3] Tell him I'm not writing to him because I'm very busy and because of the need to take care of other matters that require my immediate attention and that he should overlook this, but that I will write to him soon. Also say the same thing for me to de Paredes.

I don't have a secretary, and the situation is difficult. There's no one who wants to come here to eat roasted monkey meat without salt.

Contributions valued at fifty thousand córdobas have been assigned to the prinipal capitalists of Ocotal, Estelí, Jinotega, and Matagalpa. I know very well that they will laugh, but I also know that in regard to their state of mind I make them fear the day when any of the towns where they're established may fall into our hands.

I'm much improved from my little wound, except that the shrapnel cut some small veins and the leg has remained half stiff. I will certainly make my cane my inseparable friend. I walk now and ride, and it doesn't cause me pain, but I limp a bit. The wound is entirely closed up, and now I don't use any medicines or bindings. Also the wound hasn't had any moral effect on our cause, because it will only disappoint those timid people who are in the habit of slandering us.

When this letter reaches you the revolution on the coast will surely have taken root. Concerning the movement on the Costa Rican side, it's essential to do whatever is in your power.

If it's possible for you to send stamped paper, it would be greatly appreciated.

Warm regards to those who may ask about me.
Your most affectionate and attentive servant.
Patria y Libertad.
AUGUSTO CÉSAR SANDINO

Note: Don't be concerned about my lack of constancy, because I would like to say everything with one word. Always my compliments to your honorable family and to you my best wishes that everything will smile upon you.

A. C. SANDINO

[19, 1 p.]

1. The reference is to Teresa Villatoro.
2. This appears to be a reference to Sandino's wife, Blanca Aráuz de Sandino. RC
3. Sandino refers to his brother, Sócrates Sandino. RC

129. MILITARY OPERATIONS IN THE MONTH OF AUGUST 1930

General Headquarters "El Chipotón"
Las Segovias, Nicaragua, C.A.
September 30, 1930

RECENT BATTLES FOUGHT BY OUR ARMY AGAINST THE MERCENARY FORCES OF THE UNITED STATES OF AMERICA IN NICARAGUA

The forces of the expeditionary leaders of our army, Generals Pedro Antonio Irías and Miguel Angel Ortez, fought the enemy heroically in the place called Independencia, department of Jinotega, on last August 18. The enemy casualties were more than seventy. On our part fifteen casualties, since our army held the best positions.

On the 19th of the same month, in the place called Soledad, the enemy managed to defeat our forces after a hard-fought battle; we lost some ammunition and a certain number of animals belonging to our cavalry along with their gear.

On the 20th of the same month, in the place called El Bálsamo, there was an encounter between the family of General Pedro Altamirano and the enemy. The exchange of fire was short but bloody. The eldest son of General Pedro Altamirano, whose surname was the same and whose given name was Encarnación, died in the fight. Also dead were a little girl and a daughter-in-law of the general, and wounded were three of his children, whose names were Victorina, Melecio, and Pedro Junior. A few days later Victorina died of her wounds. On the enemy side there were seven casualties, but they remained in the field.

On the 21st of the same month Colonel Perfecto Chavarría's force set up an ambush for the enemy in the place called La Pavona, capturing from the enemy large quantities of provisions and medicines.

On the 23rd of the same month the forces of Colonel Fulgencio Hernández Báez set up an ambush for the enemy on the Ducualí River, between Palacagüina and Condega. Thirteen Yankees and five sell-out guardsmen died and twenty-five more of the enemy were wounded. Jackets, caps, and medicines were captured.

On the 28th of the same month the bloodiest battle took place involving the forces of General Pedro Altamirano and Ismael Peralta, in the place called Ias (note: this is a fluvial port of the Rio Grande), which is located on the trail running from Matagalpa to the ruins of Pos-Pos and to the port of Rio Grande. Five days earlier the enemy had numbered six hundred men, and they were in the best positions in that place. Generals Altamirano and Peralta, having four hundred men with eighteen machine guns under their command, began to pursue the enemy on the 11th of the same month, managing to catch up with them on the 27th of August at five in the afternoon, in the previously mentioned place. On the 27th there was only a light exchange of fire, but General Altamirano, having captured some enemy mail, learned of the positions where the mercenary forces were camped.

On the 28th, at nine in the morning, a slow exchange of fire took place on the river banks, formidably increasing in intensity from three in the afternoon until the darkness of night. From five in the morning of the 29th the cruel battle continued. At eleven o'clock on the same day the enemy were dislodged from their positions, our forces remaining on the field for three hours, and later the enemy recovered some of their positions, which they abandoned entirely during the night. Our men also evacuated the field in search of better opportunities.

The casualties among our forces and those of the enemy numbered more than a hundred. Items captured from the enemy included a load of books written in English, two crates of ammunition for cannon, each containing six projectiles three and a half inches in diameter and fifteen inches in length. This is the first time we have seen this class of projectiles, since they are painted green and have a cap like those that automobiles have on their gasoline tanks.

Since that bloody battle there have been many others, but of less importance, among those standing out the battle of San Rafael del Norte, led by General Pedro Blandón, as well as the battle of El Carvanal, fought by the same leader against the mercenary forces of the United States of America in Nicaragua.

Patria y Libertad.

A. C. SANDINO

P.S. The torrential rains impede rapid communications with the exterior. Farewell.

[19, 2 pp.]

130. LETTER TO COLONEL ABRAHAM RIVERA, OCTOBER 14, 1930

General Headquarters of the Army in
Defense of the National Sovereignty of
Nicaragua
October 14, 1930

Colonel Abraham Rivera
On the Coco River

Very esteemed brother in the fatherland:

We have had the pleasure of receiving all the messages you were good enough to send us, the last being the one in which you were pleased to inform me of the plan to make a journey through the mountains to a certain place advantageous to the army[. . . .]

At this time our army is being prepared for its finest projects, and it's possible that we will soon move our General Headquarters to some of the interior regions.

This possible move to those regions should bring great pleasure to the members of our army, those who because of some mission or for some other reason are still in those areas.

There's no room, certainly, for sadness or desperation, because those things are merely the offspring of indecision and cowardliness, and from that sort of thing men can't expect good results. Maintain your rational faith and confidence and try to instill the same into those around you, so that from that promising environment the atmosphere they breathe may become recharged.

Keep in mind that the divine law that rules over us is one law: *that of love.*[1] From that law of love all the rest are derived. The law of love recognizes only *justice*, her favorite daughter, who was born of her womb.

To set what is stated above upon its true foundations, I invite you to give me fifteen minutes of your attention at a time when you find yourself alone and in a state of rest.

I am giving myself the sweet illusion that you are now alone and ready to grant me the fifteen minutes of your attention that I have asked you for; imagine yourself gazing upon all the seas of the world together, and that it is ordained that a little sparrow arrives and takes a sip of water from that sea once every hundred million centuries.

When that little sparrow, in the manner indicated, has been able to drink all the water of that enormous sea, then a second of eternity will have passed. And yet, *all the time of eternity* is not sufficient to travel, at the fastest speed imaginable, through all of that thing we call space.

The first substance that existed in that immensity was *ether*, but before ether existed there was a great will, that is, a great wish for the existence of that which did not then exist, more clearly stated, *eternal love. Ether*, now, is material, and it is the vitality demonstrated by electricity, which is the vitality of mankind, that is to say, all *light (the spirit). The spirit is consubstantial with the father creator of the universe.* Therefore, keep control of yourself, dear brother Rivera, so that you may always be able to defend just causes, though you may resort to every imaginable sacrifice, because sacrifice is *love (the creator, or rather God)*.

Injustice comes from ignorance of the divine laws at the time when humanity was in embryo, and for this reason injustice has no reason to exist, because it is contrary to the law of *love*, the only law that will rule over the earth when human brotherhood arrives and men are creatures of *light*, as mandated by the father creator.

To arrive in one place from another, one must begin to walk, because, if one never begins, one never arrives. To destroy injustice it has been necessary to attack it, and for this reason we have seen many with this mission come upon the earth, among them Jesus, and every man who fights for the freedom of the nations is a follower of those doctrines.

There are men on earth who think that if they are living well it is madness to sacrifice themselves for the collective good. When this is said because of ignorance it is not as bad as when it is said with knowledge of one's own motives, because in such a case that person is animated by petty selfishness, and this is the same as despising humanity, and yet with all their scorn for humankind, they live their orgiastic existences at the cost of tears and human lives.

This is injustice, and sooner or later injustice must be overcome by *Divine Justice*. The earth was a world of atonement where for millions of centuries Divine Justice held refractory spirits to the divine law, but today the earth has accomplished its regeneration, and those refractory spirits will be cast upon other planets that are less advanced than the earth. In such a way, then, injustice will disappear from the earth and justice alone will triumph.

The earth produces everything for the joy and comfort of humankind, but, as we have said, for long millions of centuries injustice reigned over the earth, and the enormous stocks of things needed for human life have been possessed by a few lordly men, and the great majority of the peoples have lacked even that which is essential, and they have perhaps even died of hunger, after having produced with their sweat that which others waste with their gluttonous ways. But there will be justice, and the war of the oppressors of free peoples will be eliminated by the war of the liberators, and then there will be justice and therefore peace upon the earth.

Dear brother Colonel Rivera: I hope that my elucidations in this letter will not cause you to despair, because in you I have always observed a real intelligence, and it is of concern to me that the men who surround me should imbibe the greatest love of justice, because this is our standard of freedom. Soon I will write more to you and I will keep you informed of the development of our military operations on the various fronts where our army is operating. Accept a fraternal embrace from your brother who has a high regard for you.

Patria y Libertad.
A. C. SANDINO

[11, 175–77]

1. At this difficult stage in his life, Sandino's involvement with spiritism and theosophy are particularly evident. RC

131. LETTER TO THE EXPEDITIONARY LEADERS, OCTOBER 16, 1930

To all the Expeditionary Leaders of our Army

Very esteemed brothers:

Considering that the residents of the whole countryside where we operate live in desperate need of salt and medicines, which they can only obtain with peril to their lives in the villages where the mercenary enemy forces are imprisoned, and recognizing that, before entering the villages, the merchants are defying us with this salt and these medicines in the very territory where we operate; in virtue of this, all of you will authorize all residents of the countryside to denounce to our forces any shipment of merchandise that is transported from one village to another, and our forces will be under obligation to confiscate any shipment, whoever may own it, and to distribute everything confiscated to the nearest residents. The troop will take only what is needed for their immediate consumption and continue their march.

If among the individuals who are transporting the shipments there is someone who opposes giving them up to our forces, that individual will be shot. The reason for ordering the execution by shooting of anyone who is not willing to surrender a shipment or to accept what our army orders him to do, is the following: that the merchants who work in these areas, without regard for the hardships suffered by the defenders of the national sovereignty of Nicaragua, are accomplices of the Yankee invader in the looting and murdering of our people and, since they are accomplices, we should make them feel with even greater force the rigors of Justice in defense of the nation.

Those who do not wish to accept the things that our army confiscates from the traitors to the fatherland will be regarded as future traitors and, consequently, it will be necessary to have them shot.

Patria y Libertad.
A. C. SANDINO

[11, 177–78]

132. LETTER TO COLONEL ABRAHAM RIVERA, NOVEMBER 21, 1930

November 21, 1930

Colonel Abraham Rivera
Expeditionary Leader of the Coco River Region[1]

[. . .] General González will go with the same thirty men who are under his command, and with all the equipment as it was brought from Honduras, because it has occurred to me that when I make my trip into the interior it will be good for many reasons for an able force to be stationed on the river.

It doesn't matter that General González has a higher rank than yours, because he will understand the situation as a result of the explanations I will give him, and, Colonel Abraham Rivera, he will not be the expeditionary leader on the river, but instead will go there as a military inspector of the Coco River. General González is a simple man, but brave and sincere, and so he will know how to be very respectful to you as he is with me.

I have tried to arrange things so that among the young men who go with General González no family fathers will be included, so that there on the river itself they may look for their "little women" and thereby multiply the defenders of Justice[. . . .]

In my previous letter I spoke to you a little about the divine and natural laws. Surely in this respect there is nothing I can teach you, but my purpose has been to convert you into an apostle of our cause, proving to you that we aren't in this struggle merely by accident, but rather in fulfillment of the law of Justice (*the law of love*).

Since love was the first thing that existed among all the things created or that could be created, it's natural and logical that even in the most imperceptible atom of the universe an electron of love exists, because God is everywhere.

With the few explanations I allow myself to send you, I think you will know how to find confidence in our victory in everything you see: in the leaves, in the birds, in the flowers, in the sands, and even in the waters of the river itself.

I didn't know Father Reyes, whom you knew personally, but for you to know him spiritually let me say that he was a spiritist and that therefore he was prophetic when he told the people much of what is now happening, and that among those who heard him there are still some who are also witnessing events.

Patria y Libertad.
AUGUSTO CÉSAR SANDINO

[11, 186–88]

1. The source used reproduces this document in a fragmented form.

· 1931 ·

133. MANIFESTO "LIGHT AND TRUTH"

LIGHT AND TRUTH: MANIFESTO TO THE MEMBERS OF OUR
ARMY IN DEFENSE OF THE NATIONAL SOVEREIGNTY OF
NICARAGUA

A divine impulse has animated and protected our army from the start, and thus it will be until the end. That same impulse asks in the name of Justice that all our brothers, members of this army, begin to learn, within their own Light and Truth, the laws that rule the universe.

Now then, brothers: All of you display a force superior to yourselves and to all the forces of the universe. That invisible force has many names, but to us it is known by the name of God. Surely among you there are many who have hoped to find an opportunity for someone to explain to you these things that are so beautiful.

Now then, brothers: What existed in the universe before the things that can be seen or touched was ether, as the only and first substance of Nature (material). But before ether, which fills up all the universe, there existed a great will; that is, a great desire To Be on the part of that which was not, and which is known to us by the name of Love. By what has so far been explained, it can be seen that the beginning of all things is Love; that is, God, who may also be called the Father Creator of the Universe. The only daughter of Love is Divine Justice.

Injustice does not have any reason to exist in the Universe, and it was born of the envy and antagonism of men, before there was any understanding of their spirit. But men's lack of understanding is only a transition in universal life; when the majority of humanity understand that they live through the Spirit, injustice will end forever and only Divine Justice can rule, the only daughter of Love.

Now then, brothers: Many times you will have heard of a Last Judgement of the world. By Last Judgement of the world should be understood the destruction of injustice on the earth and the reign of the Spirit of Light and Truth, that is, Love.

You also will have heard that this twentieth century, that is, the Century of Enlightenment, is the epoch for which the Last Judgement of the world is prophesied.

Well, then, brothers: The century in question is made up of a hundred years and we are now passing through the first thirty-one; which means that that hecatomb that has been prophesied will have to be revealed in these last sixty-nine years that remain. It is not true that Saint Vincent must come to play his trumpet, nor is it true that the earth will explode and then later sink. No.

What will happen is the following: the oppressed people will break the chains of humiliation, with which the imperialists of the earth have sought to keep them in backwardness. The trumpets that will be heard will be the bugles of war, intoning the hymns of the freedom of the oppressed peoples against the injustice of the oppressors. The only thing that will be submerged for all time is injustice, and Love, king of Perfection, will remain, with his favorite daughter, Divine Justice.

The honor has fallen to us, brothers, that in Nicaragua we have been chosen by Divine Justice to begin the prosecution of injustice on the earth. Do not fear, my dear brothers, and be certain, very certain, and perfectly certain that very soon we will have our final triumph in Nicaragua, with which the wick of the "Proletarian Explosion" against the imperialists of the earth will be lit.

Sincerely your brother.

General Headquarters of the Army in Defense of the National Sovereignty of Nicaragua, El Chipotón, the Segovias, Nic., C.A., February 15, 1931.

Patria y Libertad.

A. C. SANDINO

[11, 206–08]

134. LETTER TO COLONEL ABRAHAM RIVERA, FEBRUARY 21, 1931

General Headquarters of the Army in
Defense of the National Sovereignty of
Nicaragua
February 21, 1931

Col. Abraham Rivera
On the Coco River

Very distinguished brother:

[. . .] Brother Estrada took your personal gift to your little namesake Barrigoncito, and along with Teresa they are still in Danlí. Teresa will also receive and make use of the two pairs of shoes that you were kind enough to send us.

In this respect I must tell you that for the good of our cause abroad, it is very possible that I will soon join up with my wife Blanca, who at the present time is in San Rafael del Norte.

I have a complete understanding of the immoral morality of the present society on earth, and yet, if we are to correct those who are immoral, we must fulfill the necessary prerequisites that will allow us to gain access to them.

In the presence of divine laws there is no matrimony other than pure and simple love without ceremonies of any kind, but we won't be able at this time to deviate from mankind's laws, and we must accept them.

I'm only speaking to you about this now so that you won't regard me as immoral in some aspects of my life. Because the person who really possesses my boundless affection is Blanca. I'm truly fond of Teresa, and I will help her all my life, but our characters are as different as heaven and earth, which proves to me that she can't be my proper wife.

Everything I've said to you in this note is of an intimate nature, and I'm saying all this to you because I've thought of you as one of the most honorable members of our army, and so that you won't be shocked by my private virtues.

I have complete faith that our victory is certain.

The practices our army uses and those also used by the enemy in the White House are about the same, but with the difference that the spirits of Light protect our army and the black spirits are those that favor the White House, which is in fact a whitewashed sepulchre.

The response that the dark spirits have given to that White House is the following: If you can close the borders where Sandino operates, you can defeat him, but if one place remains, you can't. Because his mobility is better than yours.

Now then, brother: All doubts about the victory of our cause will end for you. And after what has been said, it doesn't matter that you yourself may die along with many others, but our cause will triumph because it is the cause of justice, because it is the cause of love.

Our people themselves have become as dangerous as rogues, yet they understand, and they will be very sincere.

Our fond regards to all your esteemed family and the other brothers round about you.

Sincerely your brother.
Patria y Libertad.
A. C. SANDINO

[11, 202–3]

In response to the special question of United Press regarding General Sandino's opinion of the Managua disaster, he has stated the following:

As a human being, and especially as a Nicaraguan, this great loss of life has filled me with sorrow. In no period in history has a people suffered so much injustice at the hands of men, and now, it may well be, from the injustice of fate itself: the cruel military occupation by the United States; the inconsistency of the pretexts put forward to retain in our land the iron boot of intervention; the evil sons who have trafficked with the people's blood and the nation's honor; the reduction of public wealth by the plundering of the "protectors" who control our banks, our customs houses, our railroads; the systematic murder of all the respectable men among us who do not accept such a state of things; and above all the organized slander intended to depict us as vulgar "bandits," when the official circles of the United States know better than anyone else that we are fighting for the freedom of our people, for the reconquest of our autonomy, and so that our fatherland may again enjoy the dignity of a sovereign nation, which ours was for many years.

If the earthquake is an act of support from Providence to prevent the dismemberment of our territory, may God take into account the blood of so many victims, and add to that the blood shed by hundreds of men sacrificed in the Segovias, and may He serve to keep lit the symbolic lamp of world freedom.

Let us call upon the peoples of America to turn their gaze upon this nation of the great fatherland and, supporting the initiative begun by our general representative, Dr. Zepeda, seek to establish the foundations of a policy of continental brotherhood, and let us demand that next April 14, emptily referred to as Pan-American Day, may serve to create a collective force of nations and governments to bring an end to these flagrant violations of the rights of peoples.

Patria y Libertad.
A. C. SANDINO

[19, 2 pp.]

1. On March 31, 1931, a major earthquake destroyed much of the city of Managua. RC

136. MESSAGE TO ALL THE SANDINISTA COLUMNS, APRIL 10, 1931

Esteemed brothers:

The hour of the liquidation of the enemy before Divine Justice is coming to an end. On March 31st of this year half the city of Managua crumbled, including among other things the landing field with a large part of the airplanes and war munitions that the enemy possessed. Moreover, now that Divine Justice is herself punishing the enemy, we must complete the work of terrorizing the terrorists once and for all

Our brothers, Generals Altamirano and Peralta, now have instructions to carry out an assault upon the town of Quilalí. It appears that things are taking on the color we require.

I have news that the enemy is attempting to have a religious function performed in the town of Quilalí, and that beginning on the 12th of this month a priest will arrive to say mass and to preach gentleness to the campesinos of that town in the presence of the fatherland's invaders. With this in mind, I deem it more essential than ever to carry out an attack upon that town.

During those same days our brothers, Generals Salgado and Ortez, will launch an attack upon another town near the one you are to attack. It is almost a certainty that when this circular is in your hands, the other two brothers referred to will be completing or will be about to complete the capture of the previously mentioned town.

Gen. Headquarters of the Army in Defense of the National Sovereignty of Nic., April 10, 1931.

Patria y Libertad.
A. C. SANDINO

[11, 219]

137. CIRCULAR REPORTING THE DEATH OF GENERAL PEDRO BLANDÓN, APRIL 13, 1931

So that all members of our army may be informed of the progress of our military operations in the various sectors of the country, allow me to address to you the present circular:

Forces of ours commanded by Generals Pedro Altamirano, Ismael Peralta, Pedro Antonio Irías, Pedro Blandón, and Colonel Abraham Rivera have been maneuvering in the area of our Atlantic coast with great success since the month of February of this year.

Recently our brother General Pedro Blandón, with a powerful column, waged four hard-fought and bloody battles against the enemy in Puerto Cabezas, from whom he captured many articles of war and other objects useful to our army.

In the earlier battles General Blandón had managed to shoot eleven Yankees and fifteen National Guardsmen after disarming them, since the men who were shot were fleeing after being dislodged from their positions by our forces.

Our forces were machine-gunned and bombed by the war planes that the Yankees have on their ships sailing on Nicaragua's seas. After the enemy infantry forces had been destroyed by our forces, a bomb from the airplanes exploded, ending the life of our dear brother General Pedro Blandón. The same bomb killed the youth, Tomás Blandón, the general's nephew.

General Blandón's death was a mortal, terrible blow to our column, but nobody was discouraged. Instead they headed for Cape Gracias where they captured the port and destroyed the wireless transmitter, taking whatever they could. A few hours later Cape Gracias was also bombed by the enemy war planes, but there were no casualties on our side.

Our brother, Colonel Juan Santos Morales, became the first leader of the expeditionary column that had operated under Blandón's orders.

General Headquarters of the Army in Defense of the National Sovereignty of Nicaragua, May 4, 1931.

Patria y Libertad.

A. C. SANDINO

[10, 139]

138. LETTER TO COLONEL JUAN PABLO UMANZOR AND OTHERS REPORTING THE DEATH OF GENERAL MIGUEL ANGEL ORTEZ, MAY 22, 1931

General Headquarters of the Army in
Defense of the National Sovereignty of
Nicaragua
May 22, 1931

Colonel Juan Pablo Umanzor
Lieutenant Colonel Perfecto Chavarría
Sergeant Major Ventura Rodríguez G.

My dear brothers:

We felt terribly upset when we received the news that our very dear brother and glorious general, Miguel Angel Ortez y Guillén, fell in the battle of Palacagüina.

For us the death of our dear brother, General Pedro Blandón, was also terrible and unexpected.

Our hearts are gripped in sorrow, and within that sorrow waves of increasing anger against the enemy are constantly passing over us. It's not possible to impress on this paper all the many things we feel and would like to say to you, but I hope we can do so soon.

In this regard, would you be so good as to reorganize as follows with the following leaders: first leader of the column, Colonel Juan Pablo Umanzor; second leader of the column, Lieutenant Colonel Perfecto Chavarría; third leader of the column, Sergeant Major Ventura Rodríguez. This column will be recognized under the name *Column No. 4 of our army*.

You will march to this General Headquarters with every precaution by way of any of the routes now known to you.

When you reach Guanacaste you will attempt to speak with Lieutenant Claudio Blandón so that he can give you the guides needed to reach this General Headquarters, where everything essential is being set up for the support of those forces during the days they are here. Here you will receive the instructions and credentials appropriate for the leaders who will command that column.

Patria y Libertad.

A. C. SANDINO

[11, 235–36]

139. MANIFESTO, MAY 1931

Like an impotent and furious animal, Herbert Clark Hoover, the Yankee president, hurls insults at the leader of the army that is freeing Nicaragua. He and Stimson are the present assassins, as Coolidge and Kellogg were before them. May the North American people thank this quartet of failures, and may the parents, sons, and brothers of the marines who have died on the Segovian battlefields curse those dismal leaders now and forever.

Coolidge's insolent boasting in 1927 when he said he would disarm by force the Army in Defense of the Honor of Nicaragua has greatly hurt the prestige of the United States of America. Recently we have learned that Herbert Clark Hoover, the Yankee president who won't last beyond 1932, has promised he will capture Sandino to turn him over to justice, a verbal compensation for the drubbing our army has just given the Yankees on the Atlantic coast, leaving Logtown littered with corpses. We are not to blame in any way, because we are only defending ourselves.[1]

We are paying dearly for the North American policy in Nicaragua. From 1909 until the present time that policy has destroyed one hundred fifty thousand human lives of both sexes; it has plundered more than two-thirds of the capital of the Nicaraguan people, and it was about to colonize Central America when an awful crisis stunned and paralyzed the thrust of this wickedness.[2] Considering all this, what name do men deserve who do such things and threaten us in such a way?

Looking at things carefully, however, the Hoover administration is so deplorable that it named as secretary of state a pettifogger from the New York Bowery,[3] and not having a man to serve as minister to Nicaragua, it sent a ridiculous old fellow, Matthew Hanna, whose wife—a German, as it turns out—now runs the Yankee legation in Managua. But the government of the piracy will soon change, and in a short time all these individuals will be shot off into the air like rockets.

[10, 132–33]

1. In the month of April Sandinista columns carried out an intensive campaign in northeastern Nicaragua, causing serious damage to the North American companies and the oc-

cupation forces stationed there. Logtown, a lumber enclave owned by U.S. interests, was the scene of fierce battles and the place where General Pedro Blandón died in battle on April 13, 1931.

2. Probably a reference to the Great Depression. RC

3. A reference to Henry L. Stimson. RC

140. LETTER TO JOSÉ IDIÁQUEZ, JULY 1931

Señor José Idiáquez
Danlí, Honduras, C.A.

Peace and Love, my dear brother:

We had the pleasure to receive your very courteous note of the 7th of this month in which we had the misfortune to learn of the death of General Gregorio Ferrera.[1]

In respect to our military operations, I can tell you that they are superior to those of other periods. There have been so many battles in the last several days that one can't decide with certainty which has given us the greatest advantage, because all of them have been favorable. In our General Headquarters we have on display for anyone who wishes to see them numbers of documents, flags, maps, rings with Yankee insignias, and a multitude of objects belonging to the North American army in Nicaragua. Everything has been captured in various battles with the enemy.

The enemy suffered a real disaster in the battle of El Embocadero last July 15. Without exaggeration, more than a hundred individuals whom they dub the "National Guard" including five Yankees were annihilated with machetes. The enemy column's entire war convoy fell into our hands. Twenty-four hours later, another of our columns arrived as reinforcements,and they informed us that the picture was beautiful, deserving to be presented to the world as an example.

By the time this letter is in your hands, you will have news of new battles fought between our forces and the enemy.

All of us abundantly return your affectionate regards, and from me, your brother, accept my sincere esteem.

Patria y Libertad.

A. C. SANDINO

[11, 245]

1. Nom de guerre of General Miguel Angel Ortez, who died in the battle of Palacagüina on May 14, 1931.

141. LETTER TO GUSTAVO ALEMÁN BOLAÑOS, JULY 16, 1931[1]

July 16, 1931

Dear brother:

I hope you will not be surprised by the fraternal phrase with which the present letter begins, since it is our army's official phrase and reflects the esteem we feel for you. Our other messages will continue to reach you with the same salutation. I received your affectionate letter of the 18th of last month with which I have fully acquainted myself. I think it's good to begin by informing you that our army's general conditions are entirely superior to those of other periods, especially now that we've managed to awaken the conscience of our people, a rewarding task that I have accepted voluntarily and in which friends such as yourself have cooperated[. . . .]

Working even at night, we have recently made copies of important documents of our army, assembling them in a dossier for your publication of the work we referred to, and I have the pleasure to tell you that you have been selected by our army to publish our dossier of accumulated documents.

In this regard, by this same shipment of mail the work in question will reach you, and I ask that you proceed to publish the pamphlet or book, making all the comments and points that our documents and writings deserve in your role as author. We don't want a defense of any kind, but only hope that *justice shines*.

It's not for us to decide whether you will sell the book or pamphlet or give it away, and you will also know where to acquire the funds to print the work, but we would like to inform you in advance that we will buy a thousand copies from you at any price you estimate.

I must merely suggest to you that the book or pamphlet carry the title: *El Bandolerismo de Sandino en Nicaragua, C.A.*[2]

Before beginning to publish the collection, keep in mind that the introductory document is from a person in whom we still have hopes of some useful achievement, and his work should not be prevented for as long as he has the possibility of accomplishing something useful for our cause, but if for any reason these possibilities should vanish, it will then be time to publish the work now so often mentioned.

You also have the responsibility to try to publish this work simultaneously in various Central American newspapers.

It would be useful for us if you could publish this letter in its entirety before your pamphlet or book appears.

Thanking you for all the attention which this letter and our collection deserve from you, sincerely your brother in the fatherland.

Patria y Libertad.

A. C. SANDINO

[1, 90–91; 11, 246–47]

1. This letter to Gustavo Alemán Bolaños was reproduced in different forms in the two sources used [1, 90–91, and 11, 246–47]. The parts not common to both have been combined to create an integrated document, the first two paragraphs from the first, the rest from the second.

2. "The banditry of Sandino in Nicaragua, Central America." A work with this title never appeared, but Alemán Bolaños later published a book entitled *Sandino, el libertador*. See List of Sources. RC

142. MANIFESTO, JULY 28, 1931

Everyone knows our army is fighting against an army supplied with the most modern military equipment and all the other material resources that a governmment can provide.

Nevertheless, at the present time we control the rural areas of eight of Nicaragua's departments, and if we have not captured cities, it is because this still does not enter into our plans, but we will doubtless do so when the hour arrives. Our strategy consists of maintaining in a state of siege the villages and towns of the departments where our army operates.

The enemy has been saying that there is a shortage of food in the Segovias, but this is in the cities and towns where the mercenaries have taken refuge. In the countryside there is no hunger, and our army has more than an adequate supply of food.

Eight expeditionary columns make up the effective fighting force of our army in the places and under the orders of the following leaders: Columns number 2 and 6 under the command of Generals Carlos Salgado P. and Abraham Rivera are operating with complete success on our Atlantic coast. Column number 1 under the command of General Pedro Altamirano controls the departments of Chontales and Matagalpa. Column number 3 under the command of Pedro Antonio Irías controls the department of Jinotega. Column number 7 under the command of General Ismael Peralta controls the department of Estelí. Columns number 4 and 8 under the command of Generals Juan Gregorio Colindres and Juan Pablo Umanzor control the zones of Somoto, Ocotal, Quilalí, and El Jícaro. Column number 5 under the command of General José León Díaz controls the departments of León and Chinandega.

Our general headquarters is established in the center of the eight departments referred to. Our columns are moved about with mathematical precision, as much to the right as to the left of our general headquarters.

Our army is the most disciplined, devoted, and disinterested in the entire world, because it is conscious of its lofty historical role. It doesn't matter that backward writers call us "bandits." Time and history will be entrusted with the task of deciding whether or not the bandits are really here in the Segovias of Nicaragua where love and human brotherhood prevail. Even at those times when our army orders the execution of traitors it does so because of its great love of freedom. And only those persons are shot who commit offenses against that freedom, seeking to impose a slavery upon us that we reject with sacred fury. [. . .]

For anyone who might wish to see them, in our general headquarters we possess a large quantity of documents, flags, and a multitude of objects that once belonged to the army that is seeking to exterminate us, all of which were captured from the enemy in various battles. We have also had many casualties, but we don't try to fool the public as our opponents do, who claim our bullets only pierce the brims of their hats.

This information should suffice to keep a watchful public on the alert so that it can reject the enemy's false reports, the lies they use to confuse and intoxicate the public. Despite all this, on July 24 it was four years since our army waged its first battle in the city of Ocotal against the army of the most grotesque imperialism on earth.[1] Yesterday, as today, our impotent enemy has brandished all his weapons against us, including slander, the most powerful and reliable weapon of cowards.

I am not in any way different from any other soldier of the armies of the earth. My voice is not haughty, nor does my presence inspire terror as many persons might easily imagine, and yet, while carrying out the citizen's duty, we have had the pleasure of seeing many high leaders and officers of the proud army of the United States of America humbled under our feet, men who while seeking to destroy us have themselves been destroyed. We have proved how much more can be accomplished by the force of right, wielded with force, it's true, than by the right of brute force. My conscience is tranquil, and it enjoys the satisfaction of a duty well done. Even in my dreams I am happy, because I sleep with the contentment of a healthy child.

[1, 109–11, 115]

1. The battle of Ocotal took place on July 16, 1927. For accounts of it, see Docs. 19 and 21.

143. LETTER TO GUSTAVO ALEMÁN BOLAÑOS, AUGUST 9, 1931

Señor Gustavo Alemán Bolaños
Guatemala

My esteemed brother in the fatherland:

On this date your courteous letter dated June 29 of the current year was in my possession.

With great sadness I must inform you that in Nicaragua we haven't been fighting the Yankee intervention to put John Doe or So-and-So in the presidency of our republic. Nor have we been fighting to remove Moncada from power, nor to accept in a modified form any of the treaties that have been celebrated between the governments of the United States of America and those whom they have themselves placed in power in Nicaragua from 1909 until the present.

I thank you very much for the formulas for telegrams that you have sent us in advance so that we might send them to the Central American governments inviting them to help us to proclaim as president of our republic Señor Evaristo Carazo Hurtado, a person whose name has not even been heard mentioned among our army. I am very pleased to inform you that our army will await the world conflagration that is approaching to begin to carry out the humanitarian plan upon which it has decided for the benefit of the world proletariat.

My affectionate regards for you and your distinguished family.

General Headquarters of the Army in Defense of the National Sovereignty of Nicaragua, August 9, 1931.

Patria y Libertad.
A. C. SANDINO

[11, 253]

144. LETTER TO JOSÉ IDIÁQUEZ, AUGUST 10, 1931

General Headquarters of the Army in
Defense of the National Sovereignty of
Nicaragua
August 10, 1931

Señor José Idiáquez
Danlí, Honduras, C.A.

Peace and love, my dear brother:

With the same pleasure as always we received your courteous note dated in that place on last July 24. We also received attached to your letter that which Señor Gustavo Alemán Bolaños was good enough to send us.

Recently I wrote a note to that same Alemán Bolaños offering him a file of documents of the greatest importance to our army for the publication of a pamphlet.[1] Nevertheless, now that I am in possession of Señor Alemán Bolaños's latest letter, we have reconsidered the idea of sending him the file, and we have now decided not to send it, in view of the idiotic presumption of Señor Bolaños of formulating for us what we should say, and his ordering of what in his opinion we ought to do.[2]

Many persons have suffered from the tendency to impose their opinions upon us, among them Froylán Turcios and Gustavo Machado.[3] However, those individuals were at least serving as our representatives, whereas Gustavo Alemán Bolaños simply presumes to become our manager without having been asked. The poor devil.

Our army is not about to beg the enemy for mercy, and we have always been prepared for either death or victory, and it wouldn't be possible today now that we have awakened the conscience of our people to humiliate ourselves before the enemy, asking for or proclaiming a person as president whose name we haven't even heard spoken, and for that same reason our army could expect nothing from an individual who totally ignores our army's sacrifices. Also, I won't answer Gustavo Alemán Bolaños, and from this day on that individual is expelled from our army for having abused the affection that our army always conferred upon him.

Something more: I sincerely understand that you are worried about the border discussions between Honduras and Nicaragua, and that you hope they can be settled harmoniously among ourselves, but the Yankee assassin will not allow this, and we must see things in the light of reality. Our army recognizes as its enemy the renegade government of Nicaragua as well as the present government of Honduras, because both are the agents of the Yankee bankers, and our two nations (Honduras and Nicaragua) don't expect anything from such poor human specimens. I don't have any faith in a rupture between the government of Honduras and that of Nicaragua, and if it happened, it would certainly be in response to maneuvers of the international policy that the Yankee bankers are implementing in our Indo-Hispanic countries.

In this regard our army will perceive a single enemy bloc made up of the forces of the governments of Honduras, Nicaragua, and the United States of America. The situation would transform us into the color of an ant, and it would be advantageous for us to attack only the defeated forces of any of the three governments to add to our war supplies and to aid us in forming our new free republic for all the people of the earth.

Neither Nicaragua nor Honduras needs to engage in any border discussions, and everything being witnessed in this respect is solely a matter of the international policy of the United States of America.

Very well, if at some time you should be asked how a peaceful understanding might be reached with our army, tell them that the proposals must be completely official, within Nicaraguan territory itself, and that the persons appointed to bring us those proposals must set out with a white flag from Jinotega or San Rafael del Norte over the roads of the plains until they enter the mountains of the Naciente, where they will surely be observed by our lookouts, who in turn will pass them on to our expeditionary columns, and these will be charged with taking the would-be delegation into custody.

The persons carrying the peace proposals must be limited to three, all mounted on mules and allowed to carry the weapons of their choice, and the three individuals must understand that if they open fire while being inspected by our reserve guards, that fire will be returned by our weapons.

We have informed you of the above in advance, with the possibility that at some time the Central American governments may want to aid us in the pacification of Nicaragua. No, indeed, the situation isn't as easy as Alemán Bolaños has imagined it to be, so that with only a few badly written lines on some scraps of paper he could end a struggle that we have been carrying on for six long terrible years, with only the hope of being free, sovereign, and independent. That fellow Evaristo Carazo Hurtado is from Granada and of Conservative stock, from which the people can expect only coercion and calamities. Gustavo Alemán Bolaños is crazy, and he will never again see another letter written by our hand.

My Blanquita and all the others fully return your affectionate phrases.

Ever onward.[4]

A. C. SANDINO

[11, 254–56]

1. See Doc. 141.
2. The reference is to Alemán Bolaños's proposal to Sandino to proclaim Evaristo Carazo president of Nicaragua. See Doc. 143.
3. For the case of Froylán Turcios, see Doc. 81.
4. "Ever onward" (*Siempre mas allá*) was a slogan used on the emblem of a theosophical organization in Buenos Aires, the "Magnetic Spiritual School of the Universal Commune," founded by Joaquín Trincado, whose philosophy greatly influenced Sandino's thinking in this phase of his life. See Hodges, *Intellectual Foundations*, 40–48. In 1930 Sandino had named his general headquarters "Joaquín Trincado." See Doc. 127. RC

145. A MESSAGE TO
INDO-HISPANIC OBSERVERS,
AUGUST 20, 1931

For Indo-Hispanic Observers

We have already had the opportunity to inform the world that our army tacitly controls eight departments of our republic, but that, despite this, we do not have even one city under our control, because this is not part of our program of guerrilla warfare, and that we will do this when we deem it convenient, but that the countryside belongs to all of us and that for this same reason our army possesses food in abundance.[1]

Recently we have had news that the enemy wants to use as a tactic the disorientation of the people, publishing in the newspapers that the forces that have rudely fought the pirates and traitors in Chontales and other sectors of our republic in recent months, that those forces that threaten the towns do not belong to our army and are groups of hungry people without work.

For the sake of truth, let me point out in my role as supreme leader of our army that there does not exist in Nicaragua any movement isolated from our army, and that the cases involving discontented people that take place, even in the outskirts of Managua, are all motivated by our army's activities, and certainly such a condition will have to exist, but in the cities where the pirates and traitors to our fatherland are kept enclosed.

After the battles that took place in the cities of La Libertad and San Juan de Limay, and in Estelí, fought by our brothers Generals Pedro Altamirano, Pedro Antonio Irías, Ismael Peralta, and José León Díaz, thirty-three more hard-fought battles have taken place, among the most outstanding that which was fought by Colonel Perfecto Chavarría against the pirates and traitors in the tiny Coco River port known as Puerto de Waspuck. In that battle, which took place last July 17, six more captains of the Yankee Marine Corps and fifty-one Nicaraguan traitors died. The place where the battle was fought is several hundred miles from Cape Gracias a Dios, and that disaster which occurred there to the enemy was not witnessed by the residents of important towns, and it would not be strange if our enemies denied that more than seventy thousand rounds of ammunition of various calibers were captured in that battle, because surely they will not hesitate to say that the weapons and ammunition taken at that port were brought to us in Russian or Japanese ships.

General Headquarters of the Army in Defense of the National Sovereignty of Nicaragua, the Segovias, C.A., August 20, 1931.

Patria y Libertad.
AUGUSTO CÉSAR SANDINO

[19, 2 pp.]

1. See Doc. 142.

146. LETTER TO PEDRO JOSÉ ZEPEDA, AUGUST 20, 1931

General Headquarters, the Segovias, Nic.,
C.A.
August 20, 1931

Dr. Pedro José Zepeda
General Representative of our Army
3a de Balderas, No. 24
Mexico, D.F.

My dear companion and friend:

Concerning your statement that our declarations aren't good in which we have revealed our issuance of orders to burn our republic's cities if the government of the United States doesn't withdraw its pack of mercenary bandits from our national territory, in this respect I am happy to have this opportunity to state once again to the world and to you that our army's measures in that regard have not changed, and that nothing is responsible for that destruction except the international policy of the Washington government, and that our attitude is merely the natural consequence of that macabre policy.

Also responsible for the destruction of Nicaragua are the governments of our Spanish America, principally those of Central America. The proof of what I have said is there for all to see, and our people already understand this. Let the responsibility for the destruction of our beautiful Nicaragua fall, therefore, upon the imperialist governments of North America and Hispanic America, and in that regard *I strongly protest*, in the name of my Army and in my own name, against any responsibility for the destruction of Nicaragua that they would maliciously attribute before the nation to our invincible and glorious army. At this time this general command of our army is preparing a new plan for an offensive against the enemy in the months of November and December and during the time the Seventh Pan-American Conference is in session, and in this way it will denounce before our people all the imperialist governments of this American continent.[1]

Patria y Libertad.
A. C. SANDINO

[11, 256–57]

1. The Seventh Pan-American Conference was held in Montevideo between December 3 and 16, 1933.

147. MANIFESTO TO THE MEN
OF THE DEPARTMENT OF LEÓN,
SEPTEMBER 15, 1931

Do you know, people of León, what your name symbolizes? [. . .]

The symbol of Spain is the lion, spiritual leader of the entire globe, the reason no other nation on earth before or after can imitate Spain's great deed, which is that of discovering the continent where we live, the promised land for all free men on earth.

Our Rubén Darío spoke of our twenty-one cubs of Hispanic America, sons of old Spanish León.[1]

If the human species is the real Noah's Ark in which the instincts of every animal of the universe are enclosed, let it be understood that the lion is at the head of every instinct, the instincts being antagonistic to one another, and it is for this reason that the lion symbolizes the spirit of all of them. It always happens that when the lion roars, all the others tremble, and those which fight amongst themselves are appeased.

Our department of León is the spiritual leader of all the departments of our Nicaraguan republic.

And yet the banker assassins of North America, representatives of the golden calf of Sinai, have formed in Nicaragua the hated school of servile traitors led by Adolfo Díaz, Emiliano Chamorro, and José María Moncada.

The people of León, symbol of the spirit of the Nicaraguan people, are also being infected with servility and a spirit of betrayal toward the fatherland. For this reason, with more than adequate justification, the spirit of the Nicaraguan people has withdrawn from your department to the virgin Segovian forests, where all of you, men of the department of León, may be found, so that all good sons of Nicaragua, always standing together, may continue carrying our flag from peak to peak, the untarnished symbol of Nicaraguan León, of which you, the men of Leon, are the true guardians, before your old Spanish León, the spiritual symbol of this earth in the presence of the Father Creator of the universe.

General Headquarters of the Army in Defense of the National Sovereignty of Nicaragua, the Segovias, Nicaragua, C.A., September 15, 1931.

Patria y Libertad.

A. C. SANDINO

[11, 263–64]

1. Sandino refers to Rubén Darío's poem, "Oda a Roosevelt" (Ode to Roosevelt), in which the poet calls Spanish America "la hija del Sol" (the daughter of the Sun), then warns Theodore Roosevelt: "Tened cuidado. Vive la América española! / Hay mil cachorros sueltos del León Español!" (Take care. Spanish America lives! The Spanish Lion has a thousand cubs!) RC

148. COMMUNIQUÉ, OCTOBER 20, 1931

We have come to realize that we do not have at our disposal one single Indo-Hispanic government, much less any other nation of the globe. Nicaragua is directly and solely represented by our army and thus left to its own efforts and resources. For this reason orders have been circulated among our expeditionary columns that they may collect from nationals and foreigners everything essential for their maintenance. Many times there have been cases when, with the arrival of one of our columns at some hacienda or farm in national territory, the merchandise and provisions existing in the place were taken, and there are even cases when our soldiers take shoes and clothing from the proletariat because our brother soldiers need them more than they do, and because it isn't right that the men who are establishing the freedom of Nicaragua should go about in rags. It is because of this that many miserable people have called us "bandits," but history will see to it that justice is done to us, especially if it is remembered that the capitalist despoilers are the ones mainly and directly responsible for everything that has been happening in Nicaragua, because they brought the Yankee mercenaries to the national territory.

Avoid fires at all cost. There is no need to leave ruins behind. It would be enough if the men took screwdrivers along to unscrew doors and windows, and then burnt them along with the household equipment that must be destroyed as punishment and in order to spread terror.

This procedure is very practical and effective, and it would be good if you instilled it in your subordinates. Burned houses remain behind as a kind of accusation. Houses without doors provoke smiles, and the punishment remains visible to all.

[10, 155]

149. LETTER TO THE GUTIÉRREZ FAMILY, NOVEMBER 22, 1931

General Headquarters
November 22, 1931

To the Family of Señor Victor Gutiérrez
El Mancotal

On this date a note from Don Victor Gutiérrez for his family arrived at our military camp "Luz y Sombra," which today we allow ourselves the pleasure of sending to its destination, informing you at the same time that everything you wish, even newspapers, can be sent to that gentleman.[1]

Also permit me to inform you that Don Victor Gutiérrez, like Señores Manuel Irías and Rosendo Chavarría, was conducted by our forces to these camps because of a mistake of our secretary, because the persons who have been ordered captured are the capitalists who are identified with the enemies of our army, and we need to obtain contributions from them with which to buy war materials for the continuation of the defense of our national honor.

Nevertheless, the three persons mentioned are now in our camps, and we can't let them go unless they contribute some funds to be invested in the indicated materials, because we are convinced that if we allowed them to return to their homes they would be compelled to give a plan of our camps to the enemy. These things would have very little importance for us, because when allowing them to return we would totally change our military encampments, but it wouldn't be nice to go to so much trouble to give pleasure to the ungrateful.

On the other hand, you may be certain that the three gentlemen in question are constantly receiving lessons here in national dignity, and tomorrow they will thank God for the good fortune they have had to be among the defenders of the national sovereignty of Nicaragua.

Very attentive and faithful servant.
Patria y Libertad.
A. C. SANDINO

[11, 287–88]

1. *Luz y sombra* means "light and shadow." RC

150. NOTE TO GENERAL JUAN PABLO UMANZOR AND COLONEL SANTOS LÓPEZ ABOUT THE APPOINTMENT OF GENERAL HORACIO PORTOCARRERO TO THE PRESIDENCY, DECEMBER 12, 1931[1]

Today we are writing to Generals Juan Gregorio Colindres and Juan Santos Morales, informing them that in the city of San Salvador we have organized a committee called *Pro-Liberación de Nicaragua* and that we have appointed General Horacio Portocarrero as special delegate from this supreme command of our army to the committee referred to, and to the troops who operate in the interior of our Republic, so that in the event that our army attains military control over the country General Portocarrero may assume the presidency of the Republic of Nicaragua but will not be able to make any agreement with the enemy.

Patria y Libertad.
A. C. SANDINO

[11, 293]

1. The source used reproduces only the fragment published here.

151. INSTRUCTIONS TO
GENERAL HORACIO PORTOCARRERO,
DECEMBER 15, 1931

Instructions for General Horacio Portocarrero, in his role as special delegate of our army's supreme command to the committee favoring the liberation of Nicaragua and to the military forces operating in the interior of our country against the Yankee invasion and the traitors to the fatherland.

1. General Portocarrero, upon receiving these instructions, will be so good as to go before the Committee in Support of the Liberation of Nicaragua in that capital city and present to the members of the patriotic committee a fraternal salute in our name, at the same time informing them that we have gladly accepted their intention to acquaint themselves with our plans for the redemption of the fatherland, and that all our efforts must be directed toward the purpose of acquiring military control of Nicaragua by force of arms, and toward preventing any electoral farce that may be attempted in our country with foreign supervision. Also he will read all the documents that from this date forward are sent to General Portocarrero.

2. General Portocarrero, once recognized as special delegate of our army's supreme command to the Committee in Support of the Liberation of Nicaragua, will be so good as to ask that committee in our name for the honor, if he is persona grata whom they accept in his role as special delegate of our army's supreme command, of assuming provisionally the presidency of the Republic of Nicaragua, if our military forces can remove Moncada from power or if, as our revolutionary movement takes on increased strength in the interior, they offer us peace proposals in which the enemy agrees to turn the presidency of Nicaragua over to a person appointed by our army. Whereupon General Portocarrero will be acting as a member of our army and so will be subject to the discipline that our guidelines imply; not being able, therefore, to make any peace agreement with the enemy without the previous and direct authorization of this general command, which before authorizing it would be obliged to study carefully the proposed conditions for peace, which must be compatible with our national honor and our army's aspirations.

3. General Portocarrero has the duty to respond to any call that may

be made to him by the Committee in Support of the Liberation of Nicaragua, in his role as special delegate of our army's supreme command, whether to inform him of something that the committee requires this general command to know, or in order that he may travel to the interior of Nicaragua to organize a provisional government composed of ministers who agree to become part of the cabinet supported by our liberating weapons. In view of that hypothesis, General Portocarrero is authorized to organize a provisional government with the condition that the citizens who may compose that provisional government must sign, as members of our army, the guidelines that govern us, because whoever is not with us will be with the enemy. I allow myself at this point to indicate the names of some citizens who would be agreeable to our army, for any of the governmental portfolios, namely: Dr. Escolástico Lara, Dr. Rosendo Argüello, Dr. José Jesús Zamora, Dr. Arturo Vega, Dr. Modesto Armijo, General Juan Francisco Berrios, General Francisco Parajón, Señor José León Leiva, Señor César Augusto Terán, Señor Gustavo Alemán Bolaños, and Señor Salomón de la Selva.

4. General Portocarrero will place a printed copy of our guidelines in a good blank book that gives an impression of total seriousness, and they will sign their names therein as members of our army, as its ministers, and as the president, General Horacio Portocarrero.

5. General Portocarrero will be so good as to place himself in contact with Dr. Pedro José Zepeda, in Mexico, D.F., who at this time serves as general representative of our army, but from whom, nevertheless, we have not received satisfactory news for more than a year, for which reason he should ask him his final intentions. We also need to know if Dr. José Jesús Zamora, a resident of San Salvador, received in writing the representation of our army in that republic, which Dr. Zepeda ought to have sent him, according to instructions from this general command.

6. General Portocarrero is authorized to accept from persons and institutions disinterested support that does not involve political compromises on our part.

7. Communications should be sent to us by the same channel already known.

General Headquarters of the Army in Defense of the National Sovereignty of Nicaragua, December 15, 1931.

Patria y Libertad.

A. C. SANDINO

[11, 294–96]

1. Family portrait. Left to right: Sandino's half brother, Sócrates; his stepmother, Doña América Tiffer de Sandino; his father, Don Gregorio Sandino; and Augusto C. Sandino.

2. Sandino's mother, Margarita Calderón.

4. Henry L. Stimson, President Coolidge's special envoy to Nicaragua.

3. Photo taken following the inauguration of Adolfo Díaz as president. In foreground: Lawrence Dennis, U.S. chargé d'affaires in Managua; President Adolfo Díaz; and former president Emiliano Chamorro. Others unknown.

5. General José María Moncada.

6. Sailors and marines collecting rifles from Nicaraguan soldiers for ten dollars each, in accordance with the Tipitapa agreement.

7. Captain G. D. Hatfield, commander of the marine garrison at Ocotal.

8. Augusto C. Sandino in 1926 or 1927, during the Constitutionalist War.

9. Blanca Aráuz de Sandino.

10. "A Bandit Hut," photo taken by U.S. Marine Robert E. Moody, "Just before It was Burned."

11. Sandinista soldiers.

12. Augusto C. Sandino in Mérida, Yucatan, in July 1929, with his general staff. Front: Agustín Farabundo Martí of El Salvador, Sócrates Sandino, Augusto C. Sandino, unknown. Rear: unknown, Urbano Gilbert of the Dominican Republic, and José de Paredes of Mexico

13. Sandino with the family of Pedro José Zepeda, holding his godchild, Zepeda's son César Augusto.

14. Blanca Aráuz de Sandino (second from left) traveling on a *pipante* (longboat) on the Coco River.

15. Members of a crew of army engineers surveying the Nicaraguan canal route in 1930, with Nicaraguan workers.

16. Sandino and President Juan B. Sacasa in the Presidential Palace in Managua on February 4, 1933, after the signing of the peace agreement. Front: Dr. David Stadthagen, Sacasa, Sandino, and Dr. Salvador Calderón Ramírez. Rear: General Horacio Portocarrero, Don Sofonías Salvatierra, Dr. Pedro José Zepeda, and Dr. Crisanto Sacasa, brother of the president.

17. Sandinista and National Guard soldiers assembled in the plaza of San Rafael del Norte for the purpose of disarming part of Sandino's army in compliance with the peace agreement of February 1933.

18. In San Rafael del Norte in February 1933. Left to right: unknown, Don Gregorio Sandino, Sandino, Don Tomás Borge Delgado, and Juan Ferreti.

19. Sandino and Ramón de Belausteguigoitia.

20. Sandino and his general staff near the end of his life. Left to right: Francisco Estrada, Santos López, Sandino, Juan Pablo Umanzor, and Sócrates Sandino. All but Santos López were killed on the night of Sandino's assassination.

·1932·

152. MANIFESTO, JANUARY 1932¹

To our Nicaraguan compatriots:

What the gringos are seeking is the humiliation of our fatherland until they are able to leave. The Conservative candidacy of Díaz and Chamorro is their handiwork, because the Yankees want a new chance for rule by the yanquistas, and for the event that the Liberal yanguistas are more agreeable to them and the Liberals should win, they have ordered Moncada to make Sacasa the candidate, and they have pretended that they accept Epinosa's protestations of yanquismo. When they leave they don't want any disorderly demonstrations, which one party or the other would try to prevent, and they have even arranged things so that if there are difficulties they will be asked, by Díaz or by Sacasa, to land again and occupy the country, though they don't really want to do this, since the campaign of the Army in Defense of the National Sovereignty of Nicaragua has diminished Yankee power.

Compatriots, proceed with dignity and remember that you have been victims of the Yankees as much as of the politicians. Whoever walks in the path of those individuals and approaches the ballot boxes guarded by Yankees will achieve nothing except to render the most regrettable homage to the foreign bayonet as it flashes one final insult at Nicaragua. Compatriots, to expect dignity for our country from Chamorro and Díaz, or from Espinosa and Sacasa, is the greatest nonsense, especially now that the vanquishing Army in Defense of the National Sovereignty of Nicaragua is approaching.

Say to the invading admiral who handles you like sheep, "Get out!" Do your duty. Do not obey a single order of the marines in the electoral farce. No one is forced to go to the ballot boxes, and there is no law that compels it. Make yourselves worthy of freedom, deserving of it.

The people affiliated with the Liberal party must not think that a Conservative victory will last any longer than the time required for the people, together with the Army in Defense of the National Sovereignty of Nicaragua, to eliminate it. Conservatives must not fear a victory of the ticket headed by Sacasa, because the punitive hand of this army stands over him, and he will never remain in the presidency after January.

This is the true situation, compatriots, and the road to follow has been pointed out to you.

A. C. SANDINO

[10, 161–62]

1. The political statements in this manifesto refer to the elections that were to be held in November 1932, under the supervision of the U.S. Marine Corps.

153. LETTER TO MARCIAL RIVERA ZELEDÓN, FEBRUARY 19, 1932

Sergeant Major Marcial Rivera Zeledón

Greetings from the supreme leader, General A. C. Sandino.

This supreme command of the Army in Defense of the National Sovereignty of Nicaragua is pleased to greet you fraternally in my name and in that of all the members and brothers of this General Headquarters, for the work you carried out in making effective the list of contributions that our brother, General Francisco Estrada, put in your hands.

In this message we acknowledge receipt of the sum of 3,200 córdobas that you have turned over to this supreme command as the product of the contributions imposed upon the renegade capitalists for the needs of our brothers who fight in the Army in Defense of the National Sovereignty of Nicaragua.

This supreme command understands your report in respect to the properties that our army's system of justice was required to punish for not having complied with the clear orders of this supreme command. This supreme command is not so stupid as to believe the letters from those renegades asking for pity and moaning about a state of poverty that doesn't even exist, since they deal with the machos and the National Guard dogs as if they were princes.

This supreme command of the Army in Defense of the National Sovereignty of Nicaragua approves of the methods you used in burning the farms and haciendas to which you referred, and I will make the renegades understand that if they don't comply, in spite of this punishment, they will pay with their skins for their rebelliousness against our authorities. It's necessary for them to understand that our army enjoys the protection of Divine Justice and of various warrior spirits, and that it is a crime when those who could help turn their backs upon the struggle of our liberating army.

The traitors you "vested" in your last tour are justly executed, and this command has no comment to make, except that next time you are prohibited from going about putting little pieces of paper on the bodies, announcing that you have executed them. This General Headquarters hasn't given you any such instructions and in the future you will not write those papers giving an account of anything. . . .

Given in the General Headquarters of the Army in Defense of the National Sovereignty of Nicaragua, in Bocay, on the nineteenth day of the month of February of nineteen hundred and thirty-two.

A. C. SANDINO

[11, 306–7]

154. LETTER TO JOSÉ ZELAYA,
MARCH 11, 1932

General Headquarters of the Army in
Defense of the National Sovereignty of
Nicaragua
March 11, 1932

Señor Don José Zelaya
San Rafael del Norte

Esteemed sir:

Attached to this letter please find a receipt for the merchandise belonging to you that our forces took for the consumption of our army and to alleviate the needs of our brother campesinos who have made common cause with our Army in Defense of Nicaragua's National Dignity.

May it bring satisfaction to you to contribute (even if by force) to the maintenance of our armed protest. For your information and that of the other merchants of that place, I am attaching a copy of the circular that is in the possession of all the leaders of the forces belonging to our army.

May it be equally understood that as long as invaders exist in Nicaragua, and as long as the treaties, pacts, and conventions made between governments of the United States of America and the governments they themselves imposed upon Nicaragua remain in force, there will be no peace, nor will there be any guarantees of lives and interests. In the same vein, you must understand that we bear no responsibility, since we have been provoked and defense is our duty.

If anything is responsible for events in Nicaragua, it is the international policy of the United States and the Nicaraguans who have not hesitated to flirt with the invaders, contributing with their disgusting lack of courage to the pretext that they put forth to support their intervention in Nicaragua, saying that both important and unimportant Nicaraguans are requesting their intervention in our country. May they suffer, then, the consequences of their cowardice.

A. C. SANDINO

[11, 311–12]

155. LETTER TO GENERAL FRANCISCO ESTRADA, APRIL 28, 1932[1]

My dear brother, General Estrada:

General Irías carries instructions to place himself under your orders and to recognize you as first leader of all our expeditionary force on the whole Atlantic coast. It has also been explained to General Irías that if by means of the expedition with which I am now concerned we should manage to gain control of that coast, you will assume the office of intendant governor, choosing the location where you will establish yourself with your staff, the place from which you will direct the entire political and military movement of our Atlantic coast.

[. . .] I am sending you these newspapers, where news of the capture of Villa Nueva appears; also we have news of the taking of Ciudad Darío, and it is said that in order to gain control of it our muchachos had to burn some of the town's houses, and the airplanes put an end to the task, but only at a time when our forces were already absent.

Patria y Libertad.
A. C. SANDINO

[11, 324]

1. The source used reproduces only the two fragments published here.

156. NEWS BULLETIN OF THE DEFENDING ARMY CONCERNING OPERATIONS IN THE MONTHS OF APRIL AND ON MAY 1

To Indo-Hispanic Observers

We were correct when we stated earlier that our enemies would themselves see to the matter of publishing reports about our military movements, albeit in their own way, and these reports are the best evidence of the losses in men and weapons that they constantly suffer as the sole consequence of the international policy of the United States.

On April 4 of this year the ex-National Guardsmen belonging to the enemy forces in Kisalaya, the Atlantic coast of Nicaragua, rebelled against the Yankee filibusters who commanded them. To achieve their intentions, they killed Lieutenant Charles Lebos of Yankee nationality, and wounded Second Lieutenant Carlos Rayo. As a result of this uprising, our army obtained the following: twenty-one Springfield rifles, among them some mortars, twenty-one grenades, a Thompson machine gun with 1,600 rounds, 5,000 Springfield rounds, a .45-caliber automatic pistol with six magazines, a Browning machine gun, a Colt machine gun with the necessary equipment, and 9,000 Lewis rounds. All this was turned over by the ex-National Guardsmen Sebastián Jiménez, Felipe Briceño H., Francisco López, and Aurelio Flores, who at this time are in the service of our army. The weapons were received by Generals Estrada and Morales and Colonel Sócrates Sandino.

On the 11th of the same month of April, three gunners of the enemy garrison in Quilalí, who respond to the names Antonio García, Balbino Hoyos, and Antonio Cornejo, passed over to our ranks with their respective weapons, consisting of a Browning machine gun and two Thompson machine guns with their corresponding equipment, as well as hand grenades and Springfield rifle ammunition. All this was received by General Colindres.

On the 15th, still in April, Captain Heriberto Reyes sustained a bloody three-hour battle against the enemy in the place called San Luis, jurisdiction of Ocotal. In the battle thirty traitor dogs perished along with one of the pirates who commanded them. On our part, we lament the deaths of the brothers Alberto Cruz Maradiaga and Fausto E. García.

On the 21st the new enemy garrison stationed again in Kisalaya was attacked by our forces under the command of General Morales. This time the enemy was stronger, but nevertheless was dislodged after an hour and three-quarters of bitter combat. On our part, we regret the deaths of the brothers Sergeant Major Francisco Montenegro, Captain Zeledonio Gutiérrez, Lieutenant Marcelino Rugama, and the young student from the University of León, Nicaragua, Octavio Oviedo. Generals Morales and Estrada are continuing their march across the Atlantic interior. We also have reserve forces on the same coast. In the battle just referred to, Lieutenant Rafael César Zamora, Orlando Baldizón, and Santos Godoy were wounded.

On the same date Colonel Juan Altamirano defeated the enemy in Santa Bárbara, jurisdiction of Jinotega. The enemy left five traitor dogs and one Yankee on the battlefield. On the same day forces of that same Colonel Juan Altamirano attacked another enemy column in the place called Chagüitillo. The enemy was totally destroyed and 2,000 Springfield rounds and two .45 caliber pistols were captured from them. We had no casualties and the enemy was able to carry away his dead and wounded.

On the 21st, forces under the command of Generals Carlos Salgado P., Juan G. Colindres, and Captain Heriberto Reyes engaged the enemy in combat in La Puerta, department of Ocotal. The enemy resisted for three quarters of an hour and were defeated, leaving two Yankees and twelve traitor dogs dead on the field of battle. Captured were a Browning machine gun and five Springfield rifles, all weapons with abundant ammunition. We had no casualties in that battle. At 4 p.m. on the same day, that same force, commanded by the leaders mentioned, had another hard encounter with enemy reinforcements in the place called Los Leones, which lasted until nightfall. Upon reconnoitering the battlefield five traitor dogs and three Yankee officers were found dead. Captured were twelve Springfield rifles, three .45 caliber pistols, a mortar with six shells, and many documents important for the history of Nicaragua. On our part, we regret the deaths of the brothers Pío Melgara and Estanislao Maradiaga; wounded, Manuel Valladares.

On the 23rd, General Salgado and Captain Heriberto Reyes sustained another encounter with the enemy in the place called Los Bellorín. The enemy left seven dead on the battlefield.

The other battles occurring in April, fought in the interior of Nicaragua by General Umanzor, Colonels Tomás Blandón, Perfecto Chavarría, Ruperto Hernández Roblero, General José León Díaz, etc., have already been publicized by the enemy himself.

On the 1st of this month the same General Salgado sustained another bloody battle with the enemy in Ciudad Antigua. On our part, the brother Federico Tercero of San Marcos de Colón, Honduras, perished.

On the same date General Colindres attacked the enemy in the place called Los Bellorín. The battle lasted for three hours, the enemy leaving thirty-six dead in the field along with supplies which included fourteen woolen jackets, three caps, two suits, a pair of shoes, and a field tent. On our part we regret the death of the brother Juan Pablo Bellorín, owner of the property where the battles took place.

OUR CASUALTIES

	Dead	Wounded
San Lucas	2	0
Kisalaya	4	3
Los Leones	2	1
Ciudad Antigua	1	0
Los Bellorín	1	0
TOTAL	10	4

ENEMY CASUALTIES

	Dead	Wounded
Kisalaya	16	10
San Lucas	31	0
Santa Barbara	6	11
Chagüitillo	13	9
La Puerta	14	0
Los Leones	8	0
Los Bellorín	7	0
Los Bellorín	36	0
TOTAL	131	30

BATTLE EQUIPMENT CAPTURED FROM THE ENEMY

	Rifles	Machine Guns	Bombs	Ammunition	.45 Pistols
Kisalaya	21	3	21	15,600	1
Quilalí	0	3	5	140	0
Chagüitillo	0	0	0	3,000	2
La Puerta	5	1	0	0	0
Los Leones	13	0	6	0	3
TOTAL	39	7	32	18,740	6

Other things: I will use this opportunity to inform our compatriots in foreign countries that, today like yesterday, our army is convinced that Nicaragua will be freed only by means of bullets and at the cost of our own blood; and that, as always, we will impede by the force of right and with our weapons any electoral farce that anyone may wish to see repeated in Nicaragua with foreign supervision. General Don Horacio Portocarrero, a Nicaraguan citizen, has been designated by our army to be president of our republic, once we have achieved military control of the same, either through arms or by means of compacts in which the enemy agrees to affirm in power in Nicaragua the person designated by our army. General Portocarrero possesses high powers granted by us to organize a provisional government along with the active forces of the country who may wish to join our cause, but they will also cooperate to impede the elections that the enemy is preparing for the coming November.

Nicaraguans interested in the liberation of Nicaragua are fully accepted by our army, though without any commitment to partisan banners, and disciplined by our guidelines, which do not allow us to maintain relations with any party that considers offering candidates in elections supervised by foreign powers.

We are observing Moncada's proposals regarding the reform of the Constitution in Nicaragua as a way to legalize the sadly renowned Bryan-Chamorro agreements. Nevertheless, the last of the Nicaraguans may die and all of Nicaragua may be left in ashes, but those agreements will never be legal. [. . .]

General Headquarters of the Army in Defense of the National Sovereignty of Nicaragua. The Segovias, Nic., C.A., May 18, 1932.

Patria y Libertad.
AUGUSTO CÉSAR SANDINO

[5, 137, 143; 1, 119–20; 9, 2:171–72]

157. LETTER TO GENERALS FRANCISCO ESTRADA AND JUAN SANTOS MORALES, MAY 22, 1932

General Headquarters of the Army in
Defense of the National Sovereignty of
Nicaragua

May 22, 1932

First and Second Leaders of Column No. 3, General Francisco Estrada and Juan Santos
Morales, Respectively

The Atlantic Coast of Nicaragua

Dear brothers:

I have just received correspondence from General Morales dated the 9th of the current month, in which he informs me that up until that date he had not had contact with the general staff about the matter that concerns me.

[. . .] General Morales is obligated to acquaint General Estrada with all his movements, and, since he has not done this, he has not complied with what has been ordered by this General Command of our Army.

In this regard, General Estrada will at once order the regrouping of General Morales and his entire force at the encampment where Estrada is located. Equally, Morales will place all forces and weapons under his command under General Estrada's orders and regroup at this General Headquarters with only two of his aides. Estrada will organize the entire force in the way he sees fit, encamp them where he sees fit, and attack when he sees fit, since he has already understood everything that is to be done.

There is more: Day by day I am experiencing the enormous affliction of recognizing that all the leaders, in the majority, are becoming antagonistic toward one another and shirkers to an unspeakable extent. At this time there are ordinary soldiers of our army who are much more active than recognized leaders, which can be nothing but a very regrettable fact.

Here nobody is in a bed of flowers, and we are enduring the most tremendous sacrifices, and I swear to you that if you would like to accept the responsibility of directing this movement I will deposit it in you, and I will leave as expeditionary leader to prove to you that with a good head and a little bit of bravery and honor one can accomplish everything you think can't be done.

Sincerely your brother.
Patria y Libertad.
AUGUSTO C. SANDINO

[11, 322–23]

158. LETTER TO GENERAL FRANCISCO ESTRADA, JUNE 3, 1932[1]

General Headquarters of the Army in
Defense of the National Sovereignty of
Nicaragua

June 3, 1932

General Francisco Estrada
Encampments of Expeditionary Column No. 3

Dear Brother:

At this moment, at four in the afternoon, I have received your esteemed letter dated last May 25, and I am pleased that it arrived without incident.

Informed as I am about all the points made in your letter, allow me to tell you that if General Morales can prove that for reasons beyond his own desires he didn't communicate earlier with you, you may reconsider the order for him to regroup at this General Headquarters, but that otherwise the order remains in effect. According to news brought to us by a nephew of Captain Aguilar who campaigned with Morales, we know that the force in question fought about May 16 in Mos, or near that place at least, for which reason I suppose that at that time he could already have communicated with you.

On the other hand, if at the time this letter reaches you, you haven't yet had news from General Altamirano, I think the latter may have fought before reaching Neptuno and that for this reason he headed for Macantaca, the place where General Gómez was, and surely after meeting him they attempted the attack on that camp.

The news we have from our other leaders in the interior is flattering, and especially now that it is said that the enemy has abandoned several towns and garrisons, such as that of the Corinto hacienda of the Stadthagen family; it is also said that in Jinotega they have very greatly reduced the number of their troops.

Recently Señor Balladares, a rich and politically influential man, came to our camps from Column No. 4, asking that we grant him the post for which we had named General Horacio Portocarrero, promising us that his government would be recognized within a month.[2] He also sent us a list of persons who would make up his cabinet; among them appeared

Carlos Castro Wassmer for war minister, a certain José María Zelaya, and another group of the same men who have been involved with Moncada during his entire administration. Our reply was negative, and we restricted ourselves to telling him that if he really wanted to cooperate with us he should join General Portocarrero, the person to whom we have extended high powers for the purpose he spoke to us about. We don't know what Señor Balladares's immediate response will be.

It's almost certain that from the 10th to the 12th of this month I will make a tour of our old camps, because I have to settle many matters that concern me; I hope to have meetings in those places with Colindres and other leaders who are about to get their orders. It wouldn't be surprising if from Colindres we received some new proposals for an understanding, because we think there's a strong interest.

Concerning my health and that of my wife, fortunately at the moment it is enviable, because we are more vigorous than when you left, the result of the useful assistance we received during that distressing illness.

With the present mail I am sending you some newspapers which are the latest we have, and in them there are many reports about us and others that interest us.

In union with all the brothers nearby, I beg you to accept the sincere affection of this your brother.

Patria y Libertad.
AUGUSTO C. SANDINO

[11, 330–31]

1. The 1981 edition contains this letter in the incomplete form found in source 10, 171–72. In this edition the complete version is given.

2. On the designation of General Horacio Portocarrero to occupy the presidency of Nicaragua, see Docs. 150 and 151.

159. LETTER TO GENERAL PEDRO ALTAMIRANO, JUNE 19, 1932

First Leader of our Expeditionary Column No. 1
Divisionary General
Pedro Altamirano
Field of Military Operations

My dear brother:

[. . .] General Umanzor will arrive soon at this General Headquarters, and on Wednesday boats will leave to bring them to this camp. Previously we ordered one Señor Enrique Sánchez from León to be detained, and he was singled out to contribute a thousand córdobas which General Umanzor was waiting to receive in order to bring it with him. This Señor Enrique Sánchez is said to be the brother of Agustín Sánchez, the young man who is there with you, which I think is true. This gentleman is in El Topón, and orders have been sent to have him brought to this encampment so that we may speak to him. It could well be that we could learn something from a conversation with him which would clarify the situation in the west.

Not long ago a proposal came from one Señor Manuel Balladares, from León, asking us to grant him the personal representation of this supreme command to head a revolutionary movement in the west, and he assured me that he had war equipment and people ready to seize control of the entire country in only a month. The proposal seemed very bold to me, and we didn't accept it because two men came with him who have been Moncada's coddled pets. These men are a certain Carlos Castro Wassmer and one José María Zelaya. We have distrusted that gentleman's proposal, and, because of some newspaper clippings which we have seen, it appears that Agustín Sánchez is one of those individuals who belong to the Balladares group, and that he came on ahead to prepare the terrain. Even now there is nothing that proves that the Balladares proposals and his people aren't sincere, and it could well be that they are entirely honest, but what we can't agree to is to turn the reins of our revolutionary movement over to him. I have replied by telling them that they should join forces with General Portocarrero, who already possesses authority from this supreme command to organize our provisional government. We have still not received a reply, but we expect it soon. Colindres was eager for us to withdraw our representation from General Portocarrero and to give it to Balladares. From me a reprimand went out to Colindres for allowing himself to be so hypnotized in only a day by a man he had just met, because Balladares arrived at his encampments looking for me. Also yesterday a report came to us that a number of well-armed men have entered Nicaraguan territory by way of Somotillo, and that they are believed to be a new revolutionary group separate from our own.

For this reason I have circulated orders to all our forces who are now in the entire area of the Segovias that they are not to go into the interior and are not to withdraw very far from this region, because we want to find out what will happen to that force which has entered the country, and to find out if they are allies of ours acquired by General Portocarrero or birds of another feather.

We are expecting correspondence from Honduras, and that will determine how we will orient ourselves. For the same reason I think it would not be good for you to remove yourself very far away.

With the next mail delivery you may send the young Agustín Sánchez to this encampment, but without equipment, being so kind as to keep him under guard and to send him later. I have an interest in seeing the two brothers together and to read the reality of things in their expressions, and for me it is better that they be without weapons because if they are our enemies and they know they've been found out, they could commit a crime, since they would realize that in any event they would have to die[. . . .]

Patria y Libertad.
A. C. SANDINO

[11, 336–38]

160. LETTER TO GENERAL FRANCISCO ESTRADA, JULY 7, 1932[1]

Señor Manuel Balladares has at last agreed to join forces with General Portocarrero, and we suppose that for that purpose a conference has taken place in Tegucigalpa at about this time among many Nicaraguans interested in joining our army. We are awaiting the results of those talks.

Dr. Arturo Vega is preparing leaflets in the department of Chinandega, and I am sending you a few of the ones he sent us, which I ask you to distribute.

Recently the young Enrique Sánchez, from León, held the status of hostage in this General Headquarters, General Umanzor having levied a contribution of a thousand pesos upon him, money which according to that brother is now in his possession; for that reason the young Sánchez was freed on the 1st of this month and left for the city of Jinotega.

We are making use of the journey of the young Sánchez, who was not resentful, to send some words to the Sacasa-Argüello candidates and others of the Liberal party to the effect that they should unify themselves with our army and support our provisional government, which will call the Nicaraguan nation to elections entirely in the form of a plebiscite, and that if they don't proceed in the manner indicated to them, they will incur the greatest responsibilities.

It is ten days now that Captain José de Paredes has been staying among us, and he greets you affectionately through me; here he will remain for an indefinite period, because his actions have caused our suspicion to vanish.

Patria y Libertad.
A. C. SANDINO

[11, 334–35]

1. The 1981 edition contains these fragments of the letter to General Estrada as they appear in source 10, 173, that is, without the last paragraph and with the date on which Sánchez was granted his freedom in error.

In July the following battles were of unusual interest: Our forces of the Atlantic division under the command of Generals Francisco Estrada and Simón González attacked and captured the Vaccaro banana station in Puerto Cabezas, property of a U.S. company. Reinforcements immediately reached the enemy stationed at that camp, but our muchachos knew how to drive them back, taking possession of their trains and motorcars as well as ammunition, rifles, and machine guns. The buildings were set on fire, and the following day a flotilla of airplanes bombed our column, one of them being shot down. The bombing oriented the enemy who approached us, and a bloody battle continued almost until nightfall. The enemy's casualties are calculated at more than a hundred.

We were informed that twenty Yankee amphibious planes landed at Puerto Cabezas to pick up North American families who are residents at that port. We see this as a wise move, because the fate that awaits the North Americans there is bleak.

On that same July 14, our forces under the command of Colonel Ruperto Hernández Robledo and Sergeant Major Francisco García experienced a bloody encounter with the enemy in Los Achiotes, department of Jinotega, in which three traitor-dog lieutenants and nine Yankee pirates lost their lives. Weapons and ammunition were captured.

On the 16th, still in July, in La Rocía, department of León, our forces commanded by Colonel Zacarías Padilla fought another bloody battle and captured a large amount of weapons and food supplies.

Just now Generals Estrada and González, leaders of the Atlantic division, have informed us that large units of U.S. troops have crossed into Nicaraguan territory from the Honduran Mosquito Coast, and we are at a loss to understand how the government of Honduras would allow this, claiming as it does to be jealously independent. The report adds that they have their quarters at the banana station of the Yankee firm, the United Fruit Company, in the Honduran port of Trujillo.

J. C. Smith, a Yankee officer, gave the newspapers the following list of National Guard dead in only one battle in the Segovias. If they admit this, we don't have to say how things are going to go, or that the renegades will fertilize the earth, because the following at least are serving that purpose: Private Rigoberto Rojas, number 5,136 (numbered as if they were dealing with implements); Sergeant Juan Coronado, number 1,888; Private Lionstini Omair, number 4,764; Private Humberto Martínez, number 4,115; Private Miguel Cárdenas, number 4,073; Private Benito Zamora Rico, number 4,278; Private Manolo Cuadra, number 100.

Translation of a letter from the Yankee Captain Walter A. Gaspar to his mother, accompanied by a check for $36.85:[1]

San Rafael del Norte
Department of Jinotega
March 30, 1932.

Mr. Walter A. Gaspar
330 Wisconsin Avenue
Wankisba, Wisconsin
USA

Dearest Mama:

Just today they've notified me from Jinotega that your package arrived today by plane[. . . .] I intended to write a long and affectionate letter to you, but the war and the Sandinistas, or whatever they're called, were opposed to my wishes. Today it's six months since I came to this corner of hell, and I would have wanted to be in China all this time, where I would have felt a lot safer. I prefer to hear the roar of battle than to hear a single shot fired at me from behind [. . . .] This is life in San Rafael del Norte.

DAD

[11, 119–21]

1. Since this abbreviated letter attached to Sandino's war bulletin is signed "Dad," it might have been written to the captain's wife and not to his mother, as Sandino assumed, perhaps not knowing the meaning of the word "Dad." The uncertainty is increased by the fact that the letter appears to have been addressed to *Mr.* Walter A. Gaspar. This translation is made from the Spanish translation of the original English and so undoubtedly differs from the original. RC

162. CIRCULAR TO CIVIL AUTHORITIES, AUGUST 31, 1932

Circular to All Our Civil Authorities in
the Regions of Jinotega, Matagalpa and Estelí

My dear brothers:

Today just as yesterday we are convinced that no Nicaraguan government originating as a result of foreign supervision will defend our interests, and that, on the contrary, it will continue to support the interests of the foreigners who put it in power, contrary to every right. Sufficient cause for no Nicaraguan worthy of the name to take part in the Machiavellian elections that the enemy is preparing for the coming months of October and November of this year. I want to think and believe that in these moments of so much enlightenment there do not exist campesinos among us who want to commit the crime of high treason, guaranteeing with their own vote the enslavement of all Nicaragua, which would be the enslavement of their homes as well as of themselves.

At this very moment our army has begun to intensify its hostilities against the enemy, and at the present moment our first forces are appearing in all the departments of the Republic. As I write this, contingents of our forces continue to sally forth, and I am certain that by the time this reaches your hands the first reports of the successes achieved by our army will already be circulating, principally on the Atlantic coast and in the interior of the Republic. No less impressive will be the military movements which we will carry out in the departments of the north.

I will take advantage of this opportunity to order all our civil authorities to summon together all the civilian brothers in their dependencies so that they may use all the warlike measures available to prevent the enemy from holding elections or meetings of people in their respective jurisdictions. Moreover, if the elections and meetings of the enemy's people are not intended to occur in the place controlled by our civil authorities, our civil authorities must meet with their people and help our other brothers to prevent the elections that concern me.

General Headquarters of the Army in Defense of the National
Sovereignty of Nicaragua
The Segovias, Nic., C.A.
August 31, 1932
Patria y Libertad.
AUGUSTO CÉSAR SANDINO

[2, 61–62]

163. LETTER TO GENERAL PEDRO ALTAMIRANO, NOVEMBER 9, 1932

La Chispa
November 9, 1932

My very dear brother:

We are who we are, and we are not like anybody else, and it doesn't matter whether our representatives abroad do something or don't do something, because our cause will continue on its course, ever triumphant.

The elections are over already, and we are now waiting to learn whether it is with Sacasa or with the Conservatives that we are to continue our struggle, because, no matter who it is, the pirates are leaving on January 2.

At this time I am occupying myself by elaborating the fundamental principles for the agreement that we will present to Sacasa, if it is he who comes on stage, and if in fact he wants to arrive at an understanding with us. I will send a copy of these fundamental principles to you once they have been prepared, so that you may preserve it and keep our provisions in mind.

On the other hand, if power is with the Conservatives, I think that not even they themselves would seek agreements with us, nor we with them, and that the matter will be resolved with bullets. Meanwhile, military control of the Republic by our army will be proposed to Sacasa, for which purpose the minister of war would have to be a member of our army; also the interior minister and that of foreign relations to be held by persons designated by our Army, and for this we would choose Dr. Escolástico Lara for interior and Calderón Ramírez for foreign relations; similarly, the head of La Loma in Managua and of La Pólvora, of Granada, would have to be members of our army, *with battalions made up of our own forces.*[1] We will see now how things turn out.

For the moment our army is in magnificent condition everywhere, and the only barrier we have to overcome is the incident involving General Juan Gregorio Colindres, who certainly because of malevolent influences, taking advantage of the distance that separates himself from us, proclaimed himself president of the Republic of Nicaragua in the name of our army and in my name, without authorization from us; the funny thing about this situation is that he left this General Headquarters as first leader of our Expeditionary Column No. 12, and now he sends me a letter telling me that the people of Nicaragua and the army have proclaimed him provisional governor of the Republic, and with such a pompous name he didn't even take the trouble to sign.

Colonel Hernández Roblero and Captain Pío Arroliga with seven attendants arrived as couriers to bring us Colindres's letter, his proclamation, and his first decree as provisional governor of Nicaragua, at the same time asking me for orders on the part of General Peralta, who was the leader of the Second Column.

The same group returned at once carrying instructions to General Peralta that he is to become the first commander of Expeditionary Column No. 12 and is to capture General Colindres, Colonel Arturo Vega, and anyone he believes under suspicion, and that he bring them here and relocate himself with all his forces at this General Headquarters; likewise, a patriotic message was sent from this command to our Column No. 12. Also orders were sent to our other expeditionary columns to approach the place where these events have taken place to cooperate with General Peralta in carrying out the orders that have been distributed, and if there is armed opposition, the opponents and traitors to the army are to be executed by firing squad.

I am sending you the copy sent to me by Colindres of his first confused decree, which shows that there is an enemy hand involved trying to tangle everything up.

I'm also sending you a letter that Arturo Vega wrote to Colindres, giving him opinions and instructions; finally, I am sending you instructions that Colindres and Peralta received from this General Headquarters in their role as expeditionary leaders of our Column No. 12.

I'm sending all these documents to you so that you may read them, and you should send them back to me complete by the first mail, because all of these, the proclamation and the note that Colindres sent me, will be documents for me to justify myself, and to judge them in a Council of War; for that reason I beg you to send them to me with utmost care, without omitting a single sheet.[2]

General Irías should read those papers and give his opinion, because we will organize a Council of War made up of all the army leaders, who will judge Colindres and Vega and the other responsible persons.

This council, then, will decide the fate of the brothers who have been led astray.

Patria y Libertad.

A. C. SANDINO

[11, 372–74]

1. La Loma and La Pólvora were major fortresses, the former located on the peak of the Tiscapa volcano in Managua, at that time also the site of the presidential palace. RC

2. None of these documents have been found.

164. SANDINO'S PEACE PROPOSALS, NOVEMBER 12, 1932[1]

Principles That When Accepted Will Bring Peace to Nicaragua

1. That the first Nicaraguan citizen who, finding himself in the government of our republic, BY ANY MEANS, and who sincerely represents the interests of our nation, must ask for and obtain, even if it should be accomplished with bullets, the immediate withdrawal of the U.S. military forces of occupation in Nicaragua; AT THE SAME TIME HE MUST ACCEPT THE SUPPORT OF OUR ARMY IN DEFENSE OF THE NATIONAL SOVEREIGNTY OF NICARAGUA FOR THE MAINTENANCE OF COMPLETE ORDER IN OUR REPUBLIC.

2. That the government of Nicaragua that accepts the former principle also accept and support the idea of the undersigned to hold in the capital city of the Argentine republic a conference among representatives of the twenty-one governments of our racial America and that of the United States of America, the representative of Nicaragua to be the undersigned. And to consider in that conference everything relative to the United States project that seeks to construct an interoceanic canal and to establish a naval base in Central American territory and waters; also to clarify in the conference whether the ninety million Indo-Hispanics who make up our twenty-one racial peoples have the right or not to express their opinions regarding the transcendental project that the United States wishes to establish as its exclusive property, and what ought to be their attitude in the face of the problem that concerns me.

3. That the government of Nicaragua that accepts the first and second principles of this agreement also accept the right of the Nicaraguan people to remove it from power by force, in cases in which it fails to uphold in whole or in part the principles here stipulated.

Note: With the departure from Nicaragua of the North American pirates on the second of January, the first part of our first principle will be fulfilled; for the second part of the same first principle, which appears in capital letters, we have a separate statement that indicates the form in which our army will lend its support to the government that accepts the present agreement.

General Headquarters of the Army in Defense of the National Sovereignty of Nicaragua, The Segovias, Nic., C.A., November 12, 1932.

Patria y Libertad.
AUGUSTO CÉSAR SANDINO

[19, 1 p.]

1. These are the fundamental principles (mentioned in Doc. 163) to be presented to the Liberal candidate for the presidency, in the event that he won the election of 1932. RC

165. LETTER TO JOSÉ IDIÁQUEZ AND ALFONSO IRÍAS, NOVEMBER 1932

General Headquarters of the Army in
Defense of the National Sovereignty of
Nicaragua

Señores Don José Idiáquez and Don Alfonso Irías
Danlí

Peace and love, my dear brothers:

Your worthy notes, which you sent me through Colonel Raudales, have been received and taken into account; also I have received the correspondence that arrived for us from abroad.

Mathematically speaking, the entire movement of our army is marching triumphantly over our enemies, the only obstacle to be overcome being the incident involving our misguided brother, General Juan Gregorio Colindres, who, taking advantage of the distance that separated him from this General Headquarters, proclaimed himself head of the *provisional government of Nicaragua* as a way to play out his hand, without any authorization from our army, a stupid act that will certainly cost him his life. Because just now orders have been sent out to our brother General Ismael Peralta, who had acted as second leader of our Expeditionary Column No. 12, which General Colindres had commanded, to capture General Colindres and the deceptive Arturo Vega. They will be brought to this General Headquarters, and that will put an end to the incident as well as the stupidity of General Colindres, who clearly has been the victim of bad advice, because in General Colindres I never imagined such uncontrolled and foolish ambition. Besides, even though he was five times a deserter from our army, I always had respect, never distrust, for General Colindres; for that very reason, by assuming this attitude, which reveals a true lack of judgment, he has managed to be what he couldn't become before. Also orders have been sent out to nine of our expeditionary columns for them to cooperate with General Peralta in carrying out the decisive orders that have been circulated. Let us pray that the proclamations, decrees, and other writings that I am informed Colindres and Vega dispatched for publication in the name of our army have come into your hands and been held back, to avoid the confusion that they would certainly cause.

Other things. The elections were interrupted as it was our duty to do with the attacks on the towns of Matagalpa, Jinotega, La Concordia, San Juan de Segovia, El Jícaro, etc., etc., which I suppose the enemy press itself will have publicized.

We still don't know who was favored by the Yankee, but for us it's of no importance, because neither of them is a recognized government and the struggle will continue, except if it was Sacasa who was favored, and he is willing to accept the three principles of which you are both aware.[1] In that event, we could arrive at peace in Nicaragua as if by magic. In this regard, you have your instructions for that situation.

I am sending you some letters that you will be pleased to send on to their destinations as quickly as possible, mainly those going to Señor Mario Rivas, General Portocarrero, and Dr. Zepeda.

I sense that with every passing day Don Alfonso is losing his respect for me, his brother, because until now all my acts and procedures have been in opposition to his own wishes, as was the case when we proclaimed as head of the provisional government Don Manuel Balladares, who, as it turns out, was another impostor. But you must convince yourselves and everyone else that I don't do what I want to do, but rather what I must do, for the good progress, discipline, and triumph of our army, which in fact will be the triumph of the people of Nicaragua and of the continent in general.

The young university student fought very well in the battle of El Jícaro and was one of the first to take the positions occupied by the enemy. I still haven't seen him, but I think he will soon arrive, and it won't be difficult for me to send the present letter through him.

Ever onward.
AUGUSTO CÉSAR SANDINO

[19, 2 pp.]

1. See Doc. 164.

166. LETTER TO GENERAL PEDRO ALTAMIRANO, DECEMBER 12, 1932

My very dear brother:

[. . .] In recent days we have been exceedingly busy, mainly with the arrival of our Expeditionary Column No. 12, with Generals Peralta and Colindres. General Colindres has felt very sorry about what happened, because through his explanations we have understood that he was the victim of stupid and wicked advisers; as a result of everything that has been said, all the peril that this brother got himself into because of his mistake has vanished. Arturo Vega and de Paredes, who were Colindres's advisers, are also about to arrive at this General Headquarters with a committee which went to look for them[. . . .]

Honduras is in a state of war, and Captain Cornejo returned bringing the letters he was carrying, because he wasn't able to enter. When you arrive we will have a lot to talk about. This letter isn't long, but I suppose it will find you on the road, and besides in these moments I am getting cold from fever as a result of that same influenza[. . . .]

[11, 383–84]

167. LETTER TO GENERAL PEDRO ALTAMIRANO, DECEMBER 18, 1932

[. . .] Now there are no more warplanes in Nicaragua, because all of them left aboard a ship on the 15th of this month, and only commercial planes that don't carry machine guns or bombs are crossing the skies; I have been advised of this by Señor Sofonías Salvatierra himself, who has always demonstrated loyalty to us. In this respect, now we will no longer have air attacks, and all the precautions we take will be with regard to the enemy on the ground, but those dogs don't want to die now, and it will be hard for them to work up any eagerness to attack, and the most they will do will be to defend themselves in their positions—for as long as we have not reached a practical understanding.

Now we won't have any problems organizing cavalry units, and in the provisional headquarters that we will install, we will be able to have our taxes and well-established rural governments, so that our delegates will feel enthusiastic when they see us. Furthermore, it wouldn't be difficult for us to engage in some battles before the arrival of those persons in San Rafael del Norte, but for this we'll have to be cautious, because we have said that our attacks are not to end before an effective understanding is arrived at, and that once we reached that understanding we would suspend the orders to attack. For my part, I feel that if we could capture some towns before then, it would be much better, because the enemy would be more compelled toward the idea of an understanding.

In Honduras the war is in a delicate stage, and we know that in the capture of Danlí the Nicaraguan emigration took an active part, and one of the leaders was Colonel José Rodríguez, and they shouted vivas to Sandino and to our army, because they believe that we have sent part of our army to cooperate with the revolution; that whole country is up in flames and we can't keep up a correspondence with anybody, and only the news gets through to us.[1]

Patria y Libertad.
A. C. SANDINO

[11, 384–85]

1. Sandino refers to the civil war that preceded the dictatorial regime of Honduran president Tiburcio Carías Andino (1933–1948). RC

168. LETTER TO SOFONÍAS SALVATIERRA, DECEMBER 24, 1932

General Headquarters of the Army in
Defense of the National Sovereignty of
Nicaragua
The Segovias, Nic., C.A.
December 24, 1932

Señor Don Sofonías Salvatierra

Very distinguished sir:

Yesterday I received your interesting letter, dated in that capital city on the 23rd of last month, to which I am now responding.[1]

I take this auspicious opportunity to send you and the *Patriotic Group* that you mention our highest congratulations for your work on behalf of the restoration of our national independence, the *only cause* for which the army I am honored to command fights and will fight.[2]

We have no problem accepting the *United Committee of Those Interested in the Pacification of Nicaragua*, so long as it brings with it the official delegation of the government that seeks to legalize itself as the ruler of the Republic. Any other sort of committee that does not come vested with official powers we will not accept. Dr. Sacasa should take the opportunity that is now presented to him to reach an understanding with our army, so that he will not remain a puppet, a plaything for childish amusement. Authority favors us over Dr. Sacasa, because he abandoned us during bitter moments of our national history. Concerning his private life, the doctor deserves our esteem, but as a public man, it is our duty to remind him of his past.

Very well, then, on the basis of a possible patriotic understanding, we have appointed Señores Don Salvador Calderón Ramírez, Dr. Escolástico Lara, Dr. Pedro José Zepeda, and General Horacio Portocarrero as our delegates, to whom on this very day we are sending a patriotic summons, and we ask you to send them the statements attached to this letter.[3] Also we ask you to write to them personally, indicating to them whatever you think convenient. In passing, I suggest to you that if Dr. Sacasa decides to deal with this matter officially, our delegates' expenses during the talks leading to an understanding ought to be paid by our national treasury, because neither I nor they have the means.

We are sincerely grateful for your news from Niquinohomo. My wife, Sócrates, and I send a fraternal embrace to your distinguished family and to you.

Patria y Libertad.
AUGUSTO CÉSAR SANDINO

[8, 105–7]

1. The content of Salvatierra's letter may be inferred from Sandino's reply.
2. The "Grupo Patriótico" was an organization founded in 1932 by elements "of every political coloration," whose basic aim was to find a negotiated solution to the Nicaraguan political and military crisis. Among its members were Juan F. Gutiérrez, Salvador Buitrago Díaz, Rosendo Argüello, Francisco Maldonado, Modesto Armijo, Federico J. Lacayo, and Sofonías Salvatierra himself.
3. For the summons, see Doc. 169.

169. LETTER DESIGNATING DELEGATES TO A PEACE CONFERENCE, DECEMBER 24, 1932

To the distinguished gentlemen Don Salvador Calderón Ramírez, Dr. Escolástico Lara, Dr. Pedro José Zepeda and General Horacio Portocarrero:

Our army regards you as among the most illustrious sons of Nicaragua because your public acts have always been in conformity with the high spirit of patriotism, for which reason the army looks upon you as united by an affinity of ideas and therefore motivated to contribute to the renovation and reconstruction of the fatherland. By virtue of this, the army has resolved to state to you the following:

That today we have been informed that the Nicaraguan people in general, to the sound of the explosion of our liberating weapons, have awakened in patriotic response and are unanimously concerned that Dr. Sacasa should reach a patriotic understanding with our army. We have decided to hold peace conferences in San Rafael del Norte if Sacasa's government is free and unburdened by public or private compromises with the United States of America, and with these letters we designate you to represent us in the supposed conference; for this purpose we invest you with ample powers. The national treasury of our republic of Nicaragua will pay the costs of our journey to San Rafael del Norte. My mother-in-law, Doña Ester V. de Aráuz, will give you information about a personal interview with me before any agreement is concluded. Don Sofonías Salvatierra, in Managua, will receive you in that capital city, if the idea crystalizes; he will also write to you personally about this entire matter.

Accept our fraternal embrace.

General Headquarters of the Army in Defense of the National Sovereignty of Nicaragua, the Segovias, Nic., C.A., December 24, 1932.

Patria y Libertad.

A. C. SANDINO

[8, 107–9]

·1933·

170. LETTER TO SOFONÍAS SALVATIERRA, JANUARY 17, 1933

Provisional General Headquarters of the
Army in Defense of the National Sovereignty
of Nicaragua
The Segovias, C.A.
January 17, 1933

Señor Don Sofonías Salvatierra
San Rafael del Norte

Very esteemed Señor Salvatierra:

I received your very interesting note dated in that place on the 13th of the current month, in which you announce to us your arrival at these encampments of our army.

The present letter will serve you as a passport for our reconnaisance cavalry units and expeditionary columns, which may meet you on the road. You will make the journey accompanied by the Castelblanco brothers, about whom Blanquita will inform you. Since your entourage will surely be composed of several persons, you might be stopped by some of our expeditionary forces who are on their way to these encampments, because they have been located at places far from that zone and may not have any knowledge of your presence. In virtue of this, please carry a white flag, because with this you will be immediately identified by any of our forces, they having previously had instructions to honor it. The Castelblanco brothers will bring you to the place where I am, which is about a day's journey from there.

I consider it the highest duty of every good Nicaraguan citizen to achieve peace for Nicaragua, but the peace that dignifies and not that of the slave. For the same reason, I don't doubt that those we appointed to represent us have accepted, and let us hope that together you will be able to reach this General Headquarters.

Our sincere respect goes to you and those who may accompany you.

Patria y Libertad.

A. C. SANDINO

[8, 124–25]

171. PROTOCOL FOR PEACE,
JANUARY 20, 1933[1]

PROTOCOL FOR PEACE

The undersigned general and supreme commander of the Army in Defense of the National Sovereignty of Nicaragua formulates the following protocol for peace, to which our delegates must conform when signing the definitive peace agreement:

1. To know in depth the political program that Dr. Sacasa will carry out during the four years of his administration; to assure themselves that he will totally exclude foreign interference in the finances of Nicaragua, and to learn his attitude in respect to the so-called National Guard; likewise, to know if Dr. Sacasa has pacts of any kind signed with the North American interventionists.

2. That through the initiative of the executive, the national Congress of Nicaragua decree the creation of a new department in uncultivated national territory, contained between the zones of El Chipote and the Nicaraguan Atlantic coast, with the name of "Luz y Verdad" and with the following territorial limits: beginning at the jurisdiction of Cifuentes, Honduras, passing by the hill of El Capiro, continuing along the channel of San Pablo, passing through Los Encinos, passing through Murra, passing through El Chipote, passing through Santa Cruz de Jinotega, passing through Bocaycito, passing through Quizulí, passing through Illas, passing through Saslay, passing by the hill of Asa, passing by the hill of Cola Blanca, passing by Sandibe, reaching the sea and continuing to Karataska, going up the Patuca River, and concluding at the point of origin, Cifuentes, Honduras. Keep in mind that the creation of this new department in no way implies a sinecure for our army, and much less for the undersigned, and that the object being pursued is the general enlargement of the fatherland.[2]

3. That through the initiative of the executive, the national Congress of Nicaragua decree the complete maintenance in the new department "Luz y Verdad" of the military equipment that the Army in Defense of the National Sovereignty of Nicaragua has used during the war to dignify our national honor, and that all the civil and military authorities of the said department be appointed from among the members of our army. It is our

desire that the war matériel, which we have collected with the blood of patriots, should remain at the disposal of the departmental government of "Luz y Verdad," for a greater guarantee of order in our republic, and because the undersigned will remain in this region along with the greater part of the members who presently make up our army, where we will be prepared to repel any aggression that anyone may wish to carry out against the constituted government of Nicaragua.

4. That through the initiative of the executive, the national Congress of Nicaragua decree the removal from the national archives and the burning of all documents in which the patriotic posture of our army is described as banditry, and solemnly declare as legal that posture which the undersigned and his army assumed on May 4, 1927, when, with unmanly arrogance, the government of the United States of America threatened to disarm the Nicaraguan armies by force if they did not submit to their despotic whim. This point, which deals with the extraction from the archives and the burning of the documents that slander us, and with the Congress's declaration of the legality of the attitude of the undersigned and his army, is a question of national honor, since it is because of this attitude that Nicaragua remains a free, sovereign and independent republic.

5. In the definitive peace treaty it must be put on record that the Army in Defense of the National Sovereignty of Nicaragua is asking for the revision of the Bryan-Chamorro agreements, because it is notorious that they were entered into by a Nicaraguan government imposed by the North American intervention. Furthermore, the Army in Defense of the National Sovereignty of Nicaragua demands that the canal route through Nicaragua and the naval base that may possibly be constructed on the Gulf of Fonseca be declared the responsibility of the Indo-Hispanic nationality; for this purpose, a congress should be held with representatives of the twenty-one republics of our racial America and that of the United States of America, in the capital city of the Argentine republic. The same to have the purpose of decreeing nonintervention in the internal affairs of any of the Indo-Hispanic republics, respecting their sovereignty and independence and promoting a more brotherly approach to one another, which unites us in the common free life of the nations of this continent.

Provisional General Headquarters of the Army in Defense of the National Sovereignty of Nicaragua, the Segovias, Nic., C.A., January, 1933.

Patria y Libertad.

A. C. SANDINO

[8, 135–38]

1. This "Protocol for Peace," which Sandino presented to Sofonías Salvatierra at the

Guadalupe ranch, El Embocadero, department of Jinotega, seat of the Provisional Head-quarters of Sandino's army, constituted the point of departure for the negotiations that ended with the peace agreement of February 2, 1933.

2. Bounded as it would have been by the Patuca River on the north, this new department would have included territory now part of Honduras that was then still claimed by Nicaragua. RC

172. LETTER TO SOFONÍAS SALVATIERRA, JANUARY 25, 1933

General Headquarters of the Army in
Defense of the National Sovereignty of
Nicaragua
The Segovias, Nic., C.A.
January 25, 1933

Señor Don Sofonías Salvatierra
Managua

Señor Salvatierra:

My wife informs me that she has reached an understanding with you
and with Señor Sacasa that our positions are not to be attacked; nevertheless, we regret to inform you that on the 22d our cavalry in the "Min-
itas" under the command of General Gómez was attacked and on the
24th the same cavalry unit was attacked in Saraguazca. Those camps are
the ones chosen, as I said to you, for the grouping of our forces, and the
way to avoid clashes is for Dr. Sacasa's forces to remain in their recognized bases. In passing I will take this opportunity to inform the people
of Nicaragua through you that we are not an obstacle to peace, because
we are enemies of war, and that we are only exercising our rights to defense. My earlier telegram indicated to you that we have already ordered
our forces to suspend hostilities. It will be useful to provide our delegates
with the means by which they may hold a personal interview with me if
the situation requires it.

Very attentive and faithful servant,
Patria y Libertad.
A. C. SANDINO

[8, 161–62]

173. TELEGRAM TO THE DELEGATES
TO THE PEACE CONFERENCE,
JANUARY 27, 1933

General Headquarters of the Army in
Defense of the National Sovereignty of
Nicaragua
The Segovias, Nicaragua, C.A.
January 27, 1933

Señor Don Salvador Calderón Ramírez
Dr. Escolástico Lara
Dr. Pedro José Zepeda
General Horacio Portocarrero
Don Sofonías Salvatierra

I have just now received confidential reports that the armistice has not been declared on the part of Dr. Sacasa, and thus it can be explained why my forces are often under attack.[1] I demand seriousness on the part of Dr. Sacasa, and if there is no satisfaction in this respect, from this moment on the responsibility is Dr. Sacasa's. A response is urgent, because I don't want to be the victim of betrayals. With complete respect, your brother.

Patria y Libertad.
A. C. SANDINO

[8, 164–65]

1. For Sandino the armistice was basic to the process of achieving peace. Sofonías Salvatierra promised this to him on January 22, 1933, with the consent of the Liberal and Conservative parties and two of Sandino's delegates. In reality, the National Guard, under the leadership of General Anastasio Somoza García, regularly violated the armistice, as it systematically attacked the members and collaborators of the Army in Defense of the National Sovereignty of Nicaragua.

174. PROCLAMATION, FEBRUARY 1, 1933

PROCLAMATION

My dear brothers:

Our army, through the magnitude of its struggle, constitutes a continental moral authority, and in the environment of sympathy upon which our army can rely in the world it has brought about the complete expulsion of the North American pirates from Nicaragua. Nevertheless, upon his withdrawal the impotent invader left things arranged in such a way that Sacasa's forces have continued fighting our army, in order at the same time to foment new revolutions and to gain an opportunity to bring the filibustering armies back to Nicaragua, employing as their motive the prolongation of our struggle.

With these points in view and considering that Dr. Sacasa could in reality avoid that new conflict if he acted with good sense, I have decided, in agreement with our leaders here present, to take advantage of the arrival of our delegates at this provisional General Headquarters and of the five days of armistice that remain and are to end at 12 noon on February 5, to go personally to speak frankly with Dr. Sacasa and to resolve this problem once and for all, so that if they don't accept the patriotic principles proposed by our army, and decide instead that they would prefer to prevent my return, our whole army will continue the struggle, the blame for all this falling upon Dr. Sacasa himself.

Very well, dear brothers: Until the 5th of this month the interim supreme commander will be our brother, Doctor and General Escolástico Lara, whom our army as a whole has the duty to obey and respect in all matters concerning the service and the other military laws, for as long as all of you together unanimously acclaim him the new supreme leader.

Provisional General Headquarters of the Army in Defense of the National Sovereignty of Nicaragua, February 1, 1933

Patria y Libertad.

A. C. SANDINO

[11, 443–44]

175. ORDERS TO
THE INTERIM SUPREME COMMANDER,
FEBRUARY 1, 1933

Decisive orders to the brother, General Escolástico Lara, in his role as interim supreme commander of our army:

After the 5th of the current month, if there is no news of me, it's a sure sign that I am dead, and from then on it will be proper for all the forces here assembled to go in whatever direction they prefer and with the leader favored by each soldier.

The general is authorized to remain in the revolution or to retire to his native city.

Provisional General Headquarters of the Army in Defense of the National Sovereignty of Nicaragua, February 1, 1933.

Patria y Libertad.

A. C. SANDINO

[11, 444–45]

176. SPEECH TO THE TROOPS,
FEBRUARY 2, 1933

Brothers:

We have fought so that our country might be free of foreign interventionists. The Yankee has departed, but he shrewdly believes he will soon return, under the expectation that we will continue the struggle. And he is mistaken. I believe that peace should be established in these five days, and to establish it I have decided that the best way is for me to go to reach a direct understanding with Dr. Sacasa. I leave in my place, for the days I am absent, General Lara, a native of León, as is Dr. Sacasa. If instead of listening to me Dr. Sacasa decides to have me arrested, I will kill myself, and if I don't each of you is authorized to spit in my face as a traitor.

[8, 179–80]

177. THE TREATY OF PEACE,
FEBRUARY 2, 1933[1]

Salvador Calderón Ramírez, Pedro José Zepeda, Horacio Portocarrero, and Escolástico Lara, representatives of General Augusto César Sandino, and David Stadthagen and Crisanto Sacasa, representatives respectively of the Conservative and Liberal Nationalist parties, fully convinced of the supreme necessity of peace for the Republic, have agreed upon the following harmonious accord, which has as its basis the sincere love that the future of Nicaragua inspires in them and the high sentiments of honor to which the signers pay homage.

1. The representatives of General Augusto César Sandino declare, above all else, that the crusade in which he and his army have been engaged has served the freedom of the fatherland, and that, consequently, they now wish to affirm in his name his absolute personal disinterest and his irrevocable decision not to request nor to accept anything that might disparage the motives of his public conduct. He wishes, therefore, to establish as a principle or unalterable foundation that he does not aspire to any wealth or material advantage.

In view of the foregoing declarations of high disinterest, the representatives of the Conservative and Liberal Nationalist parties render homage to the noble and patriotic attitude of the said General Sandino.

2. General Augusto César Sandino, his delegates, and the delegates of both parties declare that by virtue of the withdrawal of the foreign forces from national territory a new era of fundamental renewal is unquestionably opening up in our public life; that this turn of events is of transcendent importance for the fate of our nation; and that, disciplined by a painful experience, they deem it an essential duty to strengthen the collective sentiment of autonomy that inspires the Nicaraguan people with unanimous enthusiasm. In order to increase that most noble tendency, the signers of the present pact regard it as convenient to emphasize, as a capital point of their respective political programs, their reverence for the Constitution and the fundamental laws of the Republic, and to maintain, by all rational, adequate, and juridical means, the full resplendence of the sovereignty and political and economic independence of Nicaragua.

3. The delegates of General Sandino and of the two parties recognize the importance of consolidating peace in a practical manner within the

territory of the Republic through the productive dedication to labor of the men who serve under the command of General Augusto César Sandino and, in the same manner, by means of the gradual abandonment of their weapons. To achieve in a secure manner the normalization of the lives of those men in productive activities under the protection of the laws and of the constituted authorities the following measures will be adopted:

a) The executive will present to the national Congress a proposal for full amnesty for political and related common offenses committed during the period from May 4, 1927, until today's date, this to be granted to all individuals of General Sandino's army who within fifteen days of the promulgation of that decree will surrender their weapons, and likewise all those who, with the authorization of General Sandino himself, promise to surrender them within three months, being included in the benefits of this amnesty one hundred persons from that army, who will be permitted to keep their weapons temporarily for the protection of the zone of uncultivated territory in which all those who have belonged to that army will have the right to establish farms and till the soil.

b) In order to represent the administrative and military authority of the government of the Republic in the departments of the north, comprising especially the zone intended for the work of the individuals of General Sandino's army, and also to receive their weapons gradually, the executive will appoint Don Sofonías Salvatierra as his delegate, to whom General Sandino, within twenty days of this date, will surrender no less than twenty-five percent of the weapons of any class that his army may possess.

c) The zone of uncultivated territory destined for their labors, to which subparagraph (a) of this accord refers, will be of sufficient size and located in the valley of the Coco or Segovia River, or in the region suitable to the government and to General Sandino, this zone being situated not less than ten leagues from towns in which there exist at the present time a municipal regime.

d) The leaders of the guard of one hundred armed men that will be allowed to exist shall be appointed by the government as emergency auxiliaries, selected in agreement with General Sandino from among the qualified members of the latter's army, but if after one year from the promulgation of the amnesty decree it should become convenient, in the judgement of the government, to maintain the aforementioned guard of one hundred armed men, or a lesser number, the appointment of the respective leaders will be carried out at the discretion of the president of the Republic.

e) The government will maintain in the entire Republic and especially in the departments of the north, for the period of at least one year, public-works projects in which it will give employment on a preferential basis to the individuals of General Sandino's army who may request it and who will submit themselves to the ordinary regimen established in those works.

4. By the act itself of signing this agreement, every kind of hostilities will cease between the forces of one and the other part, that is of the constitutional government over which Dr. Juan B. Sacasa presides and the forces of General Augusto César Sandino, for the immediate greater guarantee of Nicaraguan lives and properties; once the present pact is definitively signed, with the approval of General Sandino and the acceptance of the president of the Republic, all of General Sandino's people will come under the protection of the constituted authorities and, in consequence, will become obligated to cooperate in the preservation of public order.

5. To facilitate the disarmament of part of General Sandino's forces and to give them provisional protection, the town of San Rafael del Norte is designated, the same General Sandino assuming responsibility for the maintenance of order during the time the government regards this as convenient.

With faith in what is agreed to, two exact copies are prepared in the city of Managua, on the second day of February of one thousand nine hundred and thirty-three.

[Between the lines in General Sandino's hand: *Vale.*]

S. CALDERÓN RAMÍREZ. PEDRO JOSÉ ZEPEDA. H. PORTOCARRERO. D. STADTHAGEN. CRISANTO SACASA

Approved and ratified in all its parts. Managua, February 2, 1933. A. C. SANDINO

Accepted in all its parts. Managua, February 2, 1933. JUAN B. SA-CASA

[19, 5 pp.]

1. On February 2, 1933, Sandino flew to Managua, where he received an enthusiastic reception from the people of the city. That same night, in the presidential palace, he signed this Treaty of Peace, which was drawn up that same day. RC

178. A STATEMENT ATTRIBUTED TO SANDINO FROM *THE NEW YORK TIMES*, FEBRUARY 3, 1933

We are brothers. Let us not shed one more drop of blood. Let the Americans come here and work, but not as the owners of the country. I salute the American people.

There is no need to talk of bases for peace. I trust the nobility of Dr. Sacasa, the President of Nicaragua. We must reconstruct Nicaragua.

[14, 3 February 1933]

179. A GREETING TO
THE NORTH AMERICAN PEOPLE,
FEBRUARY 3, 1933

I send a greeting to the North American people. We need to know each other so that our continental life can be one of cooperation. The Spanish American peoples and those of the north ought to be like brothers who together watch over the continent, looking toward the Pacific and toward the Atlantic. I repeat, as brothers, but so that neither may commit an offense against the freedom or independence of the other. In this way, brothers of the American continent, the New World should be the land of genuinely free nations.

A greeting and my fraternal embrace for the people of the United States.

Patria y Libertad.
AUGUSTO C. SANDINO

[7, 22]

180. INTERVIEW WITH ADOLFO CALERO OROZCO OF *LA PRENSA*, FEBRUARY 3, 1933

In the Presidential Palace yesterday morning Doña América de Sandino was kind enough to introduce us to her adopted son as "an old friend of the family."

"A Conservative journalist?" asks the rebel of the Segovias, and he embraces us, adding, "All of us Nicaraguans are brothers now, proud possessors of a fatherland that is already free. The Liberal and the Conservative are giving way to the Nicaraguan."

We are face to face with the man who for more than five years carried on, with rifle in hand, the most talked-about autonomist rebellion in the history of Spanish America. Sandino doesn't correspond to the portrait we had invented of him. He is a man of little more than five feet in stature, weighing some one hundred thirty pounds. Small dark eyes, with a lively expression. A white complexion, a bit reddish. His skin badly cared for, and a grave countenance, even when he smiles.

He wears high dark yellow boots, khaki riding pants, and a military shirt of greenish gabardine. He doesn't wear a necktie. With his shirt collar open, a red scarf can be seen around his neck, the ends giving the appearance of a necktie hanging a few inches down over his chest. Over those scarf ends hangs a gold medal fastened by a pin, the gift of his Mexican admirers, and farther down a two-part watch chain with a round golden amulet the size of a ten dollar coin.

The general is very approachable. Talkative. Optimistic.

"I want peace in Nicaragua," he tells us, "and I've come to establish it. For years and years my companions in arms and I lived the life of the bivouac, pursued by air and by land, slandered at times by our own fellow citizens whose freedom we were seeking, but we were always full of faith in the triumph of our autonomist cause, which is the cause of justice. If the Yankee soldiers had left Nicaraguan territory, I would have wanted to make peace the following day, but incomprehension, distrust, and pessimism stood in the way."

"And when did you decide to seek peace at any cost?"

"Since Dr. Sacasa took possession of the presidency and the marines left, and this decision was confirmed for me when I received a letter from my friend Don Sofonías Salvatierra, in which he touched the most sensitive chord of my heart: love of my country."

"And do you think you won't have difficulties within your army when you try to carry out the peace agreements?"

"I have faith that they will obey my voice with the same discipline as always. The first virtues of my army have been patriotism and discipline."

"When will you return to your camp?"

"At once. The plane should already be leaving. My return is urgent; it must be done in the time allotted, and it would be dangerous to put it off. My army has very dangerous concrete orders about peace in case I don't return, and so I'm anxious not to hesitate any longer, because a delay could have serious consequences that I don't want to see."

Upon speaking these words, General Sandino turns to one of those present and asks if they will be certain to leave before 10:30. And he adds, "Before 10:30, don't forget that."

We continued our questions.

"Do you think, general, that not another shot will be fired in the Segovias?"

"It will not be fired by the autonomist army."

"Pardon the question, general, but what about the leaders who at times have been accused of committing unnecessary acts of cruelty?"

"Listen!" the rebel orders us. "This is an hour of peace and reconciliation, yet I'm not afraid to speak about those matters, always exaggerated and always attributed to my army, even when many times they were committed by our own enemies or by independent groups, who only used our flag to commit criminal acts. The autonomist army was at war with a large foreign force, to whom Nicaraguan lives were of little significance. That war had to be fought as wars are fought, and there were bullets and blood. That blood remains as a tribute to Nicaragua's freedom, and let us hope that not one more drop will be shed among brothers."

[16, 4 February 1933]

181. ORDER TO REGROUP, FEBRUARY 4, 1933

CIRCULAR TO ALL THE LEADERS, CIVIL AS WELL AS MILITARY, OF OUR ARMY IN DEFENSE OF THE NATIONAL SOVEREIGNTY OF NICARAGUA

Dear brothers:

Yesterday I returned to this provisional General Headquarters, and once again I find myself at the head of the supreme command of our army after having fully and satisfactorily arranged peace in Nicaragua.

Upon receipt of the present circular, be so good as to regroup at once with all the war equipment under your command or custody at the village of San Rafael del Norte, where I will be with the rest of our forces from the 6th of this month on, and where you will receive my personal instructions about everything concerning the peace arrangements that have just been finalized.

San Rafael del Norte has been the town chosen by us for the general regrouping of our army, where we will impart every kind of guarantee and security; furthermore, there do not now exist differences in regard to armies in Nicaragua, because we are sincerely and truly united with Dr. Sacasa, and with him our word has an effect that can lead to the satisfactory solution to any question we may wish to deal with.

With the esteem of your brother.

Provisional General Headquarters of the Army in Defense of the National Sovereignty of Nicaragua.

Patria y Libertad.

A. C. SANDINO

[11, 458]

182. MARCHING ORDERS
FOR THE PRINCIPAL LEADERS,
FEBRUARY 7, 1933

The infantry under the command of Generals Adán Gómez and Ismael Peralta will enter by way of the church of San Rafael del Norte and pass through the town until reaching the Vallecillo, the place where they will camp.

The civil force that is under the command of Generals Pedro Antonio Irías and Simón González will march by way of El Castillo, passing through the Tierras Coloradas until reaching La Brellera, the place where they will camp and get their orders.

The artillery under the command of Generals Juan Pablo Umanzor and Juan Santos Morales will remain on the street in front of the house where I will lodge. This arrangement is being taken until we have obtained quarters where they will be lodged.

The garrison under the command of the brothers Sergeant Major Marcial Rivera Zeledón and Captain Tránsito Sequeira will remain with their forces at the entrance to the church of San Rafael del Norte until the place where they will be quartered is designated.

The General Staff, that is the body of leaders who will be under my direct orders, will stay at the same place where I will be lodged.

Provisional General Headquarters, Los Potrerillos, February 7, 1933.

Patria y Libertad.
AUGUSTO CÉSAR SANDINO

[19, 1 p.]

183. ACT OF COMPLIANCE,
FEBRUARY 22, 1933

In San Rafael del Norte, at four in the afternoon on February 22, 1933, General Augusto César Sandino proceeded to verify the delivery of the weapons held by his army to the constituted government of the Republic, in virtue of the peace signed in Managua on the 2nd of the current month between the delegates of General Sandino and the representatives of the political parties. In effect, in the presence of the executive's delegate in the departments of the north, Don Sofonías Salvatierra; the delegation's military attaché, Colonel J. Rigoberto Reyes; the treasurer and his assistant and storekeeper of that same delegation, Señores Gustavo Argüello Cervantes and Julián Roiz, respectively; and Dr. Pedro José Zepeda and Dr. José Angel Rodríguez, General Sandino turned over the following weapons, which, in turn, the military attaché, Colonel Reyes, received in this same act, in the form expressed in the following record:

Weaponry turned over: 14 Springfield rifles, 55 Concón rifles, 199 Krag rifles, 23 Winchester rifles, 8 Mauser rifles, 28 unidentified rifles, 8 Remington rifles, 6 ramrod shotguns, 1 .22 caliber Remington rifle, 2 Mauser rifles without breech, 1 Springfield rifle without breech, 10 Thompson machine guns, 9 Browning machine guns, 2 Lewis machine guns, and 3,129 rounds for the previously mentioned machine guns.

Weaponry retained: In virtue of the peace agreement, an emergency body of one hundred men chosen from among those who have accompanied General Sandino has been organized, and to arm them the following have been taken from among the items previously listed: 8 Thompson machine guns, 8 Browning automatic rifles, 2 Lewis machine guns, 11 Springfield rifles, 71 Krag rifles, and 3,129 rounds for the weapons previously mentioned.

For General Sandino's personal guard: 3 Thompson machine guns, 10 Krag rifles, and the ammunition to be taken from the quantity indicated above.

Rifles that General Adán Gómez is to take along to protect himself and twelve additional men during their journey from this village to La Cruz de Rio Grande, where he will turn them over to government authority: 13 Krag rifles.

In addition, General Sandino declares that in the mountains he has a number of the so-called Concón rifles and other classes, the quantity and condition of which he cannot exactly state, but which during the two months following this date he will communicate to the government, so that the latter may dispose of them as it sees fit. The said general also declares that he has a quantity of dynamite in not very good condition, and that he will use it to break up the rapids of the Coco River to facilitate its navigation. Likewise he states that since the quantity of rifle rounds that they possess is so small, he believes they should be turned over to the one-hundred-man emergency force that has been armed by order of the government, from which quantity he will also take a proportional supply for the private guard that will be under his command, as expressed in this act. General Sandino states that in harmony with the sincere patriotic ideals that have motivated him in the late campaign, the declared weapons are the total number that his army relied upon, weapons that were almost all captured in that same campaign. With faith in what is expressed, four copies are signed. In the process of signing this act, General Sandino hands over three Bisloa shotguns, three Winchester rifles, three Concón rifles and three Krag rifles, which were brought by a platoon of the army which has been disarmed.

A. C. SANDINO. SOFONÍAS SALVATIERRA. G. ARGÜELLO. C. J. RIGOBERTO REYES. J. ROIZ R. PEDRO JOSÉ ZEPEDA. JOSÉ ANGEL RODRÍGUEZ. RONALDO DELGADILLO

[8, 211–14]

184. CONVERSATIONS WITH RAMÓN DE BELAUSTEGUIGOITIA, FEBRUARY 1933

Conversations with Sandino: The Man and His Ideas

During the approximately two weeks that I was in the camp of the army of liberty I never failed to be in daily conversation with General Sandino, who treated me from the first moment with an entirely familiar friendliness.

At times the caudillo called me in, and at other times I went to see him at his house, which was watched over by his personal guard with handheld machine guns. The general was in the habit of walking up and down in a dark room next to that used by the guard and he entered smiling, embracing me, according to his custom.

It was a simple room decorated with a calendar and a chromolithograph in which could be seen some seal hunters in a tempestuous sea of ice, firing upon those amphibians who were approaching the vessel in a state of alarm. There were also a bench and some chairs, and usually sitting on the bench were some officers who attended the interview in silence, or a few soldiers belonging to the reserve. A stack of rifles could be seen in one corner.

The general sat in a rocking chair, in which he rocked endlessly. Most noticeable in his oval but angular face was a kind of asymmetry affecting both sides of his face, which contributes, along with the corners of his mouth, to some odd facial variations. His dark eyes often radiate an affectionate sympathy, but normally a profound seriousness or an intense thoughtfulness is evident in them. The serenity of his features, the strength of his jawbones, spread wide at an angle, confirm the impression given by his conversation of a calm and positive will. His voice is smooth and convincing; he does not distrust his own ideas, and his sentences are spoken with precision, well regulated by a mind that has thought independently about the topics he communicates. His habitual gesture is to rub his hands together while holding a handkerchief in them. Rarely does he gesticulate or alter the calm tone of his voice. The impression Sandino gives, in his appearance and in his conversation, is of a spiritual elevation. He is, without doubt, a cultivator of "yoga," a disciple of the Orient.

The topics of our conversation were various and usually without much organization. I have tried to gather them together under several themes, while of course retaining an absolute authenticity regarding his concepts and his phrases so that the reader can penetrate the psychology of this extraordinary champion of liberty, who has been seen by many as a vulgar and uneducated man, perhaps also as the Pancho Villa of the Nicaraguan rebellion. But this is completely false. General Sandino is a delicate and refined spirit, a man of action as well as a seer, as we have said, and though he has a rather limited education, he is an extraordinary personality, even apart from his role as liberator.

"I see they took you for an American," he told me the first time he saw me, laughing cheerfully.

"Yes, General," I said to him, "but they were very soon convinced and nothing happened. It was all a joke."

And after we had sat down, and as the general was beginning his habitual rocking, I said to him, "In this movement what interests me most is its spiritual content, more than the episodic and the military aspects. I see that there exists in you a great faith, and I'm not sure, perhaps a religious sensitivity. I believe that all the movements that have left an impression on history have had a great religious or secular faith. The liberalism of the Anglo-Saxon peoples, united with their religious principles, seems deeper to me and more definitive than that of the French Revolution. Do you have a religion?"

Sandino: "No, religions are things of the past. We are guided by reason. What our Indians need is instruction and culture so they can know themselves, respect themselves, and love themselves."

Unwilling to accept defeat, I insisted, "You don't believe in the survival of the conscience?"

Sandino: "Of the conscience?"

I: "Yes, of the personality."

Sandino: "Yes, of the spirit, of course; the spirit survives, life never dies. From the beginning, one may assume the existence of a great will."

I: "It's all a matter of words; for me, this is religion, the transcendence of life."

Sandino: "As I'm saying to you, that will, that first great force, is love. You may call him Jehovah, God, Allah, the Creator." [. . .]

And after explaining, in agreement with his theosophic faith, the importance of humanity's spiritual guides, among whom he includes Adam, Moses, Jesus, Bolívar, [. . .] his words expressing a profound conviction and his dark eyes quickening, he continues, "Yes, each person attains his destiny. I am convinced that my soldiers and I fulfilled the destiny that was made known to us. That supreme will has brought us here together to accomplish the liberation of Nicaragua."

I: "Do you believe in destiny, in fatalism?"

Sandino: "Well, shouldn't I believe? Each of us accomplishes what he must in this world."

I: "And how do you understand, General, that primary force which moves things? As a conscious or unconscious force?"

Sandino: "As a conscious force. In the beginning there was love. That love creates, evolves. But all is eternal. And our tendency is to believe that life is not a fleeting moment, but rather an eternity across the multiple facets of the transitory."

I: "I am insisting on this point because I think every great work has been accomplished only with the assistance of a great faith, which I call religious, while you use other words for it, but which is nothing but the powerful impulse of a spiritual world. I have felt that interpenetration, that spirituality, in your army."

Sandino: "If that's all it is, we do influence one another mutually in the role we play. We are all brothers."

I: "I remember your having referred at some point to the historical significance of Napoleon and Bolívar."

Sandino: "Ah, Napoleon! He was an immense force, but there was nothing in him but egotism. Often I have started to read his biography and thrown the book down. On the other hand, the life of Bolívar has always aroused emotion in me, and it has made me cry."

Later, since the general had made a reference to the spiritual forces that affect the conduct of men, I asked him, "Do you believe, General, in forces of the kind that influence human conduct without the influence of words?"

Sandino: "Completely. I have experienced it myself, not once but often. On several occasions I have felt a kind of mental trepidation, palpitations, something odd inside myself. Once I dreamed that enemy troops had approached and that a certain individual named Pompilio who had been with me before came with them. I got up at once and gave the alarm, placing everyone under our plan of defense. Two hours later—it was still before dawn—the Americans were there, initiating the battle."

"There is a part of our body where the organ of premonition may be found."

"I would agree with that," the general continues, and grasping my head he points to the back of my neck. "You don't think this is true?"

"I don't deny any sort of possibilities of that kind. And in any case I think you may have an uncommon nervous system, a great spiritual power. I see it in your army."

And I remembered having read in a letter written by his brother, Sócrates, which Don Gregorio had showed me, that "Augusto had an enormous telepathic receptacle." And in another letter, "that he had seen his father and mother in a dream and sensed that they were very concerned."

And I added, "I have seen an admirable spiritual sense among the soldiers. Speaking with many of them, I have heard them say that justice was with them and that because of that they were victorious, even though they were so much less powerful. How have you been able to instill these principles in them?"

Sandino: "By speaking to them often about the ideals of justice and about our destiny, instilling in them the idea that we are brothers. Above all, it was when their bodies were weakened that I have tried to lift their spirits. At times even the bravest languish. It's necessary to know them, to choose them. And to drive away their fear, making them understand that death is a trifling affliction, a transition. But those ideas are assimilated through mutual penetration."

I: "Through mutual penetration?"

Sandino: "Yes, we are mutually penetrated by our mission, and so my ideas and even my voice can go to them more directly. The magnetism of a thought is transmitted. The waves flow out and are received by those disposed to understand them. During battles, when the nervous system is in a state of tension, a voice with a magnetic feeling has an enormous resonance.[. . .] Also spirits, both carnate and incarnate, take part in battles."

I: "Do you believe in the transcendence of this movement?"

The general certainly did not understand the realistic sense in which I had asked this question. In the course thus far of his supranatural impressions, if we may put it that way, his thought had unwound itself in the form of more remote and difficult concepts.

But it is not possible for us to follow his thought completely, and we will suggest only a skeleton of his ideas, which deal with unreal matters.

"I will say this to you. Spirits also engage in battle, both carnate and incarnate. [. . .] Since the beginning of the world, the earth has constantly evolved. But here, in Central America, is where I foresee a formidable transformation[. . . .] I see something I've never mentioned to you before[. . . .] I don't think this has ever been written about[. . . .] In all of Central America, in the lower regions, it's as though water had spread from one ocean to another[. . . .] I see Nicaragua engulfed in water. An immense depression coming from the Pacific[. . . .] The high volcanoes only[. . . .] It's as though one sea had emptied itself into another."

This is a fantastic description, which I have not been able to grasp completely, but which translates into a sort of vision of a great maritime catastrophe in that part of Central America. And Sandino puts his hands to his eyes, as if wanting to eradicate some vision. Again the dark tone of his voice becomes more lively.

This is the hero, Sandino, the inspired Sandino, the visionary.

Faith, I believe, is eternally childlike and creative; childlike because it unites the real world with that of the fabulous, and, unmindful of doubt, which is skepticism and old age, transports us to the fantasy world of those first years, in which perhaps, as the poet Wordsworth says, men still preserve an intimation of immortality, or of an incarnation, as the theosophists would say, which, with the years and the base reality of the senses, has not yet been erased from the mind.

And faith is creative, because mankind sees itself, not as the miserable sharecropper of a transitory life that disappears in smoke, but rather as the owner himself of the land, or more aptly, as an actor in an eternal drama that is constantly being renewed.

As I was leaving, Sandino spoke with an old soldier put in charge of carrying salt to the troops who are beginning to arrive, and as the latter departs with his loaded mule, the general says good-bye to him with a "May God keep you."

CONVERSATIONS WITH SANDINO:
SOCIAL THEMES

We had seen General Sandino while he was riding with some officers, making an inspection of the troops, and he had said to me, "Now you see, we are not soldiers, we are of the people, we are armed citizens."

Remembering these impressions regarding the social aspect of the Sandinista movement, one afternoon while we were talking and he was rocking in his chair I asked the general, "It has been said on some occasions that your rebellion has an obvious social character. You have even been accused of being communists. I understand that this last epithet has been the result of tendentious and discredited propaganda. But is there no social program?"

Sandino: "At various times efforts were made to twist this movement away from national defense, transforming it into a struggle having a more social character. I have opposed this with all my strength. This movement is national and anti-imperialist. We uphold the banner of liberty for Nicaragua and for all of Spanish America. Aside from this, on the social terrain, this movement is of the people, and we advocate the pursuit of progress in regard to social aspirations. Here, in order to influence us, some people have tried to see us as representatives of the International Federation of Labor, the Anti-Imperialist League, the Quakers[. . . .] We have always opposed this with our strong belief that this was essentially a national struggle. [Farabundo] Martí, the propagandist of communism, recognized that he couldn't win with his program, and he withdrew."

The general became quiet and thoughtful.

In some countries, such as Mexico, many have thought that the Sandinista movement was fundamentally agrarian. I have had occasion to observe during my stay in Nicaragua that property is rather well divided and that it is a land of small properties. Latifundia hardly exist, and these are not very large. Agrarianism, therefore, does not have a field of action. The few who do not have land do not die of hunger, as has been said[. . . .]

Yet with the general I stayed with the land question, asking him if he is a supporter of confirming the country's reputation of a nation of small landholdings by giving land to those who do not have it.

Sandino: "Yes, of course, and that is something that will not be hard for us to do. We have uncultivated land, perhaps the best in the country. That's the area where we've been concentrated."

The general explained his project to colonize the Coco River region, which has enormous fertility.

"Nicaragua imports a number of products that it shouldn't: cereals, oils, even meat, by way of the Atlantic coast. All this can be produced in the Coco Valley, because soon we will make the river navigable and then we will begin to open land to cultivation. There is an incredible exuberance of plant life. Wild cacao alone is available to put the land in a condition for rapid economic exploitation."

I: "Do you believe in the growth of capital?"

Sandino: "Undoubtedly capital can do its work and be accumulated, but the worker mustn't be humiliated and exploited."

I: "Do you believe in the usefulness of immigration?"

Sandino: "There exists here a great deal of land to divide up. Immigrants can teach us a lot. But on condition that they respect our rights and treat our people as equals."

The general then added jokingly that if some foreigners came there with other ideas, motivated by a spirit of unacceptable exploitation or political domination, they would go to them and put thorns on their path so that their progress wouldn't be so easy. Otherwise, all foreigners would be received as brothers, with open arms.

At that moment we recalled the admirable disinterest that General Sandino has demonstrated on every occasion, including the special stipulation of the agreement that had just been signed stating that his delegates were to indicate in his name "his absolute personal disinterest and his irrevocable decision not to request nor to accept anything that might disparage the motives of his public conduct."

I asked him, "Don't you have any ambition to possess some land of your own?"

Sandino: "Ah, people think around here that I'm going to become a big landowner. No, none of that. I will never have properties. I don't have anything. This house where I'm living belongs to my wife. Some people say that this is stupidity, but I don't have any reason to act any other way."

Remembering that General Sandino is about to have an offspring, I asked him, "And your children, if you have them?"

Sandino: "No, that's no objection. Let there be work and activity for everybody. In general I'm an advocate of having the land belong to the State. In the special case of our colonization on the Coco River, I'm inclined toward a system of cooperatives. But we will have to study all that more slowly."

"Concerning these things," the general remarked, smiling, "today I have had a case, among the many who come to tell me about their troubles, that reveals the anxious spirit of some of the people who manage money. It was a poor man with a large family who long ago had been given a loan of three hundred pesos. The man who had lent it to him is now demanding it back, and since he doesn't have it the lender wants to take away his house, his cattle, everything, and even his children as slaves. I said to the lender, 'Do you think your money is worth as much as the tears of this poor family?' Later I told the other man to go to one of the lawyers who claim they offer justice and then come back another day. I hope I can convince them. Now," added the general, "you can see what's going on around here." At that moment his mouth opened in a broad smile revealing his excellent sense of humor.

The thought of this benevolent justice, which reveals his persuasive personality, and not the sword of the guerrilla fighter, also made me smile.

I: "General, do you like nature very much?"

Sandino: "Yes."

I: "More than the city?"

Sandino: "Yes, nature inspires us and gives us strength. Everything about it teaches us. The city wears us down, diminishes us. But it's better to go to the city and help to improve it than to close one's self off selfishly in the countryside. Looking at the plants, the trees, the birds with their habits, their life [. . .] they are a constant education."

The general's clear and precise diction, the didactic impression he gives to his explanations, even the way he cuts the air with his hand, which moves incessantly and displays short, firm fingers, reveal in him, not the man of fantasy, but the man of restless and profound thought in whom there ferments a constant desire to know.

I asked him then, "Is it true that you want to engage in some studies?"

Sandino: "Yes, I'm interested in the study of nature and of the deeper relationships among things. It's for this reason that I enjoy philosophy. Naturally I'm not going to enter into a program of studies. But to know, to learn, that I will always do!"

We then began to speak on the subject of war, about how the campaign appeared to be one of extermination, and I asked him, "Were the Americans cruel?"

Sandino: "Ah, that I won't tell you! Ask that question outside there, and you will understand."

I: "General, there's talk among your enemies of unnecessary deaths, of crimes, which are attributed to a part of your army."

Sandino: "Well, if some evil is attributed, whatever it may be, I'm the only one responsible. They say there have been murders? Then I'm the murderer. That there have been injustices? Then I'm the one who's unjust. There was a need to punish not only the invaders, but those who were with them."

The general straightened himself up and spoke forcefully, and his eyes glowed with indignation.

I: "For my part, whenever people have spoken to me about these matters, I have said that freedom is not conquered with smiles for the invaders. That this is the price of freedom. But naturally, I think it's very hard for an outsider to say such things."

Sandino: "Ah, yes, the price of freedom!"

Through an association of ideas, the general went on to discuss the severity shown to his own troops in order to maintain discipline. Since this point had been raised, I asked him, "How often have you ordered your soldiers shot?"

Sandino: "Five times. Two generals, a captain, a sergeant, and a soldier. One of the generals for abuses committed. I was told that he had violated several women. I verified the facts and ordered him shot. The other because of his betrayal."

The general went on to say that since the arrival of General Sequeira he had thought he saw in him a man of questionable loyalty. One day the airplanes came unexpectedly, launching a furious bombardment. General Sandino was sitting motionless in a corner when among the exploding bombs he sensed that someone was stealthily approaching. It was Sequeira with a pistol in his hand. "He wants to kill me," Sandino thought, and he immediately took out his weapon and, rushing upon him, forced him to put the automatic back in his holster. Sequeira lost his command but continued to participate in the operations. Yet the general surprised him in a situation similar to the first. When they went out to capture him, he escaped in the direction of the American camp. Sandino sent out forces to bring him back at once, dead or alive. They brought him back dead.

I: Is it true that all your weapons, rifles or machine guns, have been taken from the enemy? What percentage do you calculate?"

Sandino: "You might say all of them, aside from a few rifles that came from Honduras and the primitive Concón rifles, which no longer work. Those who didn't have weapons waited until they were captured from the enemy, or they went into action with bombs and pistols, or they simply became part of the reserve."

I: "General, during the struggle did you have the premonition of a final moral victory?"

Sandino: "No, I believed when I undertook this enterprise that I would not survive it. I considered this necessary for Nicaragua's freedom and for raising the banner of dignity in our Indo-Hispanic countries."

I remembered having heard similar sentiments expressed among the soldiers, such as "It is better to die than to be humiliated." And "We would not have quit if the machos hadn't left."

I: "Was your wife an obstacle or a stimulus in carrying on the struggle?"

Sandino: "She was a stimulus. When I came here, after the war began, I came to know her. I became intimate with her. Her ideas and mine were the same; we identified with each other. For five years I was separated from her. Then she was able to go into the mountains. My wife's spirit has never faltered."

"But, haven't you met her?" the general added. He then called out: "Blanca! Blanca! I want to introduce you to a man with a last name so long that at first there's no way to pronounce it."

The caudillo's wife appeared. She is a very young lady with good features, a sweet manner, and a very white skin. I greeted her and she left quickly after a few brief words.

Sandino: "My wife is from this place and is ninety-five percent Spanish. Here the Spaniards mixed very little with the Indians."

I: "Generally the Spaniard has mixed with the Indians outside the places where they were very warlike. In Mexico, for example, they have mixed very little in Sonora and Sinaloa. In the rest of the country, almost completely."

Sandino: "Well, here very little. The Indian fled to the mountains. But there's some of it here. So much so, that there is a refrain that says: 'God will speak for the Indian of the Segovias.' And he has certainly spoken! They are the ones who have done a great part of all this. An Indian is timid, but cordial, sentimental, intelligent. You will see it now with your own eyes."

Then the general ordered a soldier to be called in and asked him to speak with his leader, who was sitting in the guardhouse and belonged to the same race as the Zambo Indians of the Atlantic coast.

The two spoke, and a mishmash of words of several languages, from English and French to Spanish, could be made out in the dialect.

"Now speak to him in English," he said to me. I spoke for a while and observed that the two conversed perfectly together.

"And now Spanish," he added.

Indeed, they spoke it perfectly.

Sandino: "Well, now you see that they are intelligent. But they have been entirely abandoned. There are some hundred thousand of them without communications, without schools, without anything of government. This is what I want to do with the colony, to lift them up and make true men of them."

I: "Do you believe in the transformation of societies through pressure from the State, or through individual reform?"

Sandino: "Through internal reform. The pressure of the State changes the exterior, the apparent. We believe in each one giving what he has. That each man should be a brother, and not a wolf. All the rest is mechanical pressure, outside and superficial. Naturally the State must intervene."

I: "What do your flag's colors signify?"

Sandino: "The red, freedom, the black, mourning, the skull, that we will not quit until we die."

SPANISH AMERICA, CENTRAL AMERICA, AND SPAIN

It was the usual rainy afternoon. Sandino was pacing in the dark room next to the guardroom, and when he saw me he exclaimed, "Yes, come in, we are very happy to have a Spaniard in camp, so that he can see what we are and what we have been. Yes, from Spain we have received great moral support."

I: "Positive help, that is, volunteers, would have been preferable."

Sandino: "No, you have given us something better: the feelings that come with moral support. That's worth more than if you had sent us a gunboat with soldiers and ammunition."

And he gave an account of how some time before had come to the camp a Spaniard who was a wanderer and had roamed about the world. He stayed for several days and told interesting stories about his trip and about Spain. I understood that this wanderer had later died crushed under the wheels of a moving train. No doubt he traveled economically. And the truth is I don't remember his name, though it was mentioned to me.

At that moment a letter was brought in, and I asked him to read it, interrupting the conversation, and the general said, "No, we consider you a member of our great Indo-Hispanic family, and we don't have any reserve. Look, this letter is from a priest friend of mine who was here for a long time. He's a man of free ideas. He has his family, children, a hacienda and is one of those who would say, 'Do as I say, not as I do.' "

And Sandino smiled with his kind open smile. Then he read the letter in which the priest congratulated the general for the establishment of peace, which he said should not remain half done.

I asked the general, "Could this movement have any connection wih the ideals of a united Spanish America?"

Sandino: "Yes, the great dream of Bolívar is still in view. The great ideals, all ideas, have their periods of conception and perfection until they are at last realized."

I: "Do you think this dream could be fulfilled within a generation? There is still a lack of preparation, communications, a close understanding, a harmonious sensitivity for recognizing common problems."

I remembered the situation of Central America. These small republics which not only Yankee diplomacy but also American companies, especially the fruit companies, manipulate like puppets, making and unmaking elections and, with no great effort, installing in power men they can depend upon. Just now, in the recent revolution in Honduras, they have done many extravagant things, naturally somehow to gain some advantage later on. While these countries are perhaps putting restrictions on white immigration, the companies are emptying the island of Jamaica on the Atlantic coasts to cheapen the cost of labor, and the blacks continue to increase enormously. This is how the sovereignty of the small republics is diminished.

I: "General, do you not think that Central American union is essential?"

Sandino: "Yes, absolutely essential."

I: "When do you think this may be possible?"

Sandino: "This will come soon, it will come soon."

The general became thoughtful and, not wanting to be indiscreet, I did not insist upon such a delicate point.

I remembered that President Sacasa had told me that he considered union necessary, but with time, when common ideas and communications have been adequately developed, and only on the basis of a mutual agreement, but I think there are minds among Central America's leaders who think that separation represents a morbid state, a weakness common to all, encouraged by imperialism, and those people want to establish union by force. Certainly there is a very definite kind of Central American patriotism.

Sandino: "At any rate, we don't profess an excessive nationalism. We don't want to shut ourselves up here alone. Let foreigners come, including Americans! We also don't think the whole solution is to be found in political nationalism. Above the nation, the federation, first continental, then more complete, until everything is included."

I: "What do you think of Spain?"

Sandino: "A nation predestined. Spain will be charged with the achievement of universal communication in the future."

I: "Communication?"

Sandino: "Yes, fraternization. Spain has a glorious past. There, according to legend, are buried Mary and Saint James, the brother of Jesus. Aside from that, Spain has given the world some admirable examples. The advent of the Republic has been something wonderful. Also the attitude of the king and that of the people. And regarding the colonization [. . . .] Look! Before, some time back, I looked upon Spain's colonizing work with a feeling of protest, but today I regard it with deep admiration. It's not that you're ahead of us. Spain gave us her language, her civilization, and her blood. We regard ourselves as Indian Spaniards of America."

I: "And do you believe in Spain's moral influence in the future America?"

Sandino: "No question about it. Her work hasn't ended. It will last." [. . .]

Sandino: "You have asked me for an autograph?"

I: "Yes, my general."

Sandino: "I will give it to you, with a salute to Spain."

To the Spanish people, a salute to you through the writer, Señor Belausteguigoitia, who has received impressions of our most recent efforts toward liberation.

San Rafael del Norte, February 13, 1933

A. C. SANDINO

[3, chapters 12–14]

185. MANIFESTO, MARCH 13, 1933[1]

Manifesto to the Nations of the Earth and Especially to Nicaragua

Brothers:

Above all I want to make it clear that during the seven years of war carried on for the restoration of the national autonomy of Nicaragua, we have not made political compromises with anyone[. . . .]

THE PRESENT MOMENT

I am independent of the government, and I remain in the same regions of the Segovias. I will not leave the country, because it is my intention to give moral support to Dr. Sacasa during his administration. I will use this time to organize agricultural cooperatives in these beautiful regions that for centuries have been abandoned by men of state.

CENTRAL AMERICAN TERRITORIAL DISPUTES

The Salvadoran people asked for land where all the land is monopolized, and for this they got machine-gun bullets.[2] Guatemala and Honduras have territorial problems, Honduras and Nicaragua as well, and all this is in obedience to signals from the expansionist policy of the United States; the present wars in South America obey the same signal. Everything is a game of the Wall Street bankers.

All of Central America favors union, and this is known to the vultures of the White House. Today there exist two unificationist tendencies in Central America; the first is of the people, who wish to unite because of their brotherly affinity and to defend themselves from the common enemy. [. . .] The second is the imperialist tendency, which the United States bankers are sponsoring with desire to pick a Central American traitor as leader of the five sections. President Ubico of Guatemala and General José María Moncada of Nicaragua are the strong men among the unificationists of the second tendency.[3] He who has ears, let him hear, and he who has eyes, let him see [. . .]

The Central American territorial litigations are being decided in Washington. Honduras will cede or has ceded to Guatemala her rights to disputed territory, because Nicaragua would cede or has already ceded to Honduras the territories in dispute; these things have happened during the administrations of Ubico in Guatemala and Moncada in Nicaragua, by order of the White House. He who has ears, let him hear, and he who has eyes, let him see. [. . .]

The vacant lands where we are seeking to establish agricultural cooperatives include 36,000 square kilometers, and we consider this region the federal district of Central America. Our cooperative has nothing but its workers, and it hopes to receive the support of the present government; if this should not be the case, our plans will be suspended, though the proletariat of all Central America and from any part of the world could come to this region.

THE PERSONALITY OF THE UNDERSIGNED

Because of the peace agreements signed last February 2, I have been the object of new slanders and insults written by those who, rubbing their hands together, hoped that we could win Nicaragua's independence by a single blow, no doubt forgetting the interlocking roots that the Yankee intervention has in all the countries of Spanish America and even in the world beyond, and forgetting that it is hard to untie a knot of a casting net without being forced to untie still another knot. He who has ears, let him hear, and he who has eyes, let him see the future of our racial America, and so let him make an alliance among our Spanish-speaking nations, more or less in the form that our army designed it in its *Plan for the Realization of Bolívar's Highest Dream*.[4]

Brothers: The nations of the earth and especially Nicaragua are in a position to judge our attitude during the seven years of war that we have sustained for Nicaragua's national autonomy without receiving any support or on our part having made political compromises with anybody.

Bocay, the Segovias, Nicaragua, C.A.
March 13, 1933
Patria y Libertad.
A. C. SANDINO

[20, 25 pp.]

1. As originally published, this document included verbatim copies of the documents numbered 80, 101, 106, 177, and 183 in this edition, and so, to avoid repetition, only the brief introduction and the three final selections, which reveal some of Sandino's main concerns of this period, are included here. RC

2. In 1932 more than thirty thousand campesinos of El Salvador were murdered during

the suppression of a popular uprising. One of the leaders, Agustín Farabundo Martí, a former colonel of the Army in Defense of the National Sovereignty of Nicaragua and Sandino's private secretary, was among the victims of the massacre.

3. Jorge Ubico was dictator-president from 1931 until his overthrow in 1941. RC

4. Doc. 91.

186. LETTER TO LIDIA DE BARAHONA, MARCH 15, 1933

Bocay, Rio Coco
Las Segovias de Nic., C.A.
March 15, 1933

Señora Doña Lidia de Barahona
Managua, Nicaragua

My distinguished señora:

Only today am I allowing myself to respond to your letter, dated February 10 of the present year.

Believe me, señora, for me your husband is a brother in ideas, and I could never be indifferent to his fate. But sadly I must say to you that our government is not yet autonomous, because of the political and economic intervention that cannot disappear while the governments belong to certain parties. Nevertheless, I think that for the convenience of the government itself orders will be given for the repatriation of our dynamic Dr. Barahona.

I am independent of the government, and the peace agreement was signed to avoid the return of the armed intervention, which was hardly beyond our doorstep, hoping to return within a year because it was supposed that we would continue the war among ourselves. That's the entire matter, my worthy lady. That's the secret reason that I don't leave the north, so that I may always be ready for the chance to restore our political and economic independence as well. Soon will appear a manifesto that we have sent out to the world.

I suspect you will have observed that the components of the country's military element who operated in alliance with the invaders continue to be our enemies. These things make me sad, as your husband also is, but we trust that justice will offer us inspirations for achieving the true independence of Nicaragua.

I very sincerely request that you send this letter to Dr. Barahona, and with these same words a fraternal embrace goes to him, and for you, señora, my respects.

Patria y Libertad.
A. C. SANDINO

[11, 480–81]

187. LETTER TO GUSTAVO ALEMÁN BOLAÑOS, MARCH 16, 1933

Bocay, Rio Coco
The Segovias of Nicaragua
Central America
March 16, 1933

Señor Gustavo Alemán Bolaños
9a Avenida Norte, No. 78
Guatemala City, C.A.

Esteemed brother:

In my hands is your attentive letter dated last February 7.

Referring to your opinion regarding the peace agreements signed on February 2 of this year, I will say that you are unfair and that you make yourself into my moral assassin, because you kill the illusion that I hold intact for the restoration of our national autonomy.

I haven't been the victim of anyone's pressure, and I'm the only person responsible for what is good and what is bad in those agreements. The four individuals who acted as representatives in the preliminary conferences may be called upon to testify to the circumstances that forced us to make that decision. Let's hope that when this letter reaches you, our official manifesto which for that purpose we have urgently sent out to the nations of the world will be in your hands.[1]

There's more. If the peace agreement could not have been signed because of orders that the invader left behind when he departed, I would have killed myself by my own hand in the Presidential House, so that my blood might have served as a further encouragement and a banner to the men of my army, because, although you are not aware of it, I will tell you that the disappearance of the armed intervention, though only apparent, cooled the spirits of the people because they tolerate the political and economic intervention. They don't see it, and, worse than that, they don't believe it, and this situation placed us in a difficult position. Meanwhile, the government was prepared to receive a loan of several million dollars *and to crush us with bullets and to give even greater support to the political, economic, and military intervention in this country.* And since this government was elected by the Liberals, mainly those from León, our ranks were certain to shrink, while on the other hand we were drained of economic and military resources. And so, because of everything we've mentioned, we would have suffered a calamity at a time when our troops wouldn't have been able to take refuge in Honduras because the war in that country was intense and they were murdering the Nicaraguan emigrants who in other times went there in search of refuge. We also couldn't depend upon El Salvador because the government there administered machine-gun bullets to the campesinos, and there was far less hope for us in Guatemala, as you know. In the new unificationist tendency in Central America, Ubico, Moncada, and Uncle Sam are three separate persons and one true God.

Let me remind you that in the seven years of war we never received a single round of ammunition, and we have defended ourselves by the "pure heart of Jesus," and there's no justice in demanding from us the independence of Nicaragua by a single blow. And concerning the idea that I've fallen from a pedestal that I don't even recognize, lowering myself to the level of a child, I'm in agreement. In the final analysis, I'm not even a soldier. I'm nothing but a campesino fighting for the independence of our people. Let's leave it at that and not create too much confusion for ourselves, so that we may continue working for the true independence of Nicaragua without heaping illusory honors upon ourselves, which I despise.

With my affectionate regards for your distinguished family, and do accept the sincere respect of your brother in the fatherland.

Patria y Libertad.
AUGUSTO C. SANDINO

P.S. I'm independent of the government, and the peace agreements have not been made for any personal convenience.

[1, 160–61]

1. Doc. 185.

188. CIRCULAR TO HIS LIEUTENANTS, MAY 2, 1933

CIRCULAR TO THE BROTHERS, GENERALS PEDRO ALTAMIRANO, FRANCISCO ESTRADA, UMANZOR, MORALES, GONZÁLEZ, AND IRÍAS, AND COLONELS TOMÁS BLANDÓN, ABRAHAM RIVERA, SÓCRATES SANDINO, AND RAMÓN RAUDALES

Brothers:

As you know, General Estrada and Colonel Rivera went to Managua on a special mission that was entrusted to them for the purpose of finding a way for the one hundred armed men whom we have on the river to make themselves worthy of increased confidence on the part of the government, because it's essential for us to possess that confidence in order to put ourselves in a position to proclaim the presidential candidate of our choice[. . . .]

Despite the many enemies we still have close to the government, Dr. Sacasa has nevertheless given our committee a good reception, and he agreed that the payments, which amount to a little more than 1,100 pesos per month for the hundred men, should be paid each month in a timely manner, and that they will supply one hundred uniforms so that each of the hundred men may live on the ten pesos, fifty centavos per month that correspond to the soldiers and twenty pesos for the officers. Naturally, if food were to be paid for by each of our companions, the ten pesos wouldn't be enough to feed their families too.

Colonel Rivera, who was commissioned to handle the question of establishing lumber, chicle, and rubber projects, by means of a loan of one hundred thousand pesos to be lent by the government and paid back in three years, failed in his mission, because nobody outside the country is buying lumber, chicle, or rubber.

Nevertheless, the government has granted us a quantity of provisions, machetes, and other tools so that we may establish a commissary, and so that our hundred men may buy their food there with their ten pesos per month, and the same with the others who are applying themselves to the cultivation of cereals and the washing of gold. Likewise you know that we had stationed our emergency force in Santa Cruz, El Garrobo, Bocay, and Sang, because of our hope of establishing the previously mentioned works.

Very well, then, despite the pledges of loyalty and mutual sincerity between ourselves and the government, there are people who implant distrust of us in Dr. Sacasa, and for this reason the doctor told me that they will establish a National Guard detachment with a radio in Santa Cruz, and that our first squadron should be in Wiwilí. For my part, and I believe this will merit your approval, I have decided to write to the government, thanking Sacasa for the attention he gave to our committee, telling him that we will concentrate our hundred men of the emergency force in Wiwilí only, and that they should give us the radio station, with everything required, as well as its own telegraph operator, so that he won't need to put the garrison in Santa Cruz, because that, we are certain, would have bad results for our civilians in that zone.

These are my arrangements for the days I'll spend in San Rafael del Norte waiting to give a cheerful welcome to my child. During that time it isn't at all unlikely that I'll make a brief trip to Managua to strengthen the arrangements for the benefit of the general community. In any case, I'll write to you giving you any sort of news, and if circumstances require it I'll be among you quickly. What I neglect to tell you in this letter, General Estrada, Colonel Rivera, and my brother Sócrates will clarify for you later.

It is also understood that in the entire Coco River region and its tributaries there will be the strictest guarantees of security, and that General Altamirano is appointed my general representative in Bocay and that whole region; for the same reason, every order requesting support coming from the general to the commissary or to the emergency force should be quickly received and attended to as if it were for me myself.

And General Estrada has strict instructions and an organization book, so that every person who arrives at the main Wiwilí camp is to acknowledge them. These are matters, as I have said, for when I return; also you have the obligation to communicate with Major Rafael N. Altamirano and all the people of El Chipote, indicating to them what I have ordered for the time when I return. Receive my fraternal embrace.

Guadalupe Farm, May 2, 1933
Patria y Libertad.
A. C. SANDINO

[11, 440–42]

189. DECLARATIONS TO
THE NATIONAL PRESS DURING SANDINO'S
SECOND TRIP TO MANAGUA,
MAY 21, 1933

Compelled by the sincerity of our acts, let me announce to the Nicaraguan people through the national press of Nicaragua that the fundamental purpose of my second trip to this capital was that of responding to the aspirations of many groups who desire the organization of a new party known as the Autonomist party.

The meeting for this purpose should have taken place today, Sunday, at nine o'clock in the morning, but the president of the Republic reconsidered the idea and deemed it inconvenient, since the purpose of the new party tends to reduce the strength of the opposition parties: Liberal and Conservative. For this reason we have decided to return tomorrow to the Segovias, leaving things as they are, but without desisting from the idea.

On the other hand, our attitude is unchanged insofar as it concerns our moral support for Dr. Sacasa in the maintenance of public tranquility during his administration.

Managua, May 21, 1933
Patria y Libertad.
A. C. SANDINO

[11, 496–97]

190. LETTER TO GENERAL FRANCISCO ESTRADA, MAY 24, 1933

San Rafael del Norte
May 24, 1933

General Francisco Estrada
Santa Cruz

Dear brother:

The situation of Nicaragua is the following: the National Guard is the enemy of the government and of ourselves, because it is an institution contrary to the laws and to the Constitution of the Republic; it was created by an agreement between the Liberal and Conservative parties at the behest of the North American intervention.[1] This guard tacitly considers itself superior to the government, and this is why many times the orders of the President are not respected.

Patria y Libertad.
A. C. SANDINO

[11, 495–96]

1. The National Guard began to be organized in May 1927, in compliance with the agreements reached in Tipitapa between José María Moncada and Henry L. Stimson on May 4 of that year. Nevertheless, it was not until December 22 that the governments of Nicaragua and the United States, represented by Carlos Cuadra Pasos and Dana G. Munro, respectively, signed the accord that created the National Guard.

191. LETTER TO HUMBERTO BARAHONA, MAY 27, 1933

San Rafael del Norte
May 27, 1933

Dr. Humberto Barahona
San Salvador or Costa Rica

Esteemed brother in the fatherland:

On the 17th of this month, just as I was leaving for Managua, I received your open letter, dated in San Salvador on last April 15; also copies of your letters to Dr. Manuel Pérez Alonso, Don Sofonías Salvatierra, and Señor Calderón Ramírez.

Very well, at dawn on the 18th we left this town for Managua, without reading the writings referred to. We arrived at one o'clock in the morning, and in that city I spoke with various brothers involved in the struggle who said something to me about your pamphlet. I said I had it with me and hadn't read it, but that I would busy myself with it at the first opportunity, and that if it were true that it made me a victim of an unfair attack, I would take my revenge by not responding to a single word of it.

Just now I have finished reading your writings, and I don't find anything damaging, but rather a hasty critique on your part, certainly unfair to me, because you were not aware of the countless reasons why peace was essential in Nicaragua, without anything being required of anybody, ourselves always independent of the government, as we have stated in our recent manifesto, which I imagine you will have read, and from which you will be aware of the preliminary events that led to the peace agreement. The press of those days published our reply to Don Sofonías Salvatierra, which stated to him that Dr. Sacasa should not lose the opportunity for an understanding with us, because this was essential for the health of Nicaragua.

As the theosophist you are, you must know that every human being has a mission to fulfill. [. . .] And on this occasion Dr. Sacasa has been fulfilling his [. . .] since the moment when he made an agreement with us contrary to the will of the State Department, which had the false impression that we would be eliminated by their bellicose offers to the emerging government in Nicaragua of ships and money for continuing the struggle after January 1. On the other hand, you are aware that at that time the Nicaraguan Congress tried to accept a two-million-dollar loan so that that government could continue the fight against our army. Keep in mind the danger that threatened us, and remember that that threat remains, because none of this was accepted by me, this being the destructive policy that the United States of America has used against us. For this reason your prognostication, in which you speak about Dr. Sacasa's fall from power, will come as no surprise to me.[1]

I have not renounced my rights as a citizen, and my program is alive and well and not defunct, as you suppose. Nevertheless, the duty to sacrifice one's self for the fatherland is not mine alone, and you yourself have an opportunity to follow your own advice and allow yourself to be killed. I will die but in open struggle, seeking the victory of our ideals, but I will not commit suicide because of stubbornness.

I would like to suggest to you that you get more rest and pay more attention to the progress of events in Nicaragua. As a theosophist you are obliged to know the admonitions of Zoroaster, son of Sarabatista, the founder of theosophy.

On the other hand, while you shrink from calling yourself a communist, I declare to the entire universe, with all the power of my being, that I am a rationalistic communist.

I beg you to accept in union with your esteemed family the fraternal embrace of your brother in the fatherland.

Patria y Libertad.
A. C. SANDINO

[11, 485–87]

1. President Sacasa's government was in fact overthrown in 1936 by the National Guard, led by Anastasio Somoza García, after a brief but violent military struggle. Not long afterward, Somoza made himself president, launching the Somoza dynasty that ruled until the Sandinista victory of 1979. For Sacasa's own account of Somoza's seizure of power, see his *Como y por que caí del Poder* (San Salvador, El Salvador, 1936). RC

192. BEFORE THE COFFIN OF BLANCA ARÁUZ, JUNE 2, 1933[1]

My dear brothers:

To this good woman whom we bury today, to her great spirit of love and goodness, we all owe the peace of Nicaragua. You will perhaps want to criticize me because the coffin is white, but not only the angels have the right to go to their grave in white, but also the martyrs, and this woman is a martyr of Nicaragua. Because of her the invaders haven't gone on kicking you around, nor the bandits who once arrested her in Jinotega, and it's better for me if I stop talking, because I'm beginning to lose my temper.

[15, vol. 4, no. 1082 (2 June, 1983), 2]

1. Sandino's wife Blanca died in childbirth on June 2, 1933. The surviving infant, Blanca Segovia, "the daughter of the bandit," as she was sometimes called as a child by Sandino's enemies, was brought up by Blanca's mother, Ester de Aráuz, and her sister Lucila. In 1961, accompanied by her husband, Enrique Castillo, and four sons, Blanca Segovia left Nicaragua to live in Cuba. Three sons, Augusto César, Julio César, and Walter Ramiro, returned to Nicaragua to take part in the Sandinista revolution, and soon after the victory in 1979, Blanca Segovia and her husband also returned. See "¡Habla la hija de Sandino!" in *Barricada*, Managua, 5 August 1979. RC

193. TIMID NICARAGUA:
A MESSAGE, JUNE 10, 1933

The Nicaraguans are intrepid politicians and even poets by nature, yet the conglomeration that makes up our national life presents a timid Nicaragua, though it is in fact heroic.

At the present time we have a courageous president who is without animosities, who has been able to gather into his hands the untamed convulsions of the Republic, untamed because everyone thinks he has the right to impose his authority upon him.

It has been said, I remember, that our present Constitution is the legitimate daughter, by direct descent, of the North American intervention in Nicaragua, because that Constitution was written in 1911 at a time when the country was suffering intervention, and it was signed by Adolfo Díaz, who emerged at that time as president of Nicaragua.[1] Like a newborn colt, however, the people were inexperienced, and the merchants of death could do nothing less than create the Constitution that we now have, because it is still better than any other that that Nicaraguan Congress could have reformed or revised. Only the nascent Autonomist party will be able to produce, by means of a plebiscite, a Nicaraguan Constitution for the people of Nicaragua. Therefore I believe that Nicaragua should abandon her false timidity and transform herself into the heroic sultan of the lakes.

Dr. Sacasa's popularity in the recent elections made me recognize that I should not oppose the said doctor, but rather seek to unite his popularity with the energies of our army so that the Nicaraguan people would understand our intentions, so that the main conflicting groups in the Republic, namely our army, "always spiritually united," the National Guard, and the historic parties, might cast their mututal hostility out of their minds, and so that all of us under our blue and white flag could support Dr. Sacasa and emerge from the cocoon of our timidity.

Dr. Sacasa is a politician, and I am not, for which reason I do not have a full understanding of his intentions, but for my part I know that no government, from 1909 until today, has had the opportunity that the said doctor enjoys at this moment, in the sense that, without betraying anyone, and with the Constitution in hand, he can restore our political and economic independence, but only if Nicaragua's timidity can be transformed into heroism. For my part, with our army we have given an example to the other opposition groups from the moment when we declared, "We are brothers."

It was never unknown to me that once our men had been disarmed many of our brothers in the struggle would necessarily be assassinated by the National Guard, which, because it is unconstitutional, is irresponsible. This is exactly what has happened, and today resting in peace are many of my martyred officers, men who personally came to deposit their weapons in this same village by order of the undersigned in my role as supreme leader of the Liberation Army of Nicaragua.

The patriotism of the National Guard of Nicaragua, poorly named because it is unconstitutional and therefore outside the country's laws for as long as it fails to legalize itself, is being tested in these decisive and bitter moments of our history. Also being tested is the patriotism of those heroic parties, because according to my understanding they should also support, as we do, our present government and request its compliance with point number 2 of the peace agreements of February 2 of this year.[2]

Finally, since the National Guard (unconstitutional) does not enjoy the support of any of the Republic's laws from the moment it finds itself extraneous to them, it is essential that it support Dr. Juan B. Sacasa instead of offering itself as a gambling chip in the chess game that benefits the State Department of the United States of America, through the instrumentality of the North American minister in Nicaragua. Otherwise our president has the obligation to arm the civilian population of the Republic and to order any renegade to surrender his weapons.

It is not right for men who regard themselves as free to submit to an army that is unconstitutional and outside the law. It is urgent, by my way of thinking, to provide ourselves with guarantees through our own nationality, and urgent that the Nicaraguan society not be subject to an army of men who are irresponsible, because they are outside the law.

Brothers, you Nicaraguans, accept my fraternal embrace as the soil on which you were born ceases to be the timid Nicaragua to become the heroic sultan of the lakes.

San Rafael del Norte, June 10, 1933
Patria y Libertad.
A. C. SANDINO

[11, 506–9]

1. Following the overthrow of the governments of General José Santos Zelaya (1909) and Dr. José Madriz (1910), the U.S. government imposed the Dawson Agreements (Octo-

ber 27, 1911), which ensured U.S. political and financial hegemony over Nicaragua, upon the leaders of the so-called Revolution of the Coast. One of the basic stipulations of the agreements was the election and installation of a constituent assembly intended to legitimize the new regime.

2. See Doc. 177.

194. LETTER TO RAFAEL RAMÍREZ DELGADO, JULY 16, 1933

Central Section, Wiwilí, Coco River, Nic.,
C.A.
July 16, 1933

Señor Don Rafael Ramírez Delgado
Tegucigalpa, Honduras, C.A.

Very esteemed sir:

A copy has reached me through the mail of the important book by the journalist James W. Hunter, entitled *Gandhi Speaks: The India I Desire.* You were most kind to send me that work, because everything about him, our great philosopher and defender of his nation's sovereignty, is of interest to me. With this work you have enriched our library.

In this river port from where I'm writing to you I have the satisfaction to place myself at your command; here I am dedicating myself to the establishment of a society of mutual aid and universal brotherhood. I want to offer my grain of sand in favor of the emancipation and well-being of the working class, which, as you well know, has always been exploited and looked down upon by the bureaucratic bourgeoisie. This is the problem that many men of philosophy and love seek to resolve, and now that the most excellent president of the Republic, according to the peace agreements, is offering me his protection, I want to make of these virgin and exuberant regions a place of life and a center of civilization for every family that, scourged by misery or disinherited, may face some danger in the heart of the octupus-like cities.

With nothing further, I'm pleased to wish you personal happiness.

Your most attentive and loyal servant,
AUGUSTO CÉSAR SANDINO

[2, 67]

195. LETTER TO PRESIDENT JUAN BAUTISTA SACASA, AUGUST 7, 1933

Central Section
Wiwilí, Nic., C.A.
August 7, 1933

Most Excellent President of the Republic
Dr. Juan B. Sacasa
Presidential House, Managua

Very esteemed Señor President:

The report dated the 3rd of the present month has reached us, revealing that the government's war arsenals in Managua and León were burned by criminal hands, and that you were no longer in Managua.

Upon receiving said report we have once more taken up our weapons, and at the same time we have sent orders to all our people, who are now ready to march wherever duty requires.

We have written today to General Anastasio Somoza to get information, because despite our not being sure what is going on General Juan Santos Morales will leave tomorrow for Jinotega to find out firsthand the reality of things, and if there is no further news please be so good as to inform us of that so that we may continue pursuing our agricultural labors, because at this moment we have suspended all activity, and we have a little more than six hundred men dispersed over this mountain. In passing, I am taking advantage of this opportunity to inform you that the collected weapons that we previously told you about have increased to five hundred pieces of equipment that belonged to the Honduran revolution. Nevertheless, if you find it convenient, we will happily accept any amount of ammunition for Springfields and Thompson and Lewis machine guns that you may wish to have in these encampments of yours, with the assurance that they would be fired against our enemies and in support of the national autonomy of Nicaragua.

I am not sure the present message will reach you, but I repeat that if there is no new development General Morales hopes to bring some information from you.

Fraternally,
Patria y Libertad.
AUGUSTO C. SANDINO

[11, 520–21]

196. LETTER TO ESCOLÁSTICO LARA AND NORBERTO SALINAS DE AGUILAR, OCTOBER 6, 1933

October 6, 1933
Rio Coco Cooperative
Central Section
Wiwilí, Nic., C.A.

Señores Dr. Don Escolástico Lara and
Don Norberto Salinas de Aguilar
León, Nic., C.A.

My very distinguished brothers:

Yesterday with unusual pleasure we received Colonel J. Dolores Villalobos, bearer of the letters from both of you to me, dated from last June 3 to September 9, as well as the rough draft of a letter that could be sent in our name to Dr. Vicente Toledano in Mexico City, along with some other printed matter. I have acquainted myself with the letters mentioned and the other writings. Colonel Villalobos leaves here today, taking the present letter with him.

So all right: I have acquainted myself fully with the letter from brother Salinas de Aguilar that he sends to me from Managua dated June 17, and I am pleased that between us there exist analagous projects. Moreover, I thank brother Salinas de Aguilar, with all his courage, for his defense of us that he made in the press and in the Ibero-American Student Congress that was recently held in San José, Costa Rica.

Just as the mail that now concerns me was arriving here, another package of mail, along with telegrams, which I am sending to San Rafael del Norte, was about to leave. In these I inform Dr. Sacasa of my arrival soon in Managua with the intention of conferring with him; we will try to get explanations about the conditions under which Dr. Guerrero Montalván has acquired the loan, and how we stand in regard to the unjust imprisonments that the Sandinistas are suffering in these departments. At the same time I am prepared to leave the country if there are no satisfactory explanations. For this reason I don't think it will be necessary for me to send the letter to Dr. Lombardo Toledano, since my departure from the country is almost certain, and then I will occupy myself with the manifestoes referred to, but more than anything else with demolishing through my acts any slander made against us with Machiavellian intentions, because, to speak the truth, it isn't certain that those who attack me doubt my sincerity, and what they seek is to incline us toward tendencies with which we don't agree, because we have our own ideas, and this we have proved.

I am not unaware of the dangers that my life may face in my trips through the heart of the Republic, but I will continue eluding dangers for as long as matters aren't settled in Nicaragua. By telegraph I will inform you of my arrival in Niquinohomo so that I may arrange an interview with you, either in León or in that village, where I am thinking of staying during the days I need to prepare to leave the country. Or, in the event I should return to these regions, I will pass at least a month in my native village.

I am in agreement about the inconvenience of continuing to work on the organization of the third party, and agree that we should limit ourselves to upholding Sandinismo with all its claims to moral authority, so that they may be decisive factors in the destinies of the nation at the first opportunity that presents itself. In passing, I am pleased to inform you that we will give the leadership of the renovation movement to General Escolástico Lara because this is necessary for the health of the Republic.

I will soon arrive there, for which reason I'm not more expansive in this letter, but meanwhile I request you, in my name, to acknowledge to the directors of the local council of the Liberal Republican party receipt of the letter it sent me, dated in Managua on June 1 of this year; likewise I ask you to let them know that we have the same intentions concerning General Escolástico Lara and that upon my arrival we will deal with all that in person.

Until I have the pleasure to embrace you personally, I ask you to accept the sincere esteem of this your brother.

Ever onward.
AUGUSTO C. SANDINO

[11, 535–37]

·1934·

197. CONVERSATIONS WITH
SOFONÍAS SALVATIERRA,
FEBRUARY 15–16, 1934[1]

[. . .] They are surrounding me. For about a month the Guard has been taking up positions around Wiwilí. What is this? The president is fooling me. (No, Salvatierra objected, the president is loyal.) Well then his subordinates do whatever they like. The guardsmen say they'll destroy me. Destroy [. . .] destroy [. . .] as if we didn't know what we have to do. To destroy men who are working and teaching the country how to work. They are an expense to the public treasury, petty improvised officials, whose lives consist of nothing more than eating and drinking. General Somoza wants to destroy me. And what good is General Somoza? He's important because of his rank. Later, nobody will ever look at him again. But I, yes, I am a caudillo. I can be disarmed, but not without putting up a loud scream. Out there I have only my people, because they really do believe in me. I don't want war, but how should it be possible that these people can't live in peace on their own land? The Guard is killing them. Every day it kills them. The proof that I want peace is that I go to Dr. Sacasa when he calls upon me. [. . .]

If the lives of those men aren't guaranteed, I don't know how I could suggest to them that they disarm themselves. And I don't think there's anybody in the world who could tell me that I ought to do that. In such a situation, it would be better if I left the country, and for the men to do whatever they think best. [. . .]

Many people invite me to make a revolution, and I say to him who wants war, let him make war. Peace is necessary for the country, and I won't be the one to change that. I'm told about people who don't have work. I laugh at that, because out there they hold wealth in their hands. One must go to those mountains and gather it up. [. . .]

I don't have anything to do with whether or not there is a National Guard, or anything to do with the people who lead it. I myself, as the citizen I am, am obliged to pay taxes to maintain the army or the guard, or whatever it's called. The only thing I want is for them to give us our constitutional guarantees, and for the Guard itself to be constitutionalized.

[8, 233–34; 237–38]

1. On the eve of what would be his last trip to Managua and during his stay in the capital city, Sandino held informal conversations with Sofonías Salvatierra on the topic of the constant acts of aggression that the Sandinistas were suffering from the National Guard detachments in the Segovian mountains. This document brings together some quotations that Salvatierra took personally from General Sandino. In the source used [8, 233–34, 237–38], these quotations appeared disseminated, whereas here they are offered as a coherent whole that permits appreciation of Sandino's understanding of the difficult situation in the days before his assassination.

198. INTERVIEW WITH *LA PRENSA* IN MANAGUA, FEBRUARY 18, 1934[1]

With the help of Minister Don Sofonías Salvatierra, one of our editors yesterday got an exclusive interview for *La Prensa* with General Augusto C. Sandino, in the house of the aforementioned secretary of state.

After the introduction, General Sandino ordered one of his lieutenants not to permit anyone to enter while he spoke in private with the editor, who began the interview with these words: "General Sandino, is there any truth to the declarations of yesterday afternoon, which a reporter says come from you, that you will not turn over your weapons until the Guard has become a constituted body?"

"Yes, sir, those are my words."

"Which means, then," our editor continued, "that the hundred men whom General Estrada commands will not be disarmed?"

"That troop, which is called an emergency force, is under President Sacasa's orders, and he can employ it whenever he sees fit. Those people are dependent upon him. Even today he can tell me to bring the weapons, and in a moment he will have them."

"But since those aren't the only weapons, will you persist in not turning them over?"

"One can't demand that the agreements be complied with if the other side hasn't complied as well." (And, saying this, he took from his valise a copy of the treaty of February 2, 1933.) "Here they are," he said, "I'm going to read them to you. Look, the text says that I will gradually turn over the weapons to the constituted authorities, which means I'm not obliged to turn them over. It was also stipulated to us that they would give us guarantees, and that hasn't happened either. I've brought this list of seventeen of my men whom they've assassinated during the whole of the last year, and the jails of the Segovias are still full of Sandinistas, held from the moment the agreements were signed." (He shows us the list of the dead.) "They have held General José León Díaz as a prisoner in the Ocotal headquarters since the beginning of peace. They don't even let him shave. His hair hangs down to his shoulders. Still, we have put up with everything for the sake of peace in Nicaragua."

"But the National Guard has left you in peace in Wiwilí."

"It has not allowed us to work freely. It pursues the Sandinistas who come to our camps searching for work. They haven't come to Wiwilí, of course, because we have weapons."

"Come now, General. The Guard has orders to control the region that your people occupy, as the only military body of the nation. Would you be opposed to such a thing?"

"If my intentions to back up Dr. Sacasa's government are not well understood, I will not go to war. I will abandon the country. I will issue a manifesto to the world explaining what's been happening, but in no sense will I influence my people to do as I do. The rest depends on them. I have only wanted to contribute to the country's well-being, and in no way to its desolation. I can't leave my people in the hands of illegal authorities. I insist that they continue to have protection. Let the National Guard be constitutionalized and then, yes, I will turn over my men. Or let them guarantee to me that it will be done that way, and I myself will bring the rifles to Managua in an airplane."

"General, don't you think the Guard has the obligation to maintain vigilance, since there aren't two states within one state?"

"Once things are normalized in my country, yes, sir. But the fact is that here there are not two but rather three states: the power of the president of the Republic, that of the National Guard, and my own. The Guard doesn't obey the president; we don't obey the Guard, because it isn't legal, and that's the way we are all behaving toward one another."

"A few days ago it was said that the National Guard was preparing a plan to reform its regulations in order to adapt it to the country's laws, duly approved by the Congress. What do you say to that?"

"Well, to me it seems the most sensible thing to do. That's the road that ought to be taken. Let it be given a legal form, and then we can be confident that it will not carry out hostile acts against us."

"Presently there is anxiety among the people concerning these things, and sometimes it's believed that a new domestic conflict could be the result of so many disagreements. What do you say to this?"

"I don't want war. Nothing will make me come to that. I repeat, I'll leave the country before bloodying the fatherland and bringing sorrow to many of our homes. My force has been supporting the president. This has been our purpose, and I will dedicate myself with great pleasure to the cultivation of the soil, and I will pay taxes to support the State if the Guard is included within the framework of the laws."

"When do you expect to return to the northern regions?"

"Up till now I don't know. Everything depends, as you must realize, upon our reaching a good understanding with President Sacasa."

While taking leave, our editor asked General Sandino for his authorization to publish his statements, which was granted at once. Everything, he said, which he had spoken about with reporters was for publication.

WHAT WAS STATED IN THE CAMPO DE MARTE

On the other hand, later, in the Campo de Marte, when our editor arrived at the National Guard buildings, having asked a high-ranking officer how things were going with Sandino, the latter stated that everything had been arranged and that nothing would happen to the ex-guerrilla fighter, because they had been able to isolate totally the obstacles that had stood in the way of a good understanding. Nevertheless, it has not been possible to do anything to calm the minds of the speculative public, who see in all the danger a new uncertainty that results from the obstinate and caustic manner in which this delicate national problem has been treated.

[16, 18 February 1934]

1. According to Sofonías Salvatierra [8, 238], when Sandino learned of this report, he said in a visible state of agitation, "I'm not going to give another interview to them, who put things any way they like."

199. LETTER TO PRESIDENT
JUAN BAUTISTA SACASA,
FEBRUARY 19, 1934

Managua, D.N.

February 19, 1934

Most excellent President of the Republic
Señor Dr. Juan B. Sacasa
Presidential House

Most excellent Señor President:

As you know, in the Peace Agreements signed on February 2, 1933, between you and me, with the participation of the delegates of the Conservative and Liberal nationalist parties, and of four delegates of the undersigned, in my role as supreme commander of the Army in Defense of the National Sovereignty of Nicaragua, it is stipulated in article 2 of the said agreement that the Liberal and Conservative parties would emphasize as capital points of their respective political programs their respect for the Constitution and the fundametal laws of the Republic, and maintain, by all rational and juridical means, the full resplendence of the sovereignty and political and economic independence of Nicaragua.[1]

I understand, Mr. President, that the Liberal party has come to power encountering great deficiencies in the political and economic independence of the country, and that because of this same lack of independence there exists an apolitical military institution in Nicaragua possessing regulations extraneous to our fundamental charter.

I understand that you fervently wish to lead the country within the framework of our laws, but that there is also the obstacle of the existence of two armies, that is, the National Guard, possessing unconstitutional forms and procedures, and the emergency auxiliaries whom you possess on the Coco River, under the command of Generals Francisco Estrada and Juan Santos Morales, the latter force constitutional from the moment you established it in your capacity as president of the Republic and general commander, and it is for you to decide whether it is to continue to exist or not.

Nevertheless, Mr. President, since in the same agreements there is the obligation on your part to give effective guarantees to the lives and interests of all the men who served under my orders in the recently terminated campaign that we carried out against the interventionist forces of the United States in Nicaragua, and since that indispensable guarantee could not be realized without correcting the illegal form and procedures of the, National Guard, I wish to reiterate to you the proofs of my frank and loyal cooperation in those situations in which I might in some way contribute to the maintenance of peace.

In order that you should have no difficulty in the development of your program of government from the people who served under me, and in order to offer you likewise the means to regulate the form and procedures of the National Guard, in accordance with the Constitution of the Republic, I will use my influence with the men who compose my army, so that we may give you a unanimous vote of confidence as a way to strengthen your authority and make more effective the guarantees to which we are entitled by the agreements of February 2, 1933, and so that within a set period of time you may also constitutionally readapt the regulations of the National Guard.

What is basic to this letter will be to learn from you the manner of giving us guarantees, as well as the question of the constitutionality of the Guard, and the other means of guaranteeing the lives of all the men who served under my orders in the recently terminated campaign that we carried out against the interventionist forces.

Your very attentive servant.
Ever onward.
A. C. SANDINO

[4, 101–4]

1. See Doc. 177.

200. THE ASSASSINATION
OF AUGUSTO C. SANDINO,
FEBRUARY 21, 1934[1]

A few minutes later the president came out, and a circle of distinguished friends surrounded Sandino. The Segovian hero spoke with good humor, referring to episodes of the Constitutionalist War, which all listened to with pleasure because of the interesting way he expressed himself. The president invited us to dinner, and we all went to the table, with the exception of Dr. Lara, who had some urgent professional matters to attend to. At the table Sandino was always cheerful and well-spoken. Making a good observation, he said that we had come far, because earlier the presidents had left power to go into exile, and now all were here: Don Bartolo, General Moncada, General Chamorro. Only Díaz was absent, but not because anyone had stood in his way.

With dinner over, we spoke of the formation of a company to exploit gold washings in the Coco River region. Its basic structures were outlined and the public documentation of the organization was to be authorized by Dr. Alejo Icaza Icaza on the day General Sandino returned from Niquinohomo.[2] It was ten at night when we left the Presidential House. Dr. Sacasa took leave of General Sandino with an embrace. General Portocarrero, who was there along with Señor Calderón Ramírez, was invited by Sandino to accompany us, but he announced, along with the president, that he would remain there to await General Somoza, with whom they would arrange the details of his future functions as the executive's delegate in the Segovias, since he was the one appointed according to the arrangement they had agreed to. Dr. Federico Sacasa, the president's brother, very kindly went with us to the door to say good-bye, and we entered the car: in the back seat General Sandino, Don Gregorio, and I, and in the front seat with the chauffeur the two adjutants, Generals Estrada and Umanzor.

We descended La Loma, the summit where the Presidential Palace is located, without anything out of the ordinary taking place, until we reached the foot of the hill where the sentry houses of the Campo de Marte are located, at one of which, that of the Hormiguero, on a stretch of road where the lights do not eliminate the darkness, the car was detained by a platoon of National Guardsmen pointing their machine guns at the vehicle.

"Stop the car," said the one who acted as leader. "Anyone who raises a hand will be shot," he repeated three times. "Everyone out."

We got out of the car and all gave up their weapons except Don Gregorio and myself, because we didn't possess any weapons[. . . .] On our feet by this time, they led us inside the Hormiguero prison, and they kept us there in the middle of the courtyard, constantly pointing their machine guns at us.

I observed that somebody was talking on the telephone, a Lieutenant López, I believe. And while this was going on, Sandino said more or less the following: "Why are you doing this, if we are all brothers? We have made peace, and we are seeking the restoration of Nicaragua through labor. I haven't done anything except to fight for the freedom of Nicaragua. Only three nights ago General Somoza embraced me as a sign of harmony, and before that I visited him in his house, and General Somoza has visited me. General Somoza gave me a portrait with his inscription, and I gave him one with mine. Call General Somoza, so he can come here and tell me what he wants, so he can speak to me. . . ." Nobody responded.

Moments later a platoon of Guardsmen came in, and the officer in charge said, speaking to me, "You and Señor Sandino (Don Gregorio) remain here until a further order arrives, and the others come with us."

I asked him if this was an order from the president. The purpose of this question was to remind him of the authority of the commander in chief, which they were destroying.

Hearing this, Sandino said, "No, it's a military order, and it must be respected at once," and without delay he marched off, followed by Estrada and Umanzor.

Don Gregorio and I remained on our feet in the middle of the courtyard. After a while a Guardsman brought us some chairs. For a time I didn't believe they would kill General Sandino. Many quick thoughts crossed my mind in the giddy course of those tragic moments. At times I thought they would remove him from the country, at other times that they would demand that he renounce his letter to the president and commit himself to surrendering his weapons without another word. But, though Sandino was an obstacle for many, it could never have occurred to me that they would kill him under those circumstances in which he was protected by law, by Dr. Sacasa's good faith, by the dignity of the army, by the traditional integrity of an entire nation, by universal morality. Such contempt for the honor of a civilized people, which has always been open and loyal, was not to be expected; such scorn for a government presided over by a gentleman, presided over by him and by his ancestors, could not even be imagined, all the more so because on this level of moral responsibility the leader of the Guard had ties of affinity with Dr. Sacasa that he could not violate, because he knew that this would place his relative's honor in question before the Nicaraguan nation, before decent humanity itself.[3] For this to be believed, it had to be proved by facts.

It was while I was thinking these grim thoughts that shots were heard from the eastern side of the city, which is where my Managua house is located, where Don Sócrates Sandino had been staying. A constant firing of machine guns could be heard as if in combat.

"Now they are killing them," said Don Gregorio. "It will always be true. He who becomes a redeemer dies crucified."

It was about eleven o'clock at night. At about one in the morning of the 22nd, the American minister, Mr. Arthur Bliss Lane, arrived at the prison and invited us to accompany him. He took us in his automobile to the Legation, offering us its hospitality. I informed the president by telephone, telling him that I preferred to go to the Presidential House. President Sacasa approved, and the foreign diplomat was kind enough to accompany us there.

When I reached the Government House I learned everything. While they had been arresting General Sandino, the Guardsmen, commanded by Captain Gutiérrez of San Rafael, especially chosen, it would seem, had silently laid siege to my house, setting up machine guns around it, as if to attack a fortress. When those Guardsmen heard the shots fired by those who had killed Sandino, Estrada, and Umanzor on a dark dead-end street on the edge of Managua, they also opened fire on my house from several sides at a distance of about twenty yards. Protected by the machine guns of the Republic, those who by virtue of the law are charged with defending the nation's citizens began their attack, constantly firing their weapons until they had entered the domicile, sacred and immune, according to the Constitution.

Their purpose, no doubt, was to finish off my family as well. They killed a child of about ten, a servant, and Don Sócrates Sandino, and they gravely wounded my son-in-law, Don Rolando Murillo, who died a few days later. Fortunately my wife and daughter had been in Masatepe for about a month on a health cure.

They transported the bodies to the landing field to be with the other three who had been sacrificed, and they buried them in a single grave, according to stories that circulated. They profaned the body of General Sandino, removing his clothes, a watch, a golden watch chain, and a diamond ring that he wore. Only in death could they touch the invincible warrior; only in this way could they defeat him, protected by the most shameful acts of treachery. After the massacre at my house, the guardsmen-executioners took whatever they wanted from inside the dwelling, and they ended their banquet of blood with a banquet of food and drink that they conducted in the reception room itself. The two feasts did not upset either their consciences or their stomachs. In the city the following day they made an ostentatious display of the evil work they had carried out the night before.

[8, 245–51]

1. In response to Sandino's letter of February 18 (Doc. 199), President Sacasa promised in a letter to Sandino that he would soon alter the organic law and regulations of the National Guard to bring them in line with the Constitution, and that meanwhile he would send a delegate to the northern departments who would command the forces in that region, collect the weapons outside the government's control, and protect Sandino's followers. On the afternoon of February 21, Sandino, accompanied by Dr. Escolástico Lara, Gregorio Sandino (his father), and Generals Francisco Estrada and Juan Pablo Umanzor, went by car to the presidential palace to discuss these and other matters. This account by Sofonías Salvatierra of Sandino's last hours begins just after their arrival at the presidential palace. RC

2. Sandino had planned to spend a month in his native village of Niquinohomo. RC

3. General Somoza's wife, Salvadora Debayle de Somoza, was the granddaughter of former president Roberto Sacasa and the niece of President Juan Bautista Sacasa. RC

201. THERE IS NO SEED THAT WON'T GROW IF PLANTED IN GOOD SOIL: THE FUTURE OF NICARAGUA. CONVERSATIONS WITH JOSÉ ROMÁN ON THE COCO RIVER, MARCH 1933[1]

Listen, Román, I've been in this place many times before, but never under these conditions.[2] The night so clear, the beauty and calm of the place, with a full moon that makes the waters of this millenial river sparkle, and especially without the shocking experiences of the war. I want to take advantage of the serene beauty of the landscape and this unique and indescribable tranquility to talk to you about some personal and sentimental things that, though they don't form part of our military campaign, I regard, in fact, as fundamental aspects of our struggle, which will help you to understand the essence of that struggle and the future of Nicaragua. I want to feel free to speak without pauses for taking notes, which anyway would require more light than this lovely moon can give us. It would be very hard to find a more propitious occasion than this for what I feel I must express to you, for which reason I ask you not to take notes on this occasion[. . . .] Besides, I've observed that you have a very good memory, and tomorrow or the next day you'll be able to write whatever you think convenient without any difficulty[. . . .]

Now you can see that without my hammock I'll have to pace about, sit down, and make wry faces, as Blanquita says. And about my wife, it's a shame you haven't gotten to know her. She's a beautiful person. But there will be another opportunity. Allow me to say, between the two of us here, that what's making me nervous at the moment is that I'm about to become a father. Maybe within three months. That's why she couldn't come with me this time. You can't imagine the happiness and tenderness I feel when I think that I'm about to become a father, more than anything else because I want to give my child all the care and paternal love I didn't have. The astral spirits will recognize that I'm not a resentful person.

Maybe what I just said isn't exactly true, because there's something that troubles me even more than being a father, and that's the future of

Nicaragua and my crusade, because even though the United States might have had to accept their military defeat, which to a certain extent gives some prestige to their new government, they won't so easily accept a political defeat. Of that I'm absolutely certain. I don't know in what form they will make their move, but I know that they can count on very able and subtle politicians and that ours are very corrupt, and, unfortunately, as you know, politics is not my field. Besides, the United States has a lot of money that they very well know how to use, and in politics money is a very powerful weapon. You saw how they bought Moncada and all the generals and officers and finally all the soldiers, except ours, for ten dollars a head.

I've had several proposals, which, if I had accepted them, would have given me ample means to continue the war and even take power in Nicaragua, but I knew that once the marines had withdrawn it would have been unworthy on my part to spill more of the blood of our brothers. Especially since Dr. Sacasa is an honest man whom I greatly admire and trust completely. Precisely to avoid intrigues and political pressures, I unilaterally accelerated the signing of the peace agreement.

I've thought a lot about this. For quite a bit longer than a year now, knowing that our guerrilla army was already invincible, I realized that eventually the marines would have to leave and we would be left face to face with the National Guard, an army against which our struggle isn't directed and against which we don't have any quarrel, except that I question its constitutionality and its loyalty to Nicaragua. But the more I've thought and pondered about how to avoid the dangers that such a situation implies for Nicaragua, I've come to the conclusion that it's not my task or the task of my army to try to solve a problem that doesn't yet exist except in an embryonic form. Abortion, in addition to being immoral, is also dangerous.

Look, Román, the long years of struggle, fighting under such unfavorable conditions and upholding an ideal and the country's honorable name, maybe all this is very glorious, but it's also an enormous responsibility. The purity of the cause has to be maintained at all costs. The solitude in the mountains, bearing the full weight of the campaign on my shoulders, the endless nights of vigilance and waiting, all this gives a man an extra sense through which all things acquire an added dimension, and the capacity for judgement becomes more serene. The stillness and the enormous loneliness of a man who has nobody to turn to to make the latest decisions, decisions that must be made, bring him in contact with something outside his own being. Beyond everything human! It's on the basis of these extraordinary experiences and these deep meditations, these profound thoughts, that I know positively, without any doubt whatever, that the rest of my life will be spent in these mountains among their humble inhabitants[. . . .]

It's true, poor Nicaragua has been a country damned by God[. . . .] And, frankly speaking, Nicaragua was a goddamned country for the marines, for the secretary of state, Mr. Stimpson, for Admiral Sellers, for General Logan Feland, for Mr. Knox, for President Hoover. And yet, I say this from the heart, the marines weren't to blame, I'm the first to recognize this, because like my friend Montenegro whom I spoke to you about, they only came here obeying orders. If the people of the United States had seen their boys sadly dying, without glory, without honors, and without knowing why, the North American people never would have allowed those brave boys to come here to soil their uniforms along with the prestige of that great nation in the jungles and swamps of Nicaragua[. . . .]

As I told you before, with the expulsion of the marines from Nicaragua, the problems of the nation haven't ended. There are many dangers, inside and outside the country. This, because the Americans, though they could easily grant themselves the luxury of converting a defeat into an act of generosity toward a small country, into an act of wisdom, by recognizing their mistake and withdrawing their troops, lack the liberality of spirit required to recognize the rights of others above their own commercial ambitions, and they won't stop intriguing and manipulating for the purpose of replacing armed intervention with another kind of intervention so subtle that it can't be fought with weapons, but only with the dignity and honesty of our politicians, something that now exists only to the smallest degree. This is the main internal danger, and it constitutes a condition that only in the very long term and at the cost of great sacrifices can be overcome.

This has already been said on another occasion, and maybe in other words, but allow me to repeat it because it's something I consider of fundamental importance for the future of Nicaragua. I'm absolutely convinced that there is no seed that won't grow if planted in good soil. There's no one in the world who can have any doubt about the excellence of the seed that we have planted, and I don't have the slightest doubt that the people of Nicaragua are a fertile and generous soil, and let it be known that this seed, though it will have to be sprinkled with abundant tears and the blood of our people, one day, maybe far off in the future, will unexpectedly and irresistibly bear fruit, and the longer the period of germination, the more beautiful that fruit will be. Never lose faith. You will see it! [. . .]

It's clear [. . .] that this work [of improving the lives of the Nicaraguan Indians] is difficult, but just to infuse them with dreams, with expectations, and the most elementary notions of morality and hygiene would be to achieve a great victory. There are thousands and thousands of Indians on this Atlantic coast of Nicaragua and in its river valleys, including Zumos, Zambos, Miskitos, and Caribs. Of course no official census exists, but with the help of Colonel Rivera I've been able to estimate that all together there are more than a hundred thousand. I came here by chance during my war, and I became conscious of our reality, because this is also Nicaragua, and I made myself the firm promise that as soon as the war for independence had come to an end, instead of accepting the fine invitations I have to Paris, Buenos Aires, and Mexico, where I would only go to show myself off like some movie star, tango singer, politician or showcase ambassador, instead of doing that, I would stay here on the Coco River. The wildest but most beautiful part of our country.

To free it from the barbarism into which exploitation has submerged it, first feudal-colonial and now capitalist, to do whatever is possible to civilize these poor Indians who are the marrow of our race. And as you can see, my work is beginning to bear fruit. Let's hope that at least I will leave this work well started, so that our future generations and future governments will devote themselves to this problem, which is fundamental to the economic and moral development of Nicaragua. This virgin region comprises much more than half of our national territory, and merely by civilizing it Nicaragua can be made into a worthy and respected country.

Román, listen to me well because you're young. Listen to these words because they can turn out to be prophetic. I will not leave here. I know that because of my ideas they will kill me. Not the marines, but the Nicaraguans! I know this but it doesn't matter to me, because this is my fate, the same fate that brought me here. At least I will leave the seed planted, and some day it will bear fruit.

[7, 77–79, 98–99, 160–61, 165–66]

1. Though recorded by José Román almost a year before Sandino's death, the following personal and prophetic remarks seem particularly appropriate as the final document of this book. RC

2. At this moment Sandino and José Román were sitting outside the house where Sandino was staying in the village of Bocay, overlooking the point where the Bocay River flows into the Coco. RC

BIBLIOGRAPHY

Sources

BOOKS

1. Alemán Bolaños, Gustavo. *Sandino, el libertador*. Mexico and Guatemala, 1951.
2. Arellano, Jorge Eduardo. *Augusto César Sandino, escritos literarios y documentos desconocidos*. Managua, 1980.
3. Belausteguigoitia, Ramón de. *Con Sandino en Nicaragua*. Managua, 1981.
4. Calderón Ramírez, Salvador. *Los últimos dias de Sandino*. Mexico, D.F., 1934.
5. Campos Ponce, Xavier. *Los Yankis y Sandino*. Mexico, D.F., 1962.
6. Maraboto, Emigdio. *Sandino ante el coloso*. Veracruz, Mexico, 1929.
7. Román, José. *Maldito país*. 1979.
8. Salvatierra, Sofonías. *Sandino o la tragedia de un pueblo*. Madrid, 1934.
9. Selser, Gregorio. *Sandino, general de hombres libres*. Vol. 1. Buenos Aires, 1958.
10. Selser, Gregorio. *Sandino, general de hombres libres*. Vol. 2. Buenos Aires, 1958.
11. Somoza Garcia, Anastasio. *El verdadero Sandino o el calvario de las Segovias*. Managua; Tipografía Robelo, 1936.

PERIODICALS

12. *Ariel*. Tegucigalpa. Biweekly review founded by the Honduran poet and journalist, Froylán Turcios, between 1924 and 1926.
13. *The Nation*. New York. Weekly founded in 1865.
14. *The New York Times*. New York, 1926–1934.
15. *El Nuevo Diario*. Managua. Daily newspaper founded in 1980.
16. *La Prensa*. Managua. Daily newspaper founded in 1926.
17. *Revista Conservadora*. Managua, 1963.
18. *El Universal Gráfico*. Mexico, D.F. Weekly supplement to the daily newspaper, *El Universal*.

BIBLIOGRAPHY

ARCHIVES

19. Archivo del Instituto de Estudio del Sandinismo, Pedro José Zepeda Collection.
20. Archivo del Instituto de Estudio del Sandinismo, general collection.

ADDITIONAL BIBLIOGRAPHY

Alegría, Claribel, and D. J. Flakoll. *Nicaragua: La revolución sandinista, una crónica política, 1855–1979.* Mexico, D.F., 1982.

Arellano, Jorge Eduardo, and Eduardo Pérez-Valle, eds. *Sandino: Iconográfia básica.* Managua, 1979.

Beals, Carleton. *Banana Gold.* Philadelphia, 1932.

Bermann, Mark. *Under the Big Stick: Nicaragua and the United States since 1848.* Boston, 1986.

Booth, John A. *The End and the Beginning: The Nicaraguan Revolution.* Boulder, Colorado, 1982.

Burns, E. Bradford. *At War in Nicaragua: The Reagan Doctrine and the Politics of Nostalgia.* New York, 1987.

Cox, Isaac Joslin. *Nicaragua and the United States.* Boston, 1927.

Crawley, Eduardo. *Nicaragua in Perspective.* New York, 1984.

Cuadra, Abelardo. *Hombre del Caribe: Memorias presentadas y pasadas en limpio por Sergio Ramírez.* 2d ed. San José, Costa Rica, 1979.

Cummins, Lejeune. *Quijote on a Burro: Sandino and the Marines, a Study in the Formation of Foreign Policy.* Mexico, D.F., 1958.

Denny, Harold Norman. *Dollars for Bullets: The Story of American Rule in Nicaragua.* New York, 1929.

Diederich, Bernard. *Somoza and the Legacy of U.S. Involvement in Central America.* London, 1982.

Fonseca, Carlos Amador. *Sandino: Guerrillero proletario.* Managua, n.d.

Gilbert, Gregorio Urbano. *Junto a Sandino.* Santo Domingo, Dominican Republic, 1979.

Goldwert, Marvin. *The Constabulary in the Dominican Republic and Nicaragua: Progeny and Legacy of United States Intervention.* Gainesville, Florida, 1962.

Hodges, Donald C. *Intellectual Foundations of the Nicaraguan Revolution.* Austin, Texas, 1986.

Instituto de Estudio del Sandinismo. *Ahora sé que Sandino manda.* Managua, 1986.

———. *El sandinismo: documentos básicos.* Managua, 1983.

Kamman, William. *A Search for Stability: United States Diplomacy toward Nicaragua, 1925–1933.* Notre Dame, Indiana, 1968.

Karnes, Thomas L. *The Failure of Union: Central America, 1824–1960.* Chapel Hill, N.C., 1961.

La Feber, Walter. *Inevitable Revolutions: The United States in Central America.* New York, 1984.

Macaulay, Neill. *The Sandino Affair.* Chicago, 1967.

Megee, Vernon E. "United States Military Intervention in Nicaragua." Master's thesis, University of Texas, 1963.

Millett, Richard. *Guardians of the Dynasty.* Maryknoll, New York, 1977.

Moncada, José María. *Estados Unidos en Nicaragua.* Managua, 1942.

Nalty, Bernard C. *The United States Marines in Nicaragua.* Washington, D.C., 1968.

Nearing, Scott, and Joseph Freeman. *Dollar Diplomacy.* New York, 1926.

Nogales, Rafael de. *The Looting of Nicaragua.* New York, 1928.

Ortega Saavedra, Humberto. *Cincuenta años de lucha sandinista.* Managua, 1979.

Ramírez, Sergio. "El muchacho de Niquinohomo." In Augusto C. Sandino, *El pensamiento vivo,* 1:29–64. Managua, 1984.

———. "Sandino: Clase e ideología." In Augusto C. Sandino, *El pensamiento vivo,* 2:421–41. Managua, 1984.

Ramírez Delgado, Rafael. *Jornada Libertaria de 1912 en Nicaragua.* Tegucigalpa, 1951.

Sacasa, Dr. Juan B. *Como y por que caí del poder.* San Salvador, 1936.

Sandino, Augusto C. *El pensamiento vivo.* 2 vols. Ed. Sergio Ramírez. Managua, 1984.

———. *Sandino without Frontiers.* Trans. and ed. by Karl Bermann. Hampton, Virginia, 1988.

Santos López. *Memorias del Coronel Santos López.* Managua, 1980.

Selser, Gregorio. *Sandino.* New York, 1981.

Stimson, Henry L. *American Policy in Nicaragua.* New York, 1927.

Tessendorf, K. T. *Uncle Sam in Nicaragua.* New York, 1987.

Torres, Edelberto. *Sandino.* Managua, 1983.

U.S. Department of State. *A Brief History of the Relations between the United States and Nicaragua, 1909–1928.* Washington, D.C., 1928.

Walker, Thomas W. *Nicaragua: The Land of Sandino.* 2d rev. ed. Boulder, Colorado, 1986.

Wheelock Román, Jaime. *Imperialismo y dictadura.* 5th ed. Mexico, D.F., 1980.

Wortman, Miles L. *Government and Society in Central America, 1680–1840.* New York, 1982.

Zelaya, José Santos. *La revolución de Nicaragua y los Estados Unidos.* Madrid, 1910.

INDEX

Aguinaldo, President Emilio, 83, 85n.1
air power, use of: against Chinandega,
58n.2; against Ciudad Antigua, 146–47;
against El Chipote, 163–66, 167n.1,
167n.4, 168; in Nicaragua, 73, 89, 103,
104, 115n.1, 137, 146–47, 156, 159,
167n.1, 167n.4, 174, 176, 190–91, 235,
237, 278, 367, 412, 424, 458
Alemán Bolaños, Gustavo, 380–81, 392;
letters from Sandino to, 273–76, 278,
374–75n.1, 468–69; publisher of Sandino's documents, 374–75
Alianza Popular Revolucionario Americana. See Apristas All-America Anti-Imperialist League, 288, 305, 344–45; letter from Sandino to, 200–1
Altamirano, Francisco, 207
Altamirano, General Pedro, 296, 303, 333,
350–51, 366, 367, 376, 382, 402, 407,
409–10, 470, 471; battles fought by,
338–40, 341–42; letters from Sandino
to, 265, 287, 416, 423, 424
Altamirano, Rafael N., 303
Apristas, 329–30, 331n.2
Aráuz, Ester V. de, 428, 476n.1
Aráuz, Lucila, 56–57, 476n.1
Ardila Gómez, Rubén, 274, 321, 329
Argüello, Rosendo, 392, 427n.2
Ariel (journal of Froylán Turcios), 100,
106n.1, 161
Army in Defense of the National Sovereignty of Nicaragua, 3, 17, 41, 84, 89,
117, 123, 171, 204, 338–40, 447, 477;
amnesty granted to members of, 441; antagonisms among leaders of, 405–6; archive of, 166; battle report of to Sandino, 338–40; capture of towns by, 400;
casualties of, 89, 338–40, 346, 350–51,
377, 401, 402, 403, 412; Coco River cooperative granted to, 441; compared to
U.S. forces, 128; composition of, 119;
conditions of in 1932, 414, 421; cruel
acts of, 303, 397–98, 458; described,

125; disciplinary measures imposed
upon, 134–35, 177–78, 179, 355, 458;
as emergency auxiliary, 441; espionage
system of, 176, 276; forced contributions levied by, 349, 388, 389, 397–98,
399; "grapevine telegraph" system used
by, 167n.2; Guidelines for the Organization of, 95–97, 178–79, 391, 392; interim commander of appointed by Sandino, 437, 438; Latin American
members of, 163, 164, 179, 264, 329;
medical treatment of, 159; peace agreement of with President Sacasa, 440–42;
persecuted by National Guard, 436n.1,
478, 483, 488n.1, 489–90; political positions of, 111, 270; proposal of to create new department of "Luz y Verdad,"
432–33; slogans of, 96, 143, 155; strategic advantages of, 175–76; strategy and
organization of in 1931, 374, 376–77,
382; surrender of weapons by in San Rafael del Norte, 442, 449–50; tactics of,
103, 123, 162–66, 168–69, 176, 177,
181, 276; training of, 165; weapons and
supplies (sources of), 177, 458; women
as members of, 163, 164. *See also* battles
Autonomist party, 472, 477

Baca, Arturo, 45
Balladares, Manuel, 407–11, 422
Barahona, Humberto de, 466–67; letter
from Sandino to, 474–75
Barbiaux, Justino, 25, 287n.1
Barbusse, Henri: letter from Sandino to,
305–6
battles, 122–24, 180, 190–91, 338–40,
346–47, 373; on Atlantic coast, 367,
371–72n.1, 401, 412; at Cape Gracias a
Dios, 367; of Chinandega, 45, 46; of
Ciudad Antigua, 402; of Ciudad Darío,
400; on the Coco River, 207; of Cosmate, 346; of Cuatro Esquinas, 347; on
the Ducuali River, 350; of El Bálsamo,

delegate to peace conference, 426, 428; designated president by Sandino, 404, 408n.2; instructions from Sandino to, 391–92

Pro-Liberación de Nicaragua. See Committee in Support of the Liberation of Nicaragua

Protocol for Peace. *See* Sandino, peace proposals of

Puerto Cabezas, 11, 14, 17; battles at, 367, 412; Liberal army ordered by U.S. to evacuate, 44; Liberal capital established at, 11, 279

Puerto Rico, 204–5, 310

Quezada, Carlos, 115, 120, 185, 186, 321; letter from Sandino to, 265

Quilalí: alleged destruction of, 154, 155n.2, 184; description of, 123; U.S. marines evacuated from, 278

Quintero, Ferdinando, 67n.3, 191

Ramírez, Sergio, 274; on U.S. domination of Nicaragua in 1910, 8

Raudales, Colonel Ramón, 421, 470

Reagan administration, 3–4

Reyes, Heriberto, 401, 402

Reyes, Colonel Pompilio, 47, 52, 53, 453; alleged traitor to Sandino's cause, 122, 130; letters from Sandino to, 130–32, 132n.1

Rivas, Dagoberto, 30–31, 33n.1

Rivera, Colonel Abraham, 341, 376, 470, 471, 501; letters from Sandino to, 352–53, 356–57, 363–64

Rivera Bertrand, Enrique, 322, 342–44; letter from Sandino to, 320–21

Román, José: excerpts from book of, 27–31, 103–4, 162–66, 329–31, 444, 498–501

Roosevelt, Theodore, 387n.1

Rosas Tejada, Colonel José, 67n.3, 137, 185

Sacasa, Crisanto, 441, 442

Sacasa, Federico, 494

Sacasa, Juan Bautista, 13, 44, 112, 116, 269, 334, 426, 428, 435–39, 445, 447, 470, 471, 477–78, 483, 490, 494, 499; becomes minister to Washington, 242n.3; becomes vice president, 10, 222, 241; betrayed by Moncada, 111; and Central American union, 461; estab-

lishes provisional government at Puerto Cabezas (1926), 11, 279; exiled (1925), 11; letters from Sandino to, 481–82, 492–93; ordered to evacuate Puerto Cabezas, 44; overthrow of by Somoza (1936), 475n.1; peace treaty of with Sandino (1933), 18, 440–42, 464, 466, 468, 474, 480, 489, 492–93; promises to constitutionalize National Guard, 497n.1; protests against Treaty of Tipitapa, 14, 89–90; supports Sandino during Constitutionalist War, 70

Salas, Marcial, 67n.3, 123

Salgado P., General Carlos, 138, 341, 342, 346, 366, 376, 402; battles fought by, 338–40

Salvatierra, Sofonías, 424, 427, 428, 431, 433–34n.1, 436, 446, 449–50, 474, 489, 491n.1; appointed to confer with Sandino, 441; conversations of with Sandino, 487–88; describes conference at Tipitapa, 13; describes U.S. intervention of 1927, 11–12; recommended by Sandino as presidential candidate, 112–13

San Albino mine, 43, 131, 292; seized by Sandino, 79–81

Sánchez H., Colonel Porfirio, 50, 52, 58, 88–89, 178

Sandinista Front for National Liberation (FSLN), 3

Sandino, América Tiffer de, 27, 274, 445

Sandino, Augusto C., 3–4, 5n.4, 14, 15, 67n.3, 271; on abortion, 499; accepts resignation of Froylán Turcios as representative, 228; alleged anarchism of, 17n.39; appoints delegates to peace conference, 426; appoints Escolástico Lara interim commander of army, 437, 438; assassination of, 494–97, 501; attends bull fight in Mexico, 330–31; background of, 16–17, 25–31, 41, 178, 290; beginnings of armed resistance, 56–69; bribe allegedly received by, 288–89, 305, 316; on capital punishment, 376–77; and Coco River cooperative, 460, 463, 464, 470–71, 480, 494; conditions of for ending rebellion, 16–17, 66, 71, 145, 168, 170, 174, 184, 216, 221–25, 314, 419–20, 432–33; and Constitutionalist War, 44–58, 131, 279–80, 290–91; and conversations with José Román, 498–501; and conversations with Ramón de